This volume is the first to take a systematic look at the position of women in the post-Soviet states of the former USSR. It is divided into two main parts: the first focuses on the economy, society and polity of the Russian Federation; the second gives specialists' insights into social, political, economic and military developments in the other republics of the former Soviet Union. The book pays special attention to women's own perceptions of their lives. How do factory workers, street-vendors and rural workers view their jobs? How do the women who served in Afghanistan, migrants, politicians, political activists, soldiers' mothers and feminists portray their worlds? What strategies of coping have women devised to deal with no electricity in Armenia, with unwelcome sexual advances from fathers-in-law and with violence from partners in Russia? Why did women in Georgia travel on a peace train? How has war affected lives in the Caucasus and in Central Asia? This book explores strategies of coping and forms of adaptation, noting that women are agents, as well as victims.

Post-Soviet women: from the Baltic to Central Asia

Post-Soviet women: from the Baltic to Central Asia

edited by
MARY BUCKLEY
University of Edinburgh

PUBLISHED BY THE PRESS SYNDICATE OF THE UNIVERSITY OF CAMBRIDGE
The Pitt Building, Trumpington Street, Cambridge CB2 1RP, United Kingdom

CAMBRIDGE UNIVERSITY PRESS
The Edinburgh Building, Cambridge CB2 2RU, United Kingdom
40 West 20th Street, New York, NY 10011-4211, USA
10 Stamford Road, Oakleigh, Melbourne 3166, Australia

© Cambridge University Press 1997

Post-Soviet women: from the Baltic to Central Asia succeeds and replaces
Perestroika and Soviet women, published by Cambridge University Press
in 1992 (0 521 414431 hb, 0 521 42738 X pb).

This book is in copyright. Subject to statutory exception
and to the provisions of relevant collective licensing agreements,
no reproduction of any part may take place without
the written permission of Cambridge University Press.

First published 1997

Printed in Great Britain at the University Press, Cambridge

Typeset in Sabon 10/12pt

A catalogue record for this book is available from the British Library

Library of Congress cataloguing in publication data

Post-Soviet women: from the Baltic to Central Asia / edited by Mary Buckley.
   p. cm.
Includes index.
ISBN 0 521 56320 8. – ISBN 0 521 56530 8 (pbk.)
1. Women – Russia (Federation) – Social conditions.
2. Women – Former Soviet republics – Social conditions.
3. Women – Russia (Federation) – Economic conditions.
4. Women – Former Soviet republics – Economic conditions.
I. Buckley, Mary (Mary E.A.)
HQ1665.15.P67   1997
305.42'0947–dc20   96–36259   CIP

ISBN 0 521 56320 8 hardback
ISBN 0 521 56530 8 paperback

CE

Contents

	page
List of figures	ix
List of tables	x
Notes on contributors	xi
Map	xvi

INTRODUCTION

1. Victims and agents: gender in post-Soviet states   3
   MARY BUCKLEY

PART I: WOMEN IN THE RUSSIAN FEDERATION   17

Economy   19

2. Do Russian women want to work?   21
   SARAH ASHWIN AND ELAIN BOWERS
3. Rural women and the impact of economic change   38
   SUE BRIDGER
4. Women and the culture of entrepreneurship   56
   MARTA BRUNO

Society   75

5. Images of an ideal woman: perceptions of Russian womanhood through the media, education and women's own eyes   77
   REBECCA KAY
6. 'She was asking for it': rape and domestic violence against women   99
   LYNNE ATTWOOD

7.	'For the sake of the children': gender and migration in the former Soviet Union HILARY PILKINGTON	119

Polity 141

8.	When the fighting is over: the soldiers' mothers and the Afghan madonnas KATHRYN PINNICK	143
9.	Adaptation of the Soviet Women's Committee: deputies' voices from 'Women of Russia' MARY BUCKLEY	157
10.	Women's groups in Russia OLGA LIPOVSKAYA	186

PART II: WOMEN OUTSIDE RUSSIA IN NEWLY INDEPENDENT STATES 201

11.	Women in changing societies: Latvia and Lithuania NIJOLE WHITE	203
12.	Progress on hold: the conservative faces of women in Ukraine SOLOMEA PAVLYCHKO	219
13.	Out of the kitchen into the crossfire: women in independent Armenia NORA DUDWICK	235
14.	The women's peace train in Georgia TAMARA DRAGADZE	250
15.	Between tradition and modernity: the dilemma facing contemporary Central Asian women SHIRIN AKINER	261

Index 305

Figures

		page
7:1	Who initiated migration?	123
7:2	Motivations for migration	124
7:3	Unemployment by gender and region	128
7:4	Current employment of female respondents relative to previous profession	130
7:5	Current employment of male respondents relative to previous profession	131
9:1	'Women of Russia'. 1995 election campaign poster	165

Tables

		page
9:2	Positions of responsibility in the Duma held by members of the faction 'Women of Russia': 1994–1995	167
9:3	Positions of responsibility in the Duma in 1996 held by deputies in the movement 'Women of Russia'	178
12:1	Percentages of female employees in Ukrainian Ministries	224
12:2	Social attitudes on gender roles in 1995	227
12:3	Responses on jobs for which men and women are most suited	228

Notes on contributors

Shirin Akiner is director of the Central Asia Research Forum, School of Oriental and African Studies, University of London. She is author of *Islamic peoples of the Soviet Union* (2nd rev. edn, London: Kegan Paul International, 1987) and of *Central Asia: new arc of conflict?* (London: Royal United Services Institute for Defence Studies, 1993), editor of *Mongolia today* (London: Kegan Paul International, 1990), of *Cultural tradition and change in Central Asia* (London: Kegan Paul International, 1991) and of *Political and economic trends in Central Asia* (London: British Academic Press, 1994) and co-editor of *Resistance and reform in Tibet* (Bloomington, Ind.: Indiana University Press, 1994). She is editor of the monthly *Central Asia Newsfile* and of *Labyrinth: the Central Asia Quarterly*. She has directed five British government funded projects with Kazakhstan and Uzbekistan (from 1992 to 1995) and has acted as consultant for several award-winning radio and television documentaries.

Sarah Ashwin is a lecturer in the Department of Sociology at the University of Warwick. She is currently working on a doctoral thesis on workers' organisation in Russia during the transition.

Lynne Attwood is lecturer in Russian Studies at the University of Manchester. She is author of *The new Soviet man and woman: sex role socialization in the USSR* (Basingstoke: Macmillan, 1990; Bloomington, Ind.: Indiana University Press, 1991) and editor of *Red women and the silver screen: Soviet women and cinema from the beginning to the end of the communist era* (London: Pandora, 1993).

She has contributed to a number of other books and journals on women and cinema in the Soviet Union and Russia.

Elain Bowers is a graduate student in the Department of Sociology at the University of Warwick. She is currently completing a doctoral thesis on women and work in Russia.

Sue Bridger is senior lecturer in Russian Studies at the University of Bradford. She is author of *Women in the Soviet countryside* (Cambridge: Cambridge University Press, 1987), co-editor of *Dear Comrade Editor: readers' letters to the Soviet press under perestroika* (Bloomington, Ind.: Indiana University Press, 1992), co-author of *No more heroines? Russia, women and the market* (London: Routledge, 1996) and editor of 'Women in post-communist Russia', in *Interface*, no. 1 (Bradford, Summer 1995).

Marta Bruno is a research fellow in the Russian and East European Centre at the University of Wolverhampton. She is currently completing her doctoral thesis for the Department of Geography of the University of Cambridge. She focuses on gender issues in the labour market in Russia, particularly on women in the service sector in Moscow. She is also researching into rural development in Russia and in Central Asia.

Mary Buckley is reader in Politics at the University of Edinburgh. She is author of *Redefining Russian society and polity* (Boulder, Colo.: Westview, 1993) and of *Women and ideology in the Soviet Union* (Hemel Hempstead: Harvester Wheatsheaf; Ann Arbor, Mich.: University of Michigan Press, 1989), editor of *Perestroika and Soviet women* (Cambridge: Cambridge University Press, 1992) and of *Soviet social scientists talking* (London: Macmillan, 1986) and co-editor of *Women, equality and Europe* (London: Macmillan, 1988). She is currently working on rural stakhanovism in the 1930s, funded in 1995–6 by the ESRC.

Tamara Dragadze is director of the Centre for Caucasian and Central Asian Studies in London. Third generation British, she trained in anthropology and sociology at the Universities of Kent and Oxford. She has published widely in the social sciences and in Soviet and post-Soviet studies. She is an active supporter of the National Peace Council.

Nora Dudwick is a cultural anthropologist who has been conducting fieldwork in Armenia since 1987 on issues of nationalism, armed ethnic conflict, national building and the political and social transition. She is currently a consultant to the World Bank where she has carried out poverty studies in several former socialist states with particular attention to the implications of poverty for ethnic minorities and women.

Rebecca Kay is currently completing a doctorate at the University of Bradford on 'Gender, discrimination and the role of women's organisations in contemporary Russian society'. She is co-author of *No more heroines? Russia, women and the market* (London: Routledge, 1996). An extended period of fieldwork in Russia in 1996 was funded by the Harold Hyam Wingate Foundation.

Olga Lipovskaya is chairperson of the St Petersburg Centre for Gender Issues. She has worked as a journalist and interpreter and was publisher from 1989 to 1991 of the samizdat *Zhenskoe Chtenie* (Women's Reading). She has written numerous articles in English and in Russian, including pieces for *Iskusstvo Kino* and *Rabotnitsa*. She has been interviewed on television and in newspapers. From 1988 to 1991 she was a member of the Coordinating Committee of the St Petersburg branch of the Democratic Union.

Solomea Pavlychko is a senior research associate in the Institute of Literature of the Ukrainian Academy of Sciences in Kiev. She is author of *Letters from Kiev* (New York: St Martin's Press, 1992) and of three monographs in the fields of American and English literature, published in Ukraine. She has written numerous articles on the women's movement in Ukraine and feminist critiques of Ukrainian literature.

Hilary Pilkington is lecturer in Russian Politics and Society at the Centre for Russian and East European Studies, University of Birmingham. She is author of *Russia's youth and its culture: a nation's constructors and constructed* (London: Routledge, 1994) and editor of *Gender, generation and identity in contemporary Russia* (London: Routledge, 1996). She has recently completed a study of the problems of socio-cultural adaptation of Russian-speaking forced migrants upon return to Russia from the former republics of the USSR.

Kathryn Pinnick is project manager of a European Union TACIS programme in Baku run by The Nottingham Trent University. She is co-author of *No more heroines? Russia, women and the market* (London: Routledge, 1996) and is currently researching labour relations in Azerbaidzhan.

Nijole White is lecturer in Russian and in area studies at the University of Strathclyde. She compiled *Gorbachev's Russia: a Russian reader* (London and Wellingborough: Collets, 1989) and *Time of change: a Russian reader* (London and Wellingborough: Collets, 1992). Her current research includes nationalities issues and women's studies in the Soviet successor states.

Note on transliteration

This book uses the Library of Congress transliteration system with the exception of names and words whose more customary English forms are now widely adopted. Thus El'tsin, glasnost' and Ol'ga Lipovskaia are here rendered Yel'tsin, glasnost and Olga Lipovskaya.

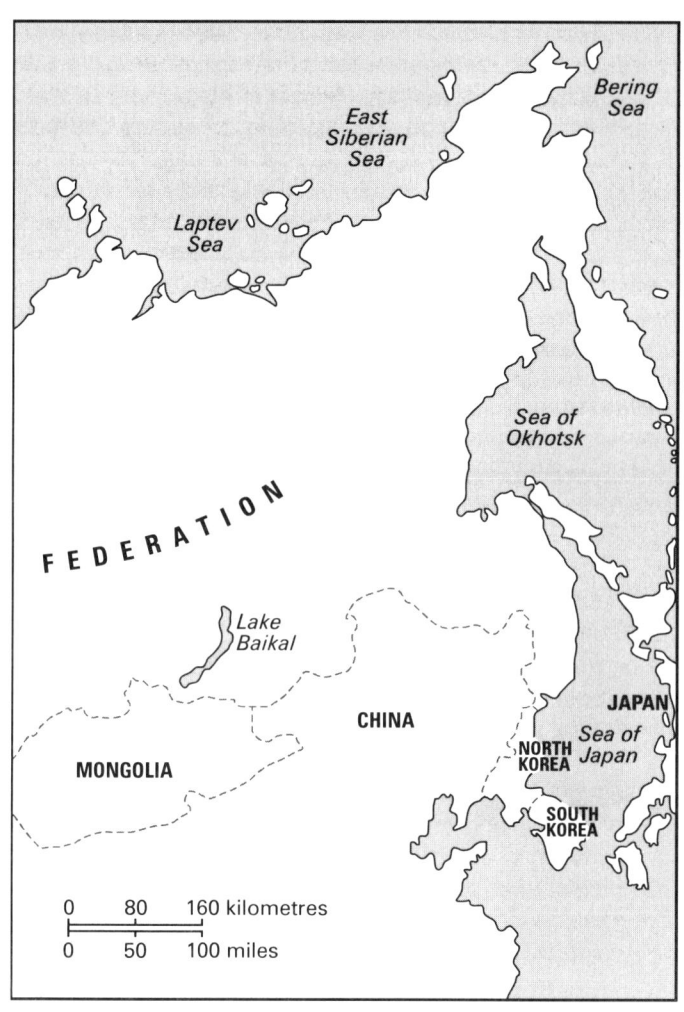

Introduction

1 Victims and agents: gender in post-Soviet states

MARY BUCKLEY

The past decade has seen tumultuous change. The Soviet empire in Eastern Europe came to an end after 'revolutions' in 1989, themselves the result of Gorbachev's encouragement of economic and political reforms in Czechoslovakia, Poland, Hungary, Bulgaria, the German Democratic Republic and Romania. Germany was reunified, the Union of Soviet Socialist Republics (USSR) disintegrated and a shaky Commonwealth of Independent States (CIS) was born. The process of perestroika instigated 'from above' by Mikhail Gorbachev after he became general secretary of the Communist Party of the Soviet Union (CPSU) in 1985 was far-reaching for Soviet citizens, for East Europeans and for the world. Gorbachev may not have intended many of its most far-reaching consequences, but once confronted by them he was forced by the weight of historical demands 'from below' to concede them.

Numerous textbooks have analysed the changes and continuities of the Soviet state.[1] Likewise, the history of perestroika and glasnost has, by now, been well told.[2] Their relevance to gender has received sufficient attention, although generally from female scholars still plugging the gaps left in conventional monographs.[3] Quite what to make of gender in chaotic transitions, from state socialism to new systems trying to adopt market mechanisms, is more hazardous.

All former Soviet republics are in periods of state building, but despite changes in economic and political direction, institutions of the past have not been shattered. Indeed, charges have been made that old bureaucracies are as secure as before and mushrooming, even though fresh legislatures have been elected. In a context of flux, lively debates have taken place about the significance of parliamentarianism versus presidentialism, with strong support for the latter. With constitutions now in place giving extensive powers to presidents, future holders of executive power have the potential to wield enormous clout whether in Turkmenistan, Russia or Ukraine. Who is president of Russia remains of immense importance to the entire post-Soviet world. Changes in Russian economic and foreign policy bear relevance to other states due to Russia's commanding geopolitical position. Russia's huge land mass, as the map on pages xvi and xvii illustrates, stretches from the Pacific, across Northern Asia and into Eastern Europe. Leaders in some Soviet republics, particularly Lithuania, Latvia, Estonia, Ukraine and Georgia, had wanted independence precisely to end Russian domination. Fear of its return has not been allayed. Nationalist proclamations made by Vladimir Zhirinovskii and others fuel apprehensions about the intent of some Russians to re-establish the borders of the former USSR. Leaders in newly independent states, however, as well as being sensitive to Russia's geopolitics, are increasingly looking to build links elsewhere. Governments in the Baltic states have turned westwards, particularly to Scandinavia. The Central Asian republics are drawn towards the Pacific and to the Indian subcontinent, to China, Korea, Japan, India, Pakistan and elsewhere. Caucasian leaders, too, look west, south and east. Leaders and business communities are directing their attention well beyond Russia, but all the time are aware of Russia's economic and strategic importance to their futures.

Gender and transition to what?

The literature on the collapse of state socialism and on transitions to new, albeit undefined systems in the general direction of 'market' economies which do not quite look like them,[4] suggests that women fare worse than men. They are the first to be laid off, are subsequently hired (if young) more quickly if 'attractive' and able to perform sexual favours, and are not taken seriously by political parties. Most party programmes ignore women, or if they receive a mention they are encouraged to return to the home.

One interpretation is that women are thus the 'victims' of transition.[5] They are vulnerable, find themselves in situations beyond their control and have their life dreams shattered. But this wholly negative picture is incomplete. Men, too, are victims of change, affected by developments around them. But since 70 per cent of the unemployed are female, the impact on gender of economic change has been differential. Women have suffered more in job losses, in a sexualisation of hiring practices, in the general spread of pornography and in violence from men. The percentage of women elected to the legislature has also fallen. So women's political representation is much lower than men's, especially since 'male' parties do not speak for women in women's voices. The argument that women should return to the home is a most repetitive one made by men for women.

Although women are more likely to be disadvantaged by economy and polity than men, it would be inaccurate to downplay the fact that men have suffered in transition. Unemployment, disorientation and soaring inflation have made huge impacts on their lives. Women and men find themselves buffeted by changing circumstances, subdued by inflation, threatened by crime and pressured to find new ways of coping.

But women and men are much more than victims. They are also agents of change and reaction. While thousands of men are 'victims' of their masculinity and have been required to fight in Tadzhikistan, Nagorno-Karabakh or in Chechnia, so thousands of men have inventively found ways of managing in new, often dire, circumstances, be it as entrepreneur, mafia thug, taxi driver in the evenings after the 'first' job is over, bodyguard or engineer securing a research grant in the West. Likewise, women have energetically sought new channels, be it as private hairdressers, tour guides, employees of McDonalds, Coca Cola and Pizza Hut or as nightclub dancers. Those with Western languages do especially well, employed by foreign firms in Russian cities and paid in dollars.

One crucial element of 'transition' is uncertainty about the future. Russia forever seems to be suffering yet another 'critical moment'. In August 1991, the critical moment was whether or not the putshchists would endure and what they would do to the 'democrats', led by Yel'tsin, holding ground in the Russian parliament. In April 1993 another critical moment was whether or not Yel'tsin would dissolve parliament for blocking his reforms, as he threatened. The building tension between the executive and the legislature was temporarily diffused by holding a referendum.[6] This, however, did not resolve deeply rooted policy differences between Yel'tsin and his parliament about the minimum wage, pensions and fidelity to the budgetary requirements of the International Monetary Fund (IMF). Yel'tsin argued that the parliament had been elected in 1990 in the Soviet state and so was inappropriate to the new Russian state. Of course, he neglected to point out that he, too, had been elected president of Russia in June 1991, also before the collapse of the USSR. Another critical moment swiftly followed in the autumn of 1993, with Yel'tsin dissolving parliament, many parliamentarians resisting and finally Yel'tsin giving the order for troops to shoot at the 'White House'. Independent for just two years, citizens of the Russian Federation witnessed their president bombard parliament; not an auspicious start for democracy in Russia or in the CIS. The story of the brutality on surrounding streets has largely been hushed up.[7]

Elections to the new Federal Assembly followed in December 1993. The lower house, or State Duma, has 450 seats, 225 of which were drawn from a party list and 225 from single-member constituencies. The upper house, or Federation Council, is a much smaller body of 178. When citizens went to vote in December 1993, they were also asked to vote in a referendum on Yel'tsin's new constitution which gave extraordinarily strong powers to the president *vis-à-vis* parliament. For many advocates of a strong parliamentary system, this spelt a constitutional return to authoritarianism. Yel'tsin had already enjoyed 'special powers' up to December 1992, granted by parliament to help him push through economic reforms. Parliament, however, had been reluctant to extend these powers further and Yel'tsin, in fact, attempted to prevent the Congress of People's Deputies from convening in December 1992.[8] Yel'tsin, to many, seemed unable to relinquish the vast powers he had accumulated. His defenders argued that what Russia needed was a strong hand to see the Federation through hard times and to steer a steady path of reform. His critics dubbed him yet another tsar.

The election results in 1993, however, shocked many. The communists, agrarians and liberal democrats in 1993 did much better than most expected. These forces opposed reform. Yel'tsin's new parliament was not radically different in composition from the previous one. Ongoing tensions, then, between executive and legislature were inevitable. Communist success in subsequent elections to the Duma in December 1995 caused anxiety among reformers who feared that Genadii Ziuganov, leader of the Communist Party of the Russian Federation (KPRF) would win in the presidential election in June. Although polls in April and May 1996 suggested that the communists were still in the lead, Yel'tsin's energetic campaign, with heavy emphasis on the dangers of returning to communist ways, saw him recover ground. In the first round of voting, he won 35 per cent of the vote compared to Ziuganov's 32 per cent and Aleksandr Lebed''s 15 per cent. By striking a deal to incorporate Lebed' in his team, he then proceeded to victory in the second round of voting which took place in July. Yel'tsin received 53.7 per cent of the vote compared to Ziuganov's 40.4 per cent. Amid power struggles in the government and renewed concern at the very last minute about his health, Yel'tsin once more assumed the presidency with questions being asked about what would really be new, how the state could cope with foreign debt, how taxes could effectively be collected and above all, what difference Lebed' would make to the army, security and foreign policy. Women's issues lacked profile in these campaigns.

Victims or agents of power?

A debate has been raging in the West about 'victim feminism' and 'power feminism'. To pick but two examples, in her book *Backlash: the undeclared war against feminism*, Susan Faludi made a convincing case that 'fear and loathing of feminism is a sort of perpetual viral condition of our culture' but not always in an 'acute stage'.[9] 'Backlash' characterised feminism as afflicting society with numerous evils – women were caught in the 'equality trap', living a 'lesser life', 'dehumanised' by careers and 'uncertain of their gender identity'.[10] Women were thus victims of an evangelical male reaction to notions of equal rights at home, at work and in politics.

By contrast, Naomi Wolf's controversial *Fire with fire: the new female power and how it will change the 21st century* insisted that, whereas the 1980s may have been years of backlash, the 1990s brought a new era of 'genderquake'. Women were now 'a political ruling class', but bearing the historical distinction of 'being the only ruling class that is unaware of its status'.[11] Women's anger at injustice had given rise to awakening and action, a 'power feminism' that was successful because women refused to let themselves be victims.

Many women in the post-Soviet states would probably be highly amused by the concept of 'genderquake', and unlikely to view one as imminent in Russia, Armenia or Uzbekistan. None the less, they have been engaged in numerous ways of seeking solutions to their plight. Although the results are mixed, the tendency is for women to find themselves working harder and harder in order to subsist. Simultaneously, women are surrounded by a male backlash against Soviet propaganda about the heroic 'emancipated woman' of the communist past. Both democrats and nationalists have railed against the inappropriateness of forced liberation 'from above' by the state. Their argument runs that woman was thereby deformed and robbed of her femininity. And many women, too, have subscribed to this view.

Generalisation and difference

Whilst one can make some generalisations about the fate of women and men as states of the former USSR are being transformed, 'gender' as a variable is further qualified by factors of nationality, age, education, geographic location and religion. 'Men' and 'women' are not homogeneous categories. There are thus variations among women and men and overlapping tendencies between them. Alongside general patterns, one can find exceptions; alongside apparent certainties are ambiguities.

Conventional social science examines tendencies and trends, with the objective of offering generalisations about behaviour patterns. This book explores many such generalisations. However, analysts should be careful not to let generalisation overpower diversity, difference and heterogeneity. The experiences of post-Soviet women are far from identical, notwithstanding certain similarities. One does not have to subscribe to post-modernism to be aware of immense variations across the post-Soviet states, although post-modernist sensitivities may prompt penetrating questions. The label 'post-Soviet', while handy for quick reference to the states once part of the USSR, inevitably obscures the variations between Georgian and Lithuanian, Russian and Kazakh. Moreover, within each state different categories of women and men lead very different lives.

The chapters which follow highlight similarities and differences across states and within states. They also note continuities and discontinuities over time. Despite attempts to promote privatisation, many elements of the old Soviet system persist, thereby sometimes redefining what leaders intended or shaping leaders' policy programmes. Moreover, many institutions and organisations did not collapse with the old system, but had to find new ways of surviving and mechanisms of adaptation in new economic and political settings.

Chapter breakdown and organisation

This book is organised according to theme and state. Hitherto, the literature on the USSR generally paid more attention to Russia than to the other fourteen republics. This was firstly because Soviet institutions were, in the main, run by Russians and Russia was effectively the empire builder. Second, some might argue that the sheer size of Russia meant that it merited disproportionately greater attention. Third, most specialists of the USSR in the West knew Russian, not Azeri or

Georgian, one consequence being that specialists on Russia far outnumbered scholars proficient in the languages of other post-Soviet states. Those who were specialists on the fourteen republics also tended to produce a separate and parallel literature.

The collapse of the USSR has thrown into sharp relief the importance of studying all the newly independent states and also different regions within states. Thus, this volume sets out to combine continued detailed discussion of Russia and Ukraine, building on past work and on fresh scrutiny of other independent states, some, such as Armenia and Georgia, having received fuller coverage in the past than others which have received relatively scant attention, including Kyrgystan (formerly Kirgizia) and Kazakhstan.

Part I concentrates entirely on Russia. Like this book's predecessor, *Perestroika and Soviet women*, it sets out to give an interdisciplinary treatment of the position of women in Russia from 1991 to the present day.[12] An interdisciplinary approach is essential for a full understanding of developments due to the interrelatedness of economics, politics, society and culture.

Given that the direction of the economy in many ways determines life opportunities, the first analysis focuses on women and work. Sarah Ashwin and Elain Bowers question the generally held assumption that female unemployment is higher than male. They point out that some recent statistics indicate the opposite and also show that female unemployment is declining. In fact, the much-predicted mass lay-offs of women have not yet occurred. They go on to discuss women's attitudes towards work and the importance for working women of the 'collective'. They conclude by predicting an accelerated 'downgrading' of female labour.

The picture in the countryside also defies stereotypes. Sue Bridger shows that, in 1991, in some regions under 10 per cent of those taking on private farms were rural people. Those keen to take up the new private farming were town-dwellers moving to the countryside. When the interest of country people in private farming grew, it tended to be former farm managers, specialists and brigade leaders, who were generally male. Women, however, were as crucial as ever for the labour power they offered, thereby perpetuating traditional patterns of the division of labour. Through the use of vivid quotations, Bridger gives rural women a voice in describing their overworked lives. Bridger goes on to stress the difficulty in calculating rural unemployment and argues that whether women are badly underpaid or unemployed, the result is similar – subsistence farming. Nora Dudwick's essay on Armenia in Part II nicely complements Bridger's analysis. Dudwick, too, maintains that subsistence agriculture is now an important survival strategy. In Armenia, privatisation has contributed to the insecurities of rural women. An additional dimension is that rural men have left Armenia to become contract workers in Russia and other Slavic states. Dudwick describes how sometimes the consequences for Armenian women are tragic, including forced sex with fathers-in-law and brothers-in-law, no money coming in, abandonment, suicide and the setting up by the male of a 'second family' in his new locality. Should women seek a similar comfort, they are branded 'prostitutes'. Double standards, worldwide, die hard whether they pertain to hiring, promotion, sexual behaviour or election to parliament.

Private business activity is engaged in by women in towns, too. Based on interviews with women entrepreneurs in Moscow, Marta Bruno argues that businesswomen developed an alternative ideology for the market mechanisms surrounding them. Woman's 'soul' and femininity were described by the women themselves as keys to their success. Male and female entrepreneurship, then, were located in different cultures. Women, Bruno suggests, had priorities other than making money, such as supporting social programmes and promoting 'Russianness'. Although women were forced into business in order to survive, once in it they held very different attitudes from male entrepreneurs and also from the wives, daughters and mistresses of businessmen. Networks of support among the women were thus vital.

How Russian women live in town and countryside does not necessarily match their ideal. Rebecca Kay opens the section on 'society' by introducing media images of womanhood and women's own perceptions of what constitutes an ideal. Drawing on letters written by women in 1992 entering a competition on 'The Perfect You', Kay shows that women tended to see their ideal man as strong and reliable, there to protect the weaker woman. Although there were shades of different opinion, the idea of woman as homemaker was not challenged. The ideal woman was guardian of the hearth, a perfect hostess, enjoying life with an ideal man. Kay also examines attitudes towards marriage, parenthood and paid work. She concludes that many of the beliefs held by young women have deep roots in the Soviet past.

Ideal men, however, appear to be wanting. Lynne Attwood's chapter underlines the extensiveness of violence against women in Russia. Official statistics on women murdered by husbands and lovers are alarmingly high, making the much-publicised mafia killings pale by comparison. Attwood notes the appalling old myths that persist in the justification of rape. She discusses policies on rape and male violence in Soviet and post-Soviet Russia, media treatment of violence and the recent development of hotlines and crisis centres.

Linked to this theme of ideal men and women, the idea has developed among forced migrants in Russia that 'men were men' and women were appropriately 'respected' only in the republic from which they have come. The life of migration and adaptation was perceived to have robbed women of their femininity and made them 'nasty'. Men, their womenfolk felt, now drank more than before and behaved more crudely. In her chapter on migration, Hilary Pilkington underscores its gendered aspects and, based on her own fieldwork in Central Russia and the Middle Volga, she challenges some of the mainstream conclusions of recent Russian research.

Disruption in daily life and the need to adjust to new realities has been suffered by the Afghan madonnas as well as by forced migrants. Kathryn Pinnick introduces readers to the *afganki*, the rarely mentioned women who served in the Soviet war in Afghanistan. Although the war is now over, the policies surrounding it and the consequences for those who participated have resonance for the war in Chechnia. These women lacked financial benefits, received no recognition and were tarred with the media suggestion that they were prostitutes not heroines; so they formed Anika, an organisation to press for the same status as men who fought in the war. The *afganki* were thus forced into political action in order to fight for their rights. Pinnick also discusses the political action pursued by the soldiers' mothers. This chapter neatly links social problems and political action.

Whereas the *afganki* became politicised in order to defend themselves, the former Soviet Women's Committee, renamed the Union of Women of Russia, entered the conventional political arena in 1993, as one of three members of a new political movement, 'Women of Russia'. Surprising success in the 1993 elections to the Duma resulted in twenty-three deputies from Women of Russia entering the lower house of the Federal Assembly. Chapter nine discusses how the Soviet Women's Committee adapted itself to changing economic and political circumstances. In addition, based on interviews conducted in 1995 and 1996 with deputies who had been members from 1994 to 1995 of the faction 'Women of Russia' in the Duma, Buckley examines their perceptions of success, of shortcomings, of the 'female' contribution to politics and of whether or not a women's party is needed. She also looks at the 1993 and 1995 election campaigns and reactions to the poor result of 1995 which meant that just three of the original twenty-three deputies were re-elected.

Some Russian feminists are critical of Women of Russia. In her contribution on women's groups in Russia, Olga Lipovskaya questions whether the movement developed a clear political platform, and attributes failure in the 1995 elections to this and to an inability on the part of Women of Russia to show positive results of their work in the Duma. But Lipovskaya's chapter is much broader. She describes how political activism expanded after the collapse of the USSR and how projects linking West and East developed. She goes on to examine what she classifies as 'introvert' and 'extrovert' groups. Feminist groups remain a tiny category, she emphasises, and feminism continues to be unpopular in Russia. None the less, there have been several positive developments since 1992.

Feminist ideas are making greater inroads into the newly independent states of Lithuania and Latvia. These two states, along with Estonia, immediately demanded independence after the failed *coup* of August 1991 and were granted it. All three had been calling for sovereignty since 1990. These three Baltic states expressed no wish to join the Commonwealth of Independent States which was established in December 1991 and which now boasts a membership of all other former republics of the USSR.

Nijole White's overview of the position of women in Latvia and Lithuania, which begins Part II on the newly independent states, looks at paid employment, abortion policy, political activity and the development of women's studies. White notes that Baltic women choose to look to Scandinavia and to the USA for inspiration, not to Russia. She optimistically concludes that women's movements in Latvia and Lithuania are strong enough to begin to influence policy making.

A more pessimistic note is struck by Solomea Pavlychko, writing on conservatism in Ukraine. She maintains that the euphoria of 1990 and 1991 is dead and that apathy has set in against a backdrop of economic crisis. Political parties lack strong women personalities and amount to exclusively male clubs. Segmentation of the labour force according to gender persists and discrimination against women is poorly recognised by society. Although the number of women's organisations has increased, they tend to be small and lacking in influence. They are even rarer, however, in Central Asia where, as Shirin Akiner points out, they made only fleeting appearances in 1991 and 1992 and failed to sustain themselves.

Even bleaker, at first sight, is the predicament of women in Armenia, shaped as it has been by earthquake in 1988 and by war over Nagorno-Karabakh. Industrial capacity has been badly damaged, unemployment has increased and fuel supplies are unpredictable. Nora Dudwick graphically describes the coping strategies which have resulted. She analyses how families have redefined their responsibilities, often resulting in a destabilisation of relations of authority. Dudwick notes that, as elsewhere, women have generally been excluded from the first post-communist government and those tiny women's parties which have been set up tend not to champion women's rights. Surprisingly, however, the women's party Shamiram won eight seats in 1995 in the National Assembly, faring better than Women of Russia in the same year, discussed in chapter nine. Society, however, seems to have dismissed these women as 'prostitutes'. As Kathryn Pinnick's chapter on the *afganki* observed, this label is freely applied to women who break out of accepted stereotypes.

War has cruelly hit populations in the Caucasian states of Armenia, Azerbaidzhan and Georgia and also Tadzhikistan in Central Asia. Dudwick ends her chapter with a discussion of the revived discourse of genocide in Armenia and notes that the individuals who do benefit from war are men, through looting, war-profiteering and jobs in the expanding war bureaucracy. Regrettably, a chapter on Azerbaidzhan with whom Armenia has been at war over the disputed territory of Nagorno-Karabakh (within Azerbaidzhan under Soviet rule, but where Armenians constitute the majority of the population) has not been included. This omission was not the editor's intent, and should not be interpreted as a partisan statement on the hostilities between Armenia and Azerbaidzhan. Specialists on the newly independent states are few and no one could be found to meet the publisher's deadline. The most welcome recent injection of government money into an expansion of posts in the post-Soviet field in English universities (regrettably not in Scotland, Wales or Northern Ireland) may overcome this type of shortcoming in future years.

Focusing on one particular response of women in Georgia to the war in Abkhazia, Tamara Dragadze documents a development with which most women in the West will not be familiar. Beginning in September 1993, a Women's peace train set out from Tbilisi, the Georgian capital, to Sukhumi, capital of Abkhazia, an autonomous republic within Georgia but where Abkhaz citizens were demanding independence from Georgia and had been receiving support from Russia. Pursuing peace, looking for sons, concerned about Georgian unity, evoking the commonality of mothers, or all four, women boarded the train along its route. Dragadze describes its course, captures the perceptions of some of those involved by quoting them and notes how mothers in the Caucasus are especially recognised as having a right to intervene in war in an attempt to stop men fighting. Dragadze raises general issues, which need to be confronted by scholars and feminists, concerning women's roles as peacemakers, and as both victims and perpetrators of violence.

In Central Asia, war in the former Yugoslavia, the Caucasus and particularly in Tadzhikistan are horrific lessons of where a loss of shared values and a breakdown in social control can lead. Shirin Akiner convincingly argues that civil war in Tadzhikistan has prompted 'an almost maniacal insistence' on the need to preserve stability. Hitherto, the Central Asian states have received less detailed attention than Russia. For this reason, Akiner gives a thorough historical overview of the development of these states and the relevance of Islam to women before, during and after the Soviet period.[13] She maintains that, while most Central Asians are happy to see Islam reintroduced, they prefer its separation from the state. Some women have chosen to follow an Islamic way of life, but there appears in some areas to be a growing tendency for men to impose religious norms on women. Akiner opens what may become a lively debate on whether passivity is a suitable coping strategy for women. She suggests that it may be a choice rather than a failure to choose. Moreover, it could be a 'sophisticated' response, designed to safeguard continuity, identity and community life at a time of severe flux.

Conclusion

These chapters are all written by specialists who frequently travel to or live in the regions they discuss. These scholars possess the necessary linguistic skills, conduct field work and interviews, and are deeply immersed in the histories of the different cultures concerned. It is my conviction that only such specialists can get close to the trends, complexities and ambiguities of recent socio-economic and political changes and appreciate their broader significance with any depth.

The approaches taken here are varied and the conclusions drawn are not necessarily consistent. No attempt has been made to impose a uniformity of interpretation. As a result, debates about the extent of female unemployment are likely to continue, following on from the points made in chapters two, three, eleven, twelve and thirteen. Most profitably the themes of 'victim', 'agency', 'adaptation' and 'coping strategies' could be further developed, and not just in the subfield of gender relations. These weave through most chapters. The last chapter also raises the question of the significance of passivity for women across cultural settings.

More broadly, comparative analysis across states could build on the firm base offered here. Indeed, similarities and differences have already presented themselves with regard to continuities and discontinuities with the Soviet past, segmentations in the labour force, the relative absence of women from formal political arenas, the consequences of rural privatisation and urban entrepreneurialism and the differential impacts of war and migration on women and men. Above all, the subjective dimension of women's perceptions and appraisals, whether of their role in a factory, in the fields, on a stall selling fruit, of their participation in the Duma, of their dreams of an ideal man, of how to cope with no electricity, of how to avoid the sexual advances of their father-in-law, of why they are on a peace train and of how to deal in some areas with Islamic norms newly imposed on them, are essential if we are to grasp what change means to them. An ongoing lesson for Westerners, particularly for feminists unfamiliar with states of the former USSR, is never to assume a priori the meanings of particular actions nor to attempt to graft Western values onto post-Soviet behaviours. Invariably, they do not fit. Even though some communalities and overlap may obtain, much remains significantly different and only first-hand investigation can establish the subtleties of these differences.

Notes

1 See, for example, Gordon B. Smith, *Soviet politics: struggling with change* (2nd edn, London: Macmillan, 1992); Jerry F. Hough and Merle Fainsod, *How the Soviet Union is governed* (Cambridge, Mass.: Harvard University Press, 1982); Stephen White, Alex Pravda and Zvi Gitelman (eds.), *Developments in Soviet politics* (London: Macmillan, 1990); Mary McAuley, *Soviet politics, 1917–1991* (Oxford: Oxford University Press, 1992).
2 Richard Sakwa, *Gorbachev and his reforms, 1985–1990* (London: Philip Allan, 1990); Stephen White, *After Gorbachev* (Cambridge: Cambridge University Press, 1993); Mary Buckley, *Redefining Russian society and polity* (Boulder, Colo: Westview, 1993).
3 See Mary Buckley, *Women and ideology in the Soviet Union* (Hemel Hempstead: Harvester/Wheatsheaf; Ann Arbor, Mich.: University of

Michigan Press, 1989), pp. 191–223; Mary Buckley (ed.), *Perestroika and Soviet women* (Cambridge: Cambridge University Press, 1992); Sue Bridger, 'Young women and perestroika' in Linda Edmondson (ed.), *Women and society in Russia and the Soviet Union* (Cambridge: Cambridge University Press, 1992), pp. 178–201; Mary Buckley, 'Glasnost' and the woman question' in Edmondson, *ibid.*, pp. 202–26; Mary Buckley, 'Gender and reform' in Catherine Merridale and Chris Ward (eds.), *Perestroika in historical perspective* (Dunton Green: Edward Arnold, 1991), pp. 67–80; Mary Buckley, 'What does perestroika mean for women?' in Jon Bloomfield (ed.), *The Soviet revolution: perestroika and the remaking of socialism* (London: Lawrence and Wishart, 1989), pp. 151–75; and Rosalind Marsh (ed.), *Women in Russia and Ukraine* (Cambridge: Cambridge University Press, 1996).

4 Several characteristics from 1991 to 1996 made it hard for capitalist economies to develop smoothly. These included: undeveloped banking systems (in which former state industries often set up their own banks, then lent to themselves at negative rates of interest); prices fixed by racketeers in some markets; former communist bosses taking control of state industries, generating immediate monopolies; lack of legality and a failure of the system to defend the rights of the individual; and an inability on the part of the state to collect taxes.

5 For discussion of the recent difficulties faced by women throughout Eastern Europe, see Marilyn Rueschemeyer (ed.), *Women in the politics of postcommunist Eastern Europe*, (Ardmonk, N.Y.: M.E. Sharpe, 1993). For analysis of the place of feminism in these states, see Nanette Funk and Magda Mueller (eds.), *Gender politics and post-communism: reflections from Eastern Europe and the former Soviet Union* (New York and London: Routledge, 1993). For analysis of earlier years, see Chris Corrin (ed.), *Superwoman and the double burden* (London: Scarlet Press, 1992).

6 For a fuller discussion, see Richard Sakwa, *Russian politics and society* (London: Routledge, 1933), pp. 63–73.

7 Jonathan Steele, *Eternal Russia* (London: Faber and Faber, 1995), pp. 382–7.

8 For further details, consult Sakwa, *Russian politics and society*, pp. 68–73.

9 Susan Faludi, *Backlash: the undeclared war against feminism* (London: Vintage, 1991), p. 13.

10 *Ibid.*, p. 5.

11 Naomi Wolf, *Fire with fire: the new female power and how it will change the 21st century* (London: Chatto and Windus, 1993), p. xiv.

12 Buckley (ed.), *Perestroika and Soviet women.*

13 For years scholars relied heavily on Gregory J. Massell, *The surrogate proletariat: moslem women and revolutionary strategies in Soviet Central Asia, 1919–1929* (Princeton, N.J.: Princeton University Press, 1974).

PART 1

Women in the Russian Federation

Economy

2 Do Russian women want to work?

SARAH ASHWIN and ELAIN BOWERS

From the very beginning of change in the Soviet Union it was predicted that economic and political reforms would have a significant impact on women.[1] In particular, there was an expectation that unemployment would be an inevitable consequence of restructuring, and that women would be the worst afflicted by this: 'that unemployment was primarily a female problem became practically a universally accepted point of view in Russian society from the moment when unemployment was legalised in July 1991'.[2] With the threat of mass unemployment, the negative aspects of women's work received more and more attention in the media and policy-making circles. This change in emphasis partly reflected a wish to protect men from unemployment and was also seen as socially desirable in itself. The Russian commentator Larissa Lissyutkina, for example, has argued that 'emancipation for Soviet women is not based upon a demand to work. On the contrary, liberation is perceived by many as the right not to work.'[3] It also seemed that a reduction of women's employment would make economic sense, since the cost of social provision for women, such as maternity leave and child care, is said to make 'the female labour force an extremely unattractive proposition for employers'.[4] A logical answer to the great problem of economic reform – mass unemployment – therefore seemed to be that, instead of attempting to combine several roles, women should be allowed to fulfil their biological destiny as wives and mothers.

Early statistics did seem to show that women were indeed the majority of the unemployed. For example, Natal'ia Rimashevskaia states, without giving her source, that between 1989 and 1991, 60 per cent of those made redundant were women, rising to 80 per cent amongst managerial workers.[5] Mezentseva also argued that, during the first stage of restructuring, 'as a result of a drop in production and the closure of a whole range of technically obsolete and uncompetitive sectors, the trend towards shifting women from paid to unpaid domestic labour is likely to intensify'.[6] Thus, women would 'have to content themselves with jobs offering few career prospects or chances for job promotion. As a result of these changes, women's part in decision making and management will be reduced to a minimum: women will work outside the home for economic reasons only.'[7]

Not only was a reduction of female labour participation rates widely predicted, many commentators also felt that this was desirable: men should be given jobs first and women should return to what Mikhail Gorbachev called their 'purely womanly mission'.[8] The implication was that, while some women might choose to have a career, the majority of women would prefer to stay at home and look after their children and husbands. Nanette Funk contends, for example, that, while paid work 'provides some benefits and satisfactions, such as friendship, solidarity, relief from boredom at home, some economic goods, and a degree of respect and autonomy', it nevertheless involves ' "gender alienation," having to be "like a man" ... is all too often boring and absurd and provides only limited autonomy, given low salaries ... [I]n spite of the benefits, the harm it generates is above any acceptable threshold'.[9] Similarly, Hilary Pilkington assumes that their status as 'second class workers ... encourages women to see work as materially necessary but undesirable, and thus to favour options to "return to their womanly mission" in the home'.[10]

In the same vein, Lissyutkina argues that in the past the only possible form of protest was an escape into private life; the house and, in particular, its kitchen was the only free sphere in society. 'The Russian kitchen was a front of massive resistance to the totalitarian regime and is perceived with sentimental nostalgia today'.

[Women] by no means perceive their kitchen ... as a narrow corridor cut off from the world ... in the kitchen one is surrounded by intimacy, publicity and intellectual creativity ... in the kitchen life gushes forth ... [and] quite a few more women wish to return to the kitchen in order to be relieved of doing road work, boring office jobs, construction jobs or factory work.[11]

For Lissyutkina 'every experience of life during the Soviet regime made the idea of emancipation unacceptable to women'.[12] Furthermore, 'if Russian women had something to lose in their communist past, they would undoubtedly have found a way to fight for it. The absence of any fight means no special values were left.'[13]

The images of 'happy housewives' conveyed in this account contrast markedly with economic realities, however. Overcrowding, poor facilities and the claustrophobia of most accommodation mean that workers often see their work as an escape. The kitchen may be an arena of creativity and discussion for the intelligentsia but workers gain more stimulation and companionship from their work collective. As Sergei Alasheev, one of a new generation of sociologists, specialising in the ethnography of the post-Soviet enterprise, argues, 'workers get more satisfaction from carrying out their work responsibilities, and sometimes much more, than from the time they spend with their families'.[14] Finally, it is by no means clear that Russian women are as passive as is implied by these arguments, and they are in fact attempting to hold onto their jobs for a number of reasons, something which is reflected in the employment statistics.

Does unemployment have a 'female face'?

Despite the gloomy prognoses of the early 1990s, unemployment in Russia does not seem so far to have afflicted women disproportionately. According to the survey data produced by the state statistical service, Goskomstat, there are fewer women unemployed than men, and the percentage of women among the unemployed population is declining: in October 1992, men accounted for 50.5 per cent of the unemployed and women 49.5 per cent, while by March 1995 the figures were 55.3 per cent for men and 44.7 per cent for women. The survey figures do differ substantially from those for the registered unemployed, among whom women still constitute a majority, although even here the proportion of women is declining: in December 1992 they made up 72.2 per cent of the registered unemployed, but by March 1995 this figure had declined to 62.3 per cent.[15] Women accounted for just under half of the workers newly registered as unemployed in the first three quarters of 1995, while making up a substantial majority (71.7 per cent) of white-collar registrations.[16] The fact that women appear more inclined to register as unemployed may be connected with the fact that men generally receive higher wages than women and see themselves as the primary breadwinners: the paltry levels of benefit on offer are therefore less likely to tempt them into what is still seen as the humiliation of registration, although the figures would suggest that this is gradually changing. It seems that unemployed men also earn significantly more than unemployed women from subsidiary economic activity,[17] and so are less eligible to register for benefit. In any case, of these two sets of statistics, it is the survey data which is considered to be internationally comparable: the unemployment rate found by the survey is five times higher than the level of registered unemployment.[18]

Other evidence also supports the conclusion that unemployment in Russia is far from being predominantly a 'woman's problem'. According to Goskomstat figures for the first three quarters of 1995, for example, 50.5 per cent of those placed in jobs by the Federal Employment Service (hereafter FES) were women. Meanwhile, although women do tend to be unemployed slightly longer than men, the differences are quite marginal: according to the FES figures for 1994, 8 per cent of the men registered were unemployed for over a year, while the figure for women was 10 per cent. In that year the average duration of unemployment for women registered with the service was 5.65 months, while for men it was 5.28 months.[19] Unemployed men took an average of 7.2 months to find a job, women an average 8.2 months.[20] In addition to this, in the regions of Russia most severely affected by unemployment, such as Ivanovo, men tend to account for a greater proportion of the unemployed than women.[21] According to the FES figures for 1 July 1994, women accounted for only 40 per cent of the unemployed in the textile centre of Ivanovo, often known as the 'town of single women' because of its predominantly female workforce.[22] Although women workers in Ivanovo have been afflicted by the privations associated with working short time or being sent on administrative vacation, this cannot be equated with what Russians often refer to as 'being thrown out on the street'. In other regions, where the industries are more male dominated, women often make up a far greater proportion of the registered unemployed: in Kemerovo oblast, where the Kuzbass coal basin is located and which has a low rate of unemployment, they account for 81 per cent of the total, for example. This underlines the fact that women cannot be assumed to be the primary victims of economic reform: in some regions this is the case, but not in others.

The fact that the much-predicted mass lay-offs of women have not materialised is partly explained by the fact that enterprises have to date generally avoided making large-scale compulsory redundancies. Instead, they have attempted to preserve the 'backbone' of their labour collectives, and have used strategies such as administrative leave, forced retirement of working pensioners and late payment of wages to reduce labour costs.[23] This is reflected in the unemployment statistics: according to the Goskomstat survey for March 1995, 36 per cent of the unemployed left their jobs voluntarily, as compared with 33 per cent who left because of redundancy or the liquidation of their enterprise. What the same set of figures also highlights is that women are less likely than men to leave work voluntarily: only 31 per cent of unemployed women had done so as compared with 40 per cent of unemployed men, with 39 per cent of women as against 29 per cent of men having lost their jobs as a result of redundancy.[24] Amongst the registered unemployed only 12.8 per cent of those applying to the Employment Service in the first three quarters of 1995 had officially lost their jobs as a result of redundancy, but 73.1 per cent of these were women.[25] This suggests that, where they can, women are tenaciously hanging on to their jobs, being much more likely than men to hold on until forced to leave.[26]

This interpretation is also supported by statistics on employment. These show that men have been leaving industry in greater numbers than women: the percentages of women working in nearly all branches of industry, with the exception of engineering, have increased since 1991 and the trend is most marked in those industries, such as metallurgy and wood processing, where overall employment has been most sharply reduced. In metallurgy, the percentage of female employees has increased from 36.9 per cent in 1991 to 40.9 per cent in 1994, while in wood processing the percentage increased from 39.4 to 46.2 over the same period.[27] It may be that many men are leaving industry to find better-paid work in the private sector,[28] while women are too scared to leave their traditional employment because of their more insecure labour market prospects. But this in no way contradicts the other implication of these figures: that women are not succumbing to the call of the home in the face of late payment of wages, compulsory unpaid leave, deteriorating wages and working conditions, but are doing their best to remain in paid employment.

Survey data has long supported the conclusion that women are by no means eager to leave the labour market. Both Judith Shapiro[29] and Rimashevskaia[30] cite evidence from surveys which show that, even if men's wages were sufficient to support the family, the majority of women would want to keep on working. Mezentseva[31] points to survey data which shows that while 81 per cent of those surveyed wanted to work a shorter day, only 4 per cent of engineers and technical staff, and 3 per cent of shop floor workers, said they would stop working altogether. Even given the often appalling conditions under which women work, there is enough evidence to show that women will not willingly give up the economic independence that work affords them. These attitudes have not changed as the economic climate has deteriorated. The July 1995 survey conducted by the Russian Centre for Public Opinion Research (VTsIOM) indicates that women show similar levels of commitment to work as men, and demonstrate no particular hankering for the comfort of home and hearth. Similar numbers of men and women opted for the statement 'Work is important and interesting to me irrespective of pay' (14.0 per cent and 14.7 per cent, respectively), as they did for its opposite, 'Work is an unpleasant occupation. If I could I wouldn't work at all' (3.9 per cent and 5.3 per cent, respectively). There was slightly more variation in the responses of men and women to the more moderate statements 'Work is important but there are other things more important to me' (15.8 per cent for men and 23.3 per cent for women) and 'Work is a means to earn a living; the better they pay the more I work' (62.4 per cent for men and 52 per cent for women), but, if anything, these figures suggest that women are less likely than men to have a purely instrumental attitude to their work.[32] It is true that, despite the high participation rate of women in the Russian labour market, twice as many women as men are economically inactive, but only 11.7 per cent of these women are 'people running a household': 65.4 per cent are retired and 17.1 per cent are students. The main reason why there are so many more inactive women than men is because Russian women now expect to live more than ten years longer than men – the inactive men are dead, so they do not figure in the statistics. Thus, the Russian women who are at home are predominantly not housewives, but grandmothers. The average age of economically inactive women is 49.6 years; that of economically inactive men is 44.8.[33]

Women and work

The survey and statistical data can only tell us so much, however. Unemployment levels, for example, are not necessarily an accurate reflection of who is hardest hit economically by restructuring. Unemployment itself is not a particularly useful indicator of welfare in Russia, as is underlined by the fact that, according to an analysis of the eight VTsIOM surveys carried out between January 1994 and March 1995, 30 per cent of those calling themselves 'unemployed' in these surveys were actually working more than twenty-eight hours a week, and many of the unemployed earned considerably more from subsidiary activity alone than those in full-time work earned from all sources.[34] The survey data on women's desire or otherwise to stay in paid employment is, as argued above, quite consistent. But surveys which ask women to choose between a series of predetermined statements on their attitude to work can only provide a very limited idea of the meaning of work in women's lives. The following section aims to increase understanding of the significance of paid work for Russian women workers by presenting the results of qualitative research carried out in three contrasting regions and industries. In-depth interviews were conducted with twenty women working in engineering and manufacturing enterprises in Samara; thirty women from a coal mine in the Kuzbass coal basin of Western Siberia and forty women from a printing enterprise in Syktyvkar in the Komi Republic.[35] In all cases a number of interviews were also conducted with men. A great deal of information was also gathered through informal social contact and discussions. The women interviewed ranged from engineers and administrators to unskilled manual workers, although the section below mainly focuses on the experience of workers, both skilled and unskilled.

What is most striking about the data is the similarity between attitudes of women working in different industries and regions. There was a remarkable consistency in the terms in which the women talked about the place of work in their lives; all of them saw their status as workers and members of 'labour collectives' as crucial to their sense of identity. Work provided a release from the monotony of home life, was a source of companionship and support, and participation in social production was seen as inherently valuable.[36]

The idea of home as a refuge had very little resonance among the women workers that we interviewed. First of all, living conditions for many of the workers hardly corresponded to the cosy kitchen of the Lissyutkina imagination. The case of the following print worker from Syktyvkar is by no means exceptional.

We live in a hostel obtained from my husband's work. We have twelve square metres for four people ... and there are no prospects to get a flat ... we've lived there for twelve years ... it's very difficult to live there; there is no place to rest after I've finished work for the day ... there are seventeen rooms sharing one kitchen with an average of four in each room ... there are only two cookers with four rings each.

Moreover, women workers often consider their domestic burden to be at least as onerous as their duties at work. However difficult work could be, as one of the workers from the lamp room at a Kuzbass mine argued, the problem with housework was that it was never-ending and thankless: 'You cook a meal, it gets eaten, and then what have you got to show for it?' This view was widely held and not only by women. The following married couple, workers from an aviation enterprise in Samara, claimed:

VIKTOR: In some cases it's better for women to work than to stay at home because it's too difficult at home ... contacts are too restricted and it's boring. Everyday life is so complex that sometimes it's harder than work.

OLGA: Sometimes when women go to work they say they have come for a rest ... home is very tiring and it's difficult to be satisfied with the results of work at home ... there is no end to it and you can't see the results.

VIKTOR: We just exchange two types of tiring work ... at work we have a rest from a boring home life and at home we have a rest from badly organised work.

However, in addition to escaping from their home lives, many workers, contrary to what has often been argued,[37] actually enjoyed the content of their work. This was most marked in the printing works, where jobs, although they were dirty and heavy, required a certain level of skill and creativity. In contrast to the widely held idea that women are technologically illiterate, many of the women displayed as much attachment to 'their' machines as any of the men. This, for example, was a printer, talking about her relationship with her machine: 'As a printer I could repair my machine and I loved my machine. Everyday I stayed behind after work to clean it and do small repairs, and even when we had Subbotniks [unpaid extra work on Saturdays] I still tried to clean my machine even when I wasn't supposed to.' Even in industrial enterprises where the work was apparently less creative, women often displayed the same attachment to their machines and their work.[38] The work of recharging and checking the miners' lamps in the lamp room of the mine, for example, is quite routine, but it is taken very seriously by the women who do it, as is made clear by the following comments of a forewoman on the qualities required to be a labour brigadier in the collective:

There is someone who's been working in the collective for about four years and she knows everything, understands everything, is keen and asks questions and so on – well, I could appoint her. I tried to recently but the person concerned said, 'Oh no I couldn't, I don't know the work well enough yet.' She does, she's just nervous ... There are those ... who want to know everything – how this works, how that works, what to do in this situation, that situation and so on. You have to choose people who are interested in the work because they have to set an example to the others.

Where work was not inherently rewarding, workers valued the fact that they felt needed within their labour collectives. As the following printer argued, 'I'd go mad staring at four walls all day ... we work at home as well but without any thanks ... not that we're thanked here either but at least here we feel needed, unlike at home.' Feeling needed was intrinsically linked to the feeling of companionship that most women gained within their collectives. This print worker's enthusiasm for the social life of her enterprise was typical:

If you love your job you can't stay at home and two days on the weekend is enough for a rest ... I probably wouldn't give up work even if I could ... it's my character ... I can't live without people ... I was home for eighteen months with both the children ... eighteen months is not so long ... it just flew by and I was soon back at work ... Most women want to work ... although the conditions are not so good ... you need something else ... and if all women stayed at home who would work? ... I can't even take a holiday.

Indeed, the women mine-workers had re-appropriated the Soviet era expression 'Off to work, like to a holiday' (*na rabotu kak na prazdnik*), which made joking reference to the supposedly endemic slacking among Soviet workers. This expression cropped up several times in interviews with women workers from a variety of collectives, but it was not employed ironically. Instead, it was both posited as an ideal and used descriptively. One worker from the lamp room, for example, talking about what she felt was the wonderful atmosphere that had prevailed in her collective before the forewoman had decided to break up established shift teams, claimed,

I used to look forward to going to work – I went to work *kak na prazdnik*. If I had any problems I used to get to work and tell the girls about it and they'd say, 'Don't worry Liuda, it'll all work out' and I already used to feel better. We all used to help each other. For example, we used to fight over the floor cloth: I'd say, 'look you have a rest; I'll do the floor today' and they'd say, 'No Liuda, you're always doing it, let us do it.'

Not only did women value the companionship offered by their collectives, they also felt that membership of the labour collective was something valuable in itself. Workers did not experience the Communist Party's emphasis on collectivism as an inauthentic imposition. They have, however, adapted such ideas in the light of their own experience. This woman mine-worker treated the idea of the collective with a reverence that the communist authorities would have found very pleasing, although for her the collective was not a cell in the construction of the communist future but a vital support network: 'We all know each others' problems here. The collective is your second family. You come to work and you can express (*vyskazat'*) your feelings, talk about your problems and then you'll feel better. That is how it should be.'

The idea of the collective as a family constantly recurred in interviews, which contradicts Lissyutkina's assertion that women feel that there are no values from the past worth preserving. Where workers felt that collectivism had waned during the transition period, as a significant proportion of them claimed it had, they were disturbed and saddened by this. As one forewoman from the print works commented, 'We had a very good collective and it was as a family; it was very good and small and we were all together ... now people are more separated and there are not such good relations, not such a close collective ... maybe it's because of the situation in the country as a whole ... because of the changes.' Given this attachment to the collective, it seems that women workers will, as the statistics suggest they are doing, retain their work within enterprises for as long as it is possible for them to do so. Seventy years of propaganda telling women that work was a path to freedom and the most worthy of endeavours has certainly left its mark: women will not withdraw from the labour market in the near future unless they are forced to do so.

Will women be forced out of work in the future?

As has already been discussed, policy makers tend to be ideologically sympathetic to the idea that the reduction in the labour force necessitated by restructuring could be achieved through a reduction in female labour participation rates. And this view is by no means confined to politicians: it is also common among male managers and workers. Within an ideological climate in which essentialist conceptions of sexual difference prevail, there will be strong moral pressure on women to leave the jobs for the boys. It is quite clear from interviews with male workers and managers that, while they accept the necessity for women to work when there are no men available, the same would not be true in a situation of high male unemployment. Most discussion of female employment has assumed that economic imperatives also dictate that women will be excluded from work because they are more expensive to employ. Women are, however, notoriously ready to accept lower wages and to work in worse conditions than men – in fact, bad working conditions are often actively sought by women since 'danger money' is a welcome supplement to low wages. The following section explores whether economic imperatives and ideology do in fact tend in the same direction.

Despite the fact that, according to communist ideology, women belonged in the workplace, the traditional gender division of labour was rarely challenged, either at home or at work. For this reason, the majority of men have an ambiguous attitude to women's work: they accept women's presence within the workplace on a daily basis, but retain the idea that, in a 'civilised' world, women would either stay at home or do clean, light work.[39] This, for example, was the view of a young male printer:

> Men and women should do different work, and heavy work is men's work ... and work which has long hours and night shifts and harmful conditions because women must be beautiful and weak and must not look like horses ... for example, bus drivers. Bus no. 4 has a woman driver, but imagine her in dirty overalls under the bus, covered in oil and then preparing to go to the theatre. She would smell. On the other hand, a man must be proud of his position and profession and that he earns the money for them to go to the theatre.

His view was echoed by the following miner (who is married to the enthusiastic worker referred to by the forewoman of the lamp room, quoted above):

> My wife gets very tired, she only goes to work for the money. All women only work at the mine for the money. [For] very, very low wages. At other enterprises the pay is even lower. What else is there to say? Here all women work, regardless of whether it's clean or dirty work. They only work for the money. They can work up to their waists in dirt, as long as they get paid.

Given such views, it is quite clear how most male workers would react if there was a choice between the loss of male or female jobs at a given enterprise. Certainly there is little ambiguity in the position of this fitter at the printing enterprise in Syktyvkar: 'Printing is men's work and I don't understand why there are women here. Women must be women and they cannot feel themselves to be women working here.'

As argued above, some commentators have assumed that as well as facing discrimination in the labour market of the future, women will also be disadvantaged by the fact that they are 'expensive'. This is a view which is shared by many enterprise managers. As one Samara personnel manager put it, 'work in an engineering enterprise is not for women; they're either on maternity leave, or on sick leave, or on some other type of leave'.[40] The following lament of a director of a small wood-processing and paper-producing enterprise about the cost of employing women is also characteristic:

> Discrimination against women is not allowed. But women have a right to a shorter working day and that means that it's better to employ men than women because women disrupt production. You can't interrupt production or allow women to stop work earlier than men ... there is an All-Russian Law for women in the north ... if you have men and women working on one operation ... it means you are paying women more because they work fewer hours ... and enterprises need workers who will work longer and are cheaper ... I don't have this problem in my enterprise because women and men have equal pay and no one disagrees ... if the state wants to support women they should pay this money from the budget and not force entrepreneurs to pay it ... we pay high taxes ... and this all leads to an increase in the cost of production ... the state made this provision but we are paying for it.

In spite of these considerable disadvantages, however, 50 per cent of the workforce of this director's enterprise were women. Furthermore, he also conceded in the interview that 'There are several types of work where women work better than men ... and the quality of their work is higher'. The fact that the same manager can argue that women are expensive, while also employing a large number of them and respecting the quality of their work, highlights the existence of countervailing tendencies amid the widespread hostility to women's employment.

For although many managers would concur with these comments about the expense of employing women, women continued to be employed by the very same managers and for good reason. They do jobs that men would refuse to do for the pay on offer, and they are also seen as well disciplined and easy to control. The gendering of jobs in Russia is a complex issue,[41] but there is one iron law: almost regardless of the physical strength required for a job, if it is low paid and low status it will become a 'woman's job'. This is understood and accepted by both men and women in industry. This shop chief certainly knew why the workers in her shop were women: 'It's heavy work and I don't like to see women working here, especially the linotype which is very harmful ... the printers should be men as well ... really it just turned out long ago that it was low paid and not very important, perhaps. They pay us, but only enough not to let us die.' The forewoman from the central boiler house (*kotel'naia*) at the mine was similarly clear about the reason why women were doing the heavy work in her collective: 'Yes, it's hard work for women but men would not do it for the pay that we get.' The fact that women are prepared to accept lower pay than men is reflected in the fact that men are leaving industrial employment in greater numbers than women.[42]

While women are often characterised as unreliable because of pregnancy, child care and other 'women's problems', they are also paradoxically regarded as more reliable than men. As Alasheev argues, 'women are the most categorical exponents of the norms of a conscientious attitude to work'.[43] This comes across strongly in the following quote from the director of the printing enterprise: 'We have no problems with women ... they work like bees, and with men every day there are problems. They deviate from the timetable, there are problems with labour discipline and we have wonderful women. We have problems with the kindergarten, but very rarely with the women themselves.' Similarly, the forewoman of the lamp room at the mine was categorical in her assessment of the qualities of her all-female collective. Asked if there was any absenteeism in her collective, she replied, 'Of course not. Why "of course"? Because women are serious. Once they've got work they try very hard to keep it ... this work is hard and dirty but we are still very scared to lose it.' While we would argue that women are by no means as passive as these quotations would imply,[44] the perception of them as quiescent and responsible workers increases their chances of employment in a period in which managers are supposed to be breaking away from the old discredited Soviet industrial culture.

Conclusion

The discussion above makes it clear that, while there are strong ideological and some economic reasons why women may be gradually pushed out of the labour market, there are also reasons why they may be able to remain within the industrial workforce. The question, however, is what sort of work they will be doing? What is likely to happen is that the majority of women will become even more ghettoised than they were in the past, in low-paid undesirable employment, while a small minority might be able to take advantage of the changes. As Monousova argues, currently there is 'a marked tendency for men to take over the better paid occupations and to move into the more prosperous enterprises, while women have been left behind, or have moved in the opposite direction'.[45] (Precisely this process could be observed in the printing enterprise in Syktyvkar where, as soon as new technology was introduced which involved more complex but physically lighter and cleaner work, men were brought in to 'man' the new machines at much higher pay rates than the women were receiving on the old machines.) While this is nothing new, in the present period of economic restructuring such 'downgrading' of women is likely to be both more general and more rapid.

What is clear is that the vast majority of women want to remain in work, and at present will put up with terrible working conditions and extremely low wages rather than give up their jobs. So the real question is not whether they are going to work or not, but whether they will be able to organise in defence of their rights and to improve their wages and working conditions. This raises the important question of the relationship between women's consciousness of themselves as women and as workers: at present, women have shown their readiness to defend their rights as workers, often playing a significant role in the workers' movement,[46] but until they do so specifically as women they will remain in a subordinate position at work.

Notes

1 We would like to thank all our Russian colleagues, and particularly Galina Monousova, for providing us with the most recent statistical data on women's employment.
2 Centre for Labour Market Research, *Polozhenie zhenshchin v reformiruemoi ekonomike: opyt Rossii* (Moscow, 1995), p. 26.
3 Larissa Lissyutkina, 'Soviet women at the crossroads of perestroika' in Nanette Funk and Magda Mueller (eds.), *Gender politics and post-communism: reflections from Eastern Europe and the former Soviet Union* (New York and London: Routledge, 1993), p. 276.
4 Yelena Mezentseva, 'What does the future hold? (Some thoughts on the prospects for women's employment)' in Anastasia Posadskaya (ed.), *Women in Russia: a new era in Russian feminism* (London: Verso, 1994), p. 77.
5 Natal'ia Rimashevskaia, 'Perestroika and the status of women in the Soviet Union' in Shirin Rai, Hilary Pilkington and Annie Phizacklea (eds.), *Women in the face of change: the Soviet Union, Eastern Europe and China* (London: Routledge, 1992), p. 16.
6 Menzentseva, 'What does the future hold?' p. 77.
7 *Ibid.*, p. 83.
8 Mikhail Gorbachev, *Perestroika* (London: Collins, 1987), p. 177.
9 Nanette Funk, 'Feminism East and West' in Funk and Mueller (eds.), *Gender politics and post-communism*, p. 322.
10 Hilary Pilkington, 'Russia and the former Soviet Republics. Behind the mask of Soviet unity: realities of women's lives' in Chris Corrin (ed.), *Superwomen and the double burden* (London: Scarlet Press, 1992), p. 200.

11 Lissyutkina, 'Soviet women', p. 276. Anastasia Posadskaya warned at the time that 'the programme of women's removal from hazardous working conditions ... might turn into the programme of the removal of women from production' (Anastasia Posadskaya, 'Changes in gender discourses and policies in the former Soviet Union' in Valentine Moghadam (ed.), *Democratic reform and the position of women in transition economies* (Oxford: Clarendon Press, 1993, p. 168).
12 Lissyutkina, 'Soviet women', p. 277.
13 *Ibid.*, p. 285.
14 Sergei Alesheev, 'On a particular kind of love and the specificity of Soviet production' in Simon Clarke (ed.), *Management and industry in Russia: formal and informal relations in the period of transition* (Aldershot: Edward Elgar, 1995), p. 70.
15 Goskomstat, *Information statistical bulletin no. 9 August 1995* (Moscow, 1995).
16 Goskomstat, *Survey of those applying to the employment service (form 1-T.)*, Moscow, 17 November 1995. Nevertheless, the view that unemployment is a female problem persists. Sue Bridger and her colleagues assert, without giving any reference, that 'At least 70 per cent of Russia's unemployed are women and this was already very much the case as early as 1992' (Sue Bridger, Rebecca Kay and Kathryn Pinnick, *No more heroines? Russia, Women and the market* (London: Routledge, 1996), p. 51). In July 1994, women still amounted to 77 per cent of the 12,245 registered unemployed in Moscow city and 68 per cent in Moscow region (Federal Employment Service, *Rynok truda v Rossii (January–June 1994)*, vol. 3 (Moscow, 1994)). This is where Bridger and her colleagues did their research and where unemployment is particularly a female white-collar problem (46 per cent of Moscow's unemployed women had higher education, against the national average of 12 per cent), but Moscow is hardly Russia.
17 VTsIOM, *Ekonomicheskie i sotsialnye peremeny: monitoring obshchestvennogo mneniia* 4, July–August 1995, p. 38.
18 Centre for Labour Market Research, *Polozhenie zhenshchin*, p. 26. These figures do not take into account women who are working on short time or are on administrative leave. But the point about such workers is that they are *not yet* unemployed. It is not possible in a volatile economic situation to make predictions about whom among those on administrative vacation or short time will eventually become unemployed. This is confirmed by longitudinal research on industrial enterprises which shows that enterprises apparently on the verge of collapse are often able to crawl back from the brink. For examples, see Simon Clarke (ed.), *The Russian industrial enterprise in transition* (Aldershot: Edward Elgar, 1996). The fact that women are prepared to hold on to their jobs even when faced with problems such as short time is discussed below.

19 Federal Employment Service, *Rabochaia sila na rynke truda v 1994g.* (Moscow, 1995).
20 Goskomstat, *Information statistical bulletin no. 9 August 1995* (Moscow, 1995).
21 Centre for Labour Market Research, *Polozhenie zhenshchin*, p. 28.
22 Federal Employment Service, *Rynok truda v Rossii (January–June 1994)*, vol. 3 (Moscow, 1994).
23 For a detailed example of the type of strategies employed by enterprises, see Tanya Metalina, 'Employment policy in an industrial enterprise' in Simon Clarke (ed.), *Labour relations in transition* (Aldershot: Edward Elgar, 1996), pp. 119–45.
24 Employers have many ways of persuading people to leave voluntarily, so a significant proportion of those made redundant are officially recorded as voluntary severances. Women are also much less likely than men to lose their jobs for disciplinary reasons.
25 Goskomstat, *Survey of those applying to the employment service (form 1-T)*.
26 Research on unemployed women has indicated that they generally feel that working fewer hours for less money is preferable to being made unemployed. Elena B. Gruzdeva, *Zhenskaia bezrabotitsa v Rossii (1991–1994gg.)* (Moscow: IMEMO RAN, 1995), pp. 63–4.
27 Centre for Labour Market Research, *Polozhenie zhenshchin*, p. 8.
28 There has been no systematic research on the destinations of men leaving industrial employment.
29 Judith Shapiro, 'The industrial labour force' in Mary Buckley (ed.), *Perestroika and Soviet women* (Cambridge: Cambridge University Press, 1992), pp. 21–2.
30 Rimashevskaia, 'Perestroika and the status of women in the Soviet Union', p. 15.
31 Yelena Mezentseva, 'Equal opportunities or protectionist measures? The choice facing women', in Posadskaya (ed.), *Women in Russia*, pp. 119–21.
32 VTsIOM, 1995, *Ekonomicheskie i sotsialnye peremeny: monitoring obshchestvennogo mneniia* no. 5, September–October 1995, p. 85.
33 Goskomstat, *Information Statistical Bulletin no. 9 August 1995*.
34 VTsIOM, 1995, *Ekonomicheskie i sotsialnye peremeny: monitoring obshchestvennogo mneniia* no. 4, July–August 1995, p. 38.
35 Women make up 15–20 per cent of those employed in the average mine. They are employed in the mine administration, mainly in low-grade clerical work; in auxiliary collectives such as the *lampovaia* (lamp room), *kotel'naia* (boiler house), the coal improvement facilities, building brigades, the ventilation and lift-operating workshops; in mine services such as the canteens, laundries, hairdressers, kindergartens and prophylactic health centres. Although printing is considered to be men's work in Russia, the majority of the workers in the enterprise studied were women.

36 This is reflected in the qualitative material presented by Elena Gruzdeva who interviewed a total of thirty-one unemployed women, from a variety of backgrounds, registered with the employment service. Work had clearly been very important to the respondents, as is starkly illustrated by their comments on the experience of unemployment: 'It's so hard to be at home without work that I went out and wandered the streets'; '[It's] a horrendous state. I had the feeling that I'd flown away from life (*vyletela iz zhizni*)' (Gruzdeva, *Zhenskaia bezrabotitsa*, p. 61).
37 Donald Filtzer, for example, argues that women workers 'gain little intrinsic fulfilment from the content of ... work itself' (Donald Filtzer, *Soviet workers and the collapse of perestroika: the Soviet labour process and Gorbachev's reforms 1985–1991* (Cambridge: Cambridge University Press, 1994), pp. 171–2).
38 For further examples of this from enterprises in Samara, see Alasheev, 'On a particular kind of love', pp. 72–3.
39 Notwithstanding their positive assessments of work, many women also hold contradictory views about the suitability of different types of work for *women in general* (as opposed to themselves). Statements such as 'women should not really do this work but I'm used to it' are very common. For more details, see Elain Bowers, 'Gender stereotyping and the gender division of labour in Russia' in Simon Clarke (ed.), *Conflict and change in the Russian industrial enterprise* (Aldershot: Edward Elgar, 1996), pp. 191–209.
40 Quoted in Irina Kozina and Vadim Borisov, 'The changing status of workers in the enterprise' in Clarke (ed.) *Conflict and change in the Russian industrial enterprise*, p. 157.
41 See Bowers, 'Gender stereotyping'.
42 Centre for Labour Market Research, *Polozhenie zhenshchin*, p. 8.
43 Alasheev 'On a particular kind of love', p. 78.
44 For examples of women's activism, see Galina Monousova, 'Gender differentiation and industrial relations' in Clarke (ed.) *Conflict and change in the Russian industrial enterprise*, pp. 162–90.
45 *Ibid.*, p. 157.
46 Although the most dramatic examples of independent workers' mobilisation have been in traditional 'male' professions such as mining and the aviation industry, women are often involved in small-scale struggles in defence of their rights *as workers*. For examples, see Monousova, 'Gender differentiation'. Moreover, although women's role in the miners' strike activity has not received much attention in the literature, women workers are often active in pushing the men to strike. Meanwhile, at the mine under discussion in this paper, the women had been involved in a struggle to change the shift system at the mine and female workers at one of the mine's kindergarten have resisted being transferred to the under-funded local authority.

3 Rural women and the impact of economic change

SUE BRIDGER

In the final years of the USSR's existence, the question of land ownership and the future of the country's troubled collective and state farms became one of the central battles in political and economic policy. The decision to revitalise agriculture by fostering personal initiative inevitably clashed with the vested interests and ideological constraints which had characterised the decades of state planning. Even as late as 1990, as Russia's parliament developed its legislation on land and private farming, these forces were still very much in evidence. Defending continued restrictions on land sales, for example, Boris Yel'tsin was moved to comment, 'The land is like a mother; you don't sell your mother.'[1] Within twelve months, however, with the demise of the USSR, the situation already appeared dramatically different. Not only was the establishment of new private farms to be heavily promoted, but the entire state and collective farm sector was to be completely reorganised.

Market reforms and agricultural reorganisation

In the autumn of 1991, the country had some 30,000 peasant farms. Their contribution to agriculture was, however, extremely modest: the farms occupied just over 1 per cent of agricultural land, accounted for less than 2 per cent of agricultural production and involved less than 1 per cent of the farming workforce. In the initial period of market reforms in Russia, the numbers increased rapidly, reaching 270,000 within two years.[2] Since then, the development of private farming has continued to receive official backing; there has, in fact, been a marked slowing down of growth accompanied by bankruptcies and the abandonment of land by unsuccessful private farmers in the increasingly difficult economic climate.

However much private farming might have been seen as the way forward, the future of the state and collective farms could not be ignored, if only because they employed over 25 million people. In December 1991, the Russian government initiated a massive and rapid shake-up of agriculture which was to involve the liquidation of loss-making farms and the restructuring of all others. A reorganisation committee of workers, managers and state representatives for each farm was to decide on its future shape: it could be broken up into individual private farms, converted into a genuine producer cooperative in which all its former employees could have a stake, or turned into a joint stock company.[3] Combinations of all or any of these three were also to be allowed. Employees, pensioners and socio-cultural workers on the farm's territory were to be entitled to a free share of the farm's land which, if they wished, they could choose to convert into an independent private farm of their own.

Inevitably, reorganisation proceeded far more slowly than envisaged. The vast majority of farms were converted into joint stock companies, whilst a substantial proportion even opted to retain their existing status, apparently in contravention of the government decrees. Where former state and collective farms were transformed into joint stock companies, the change often effectively appeared to be in name only. Power and authority on the farms, far from being devolved to those who worked the land, was often more highly concentrated than before. Reports from the countryside suggested that, in many cases, effective control of farming had, for some time, been passing from the ministries and local party committees and into the hands of the farm managers.[4] When the time came for major decisions about the future, therefore, rank-and-file farmworkers were likely to feel that everything had already been sewn up without them and to display a marked apathy in the face of reorganisation. As journalists reporting on the reforms often observed, after more than sixty years of collectivisation, rural people no longer trusted anyone to act in their interests and, moreover, felt understandably powerless to secure genuine change. In the words of one observer, 'concern for anything other than their plot and their cow has either been handed over entirely to management or has been usurped by them'.[5]

Finally, this attempted transformation of agriculture was taking place against a background of an increasingly critical situation throughout the Russian economy. Runaway inflation, the breakdown of established channels of supply and the failure of government both to agree prices and actually to pay for agricultural products had an immediate impact on farming, reducing the availability of fuel, fertilisers and animal feed, and leading to a sharp decline in output. As agriculture moved into a state of deep depression, it was inevitable that the consequences would be experienced directly by the millions employed on the land.

The new peasant farmers: 'masters' of the land?

From the very beginnings under Gorbachev of farm leasing, the precursor of full-scale private farming, setting up a new peasant farm had been viewed as an essentially male activity. The entire language which surrounded the issue – 'making the peasant the master of the land' – was couched in masculine terms and reinforced by the media images used to illustrate the progress of reform. Whilst there were some early examples of women, notably with a background in dairying, who personally took on leasing contracts with the aid of other, male and female, family members, the archetypal farming family of the new breed was almost invariably presented as man plus wife plus children, uniting, where necessary, with other similar family units.

The underlying reasons for this had little to do with traditional peasant notions of who should be the 'head of the household'. By the time of the USSR's demise, the single most remarkable feature of the new 'peasants' was how very far removed they were from the image which the word conjures up: around two-thirds of the new private farming families were of urban origin and, in most cases, registered their farm in the husband's name on the land they were newly settling. In some regions the proportion of rural people taking on private farms was less than 10 per cent.[6] The caution displayed by rural people in the face of the promotion of leasing initially changed little with the advent of privatisation, not least because of the problems and complications faced by anyone intending to take on a private farm. As the proportion of rural people amongst the new private farmers began to grow, however, it was primarily thanks to those who had stood closest to the socialised economy's supply lines and could expect to make good use of their contacts. As a result, new peasant farmers from rural backgrounds were themselves largely atypical of the rural population: in Novgorod region, for example, a third of all the independent farmers were former managers, brigade leaders and agricultural specialists from state and collective farms, occupational groups in which men were predominant. Concern was expressed that, by the time the mass of the rural population had overcome its mistrust of private farming, much of the best land would already have been acquired either by city people or by their former bosses deserting the sinking ship of socialised agriculture.[7] What this pattern of development also ensured was the continued predominance of men as the leading figures in private farming, with their wives and children tagging along behind.

Not that women's active participation was unnecessary on the new peasant farms: although the land was more than likely to be registered in the man's name, women's labour was seen as essential for performing what had come to be viewed as 'women's' farming activities. Whilst men were likely to take charge of all the tasks involving arable farming and, hence, the use of machinery, women would usually be heavily engaged in the care of livestock. Given the size and financial constraints of most peasant farms and their relatively small numbers of animals, very few of the new livestock units could be fully mechanised. As a result, milking, feeding and watering became essentially manual tasks entrusted primarily to women. The new peasant farms were therefore reproducing the familiar working practices of the collective farms, in which men drove tractors and women wielded pitchforks, although, if anything, in an even more extreme form.

The need for women as subordinate but essential workers was underlined in personal advertisements which began to be placed in the rural press by men who had taken on land but felt a need for female help. Their requests would usually appear in the lonely hearts columns as an appeal, not for a co-worker, but for a wife. Inevitably, the development of private farming was running up against all the problems of the ageing villages, of which the total absence of younger women, for marriage or work, or both, might well seem the most pressing:

Four of us – three bachelors of forty-four, forty-two and twenty-one and myself, a single father with a three-year-old daughter – decided to set up our own farm. We've got plenty of energy and enthusiasm but the trouble is that things don't go well without women to help. You just don't feel the same motivation. Please help us by publishing our letter, perhaps our northern lands will attract someone. I won't pretend that life's a picnic up here. There's no nursery yet and the school's quite a long way away, but it's a beautiful spot with the forest and the river. Anyone who isn't afraid of difficulties and would take the risk of coming here wouldn't regret it. We'd be delighted to welcome women from twenty to forty, with or without children.[8]

Others were perhaps even more optimistic, certainly more precise, in setting out the needs of the farm, if not their own; one, for example, specified 'a serious woman economist under 45 ... preferably with English as there is quite a lot of business correspondence'.[9] Evidently, the demands placed on the new peasant pioneers left little room for sentiment.

Women on the former state and collective farms

If the new private farms appeared to be offering women more manual labour than ever, the situation was certainly little better on the former state and collective farms. When so many of them had remained almost exactly as they were before, despite their supposed privatisation, there were few grounds for optimism that women's position might be improved through an ostensible change in property relations. Indeed, women who remained in the same jobs as before would almost certainly still be working in the same way: the only difference was likely to be a generally deteriorating work environment. A letter to the press from a twenty-two-year-old hairdresser described a characteristic scenario. She had helped her mother out, hand milking on a dairy unit in Vologda region, from the age of ten until her mother had sent her off to town straight after school. With the advent of privatisation she had been made redundant and, unable to find another job, had reluctantly gone home, and back to the dairy unit:

And do you imagine that anything on that unit had changed? Not a thing. Apart from the fact that there was milking machinery and some other stuff which went under the name of 'automatic manure remover' and 'feed conveyor' rusting in the yard. None of it actually worked. We just went on carting the feed on our backs as we'd always done, and mucking out with pitchforks and shovels. When you get home after work like that you're fit to drop. Then you have to go out milking again before lunch, and then again in the evening. There's not a trace left of my manicure or hairstyle or perfume, there isn't even anywhere civilised to get washed ... They did put a shower in on the unit. That was when there was a fashion for building things like saunas and showers and restrooms. But once they stopped having to put on a show these things were all permanently 'closed for repairs'. So that's how I live, and it's like a nightmare.[10]

Other women, in similar vein, described how the hours they worked and the fatigue they experienced had increased with the coming of the market reforms. As the value of wages fell dramatically, even where farms were still able to pay, women were having to take on extra jobs, even in addition to dairying, and were intensifying the work on their plots.

As this suggests, where there were elements of change in rural conditions as a result of the USSR's demise, they were frequently not for the better. In terms of its effect on the lives of rural women, it would appear to matter little whether change was occurring as a general result of the market reforms or as a specific consequence of agricultural reorganisation. Nevertheless, a constant theme in women's letters to the press on the results of change was the question of the degree of power now concentrated in the hands of the rural elite. Throughout the period of farm reorganisation, the rural press was full of reports of unfairness, high-handedness, arguments and widespread mistrust. Critics of the atrocious condition in which much of Russian agriculture now found itself blamed ill-considered, 'Bolshevik-style' reform in which all that mattered was speed and not content.[11] Whilst the question of any resulting abuse of authority potentially affected both men and women alike, women appeared to be particularly sensitive to it, complaining both about their own situations and those of male relatives.[12]

Throughout the final decades of the USSR's existence, the rural press had habitually printed letters from farming's whistleblowers describing instances of fraud, inefficiency and abuses of power by management. Frequently, an appeal to the central organs of the Soviet press – in effect, an appeal to the Communist Party centre – would ultimately bring down the wrath of local party organs on the head of the wrongdoer and vindicate the complaint. With the breakdown of party control, these constraints, such as they were, were removed and effective channels of complainant by rank-and-file farmworkers virtually ceased to exist. Journalists dealing with letters of complaint were observing that local officials and managers were only responding if they felt like it, and even then 'it's by inertia. People react because it's what they've always done, but that will have stopped completely in a year or two.'[13] By the time the ending of state ownership was on the agenda, there was, ironically, no one to champion the individual against the unbridled power of the farm managers. This situation had already been anticipated by some journalists in the rural press as early as 1990 as they realised that farm bosses, the 'local barons and big shots' as one journalist described them, could now act with impunity:

This paradox was 'explained' to me by one of 'yesterday's men' like this, 'I've seen the back of you scribblers trying to frighten us with your little articles! We've got democracy now, so I don't have to ask anyone's permission. The district Party committee used to order me to respond to criticism, so I responded. But now I don't owe anybody anything.'[14]

With the advent of privatisation, large numbers of 'yesterday's men' were becoming today's captains of enterprise, controlling the new joint stock companies.

By 1993–4, the abuse of power by farm managers featured in a significant proportion of readers' letters printed in the rural press. One magazine, *Sel'skaia Nov'*, in particular, had developed an editorial policy of continuing to take up letters of complaint much as before and attempting to seek redress on behalf of its readers by whatever channels were now available. As a means of securing a faithful readership it had much to commend it, whilst in terms of content the issues which arose made fascinating reading. Many of the complaints concerned housing. Always a sore point in the former USSR, the advent of privatisation meant that far more was now at stake and the potential for bureaucratic intrigue thus appeared to be greatly increased. Again and again, letters on this theme, the majority from women, describe illegal, unjust or callous treatment by farm managers and the fear of being thrown out of their home or their employment. As one woman described the new reality, 'It's as if the trade union committee doesn't exist. No one says anything at work. Everyone's afraid of losing their job.'[15]

Harassment and intimidation by farm managers was, of course, a phenomenon many rural people were obliged to take seriously in the past; those driven out of work on their state or collective farm would almost inevitably lose their housing and plot as well. Yet the fear of such a loss has grown dramatically in present circumstances now that there is no easy process of moving from one job to another or of simply being allocated housing to go with it. Fear of losing everything is enough to ensure the silence of the majority, irrespective of the behaviour of farm managements. Many of the women writing letters of complaint to the press make it clear that they know they are taking a risky step, often asking for their name and address to be withheld.

For all those who write in to the press, however, even with safeguards such as these, there are undoubtedly many more who feel unable to take any such step. In villages I visited in the summer of 1993 this was exactly the situation: there had been a recent local case of a woman farmworker who had made one unguarded comment in an otherwise unremarkable interview with a visiting journalist and, as a result, had been progressively edged out of both her job and her home by the joint stock company's director. The power that this

Brezhnev-period appointee to state farm management was able to wield over people's jobs, housing and such issues as the use and distribution of transport, goods and benefits of all descriptions was almost total. In circumstances such as these, the risks involved in talking about working or living conditions to anyone from outside the farm were potentially enormous, as those who spoke to me made me painfully aware. In particular, the sense of being completely tied because of the situation with housing ensured that people would keep their heads down whatever their private feelings. By comparison even with Soviet conditions, such a situation can scarcely be regarded as progress; as some commentators have remarked, the whiff of serfdom is unmistakeable as the old-style 'Soviet feudalism' is replaced by 'private, or rather, directors' feudalism'.[16]

Unemployment and poverty: a female problem

Unemployment, whilst evidently a serious concern in the countryside, has been consistently recorded at a far lower level than in the towns. If official levels of urban unemployment have failed to reflect the seriousness of the situation in much of Russia's industry, rural figures may well involve even greater levels of distortion. At the time of the major farming reorganisation in 1992, around one-sixth of Russia's official unemployed lived in rural areas. As in the cities, over 70 per cent were women, yet less than 1 per cent of Russia's unemployed women at this time were former farmworkers.[17] At a time when many farms were effectively on the verge of bankruptcy, a range of factors may explain this state of affairs. In the first place, when many urban women regarded registering as unemployed for a miserly level of benefit as scarcely worth the trouble, the disincentives for rural women to register, given the demands of homes and plots, the distance from employment centres and the cost of transport, were overwhelming. Secondly, the state and collective farms, like so many former state industrial enterprises, were keeping workers on the books and simply failing to pay them when times were tough. Finally, the major direct cause of official unemployment in the countryside was the collapse of the rural service sector and problems with rural industry.

Farm reorganisation and price liberalisation had led to a significant contraction of rural services such as nurseries, clinics and clubs. At the same time, galloping inflation in the price of machinery, fuel, feed and fertiliser had forced many farms to cut down their crop acreage and reduce livestock herds. This, in turn, had led to the closure of processing plants in the countryside. The effect of this on women's employment can be readily imagined. As women have formed the overwhelming majority of workers in rural services they have inevitably made up most of the newly unemployed. At the same time, women in the countryside have been subject to the same elements of discrimination as in the cities, whereby those with young children have been prime targets for redundancy.[18]

Whilst it is certain that official figures massively underestimate the scale of the problem, in present circumstances it would appear to be virtually impossible to calculate the real level of unemployment in the countryside. Whether women are officially unemployed, are temporarily laid off or are being either unpaid or chronically underpaid, however, the results are likely to be much the same. Inadequate income from formal employment pushes women back onto their own resources which, in the countryside, almost invariably means into subsistence farming. The key factor in determining how much women work on their plots is, of course, financial need.

Whilst living on the land offers an immediate means of subsistence, it clearly cannot provide an infallible safety net against the ravages of soaring inflation. Rural people, just like many urban dwellers, have seen their savings reduced to nought and their spending power decline dramatically in the initial years of the market reforms. With the demise of the USSR, *Krest'ianka* magazine, in particular, began publishing regular appeals from women for financial help and, especially, for second-hand children's clothes. Inevitably, the letters came overwhelmingly from rural single mothers, the disabled and pensioners:

I'm registered disabled but I try to do everything myself – I do the washing and make new things out of old clothes. My husband left me and forgot about his daughter; he doesn't send us a penny. They won't give work to people like me so we are fighting desperately for survival. I wondered whether strangers would help my daughter even if her own father doesn't want her.[19]

My daughter has suffered a dreadful tragedy. She lost both hands in an accident at work and her husband immediately left her with the four children. We are desperately fighting for survival but we don't have the strength to go on. The children aren't going to school this year because we have no money for clothes. We scarcely have enough for food. Perhaps some kind people would help us to clothe the children.[20]

It is clear from reading these desperate appeals that, if living in the countryside can provide some basic foodstuffs, it may ensure little else for the least protected groups in society. It is, perhaps, also worth pointing out that the second example quoted is by no means untypical: one of the most chilling features of these letters of appeal is the frequency with which sick or disabled women, or those with children in a similar condition, describe being abandoned by their husbands when the illness or accident occurred. For women in situations such as these, subsistence farming alone cannot be the answer: women who are pensioners, disabled, or single mothers of very young or sick children may simply not be physically capable of providing for themselves sufficiently from a private plot.

At the time of the last Soviet census in 1989, the impact of the migration of young people into the towns could be clearly seen: in the fifteen central Russian regions, between 30 and 40 per cent of the rural population were pensioners. In the Russian countryside as a whole there were three times more women than men of pensionable age; taken together, these statistics produced the phenomenon of thousands of dying villages in which virtually all the inhabitants were female pensioners.[21] This concentration of the elderly in certain rural areas has undoubtedly created additional problems as economic conditions have deteriorated. The extent to which pensioners have been affected by the market reforms has, of course, depended very largely on the kind of pension they had, although inflation has undoubtedly had a universally damaging effect on the value of savings. In purely financial terms it is arguable whether pensioners as a group have been affected as badly as large and, especially, single-parent families, for example. In the wake of farm reorganisation, however, it is not simply inflation which has hit rural pensioners hard.

As the former state and collective farms were charged with the provision of services on their territory, there was a widespread assumption that farms had a duty to look after the welfare of retired employees. Many farms took this obligation very seriously, providing regular help with winter fuel and with repairs to housing. Not all, however, were so conscientious and it was a regular feature of rural life for men with skills and access to materials to offer their services 'on the side' in exchange for bottles of vodka or home-distilled spirits. Indeed, some of the earliest and least expected casualties of Gorbachev's anti-alcohol campaign in the mid-1980s were elderly women caught distilling as a means of exchange. With farm reorganisation, the need for vodka has undoubtedly become more acute as responsibility for services has been transferred to hard-pressed local authorities and as farms have ceased to see social welfare as part of their function. Moreover, as the economic situation of the farms themselves has worsened, the money simply may not be there for 'non-essentials'. In such cases, pensioners are effectively abandoned to their own resources which, in many cases, means that they have to put up with deteriorating housing or inadequate heating.

In the published letters to the press asking for intervention in situations such as this, elderly women most frequently describe houses which are literally falling apart around them and the extreme cold they face in winter. Turning to the press, however blunt an instrument this may be, clearly remains a last recourse for those who have no one else to assist them. As inflation and the loss of free and subsidised public services have made the elderly very vulnerable, the differences between those with viable support networks and those without may become very visible. In one of the villages I visited in 1993, the comments of two women pensioners illustrated the point.[22] Whilst their pensions were actually very similar, the first had younger family members to help her:

> Prices are dreadful now. I get 15,200 roubles pension for all my years of work and the war years under occupation. How are you supposed to live? Bread and milk, that's all you can afford. Butter maybe. To heat this house in winter it takes three lorry loads of wood and each one costs 20,000 roubles. Then you've got to chop it up and prepare it all.

Despite her complaints she went on to describe her own situation as relatively good by comparison with others who were on their own. This second comment came from a woman in a family where the men had a history of alcohol abuse. As a result, she was effectively living on her own resources, as she had evidently done for most of her life. She became very upset as she described her situation:

> When I first retired I got 103 roubles and that was plenty. I could buy everything I wanted with 50 and then put 50 aside. Now I get 14,000 and I can't do anything. I need medicine but it costs 22,500 just for one packet so I can't buy any. I just have to make do with the things I've got. Everyone used to be the same. It didn't matter if you were a dairywoman or a doctor, you could buy the same clothes and live the same – there weren't these big differences between people. Life for women here now is unbearable, it's very, very hard.

In current circumstances, levels of income alone cannot offer an adequate guide to well-being. The disparity between the material comforts, health and state of mind of these near neighbours was glaringly apparent and one in which their wider family situation played a key role. The rapid descent into poverty which hit so many elderly women in the countryside from 1992 was an event for which they were neither financially nor psychologically prepared. The result, in what must be a cruel irony for some, may be that they have no choice but to buy vodka for others rather than bread for themselves whilst struggling to provide for their own needs as best they can from their plots.[23]

The private plots: is the future female?

Throughout the decades of socialised agriculture, private allotments remained a vital resource, not only for the subsistence of rural families, but also for the provision of food to the cities. It was an activity in which women were key figures.[24] In the last three years of the USSR's existence, with restrictions scrapped and a deteriorating food situation in the towns, the acreage and output of private allotments increased significantly, producing almost two-thirds of the nation's potatoes and a third of the meat and vegetables.[25] For women, this development was of considerable significance. Not only did expanding production on the plots avoid the risk factors and substantial initial investment of the new peasant farms but, perhaps most importantly, it was highly flexible and could be readily adapted from year to year. Expanding this form of production to provide both food for the family and income from the sale of produce was a very different proposition from the formal start-up of a small business with a substantial commitment to be maintained and debt to be serviced come what may.

Before the full impact of market reform made itself felt in the countryside, diversifying and developing this form of private endeavour might appear to women to be both rational and manageable; it was, after all, an activity which they knew well and which they could control by taking into account their own and their family's capacities, as one woman from a Riazan region village explained:

Before the summer season, when it's still winter, the most important thing is to weigh up your capabilities – what's my health like, was last summer too much of a strain, what sort of a mood is my husband in, is he exhausted, is he complaining about something serious which will absolutely wear him out? Will my son, who's a student, come home for the holidays or will he go to the seaside with his friends? Will my daughter and son-in-law come here on holiday and, if so, when? Have we got pumps, hoses and polythene in store to get the whole thing going? How much money do we need this year – do we need a lot, or just a little? When we've looked at all of that then we plan whether we need to make a big profit, a small one or an average one – and that decides whether we plant cucumbers on the whole allotment or just on a part of it.[26]

This description of the decision-making process involved in the management of a plot provides a classic example of the interconnection between farming for subsistence and farming for profit.

Nevertheless, with the catastrophic fall in living standards from 1992, these kinds of calculations began to give way to the demands of survival. The expansion of plots, in particular the addition of greater numbers of livestock, and the intensification of all forms of activity connected with them inevitably made enormous demands on women's time and energy. By the summer of 1993, coping with the plot was becoming a major theme in women's perceptions of their lives. The following comments were made by three women, all in their thirties, in the villages I visited at this time. All three were married and none had to rely solely on their own ability to provide for the needs of their children:

Everything's expensive. Without my plot I couldn't live. It's absolutely essential. I have chickens but lots of people have started to keep cows now. I work on the plot from morning till night ... These days we try and do everything we possibly can for ourselves, as much as possible.

I'm tied by the plot through the summer so I can't take a holiday. I had a month's leave and I managed to get to town twice. The plot is a lot of work and I can't leave it now. I never stop.

People have bigger plots than before and keep a lot more livestock because of the economic situation. They try and rely on themselves as much as they can. I have no free time at all ... I have three children and a large plot. And I don't manage. I don't manage. And it upsets me a lot.

As growing and preserving the family's vegetables and caring for livestock, especially cows, have always been viewed as 'women's work' in the Russian countryside, it has been virtually inevitable that women's prime responsibility for the plot in Soviet times should be directly extended into this major subsistence and marketing activity in the wake of the market reforms.

There are, however, other factors which leave women with prime responsibility for this area. As men were always far more involved than women in the black economy in the former USSR, they are now much more likely to be engaged in what is loosely termed 'commerce': buying and selling or dealing in services of one sort or another. As one woman from the villages I visited put it, 'Lots of people, the men that is, are involved in trading now. You don't know what they do.' The vagueness which surrounds this area may in part reflect an understandable desire to avoid trouble: women may well imply that they have no wish to know exactly what 'commerce' involves. In women's eyes, however, there is also an undoubted element of evasion surrounding these activities: whilst women see themselves as being tied to the plot, they may perceive men as simply finding new routes into additional leisure. In the countryside, leisure for men frequently means alcohol consumption, a phenomenon which appears to have become even more significant since the demise of the USSR.

If alcohol abuse has for decades been described as a major problem in the countryside, there is a widespread conviction that matters have got much worse of late. Letters to the press from rural women discussing family issues are littered with descriptions of the results of alcohol abuse, whilst rural doctors and teachers express great concern about the impact on children in particular.[27] One rural doctor whom I interviewed in 1993 described alcohol abuse as the major public health issue in his area and had no doubt where he wished to lay the blame: 'There is absolutely no basis for proper agriculture and the state knows this. That's why there's so much alcohol. It's state policy; let people drink and then they won't think about it ... When wages are so low you might as well drink them away.' Commenting that, 'to be frank, I think women's lives in the countryside are unbearable,' he went on to describe a growing number of local cases of women drinking heavily, sometimes putting themselves in hospital as a result.[28]

Despite this observation, most women in the countryside appear to see themselves as having little choice other than to feed the family, irrespective of what the men are doing. In their letters, women often comment that their husband began to drink because he was upset or depressed at the turn events were taking, yet are likely to regard this kind of behaviour as a luxury they cannot afford themselves: 'women don't have time to get depressed'.[29] Certainly, there is an element in women's descriptions of their lives in which men are seen as being either out of control, easily wounded or lacking in conscience. As one woman in the villages I visited summed it up, 'The women take absolutely everything on themselves. The men are all alcoholics, they won't do anything.'

In this environment it is therefore primarily rural women who have presided over the intensification of production on the plots, providing for their own subsistence, frequently for that of urban relatives and, in addition, a surplus for sale. It is, consequently, also women who have been organising cooperative activities, such as rotas to tend the increasing numbers of cows at pasture, to share responsibilities as the work develops. It is also women, it must be said, who are often highly active in stealing animal feed from the former state and collective farms' dairy units to support their privately owned livestock. By 1994, the plots were making an increasingly vital contribution to food production: a survey in Pskov region, for example, found the plots producing over 50 per cent of the area's milk and meat, and almost 90 per cent of the honey, potatoes and vegetables. Comparisons with the much-vaunted peasant farms were deeply unflattering: by 1996, the new peasant farms were reported to be producing 3 per cent of Russia's agricultural produce on 5 per cent of the land. Figures from 1994, meanwhile, showed the plots producing 46 per cent of gross agricultural product on 3.8 per cent of the land.[30] Looking at figures like these, prevailing attitudes and policies towards these two areas of farming were appearing increasingly difficult to justify.

Whatever the criticisms of state help to the new peasant farms, the fact remained that a system did at least exist for their support, most importantly involving access to credit and subsidies. The legal status and, hence, access to state support of those developing private plots was, however, completely different. Even though, with the passage of time, the new peasant farms and the old private plots might increasingly resemble one another, their owners were viewed through the prism of market reform ideology. As the new peasant farms tended to become smaller, the private plots were enlarging: in both cases, family members would most likely be employed elsewhere at the same time as working their land. Yet, in the one case, those involved were seen as the heroic vanguard of the market reforms and, in the other, they were the USSR's 'money-grubbing peasants', now being dismissed as the equally unenlightened lumpenproletariat of the joint stock companies. In these circumstances it is difficult to avoid the conclusion that the difference in perception also owed a great deal to the media's promotion of high profile male 'farmers' battling against the remnants of communism, compared with their disinterest in the armies of women silently getting on with a mere extension of their housework. When Russian politicians and Western commentators frequently managed to discuss the future of farming without even mentioning the private plots, this was becoming ever more ironic given the crucial role they were playing in securing the country's food supplies.

Concentrating on macroeconomics, in the view of some Russian academics, had led policy makers into the trap of being unable to see what was actually going on. As Rudolf Praust, head of the Agrarian Institute laboratory in Pskov region, observed whilst discussing the future of the private plots,

> No renaissance, no reform is possible if we do not know what is going on at the level of the family ... These moves which are being made today in peasant families, at the micro level of agricultural production, give us reason to believe that in the next four to five years these tiny, small and medium-sized family farms will *en masse* become one of the most important producers in Russia, i.e. our major providers.

To this end, he proposed that the legal and economic distinctions between the new peasant farms and the private plots be abolished and that full state support be extended to the owners of private plots with a view to developing them steadily into larger peasant farms.[31]

As far as women are concerned, if this really is the future then it is based firmly on a return to intensive manual labour, whatever the official status of the small farms on which it occurs. Yet, if the new high-risk peasant farms are not for women, the old, low-risk private plots at least have the potential to offer some financial security. Given the highly problematic nature of men's contribution to family income, especially with the evident increase in alcohol abuse, this is not to be taken lightly. Women's heavy investment of time and energy into their plots may at least bring them a measure of independence, whilst a change in legal status, if it could be attained, would at last allow for genuine recognition of what women actually achieve on the land. Developing the plots will undoubtedly come at a cost for women in terms of health, fatigue and time for other things; in the current climate in the Russian countryside, however, it may well be the best that can be expected and, as such, a price that women are increasingly prepared to pay.

Notes

1 *Izvestiia*, 4 December 1990, p. 1.
2 *RFE/RL Research Report* 25, 19 June 1992, p. 60; Iurii Govorukhin, 'Obratnoi dorogi net', *Sel'skaia Nov'* 1, January 1994, p. 5.
3 Before the demise of the USSR, legislation was approved to end the state control of enterprises and allow their conversion into joint stock companies. Shares in these companies were to be sold preferentially to the enterprise's own employees. The privatisation programme put into place

by the new Russian government permitted an enterprise's employees to acquire a controlling interest in its shares: the overwhelming majority of privatised enterprises followed this model when converting to joint stock companies. It was a model which was particularly favoured by enterprise directors as a method of privatisation which should, and indeed, did, allow them to remain in control. The transformation of state and collective farms into joint stock companies which took place from 1992 usually involved the allocation to farmworkers of shares in the farm's land and assets on the basis of length of service and annual labour input. Farming would then still be carried out collectively and the farm would be managed as before. Conversion of a state or collective farm into a joint stock company, therefore, implied the least degree of change of any of the methods of farming reorganisation.

4 Igor' Filonenko, 'Kolkhozniki, voennye i aferisty formiruiut novyi klass: sotsial'nyi portret fermera', *Nezavisimaia Gazeta*, 29 April 1992, p. 4; Iurii Evstifeev, 'Dolgaia duma – lishniaia skorb'', *Sel'skaia Nov'* 9–10 September–October 1992, pp. 12–14.
5 Evstifeev, 'Dolgaia duma – lishniaia skorb'', p. 13.
6 *Krest'ianskaia Rossiia*, 14 September 1991, p. 3.
7 *Moscow News* 43, 1991, p. 4.
8 'Bez zhenskikh ruk delo ne sporitsia', *Krest'ianka* 2, February 1992, p. 36.
9 'K dobrym liudiam', *Krest'ianka* 7–8, July–August 1992, p. 12.
10 Nina Martynova, 'Legko li v derevne byt' molodym?', *Sel'skaia Nov'* 3, March 1994, p. 14.
11 See, for example, Vasilii Vershinin, 'K rynku, no ne s zakrytymi glazami', *Sel'skaia Nov'* 3, March 1994, pp. 3–4.
12 This phenomenon was not new. It could be observed even in the heavily censored Soviet press of the Brezhnev period and, subsequently, became particularly apparent in the content of letters rural women wrote to the press with the introduction of glasnost under Gorbachev. It seems likely that women's sensitivity to the abuse of authority is related to the widespread discrimination which has kept women out of management jobs and frequently ignored their appeals for better conditions. See Susan Bridger, *Women in the Soviet countryside* (Cambridge: Cambridge University Press, 1987), pp. 82–7 and Sue Bridger, 'Rural women and glasnost', in Beatrice Farnsworth and Lynne Viola (eds.), *Russian peasant women* (Oxford: Oxford University Press, 1992), pp. 299–302.
13 Interview with Tat'iana Blazhneva, *Krest'ianka*'s letters department, 17 April 1991.
14 Iurii Govorukhin, 'Naprasnye khlopoty?', *Sel'skaia Nov'* 3, March 1991, p. 1.
15 Nina Martynova, ' "Bol'she terpet' ne mogu!" ', *Sel'skaia Nov'* 1, January 1994, p. 10.
16 R. Khairtdinov, 'Biznes po-bratski', *Sel'skaia Nov'* 8, August 1994, p. 11.

The word used by this commentator was 'barshchina', or corvée, the obligation to work for nothing for the feudal lord.
17 M. E. Baskakova, 'Sotsial'no-ekonomicheskie problemy polozheniia sel'skikh zhenshchin' in Marina Malysheva (ed.), *Gendernye aspekty sotsial'noi transformatsii* (Moscow: RAN Institut sotsial'no-ekonomicheskikh problem narodonaseleniia, 1996).
18 Vladimir Terekhov, 'Rossiiskie selianki odni nivu ne podnimut', *Nezavisimaia Gazeta*, 12 August 1993, pp. 1–2.
19 'K dobrym liudiam', *Krest'ianka* 5–6, May–June 1992, p. 6.
20 'K dobrym liudiam', *Krest'ianka* 2, February 1993, p. 8.
21 T. Levina, 'Demograficheskaia situatsiia v sel'skoi mestnosti', *Vestnik Statistiki* 1, 1992, p. 11.
22 The two villages I visited were both situated on the same former state farm. One had around 400 inhabitants and housed the central administration of the farm, the school, the shops and so on. Alongside traditional Russian houses it had several blocks of flats built by the farm with full amenities. The other village had fewer than fifty permanent residents; its traditional housing had electricity but there were no other services or utilities of any kind.
23 For a fascinating analysis of the use of vodka as a means of exchange in the countryside, see Myriam Hivon, 'Vodka: the "spirit" of exchange', *Cambridge Anthropology* 17(3), 1994.
24 See Bridger, *Women in the Soviet countryside*, pp. 106–8.
25 *Ekonomika i Zhizn'* 40, 1991, p. 15.
26 Viktor Konov, 'Reshaet-to khoziaika ...', *Sel'skaia Nov'* 11–12, November–December 1992, p. 9.
27 See, for example, Svetlana Amelekhina, 'Otkuda optimizm u sel'skogo doktora?', *Sel'skaia Nov'* 5, May 1994, pp. 16–18; also, see 'Obshchaia nasha beda', *Sel'skaia Nov'* 4, April 1994, pp. 7–9.
28 At the time these remarks were made, vodka cost 500 roubles a bottle in the village shop, less than a packet of tea, the same as 250 grammes of cheese. The average monthly wage in Russia at this period was officially put at 65,400 roubles and the subsistence minimum per head (based on a basket of nineteen basic food items) was 27,000. On the farm in question, dairy women's wages were averaging around 20,000 – although at the time they were not being paid – whilst nursery teachers were on 12,500.
29 'Avtoportret sem'i na fone rynka', *Sel'skaia Nov'* 9, September 1994, pp. 8–9.
30 Professor Vasilii Uzun, 'Farm reorganisation in Russia', paper presented at the BASEES Annual Conference 1996.
31 Tat'iana Mar'ina, 'Segodnia svoi ogorod – zavtra svoia ferma', *Sel'skaia Nov'* 9, September 1994, p. 7.

4 Women and the culture of entrepreneurship

MARTA BRUNO

> I can assure you of one thing with certainty – it is negative: my presentation will be devoid of all theory. In this fashion I hope to succeed in allowing the 'creatural' to speak for itself: inasmuch as I have succeeded in seizing and rendering this very new and disorienting language that echoes loudly through the resounding mask of an environment that has been totally transformed. I want to write a description of Moscow at the present moment in which 'all factuality is already theory' and which would thereby refrain from any deductive abstraction, from any prognostication, and even within certain limits, from my judgement – all of which, I am absolutely convinced, cannot be formulated in this case on the basis of spiritual 'data', but only on the basis of economic facts over which few people, even in Russia, have a sufficiently broad grasp.
>
> Walter Benjamin, letter to Martin Buber, 23 February 1927

Introduction

As new economic institutions and business culture and practices develop in Russia, entrepreneurship and small and medium enterprise formation have become key words and all-favourite policy recommendations in the transition process to the market. While the contradictions between the formal and informal levels of economic development are fairly widely recognised both by business actors and analysts (Russian and foreign), little attention has been given to some of the implications that these double standards are having on women's ability to access the business environment as earning producers.

The absence of community mechanisms to promote the acquisition of knowledge on the changing economic and social environment is producing a gap between an elite stratum of new 'successful' economic actors and the average citizen. The new economic elite is mainly urban based and male. Their economic success is often built on networks of access to goods, information and contacts either dating back to their professional position in Soviet times or due to their 'family background'. The dominant cultural parameters in this group tend to push women towards a non-earning and therefore wealth-indicator function as 'wives of' and 'daughters of'. Women who do work are mainly in subordinate positions and find it very difficult to move out of waged labour and set up their own companies, especially in the absence of male business-partners. Women who succeed in becoming entrepreneurs are usually limited to specific sectors, such as services or the production of cultural/educational activities or textile and fashion businesses where interference of organised crime and perceived risks are lower.

At the other end of the income spectrum, many women are looking for ways out of unemployment and underemployment by resorting to petty entrepreneurial operations or cottage industry activities. Entrepreneurialism tends to be not an informed choice but a survival strategy. The chances of long-term survival of such activities tend to be extremely low since they cannot access institutional support and seldom have the ability to expand on their own profit. What could become a successful economic activity is constrained by being a form of income supplement because of a lack of access to appropriate information and external support.

In this chapter I propose to analyse the cultural and social formation of two groups of women entrepreneurs or potential entrepreneurs – the successful ones and those who do it for survival purposes – against the wider context of institutional and political discourse and practices. I shall also be examining the breakdown of social welfare structures and of new stereotypes of feminity and changing values of women's role. Within these two groups of entrepreneurs there are further breakdowns in women's differing responses to dominant male entrepreneurial culture, which contribute either to reinforcing it or to creating a countercultural discourse on women's role in civil society.

The background for this chapter is based on research on women in the labour market in Russia and changing notions and practices of work conducted between 1991 and 1995. Over this period, I visited and interviewed Russian and foreign organisations connected with women and business (associations and clubs of women entrepreneurs, business incubators,[1] support, drop-in and training centres, international aid and technical assistance programmes, business schools and courses, state and private employment bureaux and services, local Moscow administration and federal government agencies, academic institutions, radio and television programmes and newspapers and business magazines), as well as conducting extensive ethnographic research on women and men in the service sector in Moscow. In November 1995, I interviewed some of the respondents from my previous work who had set up their own businesses, as well as interviewing women entrepreneurs, members of the associations and clubs I had contacts with and women street-vendors. The interviews quoted in this chapter are all from a set of twenty-one more formal one-to-one interviews which I was able to tape. Other interviews, especially those with street-vendors who are harder to access formally as respondents, were conducted on a group basis and through 'chats'.

The picture from above: imposing a tradition of market and capitalism in Russia

The introduction of capitalism and free-market relations in Russia is no longer a recent and uncharted event. The days when politicians, journalists and academics, both Russian and foreign, engaged in heated debates about different paths and possibilities for economic transition are gone, and by now those same people are analysing and confronting the initial results of the first five years of Russia's market romance. Critics and analysts are now busy taking in and deconstructing the first effects of privatisation, institutional reforms, labour market upheavals and the capricious behaviours of financial and commodities markets in order to construct the political economy of the new Russia's next five-year plan.

There is general consensus that the process of transition is only beginning and that Russia will have to endure a much longer period of hardship, striving and sacrifice before it will reach its object of desire, that of becoming a fully fledged market economy. But what is a market economy? And what do models of a market economy become when they meet with individuals, each with their own ways of understanding, reacting to, consuming and reproducing the new frameworks of economic relations? Increasing attention is being paid to different social groups which are playing lead parts in transforming market models into market realities: new Russians, old political elites, organised crime, youth, pensioners, workers, ethnic groups and women, whether they fall in the category of victims or of survivors, are all receiving their deserved share of importance in their choral participation in the making (or un-making) of Russian capitalism. The further question that really needs to be asked, and which I will attempt to analyse in relation to women and entrepreneurship, is that of whether the market has an intrinsic power to revolutionise culture and social relations or whether individuals are really responsible for the production and reproduction of cultural meanings and practices which engender the market. A combination of both would presumably provide a sensible answer to this question. But while the impact of the market on people has been quite extensively analysed, the impact of people on the market has not received, so far, the attention it deserves.

The initial reports of Russian women's experiences of the market are quite bleak, as Sue Bridger showed in chapter three. Women are generally acknowledged as one of the groups paying a high price in the country's process of economic restructuring. As the story goes, women have been hit in a much larger measure than men, by unemployment and downward redeployment, and are expected to suffer even more severely as the mass lay-offs in the industrial sector become an inevitable step after the completion of the privatisation of state enterprises. The inheritance of the double burden still weighs heavily on women's shoulders and exposes the weaker categories of older women and of single mothers to even greater poverty. But even other categories of women, which in the West would be less likely to suffer, seem to be caught in the downward spiral of worsening economic conditions and living standards. Most women with higher specialised education working in former state industries, branches of government administration and technical and academic institutions are frequently forced out of their jobs, if not through direct dismissal, then by the substantial lowering of their real wages.

The cornerstones of government ideology and legislation affecting women, both during perestroika and under the Yel'tsin leadership, are well known: they consisted of a mismatched cocktail of encouraging women to return to the home and engage solely in both the material and spiritual aspects of household reproduction, and also a wide assortment of usually ineffective attempts to re-train women or somehow re-direct them to different sectors of the labour market. By allowing a number of unofficial, and often illegal, practices to develop, the Soviet state let women drift towards survival strategies, unable to create any better alternatives to help them survive the transition. Failing to supply state-sector employees with sufficient and timely wages and with meaningful and useful jobs, the government turned a blind eye to employees taking on second and third jobs, spending their official work-hours in subsidiary economic activities or even using work premises and facilities to pursue alternative sources of income.

A further negative side to the relationship between the Russian state and women is usually identified in the breakdown of the social contract.[2] As a result, women can no longer rely upon social services and a distribution system that took some pressure off their shoulders. Without wanting to minimise the state's withdrawal of responsibility in the social contract, I would argue that, for at least the last decade of the Soviet regime, more and more private citizens had decreased their use of public-sector facilities, if they could afford to do so. The elements of social stratification were clear in this process. Given that the quality of public-sector services was in constant decline, all those who could, strove to find private solutions to child care, health care and consumption, while resorting to the use of networks and bribery for other needs. More than being broken, the social contract was eroded and this process happened on both contractual sides, with sections of the population constructing more efficient networks of survival for themselves.

The late Soviet system was, especially to Western eyes, the sublimation of all that was irrational and inefficient in economic and social terms, the overall expression of *russkii absurd* (Russian absurd). It was, nevertheless, a system complete with its frameworks, rules and shared practices which found a legitimacy in people's everyday lives and in their production of values and culture. The introduction of capitalism and of the market is usually seen as a clear dividing line between the old and the new, akin to the dropping of a bomb on a malfunctioning society. The popular word 'transition' is used only in relation to post-1991 events, as if the introduction of capitalism provoked a sudden crisis of values and initial period of confusion which will, with time and appropriate endeavours, clear up. In the meanwhile, various social groups, amongst which women figure large, are expected to bear the hardships necessary to the implementation of a market economy, passive victims of the new system. Falling living standards, poverty and unemployment are plights which the vast majority of the population have to confront on a daily basis; but they do not just passively submit to them. The transition to a supposedly modern free-market model presents apparent characteristics of 'exclusion' and 'inclusion' of different social groups, which, while placing Russia on the map of global capitalism, erects economic and social thresholds at the local level.

Nevertheless, when considering the argument of the introduction of capitalism and market relations to Russia from the angle of individuals' real-life experiences, there comes the realisation that it is relatively unlikely to find blue-prints outside the macroeconomic frameworks. Elements of continuity with the old regime are just as numerous as ones of change. Individuals all over Russia are busily getting on with their daily working and private lives and, in the process of doing so, engage in the production and the consumption of values and practices which at times bear resemblance with capitalist ones, at others with Soviet ones, but often are careering into uncharted directions. The heterogeneous group of Russian women entrepreneurs is, in this respect, a particularly active one.

The picture from below: women invent a tradition of proto-entrepreneurialism

One of the most visible results of the new economic conditions in Russia is that the majority of women have been pushed into entrepreneurship. In most cases, the motivation to engage in some sort of business activity stems from need rather than from choice. As already mentioned, the economic resources that women had at their disposal, be they from direct employment or from other sources of state provisions, have been severely curtailed. Traditionally, Soviet society had placed women in a position of major and often sole responsibility towards the social reproduction of the household. Furthermore, the ever-increasing aridity of the public sphere in which they were allowed, at best, a marginal position, had pushed women to invest further into the private. Economic dire straits and the generalised feeling of systemic uncertainty that has dominated in the country for the last decade, have pushed many women consciously to turn their imposed role of carer and domestic provider into a clear-cut and often passionate choice. The well-known hostility of most Russian women towards stances of Western European and North American feminist ideas does nothing but reinforce this choice.

As most Russians would argue, the urge to provide material and emotional support for the family is 'natural' to women[3] and, even though it need not be a unique endeavour in life, it is definitely a priority for many. Ironically, this same urge is also what has pushed many women to adopt and develop broad entrepreneurial attitudes towards life. These attitudes became part of the dominant culture in the Brezhnev era, a long time before the first whiff of market relations had officially been introduced to Russia. The constant difficulties in consumption and the absence of direct time-saving devices in the running of the household had turned women into able managers and specialists in marketing operations. Given that money had little *de facto* buying power, women invested their efforts in constructing complicated systems of barter of goods and favours and in cultivating networks of insider knowledge and information. While the objects of exchange, be they actual goods, personal favours or insider access to services and connections, might seem primitive by standards of developed market systems, the degree of skills required to operate successfully within this complex organisation was a highly sophisticated one.

Discussing the culture of consumption, Caroline Humphrey quotes from Katherine Verdery to describe how the formation of identity and selfhood in opposition to the regime happened through the acquisition and consumption of goods and objects.[4] 'Socialism intensified this experience'[5] and constructed patterns of motivation and desire that constituted the kernel of an entrepreneurial mentality. 'Goods must be procured with difficulty (*dobivat'*), unearthed (*otkopit'*), obtained on the side (*nalevo*), from under the counter, or from such crafty places as are known only to the dedicated.'[6]

Having lived for extended periods of time in Russia in the last years of perestroika, I experienced the crucial importance of networks of friends and acquaintances to procure even the most basic livelihood. Women were obviously the overseeing managers of the most intricate operations for the procurement of disparate supplies, services, leisure, accommodation, information and contacts. They would identify the need, tap into the most rich and fertile mental data base and provide, often through obscure paths, the solution to the problem. What appeared most striking was the lack of distinction between material and non-material objects of need that would be exchanged. Foreigners, as outsiders, were most of the time in a category that could only be at the receiving end of the process, unable to enter the system of exchange other than with limited tokens of gifts from abroad, invitations to foreign countries and other items such as language practice or accounts of foreign ways of life.

Over the years, despite the radical changes in the system of access to goods and benefits, this cultural system which is usually identified as 'Russian hospitality' but is, in reality, something much larger and more complex, has, with some shifts, stayed in place. Nevertheless, the cultural frameworks of reference have changed quite dramatically. The introduction of capitalism has had a radical modifying effect on the intrinsic value of objects. In the first place, the patterns of supplies of goods and the consequent expected behaviour for their procurement have been turned upside down. After an initial phase of exhilaration and unrestricted consumerism, many Russians started reacting negatively to Western goods as their acquisition no longer determined a self-identity in opposition with the regime.[7] On the contrary, they sought after Russian produced goods (*nashy* – ours), more familiar and 'solid'. As will be analysed in the following section, many women, and especially those who are engaged in entrepreneurial activities, tend to foster this Russo-centric vision of production.

Za dushoi (for the soul): or the de-contamination of capitalism

The diffused resistance to Western-style consumerism and consumption does not necessarily entail a rejection *in toto* of capitalism and the market. The dominant Western belief that if Russians do not want 'to be like us' then it automatically ensues that they are nostalgic for the old Soviet regime is a somewhat Manichaean and superficial one. On the one hand are the New Russians: rich, westernising and international. On the other hand are the *narod*, the grey mass hard-done by the transition, whose poverty and humiliation makes them fall easy prey to the populist and nationalistic charms of the likes of Ziuganov and Zhirinovskii. While these two tendencies do exist, there is also much else in between. Many women engaged in micro-entrepreneurial activities fall in this category. Their distinctive feature is that they are committed to business activities but have a fundamentally non-Western approach to them. Whether consciously or unconsciously understanding that many market mechanisms, as they were introduced to Russia, were structurally unfavourable to their gender, many women decided to develop an alternative ideology for their activities. According to a businesswoman in the fashion industry,

> the greatest wealth of a Russian woman in business is her soul. When a woman starts out she may not have the appropriate skills, little understanding of marketing and accounting, especially since the rules keep on changing. She may come from a totally different job and have to learn everything. But these are all things that she can pick up as she goes along. As long as a woman makes use of her culture and feminine vision she has a great chance of success. I think that women want to do business not only for themselves but because they understand that it is vital for their family and for their country.[8]

The underlying notion that women should not only maintain their 'natural' feminine attitudes when engaging in business but should further turn them into the central principle behind their work activities, is a dominant view amongst the businesswomen I interviewed, especially those who were defined as relatively successful. Tatiana Maliutina, president of the Association of Women Entrepreneurs of Russia, and Galina Chikova, one of her close associates, share a very similar view. As the opening lines to the leaflet presenting the activities of the association, they chose the following quote from Fiodor Dostoevskii: 'Woman is persistent, patient in action; she is more serious than man; she wants to do things for themselves and not for appearances. From this quarter, we shall receive great help.'[9] Galina Chikova further explained the characteristics of difference:

> There is a very big difference between male and female entrepreneurship. Men put making money in the first place, even though there are, of course, differences amongst men too. But women, in particular the members of our association, have other priorities in their livelihood. They want to support social programmes, aid the needy, the invalids, children. They want to organise charitable competitions. We recently organised an international competition for children's drawings throughout the regions. In my opinion these characteristics are all specific to women.[10]

A striking characteristic of this position is that it goes well beyond the borders of the work sphere. It affects all spheres, turning entrepreneurship into a global system of values which transcends the distinction between public and private. The approach is meaningfully summarised on the cover page of a new popular magazine, *Atlantida*, published by the Association of Women Writers and in close connection with the Association of Women Entrepreneurs of Russia.

> The world is divided between men and women. This is the only division which unites the world. Atlantida is a new Russian information association. According to its statute it includes *Atlantida* magazine, an information agency, radio and TV programmes, a publishing house, cultural and educational centres for holding international meetings, conferences and symposia. The purpose of Atlantida is to contribute to the spiritual and emotional revival of Russia, to enhance the social role of women. This will in turn contribute to the amelioration of the social climate on our planet. *Atlantida*'s main theme is harmony within a person, harmony in relations between a person and society, a society and a family, a man and a woman. It is viewed through the prism of main social situations, i.e. the four Es: ethics, ethnic relations, ecology, economics. We have named Atlantida after the lost fairyland. To find Atlantida in our souls is not an easy task, though an essential for all of us who stand now on the threshold of the Third Millennium.[11]

Women entrepreneurs propose their set of values in entrepreneurship as the one which could improve not only the economic sphere but the very identity crisis of the Russian nation. The nationalistic undertones are not constructed in open opposition to the West but rather tend to focus on notions of 'Russianness'. As a woman entrepreneur pointed out, when recounting the circumstances in which she and her friend Lena had set up a small clothes atelier, 'The most important thing for us was to be a *Rossiiskaia* (Russian)'.[12]

In more strictly economic terms, this translates into a very clear emphasis on production as opposed to commerce. As Chikhova put it,

> the majority of women entrepreneurs are engaged in production. These days many men call themselves entrepreneurs but they are not, they mainly cover functions of middlemen. Women start from zero to focus on production: they sew, they build, they engage in a number of different programmes. They do production which for us today is the most important thing.[13]

Commerce and trade are generally viewed as something not very genuine and solid, akin to a scam, in which nothing is created. This attitude is reminiscent of the dominant moral stance in Western Europe in the Middle Ages when merchants were predominantly viewed as parasites of other people's hard labour. In the dominant culture the source of value stemmed from material production.[14] Likewise, possibly because Russia is at a very early stage of capitalist development, there is a strongly rooted notion that production belongs to a higher moral order. Production is for use, and caring about production feeds directly into the same spirit of concern for the reproduction of the household which is central in Russian women's world. It is a long-term vision of the life-cycle, with implications of rebirth and growth. On the other hand, the world of commerce is one 'in which men engage with strangers in a myriad of short-term transactions and where individual competition, if not sharp practice, is acceptable'.[15]

Women entrepreneurs who adopt this culture of production tend to combine it with attempts to charge their products with values of 'Russianness'. Given that most women entrepreneurs are predominantly engaged in the light industrial sector (arts and crafts, textiles, food and services), it is relatively easy to construct a distinctive Russian style, if not in opposition, at least in contrast with what is perceived as the 'Western one' (*zapadny stil'*). This is most evident in the fashion industry where many small-scale women clothes designers are trying to reflect all the images of Russian femininity analysed above. Describing the work of members of the Association of Women

Entrepreneurs of Russia, Tatiana Maliutina underlined the importance for women of a style of dress which is 'more elegant and suitable than that what the West is proposing to us'.[16] Another clothes designer declared that, for her, every woman client was a *roman* (romance) to which she dedicated a lot of personal involvement in order to search for a style that would maintain the poetry.[17]

Another aspect of this philosophy of production are the attempts to operate as much as possible within a Russian-only environment as far as supplies of raw materials and use of technology are concerned. A woman engaged in the food sector thus described the process of production:

We try and buy all our ingredients in Russia because it is cheaper, the quality is better and we also want to support the local agriculture. We have had to buy some machinery from the West because it was impossible to find it in Russia, but it was very expensive and not really suitable because it needs a lot of maintenance. If it were available we would replace it with Russian technology ... Our products are of better quality, because I think the West is more interested in quantity.[18]

Only by avoiding, as much as possible, contamination with foreign raw materials and technology in the process of production can the product be considered truly *nash* (ours). The stress on the perceived better quality of the all-Russian product derives not so much from the intrinsic quality of the product itself but by the loaded symbolic meanings attributed to it; a strictly national process of production is the Russian version of political correctness during which an identity is built by repossessing the product. This framework of values is not necessarily reflected in the subsequent processes of selling, marketing and consuming the product. Having created a distinctive identity, many businesswomen would like to see the value of their products recognised abroad or at least by foreigners operating in Russia. Their reaction to the very real threats of international competition on the Russian market is to look for recognition and approval from the West of the fact that their products expound a meaningful set of values. For most women the accent is, rather naïvely, on the moral recognition of higher and better values rather than on the financial benefits that exporting or selling to the West would entail. As businesswoman Natasha explained, 'I would like to sell my clothes in Western countries, but unless customers knew Russia they would not understand the real quality of my clothes.'[19]

Thus quality becomes something symbolic and imagined rather than grounded in a *de facto* evaluation. Capitalist production as propounded by Russian women entrepreneurs is decontaminated of its material and soulless aspects as it is absorbed and transformed by a different culture.

Dividing lines: survival or livelihood?

As increasing numbers of women turn to business activities in order to survive, it is inevitable that the patterns of success should be heavily stratified. The notion of choice is, in many cases, severely curtailed. Many women engage in business 'not through the attractions of a "culture of enterprise" but through the unavoidable demands of economic restructuring'.[20] It would appear that being able to decide to go into business, rather than being obliged into it for basic survival needs, should already constitute a dividing line between relative success and mere 'getting by'. But what constitutes a successful entrepreneur in Russia and are the parameters of success the same for men and women?

Humphrey broadly identifies four groups amongst the New Russians:

> the old managers, their young entourages of kin and clients, the high Mafiosi, and the aspirant traders and racketeers of the kiosks. All of them love sheer wealth, but different styles are beginning to emerge. The old managers retain sober suits and put their money in opulent furniture and bushy fur coats for their wives, while their younger kin prefer sleek brand-marked Western clothing. The seriously wealthy Mafia buy private aircraft, whole plumbing systems for their houses or new kitchen systems. The aspirant traders affect black leather, dark glasses and sports clothes.[21]

Women do not really figure in these groups other than as wives, daughters or mistresses; recipients and consumers rather than originators of wealth. Increasingly, they tend to be objectified as attributes and indicators of status, obtaining visibility as a reflection of their 'belonging' to a successful male economic social actor.

This heterogeneity of styles, gender and types of activities does not really interest ordinary Russians, who tend to attribute them all together to the non-diversified group of New Russians for whom they harbour a very intense dislike. On the contrary, women entrepreneurs, be they successful businesswomen or street-traders, remain a neutral group, failing to evoke any strong passions in dominant popular culture. If anything, they meet with respect (if relatively successful) or commiseration and sympathy (if clearly driven by need). The discriminating factor for evoking such juxtaposed reactions can be found in the two groups' different relationship to money and wealth.

The introduction of capitalist-style monetary relations has had a significant impact on Russian society. In Soviet times the use of money was often a mere formality. Wage differentials were minimal compared to Western systems and currency itself had little buying power since formally there was no competition in the distributive system. Prices were fixed according to state planning, not according to mechanisms of demand and supply. As mentioned earlier, the acquisition of goods and services was mediated through insider networks, while the goods that were readily available to everyone could be purchased at prices so low that they were practically given for free. Goods had prices, but they were symbolic and non-monetary ones determined by culturally constructed notions of exchange and by established and consensual barter practices. The returns in this system of exchange were not necessarily immediate. A person might provide a friend with a favour or goods against the understanding that the friend would return something comparable, but possibly very different in nature, sometime in the future. Networks of mutual obligations were something that could be tapped into over the years, when a specific need arose.

The introduction of notions of value expressed through monetary prices came as a shock to many Russians. It threatened to undermine all the intricate webs of personal relations by offering the option of paying for something. Suddenly, people without the right connections (and therefore usually considered of a 'lower class') could skip class by simply buying goods and services. The hierarchy of social groups was subverted, if not at the top, at least in middle and lower layers. People, mainly men, who had retained economic and political power used their positions to ensure that property and access were transferred into their private hands and transformed it into monetary wealth. Even if property was nominally still state owned, it was *de facto* privately controlled. Lower down the social scale, the *kulturny* (cultured) people, the technical, academic and professional intelligentsia who had been the most successful actors and beneficiaries of the insider system of distribution through networks, saw their position of privilege crumble about them. They were suddenly outdone by groups of petty street-traders and by groups of mafiosi who made their fortunes through buying and selling on the open market and acquired status and luxury life-styles through financial means. The fact that in most regions of western and northern Russia, the successful traders belonged to ethnic groups from the southern regions of the former Soviet Union did not enhance their acceptance on the part of ordinary Russians.

Increasingly, money's buying power was seen as wiping out individuals' reliance on personal interaction and the ability to construct networks. It changed the framework and access to class and was mainly perceived as producing the rise of the *nekulturny* (uncultured). Women were particularly badly off since they were neither part of the former Soviet economic and political elite nor were they able to engage in 'violent' and dangerous trade activities. In popular imagination, men were accused of being 'speculators' (a heinous crime in Soviet times) reproducing in their business culture the *obman* (fraud) which had previously been perpetrated by the state at the expense of ordinary people.[22] The prices asked for goods were perceived as a manifestation of this fraud since they were no longer set according to consensual notions of fairness but according to monetary market rules. Furthermore, money introduced distance between owner and property, undermining the value of the personal in the processes of provision and consumption.[23]

All these elements are contributing to creating a strong counter-culture of resistance to this type of market relations. One of the peculiarities is that women street-vendors are perceived as belonging to a totally different category than equivalent male street-traders. The distinction is based on a moral stereotype: men, especially if from the southern regions, are out to make a profit at the expense of ordinary people and therefore contribute to the undermining of the Russian process of regeneration. All they want is quick personal gain. Women, on the other hand, have probably been driven onto the street by the need to support their family, pay for their children's education and livelihood or other such morally laudable motivation. Therefore the monetary price of their goods is fair because their end is long-term reproduction of the household. A woman selling women's newspapers and magazines on the street thus described the nature of her activity:

Even though my prices are higher than in the shops people still come and buy them from me. I have a regular group of women customers who come to me because they know me by now. They know how hard life is for me, standing all day in the cold, and that I do it to pay for my Zhenia's education. They don't like to give their money to the guys in the metro because they are up to no good.[24]

The counter-culture of entrepreneurship that women are producing is shared both by those who are successful in their business activities and by those who merely survive by it. Notions of competition are outdone by ones of support engendered by shared values of caring, fairness and long-term regeneration. Partly due to the strong persistence of patriarchal culture, women find it very hard to access capital to start up their business activities. This on the one hand reinforces their suspicion towards money, while on the other it leaves them with no other option but to turn back to the old networks of personal social relations in order to find opportunities. This element is present both in market relationships amongst entrepreneurs and in supplier–customer relations. As Tania, a street-vendor in her late teens described it,

me and my women friends will look after each other's stalls if one of us has something to do. In winter, we take turns to go and warm up inside ... My mother often comes to look after the stall for me, or helps me when I have to go and get the supplies. My brother doesn't really help, I don't know why; he's not really interested. I wouldn't work in a location where there were no other women because men don't do that sort of thing for you. I think that we are all in the same boat but most guys don't think that.[25]

Thus, the old networks of insider support and mutual help become crucial to counteract the impersonality of new economic relations and to engage in business enterprises. Everything is done *po znakomstvu* (through and for the sake of acquaintance). If a firm needs new employees they will be found by word of mouth. Often even customers are found through insider circulation of information about the firm's activities through existing customers and friends. There is a deeply rooted suspicion towards anybody 'from the street' (*iz ulitsi*) since there is no guarantee of shared values and intentions. As Mila, a member of the Association of Women Entrepreneurs of Russia, described it,

I think that women should work with each other as much as possible. Even if I personally haven't had any benefits from the association you can still exchange favours and information. I just want to help others. I believe in the West people would take an interest but in Russia we do a lot for emotional support (*dushchevny konfort*) ... It is good because we have few people from the street, mainly friends of friends.[26]

The degree of 'insiderism' and the quality and extent of the networks at a woman's disposal (*barter uslug*) are also fundamental to her degree of success. Women obliged to work on the street are there because they have not been able to *ustroit'sia* (settle or sort themselves out). The networks they can access are not powerful and effective enough to provide them with better opportunities. On the other hand, successful businesswomen have initially accessed their business through, or because of, some insider opportunity. Mila thus described the beginning of her business: 'my mother in law hadn't seen a friend of hers for twenty years. He had been to prison. She met him in the street and mentioned what we did. After a few days he called and ordered 150 dresses. This is how we started.'[27]

Galina Chikova, of the Association of Women Entrepreneurs of Russia, related the experience of her organisation:

> Today it is really very difficult for women to start their own enterprise. Without help from somebody it is simply impossible. When we started the association in 1991, then it was more realistic for women to start off on their own. The levels of inflation were not as high. Many women sold their cars, some jewels or something and would use it as their start-up capital, on their own, without help. Now the situation is such that you need other people's help. Of course, a lot depends on the quality of the person. There are many uniquely talented women ... If such women come to us we try to help them.[28]

Many of the women I interviewed expressed the belief that their success as entrepreneurs depended on their ability to deal with people, on the human and socialising skills that are in general more characteristic of women than of men: 'We (women) understand how to relate to people, to workers, to clients. We understand how to work.'[29] Since it is harder for women to construct safety networks through financial capacity, they construct them through personal relations. Contractual relations are acted out in a similar way. In an environment where written contracts are *de jure* binding but *de facto* completely meaningless, women speak proudly of their trustworthiness, opposing it to the frequent unreliability of male businessmen. As Galina Chikova described it,

> members of the association [of women entrepreneurs] are very active, trustworthy people. You may know that in the past we had this brotherhood of merchants. They never signed any contract but if they had shaken hands then it was already a guarantee. Today we have a totally non-legal system, in which even if we did sign a contract and you broke it would be impossible for me to defend my position. Unfortunately this nuance is very real nowadays. In this phase of transition, women entrepreneurs are very trustworthy people.[30]

An area where reliance on connections combined with 'feminine guiles' seems to serve women rather well is in their relationship to organised crime and corruption. For most businesses it is fundamental to have a roof (*krysha*), possibly a state one. This entails being under the protective umbrella of a larger organisation, be it the state or some other entity. It envisages paying bribes to officials but it should, in theory, also offer a screen against the more violent type of street mafia. Even street-vendors can fall under the state roof if they obtain a licence to trade in a given place. The licence allows them to have a stall rather than displaying goods in their hands or on the ground and spares them hasty retreats in case the local police appear. By paying the local police a bribe, the street-vendor should be, in principle, also protected from other rackets. Many women, however, mentioned the growth in numbers of organised crime groups and the breakdowns of territorial boundaries as far as spheres of protection were concerned.

Appearing more openly vulnerable to extortion, many women described how they successfully appealed to the racketeers' gallantry in order to contain their dues to the mafia. As Katia, a businesswoman who runs an art and gifts shop, described it,

> It's pure theatre. You should see how I dress when I have to go and see the people from the state mafia. All my employees can tell where I'm going and joke about it. But all in all it works, since all they want from me now is presents from the salon rather than money. They will say, 'I really don't know what to give my wife for her birthday' and I say, 'I have a pair of earrings and a necklace that would be just right' and so everything is solved. Men can't do that. They can hardly go there with their lipstick on, can they?[31]

All the women I interviewed also admitted that they did not pay all the taxes they were supposed to. Most of them pointed out that if they had to do things by the book this would cripple their businesses. Double accounting is also shielded from being investigated by the local authorities by careful manoeuvring and networking in the right places. The relative invisibility of women's economic activities thus becomes a strength in terms of avoiding the rougher illegal end of market relations, which includes crime rackets and the associated violence. Being dismissed as insignificant economic actors by dominant sexist culture allows them the space to operate unobtrusively, but often relatively successfully, in the chosen field.

Conclusion

Women in Russia are inventing a tradition of entrepreneurialism which distances itself both from the Soviet experience and from Western cultures of market relations. This tradition is also outside the boundaries of the more familiar picture of a male-dominated cowboy business environment. Women are frequently excluded from accounts of economic transformation and new business practices in Russia other than being mentioned under the heading of 'unemployment and the breakdown of the social safety net'. Current legislation is insufficient in targeting gender-related problems in the spheres of employment and social protection, and on the whole seems to be largely irrelevant to the culture that women find themselves in. More generally, legislation on wider economic issues provides the hazy framework for the development of new business practices in an environment which is predominantly male dominated. Women have to operate within this environment but are also trying to create their own pockets of business practices with a business culture that differs from the dominant one. Entrepreneurialism is a widespread, distinctive and vibrant part of women's world. Leaving aside value judgements of whether it is a 'good' culture or a 'bad' one, it is definitely unique, deeply rooted in local culture and economic and human resources. Whether characterised by success or survival, its gender specificities make it apparently invisible; but, given that women entrepreneurs seem to have a much clearer vision and commitment to the long-term human, cultural and economic cycles than the majority of men, could it be that their way of life and business could emerge as the most viable one?

Notes

I would like to thank the people who 'put me up' while researching and writing this chapter: Valentina Klimiseineite, Simon Goldberg and John Meurig Davies. Thanks to John for the unique musical background; to Michael Levett in the USA and to Julia South in the UK for sharing their work experience with me and providing precious contacts; and to all the people who helped me and talked to me in Russia. I would like to dedicate this chapter to the women in my Russian family: Nina, Zhenia and Ania.

1 A business incubator is an organisation whose task is that of providing a series of services – such as legal and economic consultancies, training, market information, premises and financing – to individuals or groups wanting to set up a new business venture. Many such programmes are being implemented in Russia under this name and are mainly funded by foreign organisations and NGOs.
2 Linda Cook, *The Soviet social contract and why it failed* (Cambridge, Mass.: Harvard University Press, 1993); Sue Bridger, Rebecca Kay and Katherine Pinnick, *No more heroines? Russia, women and the market* (London: Routledge, 1996), pp. 67–70.
3 Hilary Pilkington, 'Whose space is it anyway? Youth, gender and civil

society in the former Soviet Union' in Shirin Rai, Hilary Pilkington and Annie Phizacklea (eds.), *Women in the face of change. The Soviet Union, Eastern Europe and China* (London: Routledge, 1992), pp. 105–29; Marta Bruno, 'In search of difference: gender and stratification in Russia', *Cambridge Anthropology* 18(2), 1995, pp. 73–82; Bridger, Kay and Pinnick, *No more heroines?*, p. 35.

4 Caroline Humphrey, 'Creating a culture of disillusionment: consumption in Moscow, a chronicle of changing times' in Daniel Miller (ed.), *Worlds apart: modernity through the prism of the local* (London: Routledge, 1995), p. 56.
5 Katherine Verdery, *The transition from socialism: anthropology in Eastern Europe* (Lewis Henry Morgan Lectures, University of Rochester, 1992), p. 25.
6 Humphrey, 'Creating a culture of disillusionment', p. 57.
7 *Ibid.*
8 Interview with Larissa, fashion industry (Moscow, November 1995).
9 Document from the press conference of the Association of Women Entrepreneurs of Russia (Moscow, *Dom Zhurnalistov*, 14 November 1995).
10 Interview with Galina Chikova (Moscow, November 1995).
11 *Atlantida* 1 (Moscow, Akzent, 1994), inside front cover.
12 Interview with Mila, couturier (Moscow, November 1995).
13 Interview with Galina Chikova.
14 Jonathan Parry and Maurice Bloch, *Money and the morality of exchange* (Cambridge: Cambridge University Press, 1989).
15 *Ibid.*, p. 23.
16 Interview with Tatiana Maliutina (Moscow, November 1995).
17 Interview with Mila.
18 Interview with Olga, businesswoman in food production and retail (Moscow, November 1995).
19 Interview with Natasha, couturier (Moscow, November 1995).
20 Bridger, Kay and Pinnick, *No more heroines?*, p. 194.
21 Humphrey, 'Creating a culture of disillusionment', p. 64.
22 *Ibid.*, p. 64.
23 Parry and Bloch, *Money and the morality of exchange*, p. 5.
24 Interview with Alla, street-vendor (Moscow, November 1995).
25 Interview with Tania, street-vendor (Moscow, November 1995).
26 Interview with Mila.
27 *Ibid.*
28 Interview with Galina Chikova.
29 Interview with Lena (Moscow, November 1995).
30 Interview with Galina Chikova.
31 Interview with Katia (Moscow, November 1995).

Society

5 Images of an ideal woman: perceptions of Russian womanhood through the media, education and women's own eyes

REBECCA KAY

Public images for political ideals

The manipulation of women to fulfil the roles which suit a current political goal is by no means a new phenomenon in Russia. In fact, the promotion of a given 'ideal' of womanhood was a constant feature of the Soviet era. Whether as zealous revolutionaries, shock workers, tractor drivers or heroine mothers, Russia's women have always had a 'great mission', a vital role to play in the future development of their nation. The present exhortations to women to return to the home, to reclaim their femininity and, above all, to bear children can be seen as a direct and, perhaps, logical progression from what has gone before. In the 1970s, Brezhnev's pro-natalist policies and the promotion of theories on biologically determined sex differentiation gave official and theoretical backing to a policy of gender-defined upbringing and a division of roles, expectations and character traits along gender lines.[1] In the 1980s, glasnost revealed the terrible weight of the double burden imposed on women by a party line which ascribed to them full responsibility for the vast majority of domestic and family duties, without 'relieving' them of the obligation to engage in paid employment. None the less, Marxist–Leninist ideology, which then still held sway, combined with the economic imperatives imposed by the policy of restructuring, ensured that women continued, in that period, to form a high proportion of the labour force.[2]

With the final demise of the Soviet Union in December 1991 this position was to change dramatically: any remaining brakes on the infringement of those equal rights, which had been heralded as one of communism's greatest achievements and guaranteed on paper to women by Soviet legislation, were removed. In the new Russia of 1992, the Soviet system was publicly discredited and reviled by reformers, fear of the implications of mass unemployment loomed large and society was in a state of flux. What better solution than to promote a role for women based firmly and exclusively in the home, thus strengthening the family, increasing the birth rate and virtually halving the labour force all in one neat blow? Certainly, all these proposals had been mooted before. As redundancies began to strike, however, it rapidly became clear that this time rhetoric would be put into practice with tangible effect. Unemployment may have risen much more slowly than initially expected, yet from the very beginning a definite gender bias has been in evidence where redundancies and lay-offs have occurred: women have consistently accounted for 70–80 per cent of the unemployed.[3] This eviction of women from the labour force is only the most immediately obvious result of a series of deeply ingrained gender stereotypes and roles which continue to be advocated in Russia and which, like the traditional *matryoshka* dolls, settle snugly into one another to form a rather rigid and not universally attractive blueprint for the 'Ideal Russian Woman'.

This chapter aims to examine stereotyped images of Russian womanhood and to compare those put forward by the contemporary mass media with the ideals to which young Russian women themselves aspire. The primary research material, on which the main arguments presented here are based, is in the form of 120 letters written by Russian women in the spring of 1992 in response to a competition, entitled, 'The Perfect You', which had been launched by the Moscow Image Centre, and which invited entries describing the ideal woman.[4] The Moscow Image Centre was founded in 1989 and offers a variety of services, ranging from expensive image consultancy courses for politicians and businessmen, through training and agency work for professional models, to a programme of courses on beauty, fashion and self-presentation and a weekly drop-in session, offered free of charge to any woman interested. 'The Perfect You' competition had been used in 1992 as a device to attract women to the Image Centre. It invited women to send in their photograph and to describe both their ideal woman and themselves, and was advertised through articles in popular youth publications: the monthly magazine *Puls'*, for example, and the daily newspaper *Moskovskii Komsomolets*. The prize offered was a free course of lectures and classes at the Image Centre itself, although each entrant was promised information and advice. The competition was very successful and the letters passed on to me represent only a small fraction of the thousands of entries received.[5]

All the responses in this sample came from within the Moscow region. Eighty-two women live in the capital itself, the rest come from some of Moscow's many satellite towns. The respondents were aged between thirteen and forty, the vast majority being in their late teens and early twenties at the time when the letters were written. A range of professions and educational backgrounds are represented in the sample, but, as a result of the relatively low average age, there is a rather high proportion of students and schoolgirls. In addition to these letters I shall draw on the opinions expressed by fourteen other women, who attended courses at the Image Centre in the winter of 1993–4 and who were interviewed in spring 1994.[6]

If we are to understand the stereotyped images of women which abound in contemporary Russian society and which have become such an intricate part of Russian women's perceptions of themselves and their roles, we should bear in mind both the barrage of propaganda from the media, and the effects of the secondary school course on 'The ethics and psychology of family life' which was introduced as a compulsory subject for fifteen- to sixteen-year-olds in 1984. A large proportion of the young women who make up the research sample for this chapter will therefore have followed this course as part of their basic secondary education.

The Eleventh Five-year Plan, 1981–5, reflected a renewed concern with demographic policy and included a commitment to 'important measures to increase the prestige of motherhood and create an atmosphere of increased concern for families raising children'.[7] 'The ethics and psychology of family life' school course was clearly formulated with these aims in mind. The course textbook[8] takes the student step by step through the process of setting up a family, beginning with advice on courtship and correct relations between young men and women and progressing through marriage and the reproductive role of the family to questions of raising children. Throughout, the student is presented with writings and opinions from prominent Soviet political, literary and social figures ranging from Lenin and Kollontai to Gogol and Tolstoi as well as with information concerning Soviet legislation. The course is not about sexual education nor does it include an indepth discussion of family members' rights and responsibilities. There are, of course, the expected references to the innately 'egalitarian' nature of Soviet marriage 'partnerships' and the textbook asserts, in keeping with the party line, that the subjugation of wives to their husbands or of children to their parents has automatically been done away with by the advent of state socialism. Yet, at each stage the emphasis is clearly laid upon the cultivation of rigidly gender-defined roles and attitudes and strengthening the family as an integral part of a national demographic policy. Thus, essentially contradictory quotes 'from the chalice of wisdom' are to be found on consecutive pages. L.N. Tolstoi is quoted in support of a strict adherence to gender-based divisions, 'A woman who tries to be just like a man is just as repulsive as an effeminate man.' By contrast, Nadezhda Krupskaia insists that gender difference is of little importance since people are people: 'As a result of spiritual closeness, a man will see in a woman, and conversely a woman will see in a man, not a member of the opposite sex, but, above all, a person.'[9]

In the following sections we will look at each of the *matryoshka* doll elements in turn and examine both how that particular aspect of the 'Ideal Woman' has been sold to Russian women through the media and the education system and just how successful the sales pitch has been in each case, in terms of the opinions expressed by the women in this sample group.

The essential woman

Like any *matryoshka* doll, the 'Ideal Russian Woman' has a small but solid core. In the words of a twenty-one-year-old unemployed hairdresser, this central element at the heart of all to which she should now aspire might be called 'Woman with a Capital W', and carries a banner labelled 'Femininity'.

The problem of the so-called 'masculinisation' of Russian women and 'emasculation' of their menfolk had already come under scrutiny in the final decades of the Soviet Union's existence. In the 1970s and 1980s, gender difference became a central theme in the theorising of demographers, pedagogues and psychologists[10] and the question of 'male' and 'female' roles and personality traits is addressed at some length in 'The ethics and psychology of family life' course. In the context of a book devoted to 'Post-Soviet Women', this chapter focuses on contemporary images and stereotypes relating to Russian womanhood, with only passing references to male roles and expectations placed on men. It is clear, none the less, that rigidly defined gender roles are intrinsically interdependent and that an equally interesting study could be conducted regarding attitudes to and perceptions of masculinity and manhood.

In the 1990s, issues of femininity, masculinity and the essential nature of man and woman have left the realm of academic literature and debate and have instead become a topic of general interest, addressed regularly by the mass media and commented on with authority by every self-proclaimed pop-psychologist: 'It was, after all, decided by nature that man should provide for his family and protect it from external enemies, whilst his wife creates a cosy home, surrounds her spouse with love and care and occupies herself with raising the children. Moreover, as is well known, nature is always right.'[11] Idioms and clichés which refer to women as 'representatives of the weaker or the beautiful sex' have become commonplace, as have platitudes about the need for more beauty, more femininity and women's role in 'decorating life' and making the world a more pleasant place for others.

A conviction that 'a woman should always remain a Woman' or that 'the most important characteristic for any woman is femininity' was expressed with astonishing regularity in competition entrants' descriptions of their ideal woman and often without any further explanation. For these young women the idea that certain qualities and characteristics are appropriate to females and accentuate a woman's 'femininity' requires no further comment. In the same vein the general desirability of 'feminine' women and 'masculine' men is assumed to be self-evident. Similar statements are frequently encountered in the press. Occasionally these bald pronouncements may be elaborated more fully. In an article announcing the founding of the Image Lycee, a female journalist bemoans the depiction of Soviet women as unfeminine creatures in oversized overalls, declaring 'That's enough of being a laughing stock, we too have grace, charm and elegance.'[12] Here, the promotion of 'femininity' becomes a part of the process of rejecting the Soviet past and all its values, righting the wrongs done to Russian women by the communist regime and moving forwards to a more civilised and westernised society, as seen in the Russian-language editions of *Cosmopolitan* and *Burda Moden* currently on sale at every Moscow newspaper stand.

Beauty not brains

This rejection of the Soviet image of strong working women is a central plank in the argument for a return to the 'essentially feminine'. The new image promoted for the woman of the 1990s is one of beauty, fragility and fashion. Advertisements for slimming aids, beauty products and cosmetic surgery abound in the press and the beauty contests which burst onto Soviet screens in the late 1980s have lost none of their popularity in the new Russia.

Beauty, on the other hand, does not come without a price. Responsibility for making sure that she looks good, stays fit and never 'lets herself go' is rapidly becoming number one on the list of a woman's duties. 'There are no ugly people, just lazy ones' proclaims a twenty-two-year-old artist in her competition entry. This conviction is reflected in women's responses to questions about beauty and the growing importance of personal appearance, particularly for younger women, in terms of gaining employment. 'Every woman has a duty to look after herself and take care of her looks' was a maxim stated again and again by the women of this sample both in interview and in their letters. In competition entrants' descriptions of their ideal woman, comments on appearance ranked higher, both in terms of frequency and order of mention, than those relating to personality or intelligence, although some conceded that beauty alone is not enough: 'Her smile does not hide an empty doll-like person, she has a rich internal world and a good sympathetic heart,' says a twenty-year-old student of cybernetics. Similarly, the same artist quoted above went on to concede that, 'Beauty without brains or the reverse is boring.'

All this attention to appearance is not purely frivolous. In a social climate where job advertisements stating a preferred height and requiring 'attractiveness' from female applicants are quite acceptable, of course women will feel a pressure to 'look right'.[13] On the other hand, taking care of one's looks is often regarded not as a burden but as a release from the austerity and hardship associated with the Soviet era. Moreover, it is seen as a way of regaining a correct gender identity, which communism is feared to have destroyed: 'Of all the European countries, only in Russia has a third sex developed: "*baby*",[14] somewhere between "m" and "f".'[15]

Girls should be girls

Time and again the 'over-emancipation' of women in Soviet Russia is blamed for a whole myriad of contemporary social problems. Men, it is claimed, have become weak and emasculated as a result, and women are encouraged to be modest and retiring, to make their men feel strong by taking a back seat and, if they must lead or make decisions, to do so with tact and subtlety so that the male ego should not be offended. An article describing different 'types' of women and their respective relationships with men insists that, 'The most successful type, "the Woman-friend" ... is the most clever woman, who reasons delicately and realistically. She lets a man feel the necessity of his leadership in life, lets him take charge in the family but always under her hidden control.'[16]

In a similar vein, an agony uncle, answering the letter of a single mother concerned about her grown son's lack of interest in finding a wife, advises,

> There is such a concept as 'the son of an emancipated woman'. It is possible that your role in the family is so great and that from his childhood you were so crushing of your son's initiative, that he is now unable to identify with the male role ... Try to be less domineering with your son ... Don't show him that you are waiting for him to be married, try to show him that he is an independent man and must do as he pleases. Go to him for advice more often and, even if you are sure that your idea is more sensible, try to act as he decides.[17]

These viewpoints are also supported in a considerable number of the competition letters. The importance of modesty and of women not being too forward or showing off their intelligence, especially in male company, is stressed by several entrants. One twenty-one-year-old student writes of her ideal woman,

> If she is clever she should not aim to show this to a man. She should always listen carefully to what a man says and agree with him. She should only argue in a situation where to compromise would be impossible, in which case she will argue gently and calmly, sticking to her opinion but without foaming at the mouth.

This is not to say that all women are by any means ready to give up their autonomy without resistance. Just under half of the competition entries mention independence, self-reliance, a strong will and a sense of purpose as desirable characteristics, and issues of personal development and fulfilment are also high on many entrants' list of priorities. None the less, despite this apparent awareness of their own needs, the women of this sample seem to have accepted the altruistic role promoted as a vital element in the reassertion of women's 'true feminine nature'.

'The better half of humanity'

Women's role as caretakers and 'givers' was made very clear in 'The ethics and psychology of family life' course. In a section entitled 'To beautiful young women', male school-leavers are reported as believing that 'A girl should be caring, attentive, tender ... a good housewife, a devoted wife and an altruistic mother.'[18] Not only are women required to see to the well-being of their families, they are also regularly portrayed as having higher moral and spiritual values than men. Therefore, they are looked to as the moral guardians of society, the preservers of all that is good and just. Articles extolling the virtues of women's keener sensibilities and sharper sense of moral justice often refer to women as 'the better half of humanity'. In a speech broadcast on national television on the occasion of International Women's Day 1995, President Yel'tsin described women as 'more cultured than men'. 'Women', he went on to assert, 'are clearly made in such a way as to create naturally an atmosphere of spiritual warmth and cordiality around them'[19]

In their letters, several competition entrants reflect a sentiment akin to those described above: 'It is important that she be kind and attentive not only to those who are close to her but also to everyone around her' says a thirteen-year-old schoolgirl of her ideal woman. 'I have a dream which has become my life's goal,' proclaims a seventeen-year-old studying to enter medical college, 'I want to bring people joy, to help them to come to terms with their shortcomings so that they might regain a sense of happiness and always be smiling.'

If moral superiority and a social mission are attributed to women, these are clearly linked to their presumed nurturing nature, inherent altruism and maternal instinct. On the one hand, women may be encouraged to play a role in improving society as a whole; on the other, their first task is to create a perfect home environment for their husbands and children.

'Guardians of the family hearth'

The idea that a man should provide for and protect his family, while a woman plays the role of homemaker and mother, is not only used in arguments for removing women from the labour market. The redevelopment of a division of family roles according to gender is also seen as an important part of the re-establishment of 'proper' relations between the sexes. In fact, a traditional separation of 'men's' and 'women's' work has long been adhered to in many families, even during the period when women's employment outside the home was still taken for granted.[20] One of the major justifications for proposals to remove women from full-time paid employment prior to the collapse of Soviet rule was the well-documented gender inequality in time spent on household chores and domestic duties which left women shouldering the now notorious 'double burden'.

Far from promoting a fairer distribution of this work, 'The ethics and psychology of family life' course warned against the dangers of challenging stereotypical gender relations. Commenting on the frequency of divorces initiated by women against men who 'always helped their wives, both with the housework and with raising the children', Miroslav Plazk suggests that the cause of the problem is in this improper male behaviour. Women, he says, need a man who is 'not only an exemplary head of the family, but who will also always be a man. Although all the men who had been left by their wives were model husbands, in some way or other they had failed to impress their wives.'[21] The women interviewed in spring 1994, however, were not so keen to find an all-male macho-man for a husband as Mr Plazk supposes. When asked how they hoped to tackle household chores in their future relationships, they were almost unanimously in favour of sharing both the housework and the upbringing of children, although there was some dissent over the degree of involvement a father should have in the care of very young babies.

The women entering 'The Perfect You' competition were, on the whole, more conservative in their views. When asked to describe their ideal man, they invariably stressed the importance of his strength, reliability and ability to protect a woman: 'She will always feel his manly support, always feel that at his side she is a woman: tender, fragile even weak', writes an eighteen-year-old professional synchronised swimmer. Gallantry, courageousness and the embodiment of 'real male qualities' ranked high on the lists of demands which entrants expected their ideal women to make of a prospective partner. Similarly, the man's role as provider was promoted by many, and wealth and success in the business world were frequently required of the 'ideal man'. On the other hand, none of these attitudes was supported unanimously. Several entries underlined the need for intellectual compatibility, shared interests and mutual support, caring and respect, whilst a few women raised objections to the question of the man's role as breadwinner, woman's resulting financial dependence and the implications of this for choosing a partner. 'Since she will be financially independent,' writes a seventeen-year-old schoolleaver of her ideal woman, 'she will choose a man whom she finds interesting as a person and not as a wallet.'

The stereotype of woman as a homemaker was only very rarely challenged and encompasses more than the simple distribution of domestic tasks. Women writing letters to 'The Perfect You' competition were overwhelmingly convinced that a vital quality in a woman is the ability to keep a cosy, comfortable and welcoming household. The phrase 'guardian of the family hearth' appeared several times, as did a conviction that 'a woman's element is her home and her family'. The ideal woman, it seems, not only cleans and does the ironing, she is also, as the perfect hostess, able to create such an atmosphere of warmth and hospitality that the least-expected visitor would always be made instantly welcome with home-made offerings and pleasant conversation. These qualities and abilities were described by competition entrants regardless of the varying life-styles they ascribed to their ideal. Whether she is young and single, a high-flying professional or a full-time housewife (and she was variously described as each of these), the perfect woman, apparently, always keeps a perfect home.

Finding one's 'other half'

A conviction that finding an ideal partner would be a crucial element in the life of any woman was subscribed to by the majority of competition entrants. 'It is impossible to envisage an ideal woman without an ideal companion' was not an uncommon remark. As far as marriage was concerned, however, these women's attitudes were far less conformist. They might agree that 'love is a vital factor in the life of the ideal woman' and that without 'her other half' a woman would not be complete, yet there was no consensus that this partnership had to carry the official stamp of marriage or even that it necessarily implied a joint household. Several letters in fact, specifically stated that their ideal woman lives alone. Whilst some women laid heavy emphasis on fidelity and marriage to 'her one and only', others described their ideal woman as surrounded by male admirers as a result of her irresistible attractiveness, and as thriving on this wealth of male attention. A twenty-one-year-old medical student gave her ideal woman the following slogan: 'If in the course of a day not a single man has looked at me with interest, then the day was wasted.'

Perhaps as a result of the relative youth of the entrants, for many marriage was something for a woman to aspire to in the future. Although they did not necessarily question its desirability *per se*, for these young women getting married and raising a family clearly implied a loss of freedom and independence and as such was not a feature of their ideal scenario. A nineteen-year-old student wrote of her ideal woman, 'She might have a husband and children, but she places great value on the solitude of her home away from the fuss and bother of day-to-day life and so she is unlikely to be in a hurry to get married.'

Marriage and parenthood before the age of twenty has been a common occurrence in Russia for many years and a significant number of women have borne their first children whilst they and their husbands were still in higher education. For many this has meant great financial hardship, housing problems, additional strain on their marriage and has hindered their educational and/or professional progress. Although this tendency continues to be seen, young women are beginning to express reservations about the desirability of such an early start to family life. Despite the current uncertainties of the labour market, many young women still consider gaining a higher education as very important in terms of both personal development and future professional opportunities. Others point out that to hope that marriage will free a young woman from dependence on and subordination to her parents is often futile, since once married she will probably find not only that this relationship continues but that she is now also expected to comply with her new husband's and in-laws' wishes and requirements. Interestingly, young women frequently do not question the justice of these power relations as such, nor do they necessarily aspire fundamentally to change them in the long run. A wish to avoid the struggle they have witnessed in their mothers' generation and to retain, or at least prolong, some degree of independence and freedom does, however, prompt many to put marriage off, if only until after they have graduated.

The desire to delay marriage is also a response to the emphasis which has been placed on the family's reproductive function, the responsibility of the husband and father to provide and of the wife and mother to nurture. In a social climate where pregnancy is still frequently regarded as the logical consequence of marriage, both young women and mothers of teenage daughters often draw attention to the multiple problems facing young couples and their families. Young husbands who are not yet established career-wise are unlikely to be able to support their new families financially, whilst a young woman striving to gain an education or assert herself as an independent adult does not necessarily want immediately to cope with the physical and psychological burdens of motherhood. Certainly this would hardly be described as an 'ideal' scenario.

Motherhood: every woman's highest calling?

When Gorbachev spoke of 'returning women to their purely womanly mission' he was not suggesting anything new in terms of attitudes towards maternity, neither as the natural calling of all women, nor as a duty to the nation, particularly in times of crisis.[22] Stalin removed women's legal right to abortion in 1936 as part of a campaign to increase the number of births; privileges and benefits for mothers with many children and a medal for 'heroine mothers' of ten or more children were introduced. Women's right to abortion was only reinstated by Khrushchev in 1955 because of a realisation that, far from improving demographic trends, banning abortion had produced an alarming growth in illegal and dangerous abortions which threatened women's future fertility and, in some cases, their lives. The tradition of glorifying women's role as mothers and political concern with the falling birth rate, have continued beyond the end of the USSR: in the independent Russia, scaremongering politicians have linked the 'demographic crisis' to a possible threat to national security.[23]

Women have been displaying a definite disinterest in producing enough children to reverse the downward trend in population growth for almost as long as politicians have been trying to persuade them to do so. Throughout these periods, women have been consistently encouraged to see themselves as mothers first and foremost, yet the demographic decline continues apace, and since the demise of the Soviet Union it has only accelerated. By 1993, the number of births registered annually had been steadily falling over a six year period and had reached 1.385 million, only 56 per cent of its 1987 level and the lowest rate recorded since the Second World War.[24] This rather dramatic slide appears to end here. The figures for 1994 show 1.386 million births registered and, although no official figures were available for 1995 at the time of writing, a continued stabilisation but no reversal was clearly expected by demographers. In their annual demographic report, experts from the Centre for Demography and Human Ecology at the Scientific Research Institute for Problems of Employment of the Russian Academy of Sciences and the Russian Ministry of Labour begin by pointing out that, 'It is vital that we accept and understand that model of the family which exists in real life – urban, small and nuclear.'[25]

Since the 1970s a tendency to limit the number of children in a family to one or two has been observed, and the opinions of today's younger generation are consistent in this respect with those of their parents' generation. According to a survey of teenagers carried out by the popular newspaper *Moskovskii Komsomolets* in 1992, 65 per cent of young men and 69 per cent of young women wanted two children: 33 per cent and 17 per cent respectively only wanted one; 19 per cent overall (men and women) thought three would be a good number and only 5 per cent expressed any interest in a larger family. As the journalists responsible for the survey commented, 'The prospect of a large family is obviously not attractive to young people.'[26]

A degree of reticence and ambivalence with regard to motherhood is apparent in the responses, both written and given in interview, of several of the women from the sample group. Of the 120 competition entrants, although some expressed opinions which would surely have pleased those concerned about the falling birth rate, such as, 'One should always remember that a woman's natural destiny is to bear and raise children', barely a quarter actually mentioned motherhood as a feature of their ideal woman's life. Of the six women who indicated that they had children themselves, only one specifically stated that her ideal woman would also be or wish to be a mother. Certainly, none of the women in this sample who described their ideal woman as a mother advocated more than two or three children and several specifically stipulated that she should not have more than two.

Given the poverty and financial insecurity currently experienced by a large section of the Russian population, a reluctance to commit oneself to providing for too many mouths is hardly surprising. Nevertheless, although material concerns are frequently given as a reason for limiting the number of children in a family, this may not be the only disincentive to young women. The same survey cited above found that whilst 73 per cent of young men would like their future wives to stay at home, 89 per cent of young women were still in favour of going out to work.[27] The combination of career and family has been neither an easy nor a happy one for Russian women in the past and, having witnessed this in their mothers' generation, young women are left confused and unsure of their position and aspirations, which are not infrequently contradictory. On the one hand, the axiom that 'EVERY woman is ABOVE ALL ELSE a mother' has been forcefully instilled in them and they are for the most part reluctant to contest it. On the other hand, they realise that having a baby will restrict their options, impinge on their freedom, demand their time and attention, and hinder the personal development so many of them hunger for. 'Of course women are mothers ... Motherhood is not a choice, it is bound to happen to any woman with a proper feminine instinct' announced one young design student, interviewed in the spring of 1994. Nevertheless, she went on to say that although a good mother should devote herself to the full-time care of her pre-school children, she personally felt that to be stuck at home all day would be extremely boring. The obvious solution for the younger women who made up the bulk of this sample was to delay any decision and, temporarily at least, to ignore the issue altogether. This is reflected in the high number of letters which fail to mention motherhood at all with regards to their ideal woman.

To work or not to work?

A degree of uncertainty surrounding this issue can hardly be surprising for women living in a society which for seventy years, and within the lifetime of each of the women in this sample, was governed by an ideology proclaiming emancipation and equality for women through participation in the national economy and production. Whilst this official stance has now been replaced by a policy of promoting a domestic role for women, the conviction that work is a vital source of mental stimulation, communication and personal development remains strong in the minds of many women. Yet, whereas Soviet ideology insisted on a blanket policy of universal and compulsory employment, Russian women of the 1990s are firm in their belief in individual freedom of choice. In a great many responses, both written and oral, women were clear in advocating each woman's right to determine for herself how she will balance work and family, on the basis of her character, interests and needs.

The attitudes expressed by competition entrants concerning the ultimate desirability of a woman's employment outside the home were more diverse than those relating to any other question. Thirty-five respondents were firmly in favour of a combination of paid employment and family life, many of them advocating part-time work; twenty-two women stressed the importance of work quite heavily whilst making little or no mention of family commitments, in twenty-two letters work took precedence over family although the latter was also mentioned, whilst the reverse was true of ten other entries; only eleven women stated outright that a woman's only occupation should be her home and family; five described a lady of leisure materially supported by a man and unhampered by domestic responsibilities and fifteen entrants made no comment on this aspect of their ideal woman's life. The fairly even spread of this range of attitudes seems to contradict the findings of the *Moskovskii Komsomolets* survey cited in the previous section. In comparing the two, one should remember that whilst the newspaper survey collected responses to a specific and direct question, the opinions expressed by women from this sample emerge from their descriptions of the life-style that they would ascribe to their ideal woman. Perhaps this wider context draws out some of the confusion and contradiction in women's minds. As with the issue of motherhood, it is notable that a not insignificant number of letter-writers, over 10 per cent, chose simply to ignore the question of work altogether.

Discussion in the media about work is not as monolithic as one might expect. On the one hand, articles about unemployment often emphasise the positive aspects of a return to the home for women: 'In the West, women stay at home and look after their husbands and children, keep the house in perfect order and still find time to take an active part in social affairs. Over there women support society, over here they support industry. Can that really be right?'[28] On the other hand, articles commenting on increasing poverty note many families' reliance on a second wage-earner, whilst features in women's magazines and on women's pages frequently describe the lives of successful professional women in high-powered and atypical jobs. In March 1994, for example, the newspaper *Sem'ia* (family) launched a weekly feature which promised to focus on the lives of high-achieving women and began with an article presenting Marina Vladimirovna Korosteleva, founder of the Moscow 'Lady-Leaders' club from which the title of the feature was borrowed. The heading for this first article, 'I don't want to be a shadow', reflects a fear of personal stagnation and invisibility for women, and the column itself was promoted as aiming at 'those women who as a result of a strong character or professional talent find it difficult to satisfy themselves with the role imposed on them by society ... For those for whom personal development is important not only in the context of their families (as wives, mothers and housewives) but also in terms of their chosen professional activity.'[29]

This characterisation of the objections some women might raise to an enforced return to the private sphere mirrors almost exactly the issues addressed by many of the women who were unhappy at the prospect of giving up work completely. These concerns are not new to women but once again reflect the attitudes found by Soviet researchers in the 1960s and 1970s. Now, as then, a desire for mental stimulation, communication, personal development and a sense of independence were most commonly stated as the reasons behind a wish to carry on working, whatever one's family circumstances.

Since the ending of an official commitment to full employment for women, it has often been asserted that women continue to seek paid employment only as a result of financial necessity. Statements of this ilk are usually accompanied by expressions of regret at this state of affairs and a hope that, in the future, men's earning capacity will increase, allowing a reversal of this 'improper' tendency. Contrary to this, many competition entrants stressed the point that they did not, in fact, believe a woman should be working in order to provide for herself or her family; the role of breadwinner, they maintained, should belong to the man of the family. Nevertheless, they felt that restricting a woman's sphere of activity to the home and family alone would be harmful and suffocating to her character and wasteful of her creative potential 'For a woman', writes a twenty-one-year-old university student, 'work should not be about earning a living but rather a way to affirm herself as a fully-fledged individual'. In contrast, some of the young women interviewed in the spring of 1994, felt that total financial dependence on a man was unwise, since, in their opinion, Russian men were not altogether reliable and a woman should, therefore, work in order to retain her independence and to be able to provide for herself and her children. Economist and researcher at the Scientific Research Institute on the Family, Aleksandr Sinel'nikov, commenting on the high levels of divorce and subsequent low number of children per couple, is scathing in his appraisal of this kind of reasoning:

> They [women] realise that they may be abandoned by their husband through no fault of their own and do not want, in such a situation, to be left without a source of means for survival. This is one of the most important reasons for women's involvement in social production, which in turn leads to a decline in the birth rate and facilitates divorce on the initiative of women themselves. No longer economically dependent, they are not restrained in filing for divorce, not only from drunkards and layabouts, on whom they were in any case not materially dependent, but also from more 'decent' men, guilty only of not loving them.[30]

Whilst Sinel'nikov is clearly opposed to this kind of female 'selfishness', a generation of young women so convinced of the value of 'true love' and dedicated to finding their 'other half' might understandably beg to differ.

We have seen, then, that women are not unanimous in their positions concerning an enforced exodus of all women from the workforce. When it comes to deciding which sorts of employment are suitable for women there appears to be far more consensus, and talk of personal choice and the individual's right to decide is notable for its absence. The use of female labour for heavy or hazardous work and the impact of shift work on a woman's ability to fulfil her family role have been criticised since the advent of pro-natalist policies in the 1970s and this criticism was strengthened by the policy of glasnost in the late 1980s. Today, women themselves are adamant that strenuous physical labour and long hours are unacceptable. However, these are by no means the only criteria by which a job may be deemed unsuitable for women. In fact, the jobs which are considered appropriate have become alarmingly restricted. Women consistently limited their choice of ideal professions to modelling, fashion design and secretarial work, all of which are more concerned with a woman's external appearance than with her inner development, especially in the new world of Russian business where secretaries are typically alluded to as 'the face of the firm'.

None the less, creativity and interest were repeatedly cited as the most important factors in choosing a job by the majority of those who felt that work was an essential part of a woman's life. Professions with greater potential for intellectual stimulus, such as psychologist, teacher, journalist and doctor, were mentioned several times, as were managerial and decision-making posts in the fields of commercial enterprise and public or social organisations. Women, it seems, are not altogether ready to give up their right to work, their independence or their right to a role in decision making. In the words of the 'Lady-Leaders' feature writer, 'Our men traditionally hold the key positions in all areas and spheres (and it is no secret that they are not always worthy of this).'[31]

Mass-produced *matryoshki* or individual women?

Gender roles and characteristics as promoted in Russian society today through the media, policy and public opinions are not as simplistic or clear cut as they may seem at a first glance. Superficially it appears that there has been a complete reversal of what went before: the Soviet ideal of strong working women has been thrown out and replaced with models of femininity, domesticity and maternity. Dip a little deeper below the surface, however, and we see that things are not so different. As this chapter has attempted to show, a great many of the policies and attitudes given official backing today are firmly rooted in traditions from the Soviet period. Nor can women's own responses to and thinking on these issues be entirely divorced from that legacy, the convictions of which have, in places, survived the ideology which bore them. Moreover, claims that the totalitarian state which interfered with personal and family decisions regarding life-style choices has been swept aside and replaced with a new 'democracy' supporting individual freedom and self-determination are belied by the pervasiveness with which 'new' but equally restrictive stereotypes are now propounded.

Data indicate that attempts to convince women of a single ideal to which they must aspire have not been altogether successful. Ironically, the areas where women appear to be the most acquiescent are those relating to inner qualities and personal relations, whilst the wider-reaching stereotypes and constraints on women's life-styles, the very aspects of the promoted ideal where political interests and agendas come into play, meet with much greater resistance. Whilst women may happily aspire to ideals of beauty, may feel relieved at the prospect of being allowed to be 'weak' and to seek a man's 'strength and protection', may be pleased to imagine themselves ruling over an exquisite and perfectly ordered home, they are not prepared to see themselves limited to the private sphere only, reduced to brainless bimbos with nothing to offer but their physical attractiveness, or condemned to a life of self-sacrifice and material hardship as overworked, unappreciated mothers.

Indeed, the ready acceptance by women of some of the personal qualities promoted as inherently female has, in fact, contributed to their refusal to retire quietly from the public arena. This is rather symptomatic of the internal contradictions and lack of logic in combining the various aspects of 'womanhood' currently being put forward. As we have seen, the simultaneous promotion of fundamentally conflicting maxims was not unknown in the Soviet era. The existence of an overriding and unquestionable ideology at that time made it easier to smooth over and ignore these incongruities. Today, without the shield of a state ideology, the disparity is more glaringly obvious and women are quicker and more able to challenge it.

Women have been portrayed as morally superior, less self-centred and more conciliatory than men at a time when Russian society is in turmoil and political conflict rife. The withdrawal of women from involvement in decision making, social activity and the world of enterprise is not, therefore, universally regarded as prudent. Businesswomen are often seen to be more ready than men to use their money and influence for the good of society as a whole,[32] while social movements rely heavily on female activists. Even in politics, an area which is frequently described as too corrupt and dirty for female involvement, women are making headway: Ekaterina Lakhova, head of the 'Women of Russia' faction in the State Duma, spoke in March 1995 of a growing respect for women politicians within the parliament and described their role as one of conciliation and mediation, finding a middle path, cooling the tempers of hot-headed male politicians and promoting dialogue as opposed to monologue.[33]

Here, as with the question of women's employment outside the home, it is not only individual women but also media reporting and imagery which are often contradictory, confused and confusing. In an attempt to explain this internal conflict away, journalists, political figures and women themselves take recourse to the idea that perhaps 'certain types' of women will be able to fulfil one role in the public sphere, while the mass of women content themselves with their domestic and family lives. Yet in this very rhetoric of variety lies its own contradiction, since the 'feminine' qualities so prized for public work are attributed to all women on the basis of their biological sex with no reference to individual character traits. What is more, those women singled out as suitable for social activities outside the home are not infrequently described as 'more masculine in character'.

Whatever the characteristic or role in question, no single position is adhered to by all women. Even where the 'official' position is more clear cut, for example on the issue of motherhood, women do not necessarily conform. Seventy years of state ideology and toeing a party line has certainly left behind it a tradition of paying lip service to officially sanctioned attitudes, and the power of the media to instil certain images and phrases in the minds and on the lips of the population has been clearly documented in various societies, including our own. Yet Russian women, despite their rehearsal of certain set phrases and assertions of compliance with the accepted norms of female roles and behaviour, do not necessarily bring these to fruition, either in their own lives or in their descriptions of an ideal life-style.

Perhaps this is one of the flaws in a strategy of trying to promote a single ideal of womanhood. Whenever attempts have been made to force women into an unbending mould, whether by a totalitarian state, a 'democratic' government, the mass media or Western-style, feminist groups, there has always come a point where women themselves have rebelled. Writing on the demise of the American women's movement in the late 1980s and early 1990s, for example, feminist theorist Naomi Wolf lays great emphasis on the younger generation's rejection of a rigid set of values and characteristics dogmatically imposed by the radical feminism of the 1970s.[34] This is particularly pertinent in a society emerging from decades of totalitarian rule and in which the buzzwords 'democracy', 'individual', 'freedom' and 'choice' carry significant weight and value, especially with the younger generation. In their responses to the task of describing an 'Ideal Woman', Russian women repeatedly stress the need for individuality, to be 'unique', to 'stand out in the crowd', 'not to follow fashions blindly' but 'to find her own style'. Women are not a homogenous mass and cannot all be expected to aspire to the same goals and life styles. In the words of a seventeen-year-old medical student,

What is an ideal woman? How should this question be understood? Is a woman ideal from her own point of view or from that of those around her? I think that every woman should feel in her soul that in some way she is ideal ... and others should accept her as she presents herself and as she wants to be accepted.

Notes

1 Lynne Attwood, *The new Soviet man and woman: sex-role socialization in the USSR* (Basingstoke: Macmillan, 1990).
2 Judith Shapiro, 'The industrial labour force' in Mary Buckley (ed.), *Perestroika and Soviet women* (Cambridge: Cambridge University Press, 1992), pp. 21–3.
3 Sue Bridger, Rebecca Kay and Kathryn Pinnick, *No more heroines? Russia, women and the market* (London: Routledge, 1996), p. 40.
4 These competition entries were handed to me personally by Elena Petrovna Evseeva, fashion designer and director of the Moscow Image Centre, to whom I owe great thanks for her generosity and support. Elena Evseeva uses the term 'Lycee' to refer to the courses offered and 'Centre' to describe her entire business (such as the premises, image consultancy programme and her work with the Models' Union).
5 In the spring of 1994, when I was involved in researching the activities of the centre as a part of a research project on 'Women and Marketisation' headed by Dr Sue Bridger at the University of Bradford, a new competition had been launched and several series of free courses had been running over the previous winter. The women interviewed at that time, whose responses have also been drawn on in this chapter, were participants from some of those courses. A more detailed account of the activities of the centre can be found in the book arising from the project. Bridger, Kay and Pinnick, *No more heroines?*, pp. 182–92.
6 Clearly a sample of 144 cannot pretend to be representative of around 75

Perceptions of Russian womanhood 97

million Russian women. Nor is this sample unbiased in terms of age, geography or education, as we have seen. There is also, inevitably, a potential bias concerning the 'kind' of women who are likely to have been drawn to enter such a competition, although the reasons for entering given do vary, ranging from boredom, a general interest in the topic to a hope of 'being discovered' by the fashion industry. Nevertheless, this sample does provide a substantial body of information regarding the attitudes and personal opinions of this group of predominantly young, educated and urban women. Views which are expressed consistently in a sample of this size cannot be simply disregarded as marginal or coincidental, whatever the limitations of the sample. Moreover, as with any theme relating to personal and subjective opinions it would be hard to be entirely representative however large and random one's sample.

7 *Izvestiia*, 14 April 1982, p. 3.
8 I. Grebennikov and L. Kovin'ko, *Khrestomatiia po etike i psikhologii semeinoi zhizni* (Moscow: Prosveshchenie, 1987).
9 *Ibid.*, pp. 86–7.
10 Attwood, *The new Soviet man and woman*.
11 A. Martyniuk, 'Muza putany', *Sem'ia* 13, 1994, p. 5.
12 N. Chubarova, 'Doloi avos'ki, da zdrastvuet gratsiia!' *Pul's* 3, 1991, pp. 30–1.
13 Bridger, Kay and Pinnick, *No more heroines?*, p. 80.
14 There is no easy English translation for the Russian term '*baby*', which has its roots in Russia's peasant past. It is usually used in a derogatory manner to imply an unrefined woman with little intelligence or beauty but often with a powerful physique and stubborn mind-set. In many ways it is similar to the American 'broad'.
15 A. Bogomolov, 'Ia i loshad', ia i byk, ia i baba, i muzhik', *Moskovskii Komsomolets*, 22 July 1992, p. 4.
16 Nastoiashchaia zhenshchina', *Sudarushka*, 27 July 1993, p. 6.
17 'Anonimki dlia nashego doktora', *Pul's* 2, 1993, p. 39.
18 Grebennikov and Kovin'ko, *Khrestomatiia po etike i psikhologii semeinoi zhizni*, p. 63.
19 *Ostankino Novosti*, Ostankino Russian Television, 8 March 1995.
20 Mary Buckley, *Women and ideology in the Soviet Union* (London: Harvester Wheatsheaf, 1989), pp. 179–82.
21 M. Plazk, 'Ssora po pustiaku' in Grebennikov and Kovin'ko, *Khrestomatiia po etike i psikhologii semeinoi zhizni*, p. 156.
22 M. S. Gorbachev, *Perestroika* (London: Fontana, 1988), p. 117.
23 A. Baiduzhii 'Rossiiane mnogo boleiut i rano umiraiut', *Nezavisimaia Gazeta*, 16 July 1994, p. 1.
24 *Ibid.*
25 A. Sinel'nikov, 'Kto zainteresovan v povyshenii rozhdaemosti – gosudarstvo ili sem'ia?', *Sem'ia v Rossii* 3–4, 1995, p. 61.

26 O. Abrosova, M. Balynina and R. Skortsov, 'Liubov' v krossovkakh', *Moskovskii Komsomolets*, 6 February 1992, p. 2.
27 *Ibid*.
28 'Vperedi krutoi povorot', *Moskovskii Komsomolets*, 7 March 1992, p. 1.
29 S. Antonova, 'Ne khochu byt' ten'iu', *Sem'ia* 10, 1994, p. 4.
30 Sinel'nikov, 'Kto zainteresovan v povyshenii rozhdaemosti', p. 66.
31 Antonova, 'Ne khochu byt' ten'iu', p. 4.
32 Bridger, Kay and Pinnick, *No more heroines?*, pp. 142–3.
33 *Ostankino Novosti*, Ostankino Television Russia, 8 March 1995.
34 Naomi Wolf, *Fire with fire: the new female power and how it will change the 21st century* (London: Chatto and Windus, 1993).

6 'She was asking for it': rape and domestic violence against women

LYNNE ATTWOOD

This chapter is concerned primarily with Russian attitudes and responses to two forms of male violence against women: rape and wife battery. 14,400 cases of rape were recorded in the Russian Federation in the year 1993,[1] a figure which is thought to represent, at most, 10 per cent of the total.[2] In the same year 14,500 women were reported to have been murdered by their husbands (or male partners).[3] This constituted more than half of the total number of recorded murders in the country, and far exceeded the widely publicised mafia killings.[4] Shrouded in silence in the Soviet Union of the past, rape and domestic violence are now receiving considerable interest on the part of journalists and academics. Yet while authors applaud the new openness in Russia which allows them to tackle such formerly taboo subjects,[5] they are doing nothing to challenge past orthodoxies. Instead, their writings reproduce old myths about rape and male violence against women which have been challenged by Western research of the past two decades. Rape and other forms of male violence against women are said to have different motivations; lust in the former and anger in the latter. Both are, to a large extent, victim precipitated: women are partly responsible for the violence committed against them because of their own behaviour. Furthermore, women are natural masochists, which means they enjoy being overpowered and treated roughly.[6] Proposals for countering rape and male violence against women centre on the resurrection of a rigid differentiation of gender roles, which Western feminist theorists working in this field see as a cause of, rather than a solution to, the problem.[7]

This chapter attempts to understand Russia's approach to rape and domestic violence in the context of its broader attitudes towards gender difference. It begins with a brief outline of attitudes and policies on male violence against women from the beginning of the Soviet era until the present day, looking at the same time at the perennial concern with gender difference which existed alongside protestations of women's equality. Against this background it discusses the recent Russian literature on rape and domestic violence. Finally, it turns to the new Women's crisis centres and looks at the ways in which, as well as offering practical support to women who have suffered physical and sexual abuse, they are attempting to challenge these patriarchal notions about the causes of male violence against women.

The historical background: rape, male violence and gender differentiation in Soviet and post-Soviet Russia

The Bolsheviks aimed to create a new type of person who was committed to socialism and would place the well-being of the community above his or her personal desires. All forms of human exploitation and crime would eventually be eradicated and the Soviet Union would be a society of equals living in harmony with one another. In the meantime, some 'relics of the past' or 'vestiges of bourgeois morality' remained in the human psyche.[8] This meant that, until people had been appropriately socialised, antisocial and criminal acts would continue.

One 'relic of the past' was a conviction on the part of some men that they were superior to women by virtue of their sex, and that this gave them the right to treat women as they pleased.[9] While such ideas persisted, women needed protection. The Criminal Code of 1922 contained a number of provisions concerned with unwelcome sexual advances, while local party and trade union organisations took up cases of domestic violence.[10] Women were also encouraged to stand up for themselves and for each other. If they were fully informed about their new rights and took an active role in society, they would challenge men's view of them as inferior beings. In the words of a reformed husband in a typical 1920s short story, 'If I scold [my wife] and aim my fist at her like before, she'll simply decide not to live with me and be off: after all, she knows all the laws now.'[11]

Yet despite the Soviet Union's insistence that women were equal to men, there was an uneasy concern that this equality might erode supposedly 'natural' psychological and behavioural differences. The Soviet state had originally pledged to take over the functions of the family, but this was quietly forgotten when Stalin came to power.

Women could not be relieved of their traditional female duties, even if they also worked alongside men in factories and on farms, and they needed certain 'feminine' traits in order to perform these duties properly. Accordingly, Soviet propaganda continued to extol traditional masculine and feminine qualities, particularly during periodic pro-natal campaigns. Teachers and parents were urged to treat boys and girls differently to encourage appropriate gender differences, including 'weakness' in women and 'strength' in men. Marx himself was said to have approved of these differential 'qualities',[12] as did the population at large: men were turned off by 'mannish' behaviour in women,[13] while a woman could 'only love a man who is stronger than her'.[14] 'Female equality', then, had to coexist with 'natural' female vulnerability.

That men might use their superior strength against women was rarely acknowledged. There were few references to rape in the Soviet press, although the crime continued to be recognised in law, with the original 1922 provisions carried over into all subsequent versions of the Criminal Code, including that of post-Soviet Russia.[15] Wife battery received more attention in the press, but was blamed primarily on alcohol abuse and on those persistent 'relics of the past'. There was no attempt to understand violence against women as something structural, part of the social script of gender relations in Soviet society. This would have involved difficult questions about the possible link between male violence against women and the glorification of male forcefulness and female vulnerability.

Concern about gender difference has not diminished with Russia's move to the market. The market is said to require traditional 'masculine' qualities such as entrepreneurship and independence, which were supposedly stifled under the planned economy of the past with its emphasis on what are now held to be 'feminine' qualities: for example, collective responsibility, the obedient implementation of state decisions and conservatism.[16] What is needed, it turns out, is a yet more determined programme of gender socialisation to instil more masculine qualities in the next generation of businessmen. What role women are expected to play in the new Russia is unclear, but the market apparently has no use for the feminine qualities which educators are still being urged to develop in girls.

Women are said to form 80 per cent of the unemployed in Russia,[17] and it is increasingly common for them to be full-time housewives. This state of affairs is apparently welcomed by many so-called 'New Russians', men who have made money in private business. As the director of one women's crisis centre has noted, 'In our country it is ... considered prestigious when a wife does not have to work.'[18] Some women, aware of the harsh lives their mothers lived, are content at first with the relative ease of their own existence;[19] however, complete dependence on their husbands makes them particularly vulnerable to abuse. According to workers in the women's crisis centres, there is a definite increase in the incidence of domestic violence, and the majority of victims are full-time housewives married to New Russians.[20]

In the past, women were afforded some protection from violent husbands through the official state and party organs. Trade unions, the Komsomol, and local Communist Party organisations would reprimand or punish members who violated 'socialist morality'. Women could also appeal to the press for help: the women's magazines *Rabotnitsa* and *Krest'ianka* regularly took up cases of domestic violence. Now that the old organisations are defunct, the women's magazines are powerless to help,[21] and the police treat domestic violence as a private matter which does not concern them.[22] Women are left with the impression that they 'are now without rights ... Now men can do anything and know that there won't be any legal consequences to their violent actions.'[23]

Leaving a violent man is particularly difficult in Russia because of the chronic housing shortage and the complex *propiska* (registration) system. The Soviet Union always had an urban housing crisis; this has become worse with the 'privatisation' of much public housing and the inflated housing demands of New Russians, which has resulted in the conversion of many 'communal apartments', formerly housing several families or individuals, into single-family homes. For those without such wealth, obtaining housing is so difficult that divorced couples often have to continue living together. There is no law which requires police to remove a violent man from the apartment he shares with his wife or ex-wife if this is where he is registered to live;[24] nor are there any hostels or shelters in Russia for battered women.

The peculiarities of Russian housing also result in some women being exposed to domestic violence from men with whom they have no intimate relationship, since no attention is paid to gender when assigning people to rooms in communal apartments. One woman turned for advice to the legal section of the weekly newspaper *Nedelia*, explaining that she shared a two-room communal apartment with a violent, chronic alcoholic. She had been trying to find someone willing to exchange rooms, but this was proving impossible since nobody wanted such a neighbour. *Nedelia*'s legal expert informed her that the authorities had no obligation to rehouse her and that all she could do was go on trying to arrange an exchange herself.[25]

Women are also hampered by growing impoverishment. Those who still have work are, for the most part, in the poorly paid state sector: only 25 per cent of workers in the private sector are female,[26] and they are generally confined to relatively low-paid traditional female service posts such as secretary, assistant and receptionist. This is similar to the situation in Lithuania and Latvia, described in chapter eleven by Nijole White and is, in fact, a common pattern throughout post-Soviet states. The increasing competition for work means that women can more easily be exploited by their bosses, and sexual harassment and sexual abuse are now rife.[27] Job advertisements routinely ask female applicants for details of their physical appearance,[28] and some managers expect their secretaries to provide sexual services either for themselves or their clients.[29] The police are reported to make light of allegations of rape and sexual harassment, and there have been cases of them accepting bribes in return for dropping charges.[30]

With rising female unemployment, the return to full-time domesticity for many women, and the increasingly sharp divide between 'male' and 'female' work, one clear feature of post-Soviet Russia is a growing differentiation of gender roles. As we have noted, feminist researchers in the West have found that, in societies with the most rigid gender dichotomies, male violence against women is particularly prevalent and there are, indeed, indications that both rape and wife battery are on the increase in Russia.[31] Against this background, let us turn to the Russian literature. As rape and domestic violence are treated as separate issues (the most obvious combination of the two, marital rape, receives scant attention, and it has even been suggested that it is a contradiction in terms),[32] we will deal with them in turn.

Russian writings on rape

According to one crisis centre worker, newspapers and magazines have generally been concerned with the production of 'hot articles',[33] and much of what has appeared has been written and illustrated in a salacious manner and is of dubious accuracy. Yet the academics working in this field, who provide much of the material used in journalistic reports, offer little in the way of real analysis. We will look in detail at the work of two legal specialists, Iu. M. Antonian and A. Tkachenko, who are the principal scholars working on the subject.[34]

Antonian and Tkachenko identify three basic causes of rape. The first is a low cultural level in society. A 'civilised society', they argue, 'strictly protects the honour and dignity of woman as a symbol of its own honour'.[35] This defence becomes less effective in times of war, when rape and violence against women become common.[36] However, both are on the increase even in 'normal' life. This, they argue, stems from the fact that young people no longer embrace the sexual norms of civilised society.[37] A breakdown in moral upbringing, combined with bourgeois propaganda which disseminates ideas about sexual freedom,[38] has resulted in the development of cynical attitudes about human relations which reduces sex to a purely physical act. Although it is young men who commit rape, the 'uncivilised' behaviour of young women concerns the authors at least as much: they talk with alarm of the youthful age at which girls now begin to drink and have sexual relations, and at the new breed of 'common girls' (*obshchie devushki*) who allow themselves to be passed around the boys in their gang.[39] The question of consent is clearly not their primary concern.

The second factor is the psychological make-up of certain men. Many rapists 'look on women as inferior creatures whose wishes one does not need to consider',[40] destined only 'to serve man as the instrument of his sexual pleasure'.[41] This is, again, the result of those 'relics of the past'.[42] Other rapists act out of a pronounced fear or hatred of women; they see them 'as a hostile, aggressive, domineering force'.[43] Such men were likely to have poor relationships with their mothers, and transferred a sense of resentment to all women: they want to '"pull women from the pedestal", to punish them and violate them'.[44]

The third factor is *viktimnost'*: the behaviour of the victim. There is a complex relationship between the rapist and the woman he attacks, and 'the victim plays a significant role in the initiation ... of coercive sex crime'.[45] In 10–15 per cent of cases she has acted in a 'provocative' way: she has gone off with a man she hardly knows, either to his home or to another secluded place, and has drunk alcohol with him.[46] In 35–40 per cent of cases the victim's behaviour is not so much provocative as careless: she has put herself at risk 'by being in a deserted place late at night, where an attack is highly possible'.[47] The authors concede that it is difficult to determine exactly what constitutes provocative or careless behaviour and that a woman's natural desire to look attractive could be construed as provocation. A woman might also misjudge a situation and inadvertently allow a man to go too far, and then be unable to stop him. It is up to the courts to determine whether the man genuinely believed she had agreed to have sex.[48] However, even direct refusal on her part might be interpreted 'as dissembling or coquetry', and the man would have some justification for this, since 'many victims do play with their future rapists some kind of sexual game'.[49]

The situation is complicated still further by women's tendency towards masochism. They love men who are stronger than them, and this can extend to 'a desire, often unconscious, to be the object of violence, humiliation, coarseness, mockery and cruelty on the part of men'.[50] This makes them 'put themselves into situations in which an attack against them is very likely – for example, deserted, dark places'.[51] Even though they enjoy the experience, they then feel compelled to report it to the police so that no one will suspect the truth.[52]

A woman's previous sexual experience should not necessarily be held against her in court, the authors argue, since 'although many women begin to have a sex life before marriage, few lead a "disordered life"'.[53] Drunkenness is another matter. They refer to one case in which a woman 'in a state of extreme drunkenness, went to sleep on the side of the road in a rural place. Two young men going by on a motorbike put her in the sidecar and took her to a nearby hut, and there raped her.'[54] The implication is that men will understandably take advantage of a woman in this state.

For women who really do not want to be raped, and are sober enough to take preventative action, Antonian and Tkachenko offer the following advice. Since some men use rape as a way of overcoming a sense of inadequacy, the woman should try 'show[ing] him in some other way (not sexual) that his strength and support is essential to her'.[55] For example, one woman realised she was being followed and turned round to face the man, saying, ' "I'm so glad you're here. I am very afraid to go alone into the entranceway [of the apartment block] in the evening. Will you take me to my apartment?" She took him by the arm, and the astonished stalker took her to her apartment.' It later transpired that he was a serial rapist the police had long been after.[56] A woman might also try complimenting her attacker and expressing sympathy for him: 'You can note his strength, his clothes, his beautiful hair, his intelligence, his voice'.[57] In another case study, a man who became a serial rapist after a family tragedy came to his senses when one of his victims showed him 'sincere concern. She was the first person [I had met] for many months who was not against me ...'.[58]

Such tactics will not work on all rapists, however, so the best way of dealing with rape is to tackle its principal causes. These are laxity in sexual morals and the demise of traditional masculinity and femininity. 'In some circles', the authors explain, 'young men project a far from chivalrous appearance, and young women do not appear [*ne v obraze*] as splendid ladies.'[59] The latter is of particular concern, and so 'the careless or immoral behaviour of some women must be the object of prophylactic reinforcements'.[60] There should be 'systematic monitoring of courtyards, garrets, basements and places where doubtful company gather (people who lead depraved ways of life, homosexuals etc.)'.[61] There should be increased state intervention: more police and 'representatives of social organisations' should patrol the streets, and there should be greater psychiatric supervision of people who are seen as a potential threat, such as victims of 'significant pedagogical neglect which makes it hard for them to establish normal connections and relations with members of the opposite sex'.[62] More effort should also be made to strengthen the family, since the offspring of divorced parents become unsettled and are more prone to alcohol abuse and promiscuity.

In short, Antonian and Tkachenko's writing is replete with erroneous assumptions about rape. Although volunteers working in Women's crisis centres have found that the majority of callers know their assailants,[63] Antonian and Tkachenko portray it as a crime committed by strangers. There is no explicit suggestion that rape is a means of satisfying male sexual urges, but this notion is an undercurrent running through their work: given half a chance, boys will be boys, and the onus is on women to ensure that they do not get that chance. Women are held largely to blame for rape: if they lead 'disordered lives', drink too much, or are simply alone on dark secluded streets (something virtually unavoidable in poorly lit Russian cities), they are encouraging potential assailants. Even if they say no, they might really mean yes. In such cases, indeed, the rapist is portrayed as the real victim: he is manipulated into giving the woman what she wants and is then reported for doing so. Even when rapists have psychological disorders, women are at fault for not being sufficiently caring and loving as mothers. The concern about the collapse of moral values centres firmly on female behaviour.

The only effective way to deal with rape, according to Antonian and Tkachenko, is to strengthen the family, confine sexual practices to marriage, and ensure that men and women act in appropriately gender-defined ways. Even when a woman is actually under attack she is advised to placate her assailant by appealing to his masculine virtues.

Writings on domestic violence

As we noted earlier, in the pre-glasnost era, domestic violence was explained as a vestige of the bourgeois past which would one day be eradicated. This approach is no longer tenable and a number of scholars are now attempting to find alternative explanations for the phenomenon.

G. G. Moshak is one of the principal scholars on domestic violence. He links wife battery to the formerly high level of female participation in the work force, and the ensuing alteration in the balance of gender roles. He argues that 'Drawing women into social production, although on the whole a positive process, has had the undesired consequence of tearing wives and mothers away from family matters. The more a woman is occupied with social matters, the less attention she pays, as a rule, to family needs, and this can have a negative effect on family relations.'[64] The situation is compounded by the fact that a working wife is also financially independent of her husband, to which many men object. A sizable proportion of the population believes it is essential for men and women to have completely different social roles: 'Purely female roles include doing the housework, looking after the children, bringing them up, selflessly creating the conditions for the husband to perform his functions without hindrance'.[65] If a woman is not willing to perform such wifely duties, her husband may see 'physical punishment as morally acceptable'.[66]

The situation is exacerbated by the drop in female 'standards of behaviour'. As women have taken on 'male' roles they have also acquired some of the traits of male behaviour: they 'have begun to smoke, to drink strong spirits, to adopt a coarse and unduly free and easy manner [*razviaznost'*]'.[67] Moshak insists he is not laying all the blame for family conflict on 'members of the splendid sex',[68] but is merely pointing out that women's behaviour does play a considerable part in provoking domestic violence. The implication is that the best way of avoiding violence is for wives to give in to their husbands and do as they want.

D. A. Shestakov, an expert on spousal murder, takes a similar stance: that understanding the causes of domestic violence requires critical analysis of female emancipation.[69] In a study of male prisoners serving time for murdering their wives, he found that 60 per cent were dissatisfied with their role in the system of conjugal relations. The infringement of male authority is their motive for carrying out the crime.[70] Their wives were so independent that the men were not able to relate to them as the 'weak, splendid sex',[71] and this upset them. In 41 per cent of cases the wife had even been the head of the family, as compared with 2–4 per cent in 'normal–typical families'.[72] Even if men do not kill their wives for being insufficiently feminine, the family will not be happy: 'according to sociologists, in the majority of unsuccessful marriages the woman is the head',[73] and dysfunctional families are generally characterised by 'authoritarian behaviour on the part of the woman'.[74] The fact that comparatively few women kill their husbands – according to Shestakov's own data, only 12 per cent of spousal murders are committed by women – does not make them any less culpable. Women are less inclined towards acts of violence because they are 'designed by nature to give life and so are less aggressive'.[75] All the same, they are largely to blame for any 'family drama' which takes place.[76] Shestakov is not entirely consistent about which kind of woman is worse. In one publication he singles out 'militant feminists [*voinstvuiushchie feministki*] who think that men and women should change roles'.[77] In another, he places particular blame on those who try to have it both ways; who, 'having become strong, still want to keep all the privileges of the weak sex'.[78] In either case, it seems that a woman who wishes to avoid attack needs to respond to her partner's violence with feminine tenderness. Asked in an interview in a popular magazine how a woman could avoid being beaten by her drunken husband, Shestakov explained that the husband would not think of striking her if, instead of reproaching him, she gently offered to help him to bed.[79]

In short, Russian academics present male violence against women as an extreme but not unjustified response to the erosion of traditional patriarchal gender roles. If these roles are restored and men regain their rightful position as heads of the family, they will go back to protecting members of the 'weak, splendid sex' instead of beating them. In reality, the opposite would appear to be the case. According to the experience of workers in the women's crisis centres, the more vulnerable women are, and the more dependent on their husbands, the more likely they are to become victims of domestic abuse.

The 'women's crisis centres' and alternative approaches to rape and domestic violence

The first women's crisis centres were registered in 1993, although Nataliia Gaidarenko, director of the Moscow centre, 'Sisters',[80] had been running a part-time telephone help-line for women since 1990.

They are offshoots of the unofficial women's movement which emerged when the Communist Party lost its monopoly over social and political associations, and take a feminist line which stands in stark contrast to the attitudes we have discussed earlier. Their view is that violence against women in all of its forms, including rape, is a means of asserting male power and dominance. Rape is not a sexual crime as such but, as Susan Brownmiller put it, a 'process of intimidation by which all men keep all women in a state of fear'.[81]

There are now eleven centres operating in the Russian Federation as a whole, two of which are in Moscow. Most of them offer support and practical advice to women on a range of issues, including not only rape and domestic violence but also employment, health, education and child care. 'Sisters' is one of the more specialised, working only with women who have been sexually abused.

Concern about the paucity of reliable information about violence against women, and the attitudes and assumptions inherent in the work which has been carried out, led to the establishment, early in 1995, of the Russian Association of Crisis Centres for Women. Although as yet unregistered, the Association has already begun work on a substantial research project under the title 'REAP': the Research, Education and Advocacy Project. A report on its preliminary findings was presented to the Non-Governmental Forum of the Fourth United Nations World Conference on Women in Beijing in August 1995.[82] The aim of the project is to get a clearer idea of the extent of violence against women in Russia, how women understand and deal with it in their daily lives, and how the police, legislators, medical personnel and the general public relate to it. Questionnaires have been circulated, and in-depth interviews conducted in schools, teacher-training colleges, hospitals, orphanages, public prosecutors' offices and a number of other institutions. Ultimately it is hoped that the project will have an influence on public opinion, state policy and legislation concerning violence against women.[83]

The findings of the REAP study, and the personal experience of the volunteers working at the women's crisis centres, make it clear that Russians have taken to heart the notion that women are at least partly to blame for both rape and domestic violence. However, the REAP study detected considerable confusion amongst women about the extent of their culpability. This led the researchers to conclude that women experience an 'internal conflict' between the way society judges their behaviour and their own understandings of what is, and is not, acceptable.[84] 66.7 per cent of the male respondents and 59 per cent of the female respondents thought that women bore some responsibility for rape, but women were far less certain about what types of behaviour could be seen as provocative. Agreeing to go to a man's home to 'listen to music' was seen by both men and women as particularly irresponsible: 57 per cent of the men and 65 per cent of the women thought the woman was largely to blame for what happened thereafter. 42.4 per cent of the men and 21 per cent of the women believed that if a woman accepted an invitation from a man to go to dinner she was 'really agreeing to something much more'. However, 39.4 per cent of the men but only 7 per cent of the women thought that a woman was asking for trouble if she talked 'too freely' with a man she did not know, while 24.2 per cent of the men but only 4 per cent of the women believed the old myth that women really wanted to be raped.

Volunteers at the crisis centres report that the majority of callers suspect that their own behaviour contributed to the rape: they 'admit' that they were dressed inappropriately, were wearing too much make-up, were too trusting, or were simply alone on the streets too late at night.[85] Their confusion about their own role in the crime, combined with the justified fear that the police and the courts will criticise their behaviour, means that few women report rape. According to official figures, one in ten women go to the police. Nataliia Khodyreva, of the St Petersburg Psychological Crisis Centre for Women, suggests that the real figure is more likely one in twenty-five.[86] The first task for volunteers is to persuade callers that they were in no way at fault. As Nataliia Gaidarenko puts it, 'Even if a girl was coquettish (perhaps the rapist was someone she knew), even if she allowed him to kiss her, that does not mean she gave her consent to "all the rest".'[87]

If the crisis centres are to overturn the notion that women bring rape on themselves, there has to be a change in the way it is presented in the media. Accordingly, they have been trying to find sympathetic journalists to help them put forward an alternative view. Gaidarenko joined forces with Iuliia Vodzakovskaia of the youth newspaper *Komsomol'skaia Pravda* to produce a double-page spread on rape in April 1993. Vodzakovskaya began by relating the gruelling story of a teenage girl abandoned by her parents after she had been raped. Gaidarenko then publicised the work of 'Sisters', emphasising its non-judgemental policy in relation to callers. The newspapers' editors finished with a series of recommendations on how to raise public awareness about rape and alter criminal investigation proceedings to make them less traumatic for women. These included, perhaps surprisingly, the suggestion that capital punishment no longer be applied for any form of rape. This was justified on the grounds that if a rapist faces the death penalty he is more likely to kill the woman, since she is usually the only witness to the act.[88]

Since then, workers in the crisis centres have provided information and given interviews to a range of publications, and have ensured that a different approach to the subject is being aired. As Anna Cherniakhovskaia puts it, in an article in the Russian version of *Cosmopolitan*: 'The essence of sexual coercion is the question of control and power. Some men are not after physical intimacy ... [but] the chance to demonstrate their power.'[89]

Approximately half the respondents who took part in the REAP study, male and female, thought that women were at least partly responsible for domestic violence as well as rape. Women's own sense of culpability is again compounded by lack of sympathy on the part of the police and the legal profession. Some judges and lawyers 'react with anger to discussions of domestic violence, saying that if women would simply obey their husbands, there would be fewer beatings'.[90] In the face of such attitudes, it is hardly surprising that very few battered wives – according to one estimate, less than 2 per cent – go to the police.[91] Those who do are likely to be told that it is a family affair and the police can do nothing. One woman was only allowed to file a complaint when her violent husband turned on her mother as well.[92]

Moscow's Crisis Centre for Women takes around 200 calls per month from battered wives.[93] According to the centre's director, Marina Pisklakova, most people associate domestic violence with poverty and alcohol abuse, yet it is now most prevalent in the plush homes of New Russians, and the most likely victims are full-time housewives. Since the woman is completely dependent on the husband financially, he is able to demand her complete subordination. She is concerned solely with domestic matters. 'If he wants to talk to her, they talk. If not – she must keep quiet.'[94] Often the man puts pressure on his wife to give up her old friends, ostensibly so that she can devote herself more fully to her family; but this, Pisklakova argues, is another form of control over her.[95] It also has the effect of increasing her isolation. The situation is not helped by the fact that Russian women have a strong propensity for self-sacrifice. This can be linked to the stress on gender differences discussed earlier; as Pisklakova explains, women are 'prepared from childhood for the idea that ... they must serve a man', and this makes them more inclined to put up with abusive treatment.[96] There is also a traditional understanding that violence is a sign of jealousy and hence of love: as the old Russian proverb goes, 'If he beats me, it means he loves me.'[97]

Again, the crisis centres are attempting to tackle such attitudes through the press and through educational work. The centres' directors and volunteers have been giving interviews to journalists. (Most recently, an interview with Nataliia Khodyreva appeared in the magazine *Ogonek* in February 1996 as part of a series of articles in the magazine on domestic violence.)[98] 'Sisters' plans a programme of talks with schoolchildren and students. REAP researchers have begun discussions with teachers, schoolchildren and students on violence against women, and intend in due course to produce an educational video as well as written materials.[99] However, this in itself is far from sufficient. Women have to be in a position to leave their violent husbands. This means there has to be a network of hostels they can go to, a change in housing policy so that they have the possibility of getting their own apartments, and improved employment prospects for women so that they can support themselves and their children. There also has to be a radical alteration in the way in which domestic violence is perceived and dealt with by the police and the courts. According to an article in *Ogonek*, there is a draft law currently under consideration which aims to create a network of crisis centres, shelters and safe houses across the Russian Federation by the year 2000, as well as providing the means for counselling both victims and perpetrators of domestic violence.[100] Given the financial problems which beset the country, it is surely doubtful that the necessary funds will be found for such an ambitious project. It is not clear from the *Ogonek* article whether these crisis centres would work with those already in existence, or would constitute an alternative to them. The latter is a somewhat disturbing prospect since one of the legal experts involved in drawing up the draft law is Dmitrii Shestakov,[101] who, as we have seen, holds women largely responsible for the violence done to them by their husbands.

Conclusion

As we have seen in this chapter, while the Russian literature treats rape and domestic violence as separate phenomena, they have one distinct feature in common: the woman's own behaviour is thought to have played a considerable role in instigating the violence. She has incited male violence by, in different ways, challenging the traditional norms of femininity. In the case of rape she has been insufficiently modest; in the case of wife battery, she has been insufficiently domestic. Western feminists have suggested that rape is the logical conclusion of traditional cultural notions of masculinity and femininity, which emphasise the 'natural sexual aggressiveness of man and man's natural physical superiority over women'.[102] Yet in the mainstream Russian literature, a strict dichotomy between 'strong, active' men, and 'weak, passive' women is advanced as a possible solution to the problem. If men's superior status and strength were given more recognition, the argument goes, they would be more inclined to protect women instead of raping and battering them. Rape and domestic violence are both being used as an excuse for promoting a stricter gender dichotomy, a means for bolstering the patriarchal order which has always been so central to Soviet and, now, post-Soviet Russia.

The women's crisis centres are trying to challenge these attitudes. As well as offering practical assistance to women suffering male abuse, they are trying to get across an alternative feminist understanding of the problem, which holds that violence against women is used to reinforce male power and control, and that patriarchal norms need to be confronted rather than reinforced. Their efforts are severely hampered by financial restraints. They survive on extremely small budgets, in some cases with the help of Western organisations: 'Sisters', for example, has had some financial assistance from the Global Fund for Women, and the Moscow Crisis Centre for Women from the Soros Foundation. This support will not last indefinitely, however, and the future of the centres remains precarious. While the centres' workers feel it is important that they began as grassroots feminist organisations, they are not hopeful that they will be able to continue without some support from the authorities. As the REAP report concludes, 'the problem will not be addressed adequately until the government and the public recognise that rape and domestic violence are violations of women's human rights and must be confronted on a political and societal level'.[103]

Notes

1 'Iznasilovaniia: statisticheskii aspect', *Voprosi Statistiki* 2, 1995, p. 81.
2 Interview with Nataliia Khodyreva of the St Petersburg Psychological Crisis Centre for Women, August 1995.
3 Russian Association of Crisis Centres for Women, *Violence against women in Russia: education and advocacy project* (hereafter referred to as

REAP report), presented at the Non-Governmental Forum of the Fourth United Nations' World Conference on Women in Beijing, August 1995, p. 1.
4 'Russian women face increased violence, inequality', *Moscow Tribune*, 1 September 1995, p. 8.
5 D. A. Shestakov, *Supruzheskoe ubiistvo kak obshchestvennaia problema* (St Petersburg: Izdatel'stvo Sankt-Peterburgogo universiteta, 1992), pp. 1–2.
6 For a discussion of these ideas in Western writing on rape and violence against women, see, for example, Susan Brownmiller, *Against our will: men, women and rape* (New York: Fawcett Columbine, 1975), and Patricia Searles and Ronald J. Berger (eds.) *Rape and society* (Boulder, Colo., and Oxford: Westview Press, 1995).
7 Cited in the preface to Searles and Berger, *Rape and society*, p. 2.
8 See, for example, Iu. M. Antonian, 'Obshchii vzgliad na seksologo-kriminologicheskie issledovaniia' in Iu. M. Antonian (ed.), *Seksual'nye prestupniki* (Moscow: Ministerstvo vnutrennikh del rossiiskoi federatsii nauchno-issledovatel'skii institut, 1992) p. 10.
9 *Ibid.*, p. 10.
10 See, for example, N. Kaptel'tseva, 'U rabotnits – delegatok', *Krest'ianka* 14, July 1925, pp. 9–10, which lists wife beating as one of the problems to which women can turn to their delegates or political representatives.
11 Aleksandr Neverov, 'Strogii muzh', *Krest'ianka* 20, November 1923, pp. 17–18.
12 See Lynne Attwood, *The new Soviet man and woman: sex-role socialization in the USSR* (Basingstoke: Macmillan, 1990), pp. 133–4.
13 A. G. Khripkova and D. V. Kolesov, *Devochka-podrostok-devushka* (Moscow: Prosveshchenie, 1981), p. 120.
14 A. Kotliar, 'Myzhskaia otvetstvennost', *Vospitanie Shkol'nikov* 4, 1986, pp. 69–71.
15 Article 117 of the Criminal Code of the Russian Federation defines 'ordinary' rape as 'sexual intercourse obtained through the application of physical of physical force, mental anguish or taking advantage of the helpless state of the victim', and is punishable by three to seven years' imprisonment. If the coercion involves the threat of murder or grievous bodily harm, or if the perpetrator has a previous conviction for rape, the sentence goes up to five to ten years. If the rape is committed by a gang, or the victim is 'underage' (from twelve to eighteen years), the sentence is between five to fifteen years. If the rapist is a 'dangerous recidivist', the act has particularly severe after-effects, or the victim is a child under the age of twelve, then the penalty is eight to fifteen years' imprisonment or the death penalty. *Ugolovnyi kodeks RSFSR* (Moscow: Izdatel'stvo BEK, 1995).
16 Iu. E. Aleshina and A. S. Volovich, 'Problemy usloveniia rolei muzhiny i zhenshiny', *Voprosy Psikhologii* 4, 1991, pp. 74–82.

17 V. V. Koval, 'Women and work in Russia' in Valentina Koval (ed.), *Women in contemporary Russia* (Providence, R.I. and Oxford: Berghahn Books, 1995) p. 23.
18 Marina Pisklakova, interviewed by L. Gridina, 'V Rossiiskoi sem'e est' vse vidy nasiliia', *Torgovaia Gazeta*, 29 March 1994, p. 4.
19 Personal interview with Anna Petrushevskaia of the Moscow Crisis Centre, September 1995.
20 *Ibid.*; and L. Gridina, 'V Rossiiskoi sem'e est' vse vidy nasiliia'.
21 Personal interview with Nadezhda Aleksandrovna Nesterova and Irina Viktorovna Skliar of *Rabotnitsa* magazine, 10 August 1992.
22 *Human Rights Watch Women's Rights Monitor* 7(5), March 1995, pp. 20–4; REAP report, pp. 4, 11: interview with Anna Petrushevskaia of the Moscow Crisis Centre for Women, September 1995.
23 REAP report, p. 10.
24 See *Human Rights Watch Women's Rights Monitor* 7(5), March 1995, p. 23.
25 'Prinuditelnyi obmen kvartiry', *Nedelia* 22, 1995, p. 12.
26 Personal interview with Zoia Khotkina, Centre for Gender Studies, August 1995.
27 *Ibid.* Zoia Khotkina has recently started a research project on sexual harassment and abuse in the workplace.
28 REAP report, p. 3.
29 Personal interview with Nataliia Gaidarenko, August 1995. See also 'Russian women face increased violence, inequality', p. 8; and Anna Cherniakhovskaia, 'Seks po prinuzhdeniiu?' in *Cosmopolitan* (Russian version) no. 2, 1995, p. 89.
30 See *Human Rights Watch Women's Rights Monitor*, 7(5), March 1995, p. 26.
31 This is the conclusion drawn by women working in the crisis centres: personal interviews with Nataliia Gaidarenko, Nataliia Khodyreva, Anna Petrushevskaia, August–September 1995.
32 One male lawyer, Evgenii Tsimbal, a member of the committee formed to write the new draft provision on family violence, is quoted as having claimed, at a seminar on sexual harassment held in Moscow on 20 May 1995, that marital rape is simply not possible. See REAP report, p. 3.
33 Nataliia Khodyreva, speaking at the Women's Forum held in Dubna, Russia, November 1992, attended by the author.
34 For discussions on journalistic writings, see Lynne Attwood, 'The post-Soviet woman in the move to the market: a return to domesticity and dependence?' in Rosalind Marsh (ed.), *Women in Russia and Ukraine* (Cambridge: Cambridge University Press, 1996), pp. 255–266.
35 Iu. M. Antonian and A. A. Tkachenko, *Seksual'nye prestupleniia: Chikatilo i drugie* (Moscow: Amal'eia, 1993), p. 3.
36 *Ibid.*, p. 38.

37 *Ibid.*, p. 139.
38 Antonian, 'Obshchii vzgliad na seksologo-kriminologicheskie issledovaniia', p. 10.
39 Antonian and Tkachenko, *Seksual'nye prestupleniia*, p. 139.
40 *Ibid.*, p. 16.
41 *Ibid.*, p. 156.
42 Antonian, 'Obshchii vzgliad na seksologo-kriminologicheskie issledovaniia', p. 10.
43 Antonian and Tkachenko, *Seksual'nye prestupleniia*, p. 163.
44 *Ibid.*, p. 305.
45 *Ibid.*, p. 174.
46 *Ibid.*, p. 166.
47 *Ibid.*, p. 166.
48 *Ibid.*, p. 170.
49 *Ibid.*, p. 170.
50 *Ibid.*, p. 182.
51 *Ibid.*, p. 182.
52 *Ibid.*, p. 183.
53 *Ibid.*, p. 171.
54 *Ibid.*, p. 174.
55 *Ibid.*, p. 304.
56 *Ibid.*, pp. 304–5.
57 *Ibid.*, p. 309.
58 *Ibid.*, p. 309.
59 *Ibid.*, pp. 288–9.
60 *Ibid.*, p. 291.
61 *Ibid.*, p. 299.
62 *Ibid.*, p. 299.
63 Personal interview with Nataliia Gaidarenko, July 1993.
64 G. G. Moshak, *Prestuplenie v sem'e: istoki i profilaktika* (Kishenev: Karta Moldoveniaske, 1989), p. 9.
65 *Ibid.*, p. 11.
66 *Ibid.*, p. 9.
67 *Ibid.*, p. 11.
68 *Ibid.*, p. 11.
69 Shestakov, *Supruzheskoe ubiistvo*, p. 3.
70 *Ibid.*, p. 3.
71 *Ibid.*, p. 15.
72 *Ibid.*, p. 15.
73 *Ibid.*, p. 18. There is no mention of who these sociologists are, and contrary to the impression given by Shestakov this position is not supported by all Russian sociologists. See Attwood, *The new Soviet man and woman*, pp. 128–9.

74 Shestakov, *Supruzheskoe ubiistvo*, p. 15.
75 *Ibid.*, p. 56.
76 *Ibid.*, p. 56.
77 D. A. Shestakov, *Predotvratit' semeinuiu dramu* (Leningrad: Znanie, 1981), p. 12.
78 'Suprug opasnei killera', interview with Dmitrii Shestakov, conducted by Elena Berezina, in *Ogonek* 9, February 1996, pp. 44–5.
79 *Ibid.*
80 The full name of the centre is 'Sisters': The Moscow Assault Recovery Centre (or, in Russian, Moskovskii tsentr okazaniia pomoshchi perezhivshim nasilie).
81 Brownmiller, *Against our will*, pp. 14–15.
82 Although more than 600 questionnaires had been completed by the time of the Beijing forum, only 130 had been analysed, and the researchers stressed that their conclusions could only be seen as tentative.
83 REAP report, p. 4.
84 *Ibid.*, p. 8.
85 Personal interview with Nataliia Gaidarenko, November 1994.
86 Nataliia Khodyreva, speaking at the Women's Forum held in Dubna, Russia, November 1992. Of 248 women who had phoned the Petersburg centre that year, only two had been to the police.
87 Iuliia Vodzakovskaia and Nataliia Gaidarenko, 'Sovremennaia poves' o kapitanskoi dochke', *Komsomol'skaia Pravda*, 16 April 1993, p. 4.
88 *Ibid. Komsomol'skaia Pravda* is not alone in voicing this concern. See also K. A. Tolpekin, 'Iznasilovaniia, zavershivshiesia ubiistvom poterpevshikh: statistika i reali'nost'' in *Sostoaynie i tendentsii nastil'stvennoi prestupnosti v rossiiskoi federatsii* (Moscow: Sbornik nauchnykh trudov, nauchno-issledovatel'skii institut problem ukrepleniia zakonnosti i pravoporiadka, 1993), p. 117.
89 Cherniakhovskaia, 'Seks po prinuzhdeniiu?', p. 89.
90 REAP report, p. 3.
91 *Ibid.*, p. 3. This information was supplied by the Nizhnii Tagil crisis centre, 'Lana' (named in honour of one of its volunteers, who was herself raped and murdered in July 1995).
92 *Ibid.*, p. 4.
93 This information was provided by Anna Petrushevskaia of the Moscow Crisis Centre for Women in a personal interview, September 1995.
94 Gridina, 'V Rossiiskoi sem'e est'vse vidy nasiliia', p. 4.
95 Galina Polozhevets, 'Ia boius' svoego muzha', *Vek*, 22 April 1994. (The page number is unknown; I was provided with a photocopy of the article by the Moscow Crisis Centre for Women, which had not made a note of the page number.)
96 Quoted by Gridina, 'V Rossiiskoi sem'e est' vse vidy nasiliia'.

97 See Larisa Bogdanovich, 'B'et – znachit liubit?', *Rabotnitsa* 5–6, 1992, pp. 26–7. The same point is made in 'Knut nad supruzheskoi krovat'yu', *Ogonek* 9, February 1996, p. 43.
98 'Nasil'nika – za partul', *Ogonek* 9, February 1996, p. 47.
99 REAP report, p. 13; also discussions with members of the REAP group, August 1995.
100 'Kuda bezhat' iz domashnego ada?', *Ogonek* 9, February 1996, pp. 46–7.
101 'Suprug opasnei killera', *Ogonek* 9, February 1996, p. 44.
102 R. Herschberger, quoted by Stevi Jackson in 'The social context of rape: sexual scripts and motivation' in Searles and Berger, *Rape and society*, p. 19.
103 REAP report, p. 13.

7 'For the sake of the children': gender and migration in the former Soviet Union

HILARY PILKINGTON

Since the ethnic conflict in Baku at the end of January 1990 produced the first mass inflow into Russia of internally displaced people (40,000 mainly Armenians and Russians), post-Soviet Russia has been coming to terms with a new social group in its midst – 'refugees'.[1] Following the break up of the Soviet Union, however, periodic influxes of those in flight from ethnic and military conflict have been supplemented by a steady flow of another new social group – Russian-speaking forced migrants[2] – and the growing tide of returnees has elicited concern about potential social and political tension within Russia itself. Although suggestions that all, or most, of the 25.3 million ethnic Russians living beyond the borders of Russia in the former Soviet republics at the time of the 1989 census are likely to return to Russia over the coming years are alarmist, equally misleading are official figures which indicate that, since the beginning of formal registration of refugees and forced migrants in July 1992, just 784,014 have been registered by the Federal Migration Service of Russia (FMS).[3] It is widely accepted that between two-thirds and three-quarters of forced migrants and refugees entering Russia are simply not registered as such. Estimates of actual numbers already having returned to Russia, therefore, range between 2.5 million and 6 million.[4]

Forced migration between the former constituent republics of the USSR appears ungendered.[5] Published Federal Migration Service data on refugees and forced migrants includes gender as a category only in figures providing a sex–age breakdown of those registered, and only one academic study published to date in Russia has taken gender to be a variable worthy of note in current migratory processes.[6] It is the contention here, however, that the experience of forced migration

119

between territories of the former Soviet Union *is* gendered and this article explores the relationship between gender and forced migration in three of its aspects. Firstly, the experience of Russian-speaking forced migrant women will be examined in the light of wider academic debates about gender and migration which have begun to address: the changed roles of women after migration; the specific socio-economic and cultural positioning of female immigrants; the relationship between women and idealised homeland; and women's role in recreating the connection with the past community.[7] Secondly, the chapter seeks to locate the experience of Russian-speaking forced migrants in wider patterns of change for women in the post-Soviet space. This will entail an analysis of how forced migrant and refugee women are positioned in post-Soviet Russian society – paying particular attention to their labelling as 'burdens' on the state – as well as of the strategies devised by migrant women to overcome the difficulties they face as they reforge their lives in a new economic, social and cultural environment. Thirdly, the peripheral cultural position of forced migrants will be employed as a vantage point from which to observe the interconnection of the reforging of gender identity and the reconfiguration of the 'nation' in post-Soviet Russia.

This chapter bases its theses on: a critical study of data published by Russian governmental and non-governmental and international organisations, academic surveys and studies (Russian and Western) and Russian media reports; and the results of a qualitative sociological study of the experience of Russian-speaking forced migrants undertaken by the author in 1994. The latter consists of data emanating from 195 refugee and forced migrant respondents[8] – both male and female – in four rural settlements in the Orel region of Central Russia and the city of Ul'ianovsk in the Middle Volga.[9] All had left the former republics (primarily the Central Asian states of Tadzhikistan, Uzbekistan and Kyrgyzstan as well as Kazakhstan and Azerbaidzhan) and resettled in Russia between 1988 and 1994. They were interviewed between July and December 1994. Almost three-quarters (73 per cent) of respondents stated their nationality to be Russian; this is in line with Federal Migration Service data on the nationality of registered refugees and forced migrants. Women predominated among respondents in both rural and urban regions of fieldwork, although this reflects neither a significant gender imbalance among migrants nor the open bias of the research (the gender aspect was only one dimension of a much wider study).[10] The explanation lies rather with the greater accessibility of women during fieldwork: women were more likely to be at home, especially in rural areas; women were more prepared to 'find time' to give interviews; and men were more reluctant to talk.[11]

A woman's 'natural urge'? Gender and migratory push factors

Women predominate in current migratory processes on the territory of the former Soviet Union. An early survey of refugees and forced migrants conducted by the Institute of Sociology suggested that around 54 per cent of refugees and forced migrants were women.[12] The latest Federal Migration Service data indicate that women continue to predominate; they constitute 53 per cent of refugees and forced migrants registered between 1 July 1992 and 1 April 1995.[13] These raw demographic data are of little value, however, since they suggest no radical deviation from the overall gender balance of the Russian population.[14] Much more significant is the *role* attributed to women in forced migration.

Based on a survey of 1,948 potential migrant families in four former Union republics and two autonomous republics of the Russian Federation during the summer of 1992, Galina Vitkovskaia determines two aspects of migrational behaviour which are significantly affected by gender: women, she says, have a higher migrational intention; and women's migrational activity is – in comparison to men's – 'forced' (*prinuditel'naia*); that is, it results from fear of military and interethnic conflict or ecological catastrophe.[15] To some extent, Vitkovskaia's hypothesis is unremarkable; it follows a wider trend in migration studies which posits women as victims (refugees in flight) rather than voluntary economic migrants.[16] What is interesting about the gender analysis undertaken, however, is a series of explanatory connections Vitkovskaia makes which suggest that the role of women as initiators of migration in itself indicates the abnormal or 'forced' nature of current migratory processes.

Women are seen to have a primordial connection with the land (*rodina*) making them, 'in normal circumstances' less inclined to uproot.[17] Thus, women's current migrationary zeal is seen as evidence of social and political factors driving migration from the former republics as indicated by a gendered pattern of 'push factors'. Women, Vitkovskaia found, referred much more frequently to inter-ethnic relations as a primary motive for migration (20 per cent of women compared to only 12 per cent of men) and were a third more likely than men to name factors such as fear of the future, the change in the position of Russians in the former Soviet republics and the attraction of the ethnic comfort of Russia as motivating factors. This greater 'fear' felt by women is explained primarily by women's greater responsibility for children, as well as by women's relatively weak integration into the native ethnic environment due to the absence of close relatives and friendly inter-ethnic contacts as well as women's weaker knowledge of the local language.[18] Vitkovskaia suggests that all this is evidence that women are the ones 'sitting on their suitcases' in the former republics.

'For the children's sake': explaining women's 'suitcase mood'

The testimonies of respondents in the author's own study confirm Vitkovskaia's finding that far from 'following' their male partners, women might instigate migration from the former republic. However, in-depth interviews with refugees and forced migrants suggest that a gendered reading of 'push factors' in forced migration needs to be more complex than Vitkovskaia indicates.

The clearest evidence of this from my study is that forced migrants themselves disagree as to who instigated the move; when asked who had been the main protagonist in the decision to leave the former republic, women were equally split between seeing it as their own decision, their husband's decision or a joint decision, while men were more likely to see it as their own decision (see Figure 7:1).[19]

The link Vitkovskaia makes between migrational push and the presence of children, on the other hand, was confirmed by the interviews conducted in 1994; whereas children are generally an inhibiting variable in migrational behaviour, amongst Russian-speaking forced migrants they constitute a key *push* factor. One respondent expressed this from her personal experience of those leaving Kazakhstan: 'the children needed a school ... we needed a school, nothing else ... We could have worked there. Many of our friends who did not have children stayed. Those whose children are still little, who have just been born, who are a long way off school, they still live there.'

However, the direct correlation made by Vitkovskaia between concern about children and women's fear of ethnic conflict is more problematic. Comments made during the completion of questionnaires and in interviews suggest that although women's concern about their children is high, such concern is far from gender exclusive; the desire to protect both wives and children was frequently cited as a primary motivating factor by male respondents. Of forty-one respondents

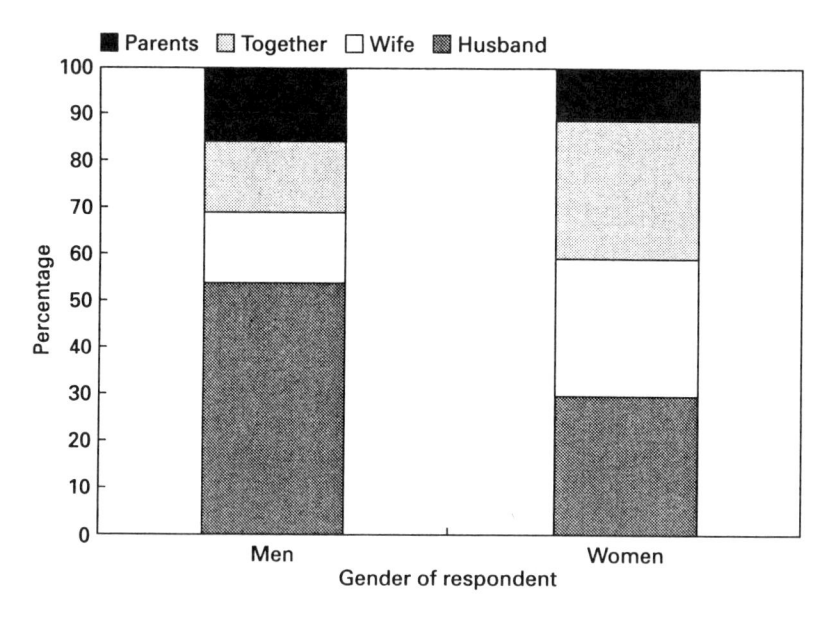

Figure 7:1 Who initiated migration? (total = 41)

(thirteen men and twenty-eight women) in one rural fieldwork location in Orel region, twelve (92 per cent) of the men and twenty-five (89 per cent) of the women mentioned 'the future of the children' as one of the major concerns in making the decision to leave their former place of residence.

Thus whilst, as is clear from Figure 7:2, the 'future of the children' is a key push factor amongst migrants, the gender distinction between women's *ethnic* and men's *economic* concerns made by Vitkovskaia should be treated more critically. Citing 'the future of the children' as a motivation for leaving the former republic welds together concerns – held by both men and women – about physical danger (children disappearing, being beaten or killed), ethnic discomfort (isolation as Russians) and the decline in long-term socio-economic prospects (tied up with perceived discrimination against Russians, primarily due to the closing of Russian-language schools); and thus the dividing line between ethnic and socio-economic motivations is far from clear.[20] Motivations are not the result of 'natural instincts' but the product of changing ethno-social, ethno-political and ethno-economic power relations reflected in concern about access to education in Russian, the introduction of the state language law and future job prospects.

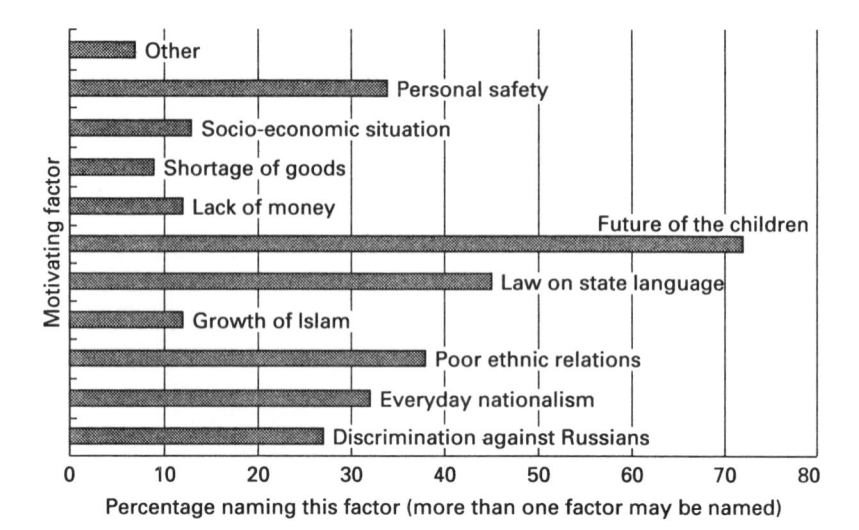

Figure 7:2 Motivations for migration in Orel region ('push factors') (total = 83)

Vitkovskaia's second explanation for women's greater motivation to leave the former republics – that women are more weakly integrated into the local community – also received no conclusive confirmation from interviewees. Although language knowledge was reported as weaker among women, this was not reinforced by any greater sense of hostility towards themselves or their family. Thus, Natal'ia Kosmarskaia argues, women might be more sensitive to 'push factors' not because they were more weakly integrated but because they bore the brunt of the psychological burden of the changing ethnic relations in the republic.[21] As Vitkovskaia herself suggests, it is not so much interpersonal ethnic relations which have deteriorated but, on the one hand, top-level political and ethnic relations and, on the other, daily interactions with 'the mass' in public places (hospitals, schools, bread shops, public transport) and it is women who are generally more extensively involved in such everyday out-of-home contacts. The fact that women were more likely to mention the deterioration in ethnic relations than men during interviews might thus be more usefully interpreted as a sign of their greater exposure to sites of everyday ethnic tension rather than of women's greater 'fear' of nationalism or greater ethnic isolation.

Finally, it is worth noting that women were significantly more likely

Gender and migration   125

to cite the 'rise of Islam' amongst their worries. Whilst this tends to be classified as an indication of ethnic discomfort in the former republic, it might perhaps be better read bearing in mind the socio-economic dimension of a resurgence of Islam for women. This is articulated by one female respondent having left Uzbekistan:

> if this Islam takes off ... then first and foremost it will be women who will lose everything. At the moment women are equal ... but, God forbid, if this Islam takes off they will be downtrodden ... They will be allowed only to bear children ... they will be just like slaves ...

As yet, there is insufficient data to draw firm conclusions about the gendered nature of migratory push factors. Nevertheless, it is important to be aware of the potential dangers of prematurely ascribing 'natural' gender differences, as Vitkovkskaia does in her argument that it is an instinctive, protective attitude towards their children borne of greater fear of ethnic conflict which is encouraging women to lead the exodus from the former republics. Such a line of reasoning suggests that the current socio-political abnormality sets women's 'natural' rootedness (centred on a closer connection to the *rodina* due to their role as mothers) in conflict with their other primordial role, as bearers and protectors of children. Not only does this potentially reinforce reactionary, essentialist gender discourse but it makes the important link in nationalist discourse between women, birth and native land (*rodina*). As Parekh argues, for nationalists, territory and nation are connected in a very real bodily relationship, and to deprive a nation of even an inch of its territory is to violate its physical and cultural integrity.[22] Given this, the set of connections between gender and migration set out above opens the way to viewing Russian-speaking women's movement from the former republics as a symbolic violation of Russia's right to continue to consider the territory of the former Soviet Union as a single space.

The resettlement of forced migrants: gender, employment and welfare provision

Alongside the growing political pressure to encourage the Russian minorities to exercise their 'right to stay', the social burden of any mass repatriation of the Russian diaspora has been emphasised increasingly by government spokespeople.[23] Thus, whilst, at the beginning of 1996, the Yel'tsin government remained formally committed to welcoming with open arms any former Soviet citizens wishing to return to Russia, some are more welcome than others. It is in this sense that the experience of forced migrant women needs to be viewed in the wider context of gender and socio-economic change in post-Soviet Russia.

It is the task of the government's Federal Migration Service – and its regional branches – to identify what proportion of forced migrants and refugees resettling in Russia will be 'adding to the economy' as opposed to constituting a burden on the state and, it would appear, the two main criteria for determining this are 'sex' and 'age'. There is a basic assumption – even in Vitkovskaia's generally sympathetic approach to the problems of female forced migrants – that women are a burden on the state. However, the real problem is identified as one of the combination of gender and age: Federal Migration Service data (for refugees and forced migrants registered in 1994) suggest that 16 per cent of female forced migrants are of pensionable age compared to just 9 per cent of men.[24] The fact that migrant women are disproportionately pensioners reinforces the current discourse of gendered state dependency which posits men as productive workers and women as recipients of state benefit. The fact that forced migrants are also more likely to have child dependents – state provision for whom is channelled via benefits for the *mother* – also raises the burden on the state and links this to women.

The gendered nature of the administration of welfare provision for forced migrants contributes to the perception of women forced migrants as dependent. The Federal Migration Service itself is headed by one of the few women to hold a top state position in Russia – Tat'iana Regent – and the majority of local level migration workers are women. The committees on family, women and children generally play an important role in migration commissions, and it would appear that much of the benefit actually paid to forced migrants is in fact given on grounds of being single mothers, pensioners, or having large families rather than accruing from the status of forced migrant or refugee itself. Women are thus the primary recipients.

Women are also more visible to the state; it is women who generally engage in the frustrating chase around offices to collate the documents necessary for registration and the receipt of status and benefit. Rather than having their efforts recognised, however, this can lead to resentment by migration workers who see some women as trying to manipulate the benefit system to their own advantage and identify single-parent, dependent migrant families as a significant 'problem'.[25]

The graduate milkmaid: gender, displacement and the labour market

The problem is not one of labelling alone, however; the experience of forced migrant women on return to Russia exemplifies the wider structural disadvantage of women in the post-Soviet environment. Forced migrant women, like other women losing their jobs in Russia, find it significantly harder to re-find employment than men. Vitkovskaia's study among 870 forced migrants resettled in Central Russia showed that, in Moscow region, 43 per cent of men were unemployed or had only temporary work, compared to 94 per cent of women. While Moscow region is far from typical, the general trend of the results was confirmed by research in Tver', Orel and Volgograd regions.[26] In the towns of Tver' region, 11 per cent of male forced migrants compared to 28 per cent of women forced migrants could not find work, whilst in the villages unemployment was 7 per cent and 16 per cent respectively.[27]

Evidence from the author's own study in 1994 confirmed this as an ongoing pattern: of the 195 respondents in Ul'ianovsk and Orel region, 17 per cent of women and 9 per cent of men seeking work could not find it.[28] However, the relatively positive results for rural areas found by Vitkovskaia were not confirmed by forced migrants interviewed in Orel and Ul'ianovsk. In fact the current study identifies a particular problem of female rural unemployment: 21 per cent of women respondents in rural areas of Orel region could not find work (see Figure 7:3). In contrast, among male respondents having resettled in Ul'ianovsk city, there was nobody without work.[29]

Women not only suffer disproportionately from unemployment, however, but also from a mismatch of skills to available jobs and a subsequent de-skilling. Comparing professional qualifications (or usual professional practice) with current employment, Figures 7:4 and 7:5 indicate the different relocations of male and female respondents in the labour market after migration to Russia.

Male forced migrants, it would appear, are much more likely to re-find employment in the same job (almost one-third). Women, in contrast, find it very difficult to continue in their old profession (just 14 per cent were working in the same kind of job). Interviews revealed that finding jobs for which they had been trained was a particular problem for women who resettled in rural areas. Women respondents frequently complained that the jobs available were 'men's jobs': 'the work here is mainly for men, men's work, the only thing [for us] is to be a milkmaid, work with livestock and that's all'. The acute problem

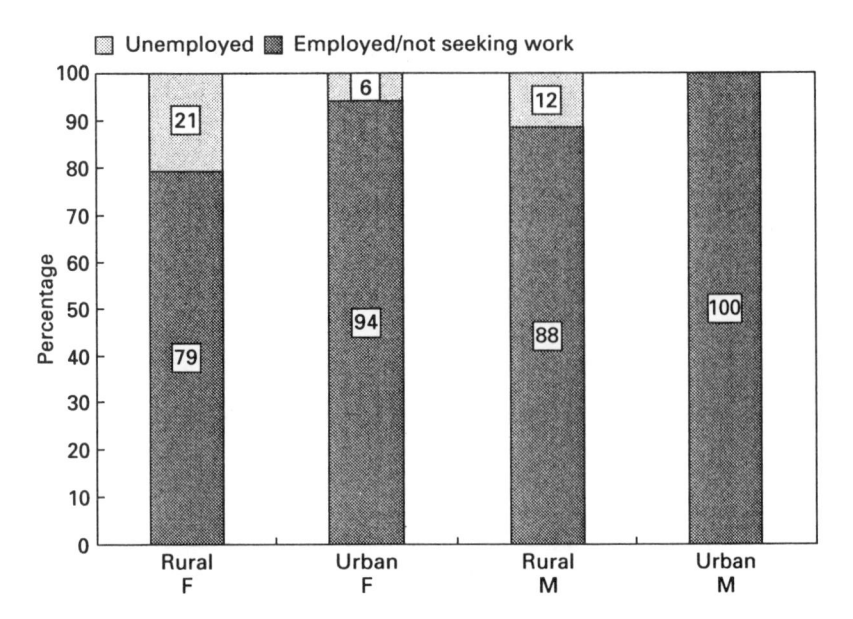

Figure 7:3 Unemployment by gender and region (total = 195)

of mismatch of skills is confirmed by both Vitkovskaia and Kosmarskaia who note that men (especially those with some kind of engineering qualification) are more likely to find work in the new place of residence akin to their urban specialism, whereas the social distance between women's pre- and post-migration occupations is much greater.[30] This results in a much higher rate of de-skilling[31] among women than men (see Figures 7:4 and 7:5).

Whilst the problems of de-skilling and unemployment are particularly acute for women resettling in rural areas, they are far from unique to them. One migration worker in Ul'ianovsk rated the problem of women's unemployment second in severity only to that of housing. Moreover, it was a problem fuelled by direct discrimination on the part of employers; other migration workers noted that one of the two main employers in the city (the aircraft builders, 'Aviastar') simply no longer hired women at all.[32] Those who had found work, meanwhile, complained that it was heavy, factory work to which they were unaccustomed, while many others (especially older women) took work as cleaners or hostel caretakers in order to secure tied accommodation. In Ul'ianovsk, six women among those interviewed had taken this option including an economist with higher education, an accountant and a pharmacist. Many other respondents had taken jobs in factories or particular workplaces where accommodation was offered in hostels. This meant families living in a single room (during interviewing the largest encountered in such circumstances was a family of seven) and sharing kitchen and bathroom facilities with a number of other families. Thus, Vitkovskaia's finding that women resettling in towns tend on the whole to be more satisfied with their new work than men[33] may well reflect, above all, the primacy of the problem of housing over employment for forced migrants resettling in urban areas, rather than any positive feelings about their employment.

The negative consequences for social integration of this professional downgrading are significant. The loss of professional status and identity discourages positive integration and is reflected in high levels of dissatisfaction with the work environment in particular and the move in general.[34] The impact on women's sense of self-worth is immense and signs of serious depression were evident among a number of respondents.[35] The importance of work for integration into the receiver society is summed up by an unemployed female respondent in Ul'ianovsk: 'now I am at home. I cannot feel myself to be a complete citizen of Russia. I must interact, I must work'.

Figures 7:4 and 7:5 indicate two further discrepancies between male and female experience worthy of further exploration: the significantly greater proportion of men than women moving into self-employment or business, and the relatively large proportion of women on maternity leave or 'not working' (15 per cent). Vitkovskaia suggests that there is a general tendency for women to be less keen to enter into entrepreneurial activity. However, from the analysis of in-depth interviews with forced migrants in both rural and urban areas of fieldwork, it would appear that, in fact, this apparent gender difference may reflect gendered modes of articulation rather than any fundamental difference in outlook and experience between the sexes. Moreover, women's apparent absence from the category of the 'self-employed' may be directly linked to the high proportion being, at least temporarily, 'at home'.

Many migrant women were taking longer maternity leave than they would have done in 'normal circumstances' in order to protect their work record or because it was financially disadvantageous to work. The latter was the result of a combination of the sudden rise in nursery school fees, extremely low wages in rural areas and the loss of extended family networks previously facilitating child care. Such women occupy their time by working on their allotments, either to

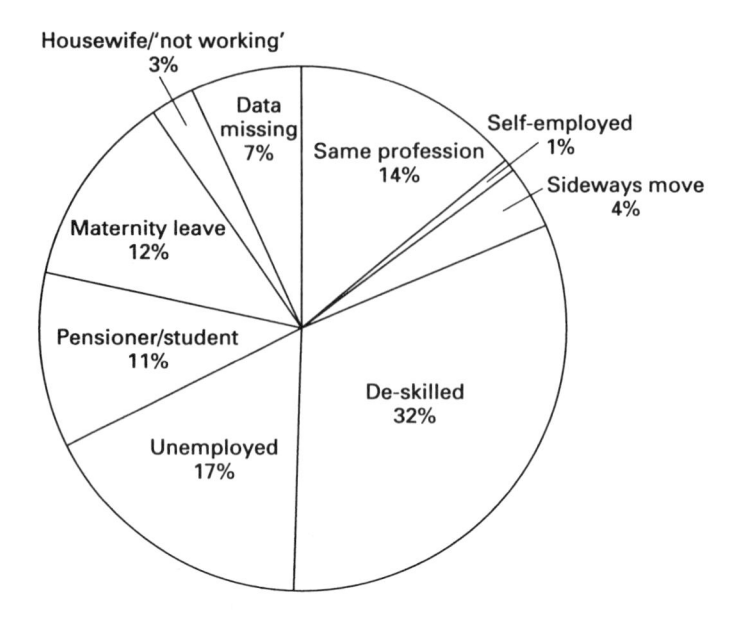

Figure 7:4   Current employment of female respondents relative to previous profession (total = 120)

feed the family or to sell produce at markets, preserving food and making clothes (sometimes for sale). However, they would describe themselves as 'on maternity leave' or 'not working at the moment', since they are conscious of the temporary, 'survival' nature of the option and would actually prefer 'a proper job'. Men in urban areas involved in similar survival strategies, however, would be more likely to describe their path as 'having gone into business' even though this business often involved only petty trade, or the process of trying to establish some kind of intermediary selling business, and in practice meant they were predominantly at home and actually undertook a good deal of the domestic burden.[36]

Secondly, far from being resistant to entrepreneurial activity, female respondents clearly identified the need to use women's skills in the provision of services on collective farms where no such services were available. As one female forced migrant in Orel region noted, 'I have always had one thought, to start up my own business of some kind, to open some kind of services complex ... Why should they come in from the town when we have everything virtually here – hairdressers

Gender and migration

Pie chart showing:
- Data missing 11%
- Same profession 32%
- Self-employed 8%
- Sideways move 15%
- De-skilled 16%
- Unemployed 9%
- Pensioner/student 9%

Figure 7:5 Current employment of male respondents relative to previous profession (total = 75)

and dress-makers; I myself, for example, love baking, love handling dough'. However, women settling in rural areas have little chance of achieving their aims; the 'double burden' of the cities is transformed into a 'triple burden' of work, children/home and the allotment. This leaves older women exhausted and desperate and younger women determined to get out of the village. The latter is expressed by one young woman forced migrant in Orel region: 'those my age are trying to get away from here, to get married. That is the aim of all young people, young women. To marry someone well-off ... and not return to the village.' However, many fail to achieve their aim and there has been a recent spate of early marriage and pregnancy between migrant young women and local youths.

The government, via its chief agency responsible for migration, the FMS, has singularly failed to provide any positive programme of retraining and utilisation of the significant skills and resources of Russian-speaking forced migrants. It has sought rather to utilise the sheer physical resources of returnees to repopulate poorly developed northern and eastern regions of the country and the depopulated rural regions of central Russia in a crude attempt to minimise potential social conflict ensuing from repatriation. Although this has affected men and women alike, the legacy of the horizontal and vertical gender structure of the Soviet labour market, combined with new gendered patterns of employment in the post-Soviet economy, means that women forced migrants currently suffer a greater mismatch of skills and opportunities. Specific programmes of retraining need to be targeted at them if a growing migrationary push by women out of initial areas of rural resettlement is to be prevented.

'I have no future here': the gender of cultural adaptation

... my future ... I have already put a cross on myself. It's all over; where am I going to go?

The above is a common response to the new environment among forced migrant women resettling in rural areas in Russia. It is partially a result of the loss of professional status discussed above, but women's identity is not solely focused on work but also on family, home, husband, friends and self. Hence the whole cultural environment into which they move must be examined to explain the desperation expressed by women who, in their thirties and forties, have written off their own lives.

In interviews, women often responded to questions about how they feel in their new environment by pointing despairingly to their surroundings; the loss of good housing, material belongings accumulated over a number of years and general financial hardship acutely affects women's own sense of self. For those women moving to rural areas, the inability to provide a comfortable family home is experienced particularly painfully, since they have consciously sacrificed other things (such as their own job prospects) in order to prioritise obtaining housing for the family. When money dries up and improvements in the house (often received as four walls and little else) cease, women come to feel like hostages in their own homes.[37]

The move from urban to rural environment, and the concomitant loss of urban culture stressing appearance and public show, also encourages a fear among women that their own youth and femininity is being lost. Above all, they fear becoming like village women, ground down by constant work and worry and unable to find the time necessary to look after their appearance. One female respondent sums up the difference between her urban and rural existence as a woman:

Like any woman I would get up in the morning ... twirl round in front of the mirror ... put my make-up on. I went to work like a human being. But now, of course, it's horrific to look at me, I am like any old village hag (*baba*) ... a woman should always be a woman. She should always be smart, beautiful, elegantly dressed ... not go out to the shop in the dirty clothes she was wearing to do the washing in ... My husband is already saying 'God, what do you look like. You could at least make up your eyes and lips.' And I would gladly put some make-up on, but for whom? For the goat ... or the pigs? ... Our youth is passing and the wrinkles won't smooth out ... how many new wrinkles have been added here, how much grey hair ...?[38]

Women feel their femininity to have been compromised not only outwardly but inwardly; this is expressed most vividly in the constant reference to having become 'nasty' (*zloi*). This term has a host of associated meanings including becoming aggressive, irritable, more likely to shout and fly off the handle, less tolerant, less affectionate and less kind. Whatever its meaning for each individual, its widespread use singles it out as a common metaphor for the perceived negative effect of the move.

Women respondents were thus highly critical of their own ability to handle the stresses of readaptation and the responsibilities of making the move work. In contrast, they suggest that men integrate and adapt better, finding it easier to develop 'a common language' with locals and fit into their new environment. This ability of men is attributed to their less 'complex' characters and the oiling of male social interaction with alcohol. In contrast, women perceive the alcohol-based culture of Russia, especially in rural areas, as being a different social order to which they cannot adapt: 'They drink ... as a matter of course. You can buy and sell anything for a bottle, they don't know the value of anything else.' But forced migrant women are also critical of men's weakness in not resisting this way of life and many women complained that their husbands had started drinking, swearing and behaving crudely only after the move. Moreover, women see the problem as one of a perverted masculinity absent from their former culture:

If a day goes by here without getting drunk it is considered a day lost. The locals, I mean. And when a person comes from somewhere else and says that he doesn't drink, they start on, "Oh, why don't you drink, you old woman!" ... And so it goes on until that person starts drinking with them.

This characterisation of masculinity in the 'historical homeland' is in stark contrast to the nostalgic references to the former republic, where 'men were men' and women were 'respected' (whilst knowing when to 'hold their tongue'). This nostalgia for the old patriarchal order is reflected in the following statement by a female forced migrant from Tadzhikistan:

in the East the man is the boss ... And when I came here ... I was surprised at first because here the woman is considered the head of the family. The woman gives the orders. And many men come to us and they wonder why the man is giving the orders because, out of habit, they turn to me. But I say, 'I don't know. The boss is over there, talk to the boss.' ... A man should be a man after all. He should be the head of the family ... the man should give the orders, be the boss so that a woman can feel a woman, and a man should be a man ...

Despite women's belief that men will always get on with each other if they have a bottle to share, male migrants themselves note difficulties in finding friends and bemoan the drinking, swearing and, above all, lack of honesty and decency among local men. Men also sometimes express a sense of inadequacy and loss of self-respect, primarily associated with loss of professional status. In general, however, men are less likely than women to admit that they have changed for the worse. At the same time, they are more likely to say that the experience has made them stronger, less naïve and more mature.

One explanation as to why men appear to suffer less of a crisis of self-esteem than women is provided by female migrants themselves who suggested that women were simply more willing to express dissatisfaction, while men were more determined to put on a brave face and 'suffer in silence'. Another reason, however, might be inferred from a broader look at the impact of migration on gendered communication. While both men and women recognise the loss of familial and acquaintance networks and the concomitant turning inwards on the nuclear family as the primary, if not sole, source of intimate social interaction, men and women appear to evaluate this differently in terms of their own identity. Men feel a greater pressure to provide for their family on their own, but associate this with the gaining of full maturity and expression of their masculinity. In contrast, women appear to miss the security of family networks and find it difficult to form meaningful friendships.[39] Women see this as an impoverishment of their social interaction, and the re-focusing of identity more exclusively around the immediate family appears to increase a sense of their own failure.

Many of the problems of cultural adaptation experienced by forced migrants are shared by men and women. Women, however, are less attracted by the romanticism of rural life in the first place and, in general, their worst fears are realised. Rather than experiencing a 'liberation' through migration, therefore, women forced migrants have their loss of professional status deepened by the loss of pride in their homes and family. The desperation which ensues leads them often to write off their own lives and focus their energies on providing the means for their children to find a way out of the village.

Conclusion

Exploring the experience of forced migrant women upon resettlement in Russia raises some challenges to existing Western interpretations of the gendered nature of migration which focus on displacement as leading to loss of masculine identity,[40] whilst having an emancipatory effect for women.[41] Whilst important in counteracting the victimology thesis of earlier assumptions about gender and refugee experience, such an interpretative framework does not help us understand the experience of Russian-speaking forced migrants returning to Russia who are largely skilled workers and professionals and who – whether men or women – experience a severe loss of social status and professional ethos after migration. However, this does not negate a gendered approach to the study of migration; rather, the experience of Russia should allow us to rethink and expand such an approach by highlighting other gender-specific experiences resulting from displacement.

The peculiarities of current processes of forced migration to Russia mean that displacement is neither pure flight to a safe haven nor a process of voluntary economic migration. Russian-speaking forced migrants resettle in a country which is supposedly culturally the 'homeland' and traditionally the economic 'big brother'; they are supposedly 'going home'. However, in reality, forced migrants return to a country in severe economic difficulty and culturally remote from the imagined community of Russia. But why should this, admittedly difficult, relocation be experienced in a gendered way?

Firstly, the economic displacement accompanying the physical one is experienced particularly acutely by women. This is due to the common move from urban to rural residence which produces a significantly grater mismatch of skills and jobs available for women; and to the changed employment environment in post-Soviet Russia in which women have become highly undesirable employees whilst high nursery school fees has made it economically unviable for many women to work. At the same time, the mechanisms of coping with the chaotic and discriminatory labour market being employed by women across Russia – survival strategies involving the taking of numerous jobs, selling possessions, shuttle-trading – are more difficult to employ when starting from scratch (you have nothing to sell), and when family and acquaintance networks have been destroyed in the process of migration.[42] Thus, forced migrant women are disadvantaged both *vis-à-vis* forced migrant men and local women.[43]

Secondly, although this study found no evidence to suggest that women's primordial link to the 'native land' made the process of uprooting and displacement inherently more difficult for women, nevertheless cultural adaptation is gendered. Women experienced the move not as a process of the widening of their horizons but as a cultural impoverishment. Although both men and women bemoaned the lack of free time for self-development and noted the increase in domestic arguments because both partners suffered from more tiredness and stress after the move, the decline in satisfaction with family life appears to affect women's sense of self-worth much more than men's. While men often bragged of having built their new house themselves, women could only point in despair at the unplastered and unpainted walls – the money to buy a tin of paint or a door had to be saved over months. Neither can women find solace in their stated aim of having moved primarily 'for the sake of the children', since their own feelings of being trapped extend to a belief that there is no future for the children in rural areas either (a feeling intensified if the children are girls). While for male forced migrants masculinity might be salvaged in their role in physically providing for the family (a kind of frontier masculinity), for women forced migrants village life appeared totally incompatible with their urban femininities and only rare exceptions among them had any positive feelings about a future there.

Finally, the discourses of gender and nation are frequently interwoven and never more so than at times when nationhood is under reconstruction or challenged by military or ethnic conflict. It is not surprising, therefore, that the redefinition of Russianness in the post-Soviet space has a gender dimension and that Russian returnees from the former Soviet republics are a significant social group in the process of its reconfiguration. Although extreme discourses of gender and nation remain on the periphery of Russian society at the moment, there is an ongoing process of redefinition of both as forced migrants reconstruct their sense of self in the new environment. Confrontation with the imagined community incites a nostalgia for the ways of old whereby 'there' is associated with all that was orderly, honest, decent and prosperous, and patriarchal norms become idealised. The reconsolidation of control mechanisms over women is not uncommon amongst migrant communities and, faced with the perceived disorder of post-Soviet society, it is not surprising, perhaps, that Russian-speaking forced migrants should cling to patriarchal gender norms which appear to restore a former order, both spatially and temporally.

Notes

1 Since these people at the time crossed no international border they were not 'refugees' according to international law, nor was there any existing Soviet legislation which defined them as such. Nevertheless, the term 'refugee' was consciously used by the press to express the outrage felt at such vivid evidence of the collapse of the fraternity of nations.
2 According to legislation passed in February 1993, qualification for the status of refugee or forced migrant is dependent on recognition of persecution or the threat of it. Refugee status is given to those proving this but who do not hold Russian citizenship; forced migrant status is reserved for Russian citizens. However, until 1994 the Federal Migration Service did not distinguish between refugees and forced migrants in their statistics.
3 These are the latest available figures and include all refugees and forced migrants registered by 1 April 1995.
4 I. Rotar', 'Russkikh pereselentsev pytaiutsia ispol'zovat' kak politicheskuiu silu', *Nezavisimaia Gazeta*, 7 June 1994, p. 3; A. Sergeev, 'Nado otdelit' politicheskikh bezhentsev ot ekonomicheskikh', *Inostranets* 18, 1995.
5 The issue of forced migration is largely constructed as one of Russia's foreign policy *vis-à-vis* the 'near abroad'. What is at stake is Russia's pride at being able to defend her 'compatriots' abroad and, via them, her ability to influence the newly independent states. Thus, Russian-speaking forced migrants symbolise the failure of Russian foreign policy in this respect and, as a result, the need to conduct a more forceful defence of the 'Russian diaspora' has become an increasingly central part of domestic political debate.
6 G. Vitkovskaia, *Vynuzhdennaia migratsiia: problemy i perspektivy*, (Moscow: Institut Narodnokhoziaistvennogo Prognozirovaniia, RAN, 1993); G. Vitkovskaia, 'Puteshestvennitsy ponevole: u zhenshchin "chemodannoe nastroenie" voznikaet chashche, chem u muzhchin', *Rossiiskoe Obozrenie* 9, 1 March 1995, pp. 5–6.
7 See, for example, G. Buijs (ed.), *Migrant women: crossing boundaries and changing identities* (Oxford: Berg, 1993).
8 Self-definition as opposed to the holding of official status was taken as the criterion for refugee and forced migrant status.
9 A combination of interviews, informal meetings, participant observation and questionnaires completed in interview format were used, the latter being conducted by Russian colleagues – Natal'ia Kosmarskaia and Tat'iana Sheikina – in the Orel region only. Findings based on responses to questionnaire questions are cited only if confirmed by interviews and all

quotations come from interviews conducted by the author. Given the variety of methods used, the different researchers involved and the essentially quantitative nature of the data, however, readers are advised to treat tabulated data with caution and refer always to varying sample size and region of origin.

10 The research was financially supported by the ESRC under the Research Grant scheme ('Going home: a socio-cultural study of Russian-speaking forced migrants', June 1994–August 1995).

11 This was partially due to a greater scepticism about the 'point' of the work; men were more likely to comment on the fact that the research would not have any practical implications and on the small size of the 'sample'. However, men also frequently noted that their wives 'talked better' and were clearly uneasy about answering personal questions. Women, on the other hand, often relished the opportunity to have somebody listen to their story and their problems; agencies helping forced migrants had neither the time nor the will to do this.

12 V. Cherviakov, V. Shapiro and F. Sheregi, *Mezhnatsional'nie konflikty i problemy bezhentsev* (part 1) (Moscow: Institute of Sociology, RAN, 1991), p. 17.

13 *Vynuzhdennie pereselentsy v Rossii: statisticheskii biulleten'* 6 (Moscow: FMS, 1995), p. 103.

14 In 1993, women constituted 53 per cent of the Russian Federation's population. See The World Bank, *Statistical handbook 1994 – States of the former USSR* (Washington DC: The World Bank, 1994), p. 492.

15 Vitkovskaia, 'Puteshestvennitsy ponevole', p. 5. Vitkovskaia found that 42 per cent of women compared to only 31 per cent of men surveyed cited such factors as the reason for migration or intended migration.

16 A similar hypothesis – that women make up a higher proportion of long-distance migration motivated by political or social conflict – is stated by American migration experts studying in- and out-migration ion Yaroslavl' region, for example. See B. Mitchneck and D. Plane, 'Migration patterns during a period of political and economic shocks in the former Soviet Union: a case study of Yaroslavl oblast', *The Professional Geographer* 47(1), February 1995, pp. 17–30, p. 23.

17 Vitkovskaia, 'Puteshestvennitsy ponevole', p. 5.

18 *Ibid.*, p. 5.

19 One explanation of this difference may be methodological. Firstly, the tendency during interviews of men to over-estimate their own role in the decision (see Figure 7:1) may be reduced by the use of self-completed questionnaires. Secondly, Vitkovskaia's survey method taps migratory *mood* rather than actual migratory practice. Interviews conducted after resettlement, on the other hand, reflect the impact of the system employed by many families of sending out advance parties (*na razvedku*) to seek out suitable places for settlement. Almost always it is the husband, or a group

of male relatives or colleagues, who constitute these advance parties and, once they have found housing and jobs, they call the family after them. Thus, with time, push and pull factors often become merged in respondents' minds so that those (the men) who 'pulled' the family to a particular place are seen also to have 'pushed' them out of the old place of residence.

20 Interestingly, both men and women refer to a greater fear for their children if they are girls and there is a particular fear of the rape of girls. However, men may also need protection; having sons, or indeed husbands, of conscription age in those former republics where armed conflict is taking place also acts as a push factor.

21 N. Kosmarskaia, 'Women and ethnicity in present-day Russia: thoughts on a given theme' in N. Yuval-Davis, H. Lutz and A. Phoenix (eds.), *Crossfires: nationalism, racism and gender in Europe* (London: Pluto Press, 1995), p. 150.

22 B. Parekh, 'Ethnocentricity of the nationalist discourse', *Nations and Nationalism*, 1(1), 1995, pp. 25–52, p. 33.

23 T. Regent, 'Tiazhelo nachinat' vse snachala ...', *Rossiiskie Vesti* 86, 6 May 1993, p. 2; A. Baiduzhii, 'Anatolii Illarionov: "Gosudarstvo ne v sostoianii obespechit' zhil'em vsekh bezhentsev"' *Nezavisimaia Gazeta*, 5 October 1993, p. 6; M. Nekrasova, '... Eto – rodina moia?', *Obshchaia Gazeta*, 5–11 August 1994; V. Mukomel', chief analyst of the Analytical Centre of the Russian Federation Presidential Apparatus, Moscow, 20 July 1995 (interview conducted by author).

24 *Vynuzhdennie pereselentsy v Rossii: statisticheskii biulleten'* 6 (Moscow: FMS, 1995), pp. 38–9.

25 Information taken from interviews and informal contacts with migration workers in Orel and Ul'ianovsk regions.

26 Vitkovskaia, 'Puteshestvennitsy ponevole, pp. 5–6.

27 Vitkovskaia, *Vynuzhdennaia migratsiia*, p. 63.

28 Those included as 'unemployed' are those actively seeking work. This excludes women on maternity leave or temporarily choosing not to seek waged work.

29 This discrepancy may be accounted for by the time-lag between the two studies. Vitkovskaia's survey was conducted earlier, when migrants were still easily absorbed into central Russia's labour-deficient rural areas. By 1994, however, lay-offs on farms were widespread, particularly in female-dominated areas of work such as administrative positions and nursery schools.

30 Kosmarskaia, 'Women and ethnicity in present-day Russia', p. 156; Vitkovskaia, 'Puteshestvennitsy ponevole', pp. 5–6.

31 The term 'de-skilling' is used here to describe a move into a job not commensurate with a respondent's qualifications and to which a lower social status is attached. It is thus distinguished from a 'sideways pro-

fessional move' whereby social and professional status is retained although a significant change in occupation takes place.
32 This information is taken from interviews conducted with district level migration service workers in Ul'ianovsk city as part of a series of expert interviews conducted with migration workers in the city in July 1995 by the Sociological Laboratory of Moscow-State University at Ul'ianovsk under the direction of Elena Omel'chenko and as part of the ESRC project referred to above.
33 Vitkovskaia, *Vynuzhdennaia migratsiia*, pp. 65–6.
34 The most frequent complaints are that: the work is dirty and heavy; the work available does not correspond to qualifications; low wages; and the lack of understanding shown by farm managers in finding lighter work for women and in allowing flexible hours to fit in with child care.
35 Of course, male forced migrants also often work outside their previous profession, experience de-skilling and, especially in rural areas, are forced to work for extremely low wages. Male respondents complain, in particular, of the loss of responsibility and the paternal mode of management on farms.
36 Such men often had early retirement pensions from previous jobs while their (younger) wives were working in their chosen profession.
37 Almost without exception, forced migrants moving to villages in Orel region where fieldwork was based had been attracted primarily by the promise of housing. Subsequently, however, they received little, or no, help in building or decorating the houses and were often deprived of the right to privatise them.
38 For balance it should be noted that one female respondent did acknowledge the liberating effect of village life where one felt free to walk around the house and garden without having to dress up.
39 In particular they cite gossiping in the village as an inhibiting factor, revealing the need to talk about personal issues within the anonymous environment of urban social relations.
40 D. Abdulrahim, 'Defining gender in a second exile: Palestinian women in West Berlin' in Buijs (ed.), *Migrant women*, pp. 55–82.
41 G. Buijs, 'Introduction' in Buijs (ed.), *Migrant women*, pp. 1–20, p. 4.
42 That these are predominantly women's survival strategies is confirmed by a recent survey in Tatarstan showing that women make up 80 per cent of shuttle traders in Kazan'. See P. Morvant, 'Tatar study on "shuttle" traders', *OMRI Daily Report* (part 1), no. 169, 30 August 1995.
43 This is apart from the bureaucratic obstacles often put in forced migrants' way, such as the loss of documentation in flight and restrictions placed on their residence rights.

Polity

8 When the fighting is over: the soldiers' mothers and the Afghan madonnas

KATHRYN PINNICK

With the war in Chechnia on Russian television news, Afghanistan cannot but be on the minds of its audience. Notwithstanding the comparisons being drawn between Moscow's strategy behind its military incursions of 1979 and 1994, the Afghanistan war continues to be of significance for post-Soviet society. It is not just that those who were directly affected by it – the servicemen, their fathers, mothers, wives and children, plus the women who served there, too – who cannot escape from its consequences. The legacy of the war is important for the whole society.

Afghanistan is associated in their minds and ours with the collapse of the Soviet Union. While military defeat in this proxy war with the United States meant that the Soviet Union had lost the Cold War, it is also synonymous with the breakdown of the domestic fabric of Soviet power. That is to say, Afghanistan is not significant because the reputation of the Soviet armed forces was discredited on its soil, but because the policies and politics of dealing with the war inside the USSR were. Mismanagement of the episode led the citizens to question the foundations on which the CPSU had placed their Motherland. Its authority was undermined in the late 1980s when the extent of its lies and misrepresentation on everything to do with the war (the battles, the human and financial cost, the fate of the returning servicemen and women) became clear. In addition, the inability of the welfare state to provide for those who had been injured or traumatised and the ineffectiveness of the public officials to facilitate the reintegration into society of the men and women who had worked in Afghanistan, revealed the shortcomings – objective and subjective – of a crumbling system.

The majority of the Soviet citizens who served in Afghanistan were men and 3 per cent were women – the *afgantsy* and *afganki*.[1] Although a minority, the latter and their experience should not be ignored; in fact, their fate on their return to the Motherland throws light on attitudes in Russia to both the war and women in general. There are many women as well as men who were directly touched by Afghanistan. During the war, it was the wives and sisters of those who served who wrote to the press and public officials demanding information on the war and asking for help with their menfolk who had returned from it. It is the fate of all these women which is the focus of this research: how are they coping in a period of economic and political transition in the new Russia which has yet to come to terms with the legacy it carries from the Soviet Union's last war? Is the fighting over?

The soldiers' mothers

'Send our sons back from Chechnia', 'Don't kill our sons', came the refrains from a group of women demonstrating on Red Square in December 1994. Alongside them were others whose sons and husbands had been killed in a previous war – Afghanistan – who meet at the eternal flame every year on 27 December to mark the anniversary of the dispatch of Soviet troops in 1979.[2] Was history repeating itself outside the Kremlin walls?

The political climate of 1994 allowed the mothers of the Russian soldiers who had been sent to Grozny to mobilise themselves outside the seat of Russian power and give an immediate response in the form of banners of protest against Moscow's military assault on the breakaway republic. They had learnt from the experience of their older sisters, who had remained silent in 1979. Other than that of Andrei Sakharov, the only voice of protest in the Soviet Union against the intervention into Afghanistan in 1979 came from a group of women in Leningrad – 'Maria'. Exile was the authorities' response to them, as their 'anti-Soviet' stance on Afghanistan came as the last straw on top of their 'subversive' feminist agenda.[3]

From 1979 until 1988, families were kept ignorant of what it meant seeing their sons off 'to carry out their internationalist duty in Afghanistan'. In 1994, the mission 'to restore the constitutional order in Chechnia' rang an all too familiar bell. A different generation of mothers were saying farewell to their sons in the same way but now, having reached a new stage of political maturity, they no longer trusted the reassurances of the powers-that-be. The change in social control meant they were no longer disqualified from organising themselves and could openly show their opposition to their government's decision.

They also chose a traditional form of political action from the Soviet era: writing letters to the press and to the country's leaders. Since military units began to be dispatched to the territory of the Chechen republic, President Yel'tsin's office has received letters from mothers of the soldiers demanding that the hostilities be stopped immediately, that their sons be returned to base and that efforts be made to settle the conflict by political means.[4] The appeals have come from all organisational levels of a nationwide social movement from local committees of soldiers' mothers to the co-ordinating council of the Committee of Soldiers' Mothers of Russia.

The Committee of Soldiers' Mothers was founded in 1989 by a group of women whose sons had died in peacetime service. Glasnost in the press brought to light cases of *dedovshchina* – bullying and brutality towards new recruits by older soldiers. More soldiers died as a result of this in the 1980s than did in Afghanistan.[5] The women staged hunger strikes and demonstrations (in 1990, 250 women from fifty-six cities gathered in Red Square). The women's spotlight in the press and permanent presence on Pushkin Square in Moscow had a political impact. Public awareness grew of the terrible conditions for conscripts in armed service and pressure was put on the authorities. Gorbachev met them and set up a commission under the Congress of People's Deputies to investigate the thousands of complaints received from mothers.

In 1994, Yel'tsin commissioned a report from his staff, 'On appeals from soldiers' mothers', which concluded that the 'emotionalism' of these women's groups was being exploited by political parties and movements 'to advance their own political demands'.[6] The women did, in fact, hold joint public meetings with some parties but this was due to political astuteness rather than *naïveté*; the women built alliances in order to gain sympathy and legitimacy.[7]

They have always been accused of inciting 'anti-army hysteria'[8] and been seen as pacifist and 'anti-patriotic' by the senior military personnel accustomed to the armed forces being an accountable pillar of society. What the military and political leadership found alarming about the women's outspokenness, both in the late 1980s and now they are the focus of attention again in the mid 1990s, is the fuel they give to pressures for military reform. The public outcry which they led over *dedovshchina* added steam to the anti-conscription movement in the late 1980s. The political nerve centre was also touched as this movement tied in with nationalistic and self-determination pressures from the Soviet republics; rejection of the draft was particularly strong in Estonia, Lithuania, Latvia and Georgia. The women's voice on Chechnia (and their threat to disrupt the call-up procedure on a nationwide level by inciting conscripts to go absent without leave) has brought debate on conscription, exemption from it, alternative service and the issue of establishing a professional army back into the open. However persuasive the arguments for ending conscription (the women's original line back in the late 1980s was that *dedovshchina* would not occur in a professional armed force), Russia is not yet ready either economically or politically for this. There is some contract service but, primarily due to the low pay plus the terrible conditions, it is not popular enough to fill the ranks. Nevertheless, it was announced in February 1996 that the number of regular soldiers would be cut to create a leaner armed force with more specially trained officers.[9]

Perhaps the women influenced this decision in part. The women do have a broader political agenda beyond the immediate concern of their sons' welfare. It is not that their protest is against a Russian imperialist strategy of halting separatism of the Federation's regions or of quashing Islamic insurgency, but the women are outspoken on what they see as the cynical attitude of Russian military strategists towards their own soldiers.

The members of the committees of soldiers' mothers are women who are concerned about the experience to be had by the young men conscripted into the ranks of the Russian Federation armed forces. On this basis, they can be viewed as an interest group which leads pressures within society for military reform. They have proved themselves capable of influencing public and polity alike through the chosen, familiar, means of demonstrations, petitioning with letters and giving interviews to the press. The soldiers' mothers (and Afghan mothers to be discussed below) have a certain moral authority; they have impressed their standpoint onto other members of society – in particular their peers, other mothers of conscription-age young men. Their strong influence can perhaps be explained by 'motherhood' in Russia being a strong symbol and one which evokes emotion, patriarchal as the country is. The relationship between mother and son is a special and intense one, all the more so since the low birth rate means a son would normally be the only son and often the only child.

It is the women who remain the most vocal and most active part of society on the Chechnia war. However, even though the war is recognised by the majority of the population to be atrocious and unjustifiable, there has been no widespread anti-war protest. That there was none over Afghanistan to compare to the demonstrations in the USA over Vietnam was understandable in the context of the level of social control in the USSR; more protests on the streets over Chechnia might have been expected – yet the women's seems to be the only voice. That they have influenced public opinion at all in a society tired of politics and upheaval is impressive.

Widows and mothers of soldiers killed in Afghanistan

Separate from the organisational structure of the soldiers' mothers committees are the women whose sons and husbands were killed in Afghanistan. Initially, all these women were united in one group, but the widows and mothers of fallen *afgantsy* defined their own interest and set up a separate organisation in which to express it.

The Afghanistan mothers and widows do represent a specifically Afghan interest and are mainly concerned with supporting each other in practical and emotional ways. The rationale behind the formation of the Moscow Council of Mothers and Widows (to take a leading example of one such body) was to create a focal point in a society which was callous at worst, disinterested at best, for sharing sorrows and concerns with others in the same position. It was set up in 1989 with three main aims: to provide social protection for the families of the casualties (finding jobs or providing material assistance), to provide medical rehabilitation and to ensure remembrance of those who lost their lives. They lobby parliament, president and public opinion for greater rights and social security benefits. The chair of the Moscow committee, Alexandra Ivanova,[10] maintains that the state has largely ignored them and only provides a meagre level of support, insufficient for helping their psychological state and the process of coming to terms with their loss.

The bereaved mothers may remain emotionally disturbed and some find it hard to accept that their sons have died. One mother locked an *afganets*, the best friend of her fallen son, into her flat and refused to release him, saying *he* would now be her son.[11] Others refuse to believe their sons are dead, and expect them to come home one day. There are some mothers like these in Moscow whose sons are on the official list of fatalities but live on in despair and the hope that they will return one day; they will not give a photograph of their son to the compilers of a book on the Muscovites who lost their lives in Afghanistan. This is being edited by the Moscow Council of Afghanistan Mothers and Widows and the Liublinsk Internationalist-Servicemen Museum. Their objective is to preserve the memory of the fallen and thereby further facilitate the process of society's recognition of the legacy of the conflict.[12]

It is clear that the women could benefit from counselling, but the state (either through the Ministry of Defence or the Ministry of Social Security) has not provided anything for them in the way of a rehabilitation programme. An understanding of the value of trauma counselling did not exist in the Soviet period; there were no trained specialists and no element in the health or social security budgets to accommodate it. However, by the time the decision was taken to withdraw the Soviet troops, and as contact was established by some of the Afghanistan former servicemen organisations with US Vietnam veteran groups, things changed slightly. Some male *afgantsy* were counselled for post-traumatic stress syndrome by American doctors and there were signs of recognition within post-Soviet society of the importance of this. There has been no bereavement counselling for the parents of the dead. A small number of the mothers and widows have attended the Rus sanatorium in Moscow region which used to be for the CPSU elite but which now provides medical treatment – including psychological – for the *afgantsy*. The families occasionally receive *putevki* or passes from the Ministry of Defence to spend a week there. On one occasion last year, to add insult to injury, the Ministry neglected to provide transport for a group of widows to get there, on the assumption that their husbands would take them.[13]

As a result of the absence of professional medical help, many of the mothers and widows have turned to the Church for solace. Of course, it is not only these women who have found a new faith; the revived interest in the Church is widespread in Russian society, particularly amongst women. The collapse of the old belief system – communism with its fundamentals of collectivism at home and internationalism abroad – poses a particular problem for those who lost a son *for* that very system. This is one element of their activities which may seem paradoxical, but in essence reflects their confusion over this problem.

By the time of the troop withdrawal, the Afghan mothers became critical of the way the war was waged (such as the deployment of ill-prepared young conscripts) and they have become more convinced of this in the post-war, post-Soviet period. However, they are still avidly patriotic and continue to see their sons as heroes in spite of the war having been discredited. Furthermore, women whose own sons and husbands had been killed in a distant and futile war have been active supporters of the military-patriotic education of young people. Their involvement took the form of visiting schools and colleges to talk about their sons.[14] This continued in the first few post-Soviet years, although the mothers' message became a more distinctly anti-war one which they delivered without belittling their sons' roles in Afghanistan and without questioning the duty of each male teenager to serve his country. They did not see any contradiction in this. In this period they also called for an end to hostilities in the other hot spots in the former Soviet Union. They appealed to *afgantsy* in Transcaucasia to stop joining in the fighting there. 'Your hands which have already held weapons, must not hold them again ... Kneeling before you, we beg you: give up your weapons, and go home'.[15]

They were involved in this military-patriotic education until as late as 1993. Yet by 1994, they had moved closer to the pacifism of the soldiers' mothers and were giving advice to young men and their mothers on how to avoid military service. Some of them now regret that they acted on requests to make a contribution to the state's military socialisation programme, as they are now sceptical about the authorities' objectives at the time and feel they were exploited in their grief. This change in attitude reflects their growing disenchantment with the authorities – military and political. Nevertheless, they continue to believe that the state should resolve their problems and they do have some contact with the part of the male *afgantsy* network which is primarily a state or official structure – for example, representatives from the Ministry of Defence and the CIS committee for internationalist-servicemen. The latter is supporting them in the post-Soviet period in their demands for better state benefits such as an additional monthly sum for those who lost their family's breadwinner, exemption from the privatisation fee for their flats and exemption from income tax.[16] At least the bereaved parents and wives do receive payments from the state in recognition of the loss of their sons or husbands, although such social security benefits amount to very little in a time of social and economic uncertainties where the social safety net has been pulled away from under the feet of growing ranks of benefit claimants.

The Moscow Mothers' Council has begun looking for sponsorship in the private sector, primarily pinning their hopes on receiving donations from some individual *afgantsy* organisations. The women have nothing to do with the largest part of the Afghan movement – the

Union of Afghan Veterans (UAV) – which, in the mothers' eyes, is primarily a commercial outfit whose management ostensibly misdirects profits away from the relief of the needs of bereaved families. The UAV comprises organisations incorporating businesses which were set up with the aim of making money to help themselves and their disabled comrades-in-arms. Many of them are thriving due to their special profit-tax exemption status which was granted to them by President Yel'tsin in 1991. This generous provision, which has in fact allowed many *afgantsy* to move from a position of being social outcasts to one of successful entrepreneurs, has caused disquiet and envy from the female contingent of the Afghan movement who do not have the same privilege.

The Afghan madonnas

Another group of Afghan war females do not receive even such a meagre payment. The *afganki* – or women who served in Afghanistan in a support role (in the kitchens or laundry, or as translators or radio operators) – are not entitled to any of the privileges accorded to others who were affected by the war in Afghanistan. They have no recognition from the state that their personal well-being has deteriorated as a result of having worked in Afghanistan. They get no 'pension' from the Ministry of Defence which all the ex-servicemen receive and only those of them who are classed as having a disability (including psychological problems) are entitled to a small sum from the Ministry of Social Security.

Women with this fate living in Moscow and Moscow region have come together in an organisation – Anika – to fight for the right to have the same status in law as the men who served in Afghanistan. Their efforts to achieve this mainly take the form of petitioning parliament. The women have found no understanding of their plight or help in influencing the legislature from the male-dominated Afghan movement. Yet, in contrast to the widows and mothers, the *afganki* have accepted the situation and, instead of complaining and bearing a grudge against the state and the *afgantsy* Union, these women have struck out on their own.

Anika is a Moscow-based non-governmental organisation (registered as the Moscow Committee of Women Disabled in the Afghanistan War) which was set up by Liubov' Iakovleva in 1991. It was originally planned that the body be called 'Nika' after the goddess of victory but, as Iakovleva rationalises, there was no victory in this war and none of the women who served there became goddesses. So it was decided to add the letter 'A' to represent Afghanistan: thus they came to be called 'Anika'.

Having suffered a spinal injury from an explosion in Afghanistan, Liubov' could not return to her former career as an equestrian.[17] For her first couple of years back in the homeland, suffering physiologically and mentally from the experience, she lived at a dacha, working the land and reflecting on what she should do with the rest of her life. She was well aware of the difficulties of settling back into civilian life in a society which believed that no women had been *sent* to Afghanistan but that they had gone of their own free will, motivated by self-interest.[18]

The female contingent of Soviet personnel in Afghanistan were dubbed the 'Afghan madonnas' by an article in *Pravda* in 1987. The writer proposed that there were a range of reasons why they chose to go there: 'Some come to test their strength of character, others come with the aim of improving their material position and others come looking for their mission in life. However, there is one thing that united them all: they all come here to work.'[19]

Many of the women felt that this nickname and the article did them a disservice in questioning their motives, since public opinion often tarred them all with the same brush, deeming them all to be prostitutes or self-seekers. One young woman told her mother not to tell people loudly and proudly that her daughter was serving in Afghanistan, if she did not want to hear her called a whore.[20]

Iakovleva and others had, in fact, been recruited by the Ministry of Defence and were classed as volunteers. They received an average (low) Soviet salary but in addition were given hard currency cheques. There was an assumption back home that they worked as prostitutes during the war. There undoubtedly were cases of women who did more than provide a cooking and cleaning service but prostitution was not necessarily the form this took. More alarmingly, there were cases when the women were put in a situation where their position and integrity were compromised and they were forced into sexual encounters.[21]

The allegations against, and unjustified bad reputation accorded to, the *afganki* has weighed heavily against the women and explains why the public and servicemen do not see them as heroines, and the reluctance of the bureaucrats to give them benefits on their return. There are objective factors to account for this, too. These women are not entitled to the same privileges as the men for two reasons – firstly, they volunteered to go to work in Afghanistan and, secondly, they are non-military personnel. Although they were classed as volunteers for this work, they were nevertheless recruited and selected by the same military commissariats which sent the servicemen. The women argue that the only voluntary aspect was the very first step they made of expressing an interest in going. After that, the element of free will ended and they fell under the full command and control of the armed forces and were in identical circumstances to all military personnel.

As *Komsomol'skaia Pravda* commented, 'It is such an insult... they worked on the same terrain and under the same conditions – in fact, often in worse conditions – than many of the officers'.[22] Iakovleva believes that the inequality is unjust since the armed forces had a specific aim in mind in recruiting women such as herself to go there. The tactic of the military was that there should be a presence of civilian women amongst the Soviet Union's limited contingent to bring a sense of normality in order to relieve the stress of the war situation experienced by the young conscript servicemen and officers.

The women would like all the legislation which grants these privileges only to the male participants to be rewritten with the beneficiaries named 'all participants in the Afghan war' so that the female voluntary contingent would be included.[23] The women are still, in 1996, ineligible, even though society is aware of the consequences of it; the female volunteers still have no recompense and no recognition for their participation in the same war. It is not surprising that they feel alienated and isolated. Liubov' Iakovleva sought and found women in the same position as herself (with physiological and, primarily, psychological trauma) by putting out messages in the media (having failed to obtain any reliable data from the Ministry of Social Security and the Ministry of Defence). She was not surprised to find that the majority of them were suffering psychologically, had remained single, were out of work and in dire financial circumstances. They suffer from post-traumatic stress syndrome just as do the men.

Anika's aim is to provide social, medical and psychological rehabilitation and to improve its members' material well-being through commercial activity. The women know they must rely on themselves. As Iakovleva commented in an interview with *Krest'ianka* magazine, 'the most important thing is that the women who were in that war have to acquire a sense of their own self-worth and must not write themselves off. They must stand up to the last.'[24]

This article was published in 1992 and highlighted the plight of the *afganki*. An indication of the lack of interest from the readership (and society as a whole) is that the article only inspired four people to write to the editors in response. In another effort to influence public opinion, the women appeared in a short television documentary film in 1995. They are seeking sponsors because they need capital in order to realise their main project: the establishment of a small farm which will allow a group of them to be self-sufficient. They need money, land and building materials, intending to build their own home by themselves, then to till the land and produce fruit and vegetables to consume and sell. They have failed to secure bank loans and neither have they been allocated any land by the Moscow region authorities. Iakovleva feels that they are discriminated against not only because of their unclear status but because they are women.

Iakovleva sees the intractability of the state and government towards her organisation as inevitable, considering the government's overall attitude to women. Jobs and bank loans in 1990s Russia are primarily for the men.[25] Anika's leaders are more aware of their gender as a factor in state policy than the Afghan and soldiers' mothers' committees. This might explain their isolation from these other women's groups; they do not see eye-to-eye with them and do not cooperate on any of their campaigns. The mothers who lost their sons fight their battle for state help in the name of their sons and, in contrast to Anika, have nothing resembling a feminist agenda. Neither does Anika have any contact with any other Afghanistan-related organisation. The only time the UAV contacted Anika was when its president, Alexander Kotenov, was canvassing for votes for his candidacy as a deputy in 1993 and 1995. Iakovleva and her friends were stunned at the insolence of this approach and, in their scepticism, knew that anything he promised them would not come to fruition. To Anika the Afghan movement seems male-dominated, with no place in it for the women who provided support for the servicemen in Afghanistan.

The Anika women seem to have come to terms with being ignored and appear too tired of this ignorance to put more effort into fighting it. Their desire to set up as a self-sufficient unit is almost tantamount to removing themselves from society and is their reaction to what they feel to be prejudice against, and misapprehension of them. It is hard to gauge social attitudes towards this group in Russia today; the *afganki* are just one of the many social groups in need. Since they are a small one and since their fate is connected with a phenomenon with which society has not yet come to terms, they are largely unrecognised.

Coming to terms with the war

Russian state and society as a whole is not yet reconciled with the Afghanistan war and does not know how to deal – in both psychological and practical terms – with its fellow citizens who participated in, and who were affected by it. Everyone recognises it was a mistake to send the troops there; there are some, like the bereaved mothers, who continue to see them as heroes and patriots, and, on the whole, society is not mature enough to apportion blame for what happened to the members of the Soviet contingent. However, politicians, legislators and public opinion have not done enough for all of those whose lives have been turned upside down as a result of the war; many of the problems of the servicemen have been addressed, but the women are left wanting. It is not just the dire straits of the state welfare budget or the patriarchal nature of society that is the cause; Russia is reluctant to take responsibility for the mistakes of the Soviet Union.

There is still a learning experience being absorbed regarding the significance and legacy of the Soviet Union's last war, and in this it is women who are playing the leading role. The Moscow museum on the Afghanistan war is run by three dedicated women who, unlike the others mentioned above, were not touched by the war directly. Yet they understand the importance of having a permanent exhibition about the war and its participants for the public to visit in order to learn and understand what it was (and is) all about. The museum was originally based in a single room on the premises of the Liublinsk district internationalist-servicemen's committee – distant in physical and political terms from the centre. The director puts most of her efforts into finding new premises, big enough to house all the exhibits which were so numerous they had to be stored away elsewhere, and in a central location to increase the museum's accessibility and thereby its political impact.[26] The museum staff have sought to make the display an objective one, with information about all sides of the conflict and about the continuing legacy for both Afghanistan and the post-Soviet Union. It could also help the plight of the women touched by the war to be better understood.

Other than the museum, other forms of public relations activity would facilitate this process. For example, if the museum staff, the soldiers' mothers and Anika had advice or the opportunity to undergo training on business start-ups, publicity and fund-raising they would be better qualified to channel their efforts both to increase public awareness and also to find greater success in realising their plans.

Their desire and potential to do so cannot be questioned. Having shown strength in a climate of economic and political uncertainty, the members of the groups of women discussed are proving resourceful in the face of discrimination (whether they themselves recognise it to be so or not) and capable of influencing others in society. Their coming together in self-help groups and participation in wider political movements represent a striking demonstration of womanpower and social-political clout. That the reason for the activism of these particular women was a war in which they were afflicted by loss and trauma adds all the more poignancy.

The war in Afghanistan may be over for the Russians, but the legacy continues to be felt. The conflict in Chechnia goes on and neither the outcome nor the consequences for individuals touched by it can be predicted. However, the outspokenness shown by women so far in the face of this adversity indicates that we have not heard the last of them yet. It is women who will make the consequences of wars known and who will struggle in order that society and polity do not ignore them.

Notes

1 The colloquial, but universally applied, term for the soldiers who served in Afghanistan is *afganets* (plural: *afgantsy*). The female equivalent is *afganka*.
2 James Meek, 'Mothers Weep for Russia's sons and war's eternal hunger', *The Guardian*, 28 December 1994, p. 11.
3 Julia Wishnevsky 'The Samizdat Almanac of Soviet Feminists', *Report on the USSR*, Radio Liberty, 15 April 1980.
4 'Emotionalism of soldiers' mothers', *The current digest of the post-Soviet press* 47(5), 1995, p. 21.
5 Peter Pringle, 'Death without glory', *The Independent Magazine*, 19 October 1991, pp. 26–30.
6 'Emotionalism of soldiers' mothers', p. 21.
7 Mark Galeotti, *Afghanistan: the Soviet Union's last war* (London: Frank Cass, 1995), p. 98.
8 Pringle, 'Death without glory', pp. 26–30.
9 Christopher Bellamy, 'Russia scraps mass army for elite force', *The Independent*, 19 February 1996, p. 11.
10 Alexandra Ivanova, chair, Moscow Council of Mothers and Widows of servicemen who died in Afghanistan, in interview with the author, 1994.
11 P. Naysmith, 'Blood brothers', Soundtrack series, BBC Radio 4, 11 March 1990.

12 Raisa Chibisova, director, Museum of Internationalist-Servicemen, Moscow, in interview with the author, 1995.
13 Alexandra Ivanova, in interview with the author, 1994.
14 Alexander Oliinik, 'Podstavim plecho drug drugu', *Krasnaia Zvezda*, 13 February 1993, p. 3.
15 'Pozhaleite nas, synov'ia', *Kontingent* 3, 1991, p. 1.
16 Oliinik, 'Podstavim plecho drug drugu', p. 3.
17 Interview with Liubov' Iakovleva, 1993. Iakovleva was chair of Anika in these years.
18 Liudmilla Bychenkova, 'My vernulis' s voiny, nas ne zhdali', *Krest'ianka* February 1992, pp. 4–6.
19 'Afganskie Madonny', *Pravda*, 29 October 1987, p. 3.
20 N. Orlova, 'Vernite syna', *Moskovskii Komsomolets*, 14 November 1989, p. 2.
21 Afghanistan was no exception to the established war phenomenon of rape of the local population by occupying forces (L. Meizerkina, 'Prizvanie odisseia i uchast' penelopy', unpublished paper, Institut Sotsiologii, Akademii Nauk, Moskva, 1995). This is, of course, another of the aspects of the Soviet armed forces' operations in Afghanistan which have remained covered up.
22 M. Guseinov, 'Zhenshchiny na voine?', *Komsomol'skaia Pravda*, 14 June 1988, p. 2.
23 Interview with Liubov' Iakovleva, 1993.
24 Quoted in Bychenkova, 'My vernulis' s voiny, nas ne zhdali', pp. 4–6.
25 Interview with Liubov' Iakovleva, 1993.
26 Raisa Chibisova, in interview with the author, 1995.

9 Adaptation of the Soviet Women's Committee: deputies' voices from 'Women of Russia'

MARY BUCKLEY

> Better an old woman with a rolling pin than a peasant man with a sub-machine-gun
>
> Male voter, 1993

The great historical divides of 1917 and 1991 are significant for heralding changes in ideological, political and economic directions. But simultaneously these important years are false divides. Much stayed the same after the revolutionary rupture of 1917 and the failed *coup* of August 1991. Continuities in the social fabric were especially strong, notwithstanding modifications and adaptations. Whilst some attitudes altered, traditional notions of gender roles persisted, too, especially among older generations.

After 1991, institutions of the USSR did not all collapse. They frequently persisted under new names, run by the same people, but in a redefined context. The main aims of those in charge were for their organisations to survive, readjust, consolidate and be successful. Although 'victims' of the shifting and precarious circumstances in which they found themselves, directors, chairpersons, employees and organisers had to find inventive ways to guarantee the persistence of their various institutions. Broader socio-economic and political contexts constrained and shaped the opportunities available to these agents of adaptation.

The Soviet Women's Committee (SWC) has reasonably successfully set about redefining its role to guarantee survival in rapidly changing, sometimes chaotic, economic and political systems. In the independent Russian Federation, the SWC renamed itself the Union of Women of Russia (*Soiuz Zhenshchin Rossii*). In the 1993 elections, it joined forces with the Association of Women Entrepreneurs of Russia (*Assotsiatsiia Zhenshchin-predprinimatelei Rossii*) and Women of the Fleet (*Zhenshchin Voenno-Morskogo Flota*) and fielded thirty-six candidates under the umbrella movement 'Women of Russia'.[1] This movement registered with the Ministry of Justice of the Russian Federation on 11 October 1993.

In order to qualify to run in the 1993 elections, organisations had to gather 100,000 signatures across several regions of Russia. The vast network of *zhensovety*, or women's councils, across the land made this possible and relatively easy. Although twenty-one political parties and movements succeeded in gathering the requisite number of signatures, eight were subsequently disqualified for not having obtained a spread of region. Thus, Women of Russia went into the 1993 elections as one of thirteen contenders. They won 8.1 per cent of the vote on the party list for the State Duma. Then in the elections of December 1995, with two years' parliamentary experience behind them and with a growing confidence, Women of Russia easily again collected the necessary number of signatures in order to run, and put up eighty candidates. To their disappointment, they won only 4.6 per cent of the vote. Not reaching the 5 per cent barrier meant that they were ineligible for any seats at all on the party list. Just three women from the faction won seats, elected in the single-member constituencies.

This chapter examines how deputies in Women of Russia viewed their successes and shortcomings in the Duma, how they evaluated their political roles and how they assessed the 'female' contribution to Russian politics in the early 1990s. Data include interviews with thirteen deputies of the 1994–5 Duma (conducted between 1991 and early 1996, either in person or over the telephone), material in newspapers and bulletins issued by Women of Russia and, more broadly, the Russian press and television. A starting assumption of this discussion is that social scientists cannot fully grasp the dynamics of change without considering the perceptions of those active in the process. Study of political behaviour *tout court* is insufficient for understanding. Thorough analysis must include study of how political actors conceptualise reality, define their roles in it and evaluate the options available to them. Scrutiny of discourse, as well as examination of events, provides a richer tapestry of changes and continuities since it incorporates a necessary subjective dimension. Without this, observers from the outside can easily misconstrue meanings, too readily grafting onto developments their own assumptions and reasoning which belong to other systems and cultures.

Study of perceptions of political roles can also shed light on questions of empirical political theory. For example, theorists of party systems have long posited that out of parliamentary factions grow political parties. Among the frequently cited cases are Tory and Whig factions in the nineteenth-century British parliament. Study of the faction Women of Russia in the Duma of 1994 and 1995 prompts deeper questioning of this claim and shows contradictory views among deputies concerning whether a party should develop. Instead, three broad opinions existed: that a party was likely to be formed from the movement; that a party was unnecessary since a political movement was more appropriate for women; and that the movement was likely to disband in two or three years with its members dispersing into a broad spectrum of already existing 'male' parties. But before addressing these central questions, a brief sketch of the Soviet Women's Committee is in order.

The Soviet Women's Committee

The Soviet Women's Committee was one of the institutional pillars of the old regime. It became established after the Second World War and grew out of the Soviet Women's Anti-Fascist Committee formed in 1941. The SWC's main purpose was to develop links with women's organisations in other countries in furtherance of 'peace, friendship and mutual understanding'.[2] Over the years it formally hosted delegations of foreign women, but quickly developed the reputation of failing to be critical about the predicament of Soviet women. As an arm of the CPSU, it lauded the achievements of Soviet socialism for women, not its failures. Foreign visitors who tried to broach topics such as the lack of contraception or the huge number of abortions performed, were often met with blank gazes, denials or quick acknowledgement and a speedy change of topic. The USSR, before glasnost, did not permit lively and freewheeling discussion about such delicate matters, notwithstanding a limited official debate in the late 1960s and 1970s about how women could best combine their roles in production and reproduction.[3] In this context, the SWC was generally viewed as an apologist for the regime, toeing party lines rather than challenging them. In what Gorbachev labelled (not entirely correctly) 'the years of stagnation', Valentina Tereshkova, pilot and astronaut, was chairperson of the SWC. She held this post from 1968 to 1987, when Zoia Pukhova succeeded her.

During the Gorbachev era, particularly towards its close, the Soviet

Women's Committee began to be more critical about women's lot. Pukhova delivered an especially trenchant critique at the Twenty-Eighth Party Congress in 1990.[4] Like her successor, Alevtina Fedulova, she was seen by feminists outside the SWC as a typical communist *apparatchik* with questionable feminist credentials. Both, however, are serious and hard-working women, committed to making women's working lives better. They may not have savoured the theoretical arguments of feminist debate, nor put issues such as violence against women high enough up their agendas to satisfy their critics, but they did attempt to redefine some discourses on women, particularly more official ones. Pukhova, moreover, had not enjoyed the relatively luxurious career paths of elite professionals and intellectuals – she had worked her way up from a weaver on the shop floor to factory director. Fedulova, by contrast, graduated from Moscow oblast pedagogical institute and worked as a teacher before becoming a member of the Central Committee of the Komsomol, followed by chairperson of the Central Committee of the All-Union Pioneer Organisation.[5]

In 1990 and 1991, the SWC was forced to adapt its role. In a context in which the CPSU was losing its legitimacy as thousands flocked to leave it, the SWC had to reconsider its attitude toward economy and market opportunities. As new groups, movements and parties mushroomed, the SWC had to develop a sense of its own restructured identity and purpose. With huge cuts in its budget, it was forced to seek Western sponsors. Their money enabled the SWC to run courses to train Soviet women to move into business. Quite an ideological volte-face in role thus took place. An erstwhile defender of Soviet socialism for emancipating women and one-time critic of the evils of capitalism for degrading women and discriminating against them, became a new champion of the right to success through small businesses.[6]

By the time the process of state disintegration was complete, leaders of the SWC had, for at least two years, been rethinking its direction. Thus, developments after 1991 were really a continuation of what had started earlier. In 1990 in Moscow, Pukhova told this author that women had to become more active in politics.[7] Then in 1991, Fedulova stressed in interview that women had to learn to develop self-confidence in both business and politics. One new aim of the SWC was to train women to become successful entrepreneurs and leaders. Fedulova insisted that 'every day we need to find new ways to find solutions. Women should not be social invalids. Help should come from the state, but not only from the state. So that women can compete with men, they must have social protection, but must be helped to enter the market.'[8] Fedulova went on to regret that 'psychologically women are not prepared'. In particular, 'special knowledge is wanting'. Ways of addressing this included monthly open lectures, business training courses funded by the Netherlands, special schools sponsored by partners in Australia, as well as the SWC's own courses for women entrepreneurs. In addition, a *politklub* was designed by the SWC to train leaders and, with help from Finland, a school for women leaders would instruct in how to prepare for elections.[9]

In the 1993 elections, Ekaterina Lakhova became a prominent political actor alongside Fedulova. She had previously been state secretary for families, mothers and children and also presidential advisor to Yel'tsin. Before embarking upon a political career in Moscow she had been a doctor in Ekaterinburg (previously Sverdlovsk). When I interviewed Lakhova in the Russian parliament in 1991 she stressed the need to end all forms of discrimination. She also contended that 'we need to change ideology. Women must do something "from below"', but 'our main problem is that we understand problems badly'. Moreover, 'women need information. Women should not wait, but should act for themselves. What do we need? For women to change.'[10] In a subsequent interview in the Kremlin in 1992, Lakhova reiterated these views,[11] and by 1995, her ideas had become sharper and more radical. She then declared, 'all parties are dominated by men. Male politics is dirty. We want to make it cleaner.'[12]

Russian parliaments

Gorbachev brought revolutionary change to the Soviet electoral system. After a tiny experiment in voter choice in 1987 which affected just 1 per cent of constituencies, a new electoral law passed in December 1988 paved the way for historic elections in March 1989 to a new Congress of People's Deputies. These were followed by even freer elections in the fifteen republics in late 1989 and 1990. Multi-candidate choice was offered in most seats, thereby shattering the stultified no-choice system of the past. Notwithstanding 750 'saved' seats out of 2,250 in the March 1989 elections and also in two republics of the fifteen in elections in 1989–90 to republican supreme soviets, and despite certain irregularities, these two sets of elections were truly historic and catalysts of accelerated political change.[13]

The first parliament of the newly independent Russian Federation had been elected before the collapse of the USSR and was not re-elected until December 1993. The loss of quotas of representation for women in most of the republican legislatures meant that the female presence in politics had already sharply declined. On average, in the USSR of the 1970s and 1980s, 35 per cent of the people's deputies on republic-level supreme soviets had been women. With freer elections, this figure fell to 5.4 per cent in Russia, 7 per cent in Ukraine and a higher 15 per cent in Uzbekistan where a quota was retained.[14] Coupled with the inattention to women's issues in most of the programmes of new parties, this meant a new invisibility of women parliamentarians and a low salience of women's issues. Although many female deputies had previously been mere tokens, saying 'yes' to party lines, new female deputies were in tiny minorities at a time when the automatic CPSU lines on social protection for women and encouragement to be employed outside the home were coming under attack. As women's unemployment grew, the number of women in parliament was falling. There was no causal link between these two developments; but their coincidence meant that, as women found themselves in increasingly vulnerable economic positions, likely defenders of their interests in parliament were decreasing in number.

The Russian Federal Assembly has a lower house called the State Duma and an upper house known as the Federation Council. The former has 450 seats and the latter a smaller 178. Half of the 450 seats to the State Duma were elected by party list, inspired by the German system. All thirteen organisations running for the Duma in 1993 put forward lists of names for these 225 seats. Women of Russia was the only 'all female' list. Other parties included very low numbers of women – the first woman on the list of the Agrarian Party, for example, was in seventieth place. Likewise, Sergei Shakhrai's Party of Russian Unity and Concord put its first woman in sixtieth place. Low rankings ensured women would not be returned. Of 194 candidates for Shakrai's party, only six were women. If parties won over the 5 per cent hurdle required for access to any of the 225 list seats, then the first twelve names on their list won seats. Five parties, however, had no women at all among their first twelve names. These were: the Liberal Democratic Party; the Agrarian Party; the Russian Movement for Democratic Reforms; the Party of Russian Unity and Concord; and the Future of Russia – New Names. Women of Russia won twenty-one seats on the party list, amounting to 8.13 per cent of votes. They came fourth on the party list after Zhirinovskii's Liberal Democratic Party (fifty-nine seats on the party list), Gaidar's Russia's Choice (forty seats) and the Communist Party of the Russian Federation (sixty-five seats).[15] One Russian commentator has remarked that the success of Women of Russia was 'one of the greatest surprises' of the 1993 elections.[16] Women, however, did less well in their fight for the 225 seats to the Duma elected in constituencies. These seats were less tightly tied to party affiliation. Here, Women of Russia gained a further two seats, bringing their initial total in the Duma to twenty-three.[17]

By the time of the 1995 elections, other parties were a little more sensitive to the 'female factor'. This led them to give a slightly increased visibility to women on their party lists and to rank them higher. For example, Iavlinskii's Iabloko put women in third and sixth places on the list, Gaidar's The Democratic Choice of Russia put an actress in third place, Chernomyrdin's Our Home is Russia gave fifth and seventh places to women, the bloc of Ivan Rybkin put a woman in fifth place and Zhirinovskii's Liberal Democratic Party of Russia gave tenth place to a woman. While women were hardly present in equal numbers to men, there was a trend away from all-male party lists.[18]

On the eve of the 1995 elections, hopes were high among deputies in Women of Russia. As Fedulova put it, they expected 'victory'.[19] Most expressed the view that they would win on the party list, but were reluctant to predict their overall percentage.[20] Irina Vybornova, however, was bold enough to hope for an optimum of 10–12 per cent.[21] Some opinion polls had put Women of Russia in second place with a high 9 per cent of the vote.

But with just three deputies from the single-member constituencies taking their seats in the new Duma (all of whom were on the party list, but had chosen to run in constituencies as well), the faction Women of Russia could no longer exist, not meeting the required size for those elected in constituencies. Members of Women of Russia thus greeted the 1995 election results with dismay, contrasting with their euphoria after the 1993 results, but none the less expressing immediate commitment to a comeback in the next elections to the Duma.[22]

Women of Russia's 1993 election campaign

Members of Women of Russia expressed surprise at their electoral success in 1993. 'We expected about 4 per cent of the vote,' said Natal'ia Sinitsina of the information bureau of the Union of Women of Russia. Looking back, she noted that 'it was all very tense. People had become so sick of Russia's Choice since so much attention had been concentrated on them.' Excited in her reflections, she added how quickly the movement Women of Russia had managed to secure the necessary 100,000 qualifying nomination signatures in order to run. 'We did it in a week.' In fact, 'one man rang in and said he would help acquire signatures', allegedly saying, 'better an old woman with a rolling pin than a peasant man with a sub-machine-gun' (*luchshe baba so skalkoi chem muzhik s avtomatom*).[23]

Like other contenders in the elections, Women of Russia took advantage of the television time allotted to them. On air, Lakhova and Fedulova tried to create an image of brightness and seriousness. They wore colourful yellow and red suits, a challenge to the dark and dowdy image of the Soviet past. They rarely smiled, however, for which they were criticised. In response, Fedulova argued that there was nothing to smile about yet, given the predicament of Russian citizens.[24]

Fedulova and Lakhova, in turns, outlined their centrist policy priorities. Fedulova explained that Women of Russia were 'for economic reform, for new market relations'. She quickly qualified this with 'but we are for life. We want to live now.' Reforms had not been efficient. Social protection was needed and had a role to play in the privatisation of housing, in education and in healthcare. A serious problem was that 'social guarantees' had been lost. Above all, women in light industry had to be protected. Lakhova concentrated more forcefully on questions about unemployment, arguing that 'apart from us, I don't think that anyone stands for women's rights'. In 1993, women already made up 70 per cent of the unemployed.[25]

As well as indicating the consequences of reform for women, Fedulova and Lakhova suggested that their policies would benefit everyone. Women of Russia would defend the interests of men and women. The loud message, however, was that they were the only contenders in the 1993 elections to take women seriously.[26] Many women must have been persuaded that this was indeed the case.

So who voted for Women of Russia? In all, 369,918 voters gave their support. Although 8.13 per cent was the overall percentage, in thirty-two of Russia's regions, Women of Russia received more than 10 per cent of the vote, peaking in one at 17.3 per cent. Svetlana Aivasova has shown that, in the 1993 elections, 82 per cent of Women of Russia's supporters were women, 19 per cent of whom were aged from eighteen to twenty-nine and 37 per cent from thirty to forty-four. Twenty two per cent of those who voted for Women of Russia had

Deputies' voices from 'Women of Russia' 165

'Women of Russia'

One of Women of Russia's posters in the 1995 election campaign. From left to right and top to bottom: Alevtina Fedulova, Irina Vybornova, Galina Parshentseva, Svetlana Orlova, Ekaterina Lakhova (middle), Liudmila Zavadskaia, Marina Dobrovol′skaia, Elena Chepurnykh, Antonina Zhilina (under Lakhova), Galina Klimantova (bottom right), Fanuza Arslanova and Natal′ia Malakhatkina.

received some higher education. Broken down according to social category, 30 per cent were workers, 27 per cent employees, 13 per cent engineering-technical workers, 3 per cent peasants, 8 per cent intellectuals, 1 per cent bureaucrats, 1 per cent business persons, 1 per cent from the military and 16 per cent pensioners.[27]

Women of Russia in the Duma, 1994–5

Of the twenty-three women elected to the State Duma on the party list, there were nine teachers, six in healthcare, four entrepreneurs, three lawyers and one actress.[28] The youngest was Marina Dobrovol'skaia, aged thirty-two, and the oldest Alevtina Fedulova, at fifty-four. The remainder fell into the forty to fifty age-bracket, underlining the fact that this was a movement run by middle-aged professional women. Like other movements and parties, women of Russia formed a faction within the parliament, with Ekaterina Lakhova as its chair. The faction established a small bureau of four others – Alevtina Fedulova, Antonina Zhilina, Galina Klimantova and Natal'ia Malakhatkina.[29] Fedulova was elected to the prominent position of deputy chair of the Duma, giving her a high profile and active role.

Like all parliaments, the State Duma has committees and subcommittees. Members of Women of Russia were allocated the positions listed in Table 9:1. Raisa Skripitsina explained to me that the deputies were initially assigned places on committees appropriate to their backgrounds and specialities. This was done at a meeting of the faction and the Duma then approved the arrangements suggested.[30] Initially, deputies expected women to want positions on social committees, but Marina Dobrovol'skaia stressed that women quickly made it clear that they wanted traditionally 'serious' committees too, including the budget, defence, economic policy and state security. This showed that 'women are able to work professionally everywhere'.[31] A spread of membership on different committees was also beneficial, said Skripitsina, since it meant questions important to Women of Russia were raised across committees and also female deputies could bring back a range of information to internal discussions of the faction.[32]

Those interviewed had a strong sense of the importance of their committees. On the defence committee, Marina Dobrovol'skaia emphasised the seriousness of her work in discussing the possible

Table 9:2 *Positions of responsibility in the Duma held by members of the faction 'Women of Russia': 1994–5*

Deputy chair of the State Duma	Alevtina Fedulova
Chair of the faction 'Women of Russia'	Ekaterina Lakhova
Chair of the committee for women, the family and youth	Galina Klimantova
Chair of the subcommittee on pensions and state payments	Anna Vlasova
Member of the committee for defence; chair of the subcommittee on social and legal protection for servicemen and their families	Marina Dobrovol'skaia
Member of the committee for legislation and legal reform; chair of the subcommittee on rights of the individual and federal law	Liudmila Zavadskaia
Deputy chair of the committee for health protection	Valentina Kozhukhova
Member of the committee for health protection; chair of the subcommittee for medical rehabilitation of the population	Natal'ia Malakhatkina
Member of the committee for health protection; chair of the subcommittee for the legal basis of medical products	Valentina Martynova
Member of the committee on security; chair of the subcommittee for the budgetary planning of security	Galina Parshentseva
Member of the committee for women, the family and youth; chair of the subcommittee for family and demographic policy	Raisa Skripitsina
Member of the committee for women, the family and youth; chair of the subcommittee for children and youth	Elena Chepurnykh
Member of the committee for international affairs; chair of the subcommittee for culture	Galina Chubkova
Member of the committee for cooperation of independent states and communications with compatriots; member of the subcommittee on the Ukraine, Moldavia and Belarus; chair of the commission of the State Duma for refugees and needy migrants	Zhanna Lozinskaia
Member of the committee for the budget, taxes, banks and finance	Antonina Zhilina
Member of the committee on the budget, taxes, banks and finance; member of the	

subcommittee for tax and customs law	Svetlana Orlova
Member of the committee on economic policy	Fanuza Arslanova
Member of the committee for geopolitics; chair of the subcommittee for the economic security of Russia	Irina Vybornova

Source: Zhenshchiny Rossii, *Informatsionnyi Biulleten'* 5, September 1995.

widening of NATO and the fate of the Black Sea Fleet. She felt that she tackled these 'purely male questions' with a high standard of professionalism. When asked how the men on the committee treated her and whether they respected men more than women, she responded, 'I am the only woman. I feel myself to be suitable and am comfortable. But I worked for thirteen years for the General Staff and am used to a "male collective". You forget whether you are male or female there and work professionally.' When I asked how easily she could influence the agenda, she responded, 'Like thinkers support me.'[33]

The gender composition of the committee for women, the family and youth was quite different: here sat eleven women and four men. Skripitsina believed that 'we have good men from different parties – a communist, liberal democrat, a deputy from Iabloko and from Russia's Choice. Men listen to us and take ideas into their own parties.'[34]

Like Dobrovol'skaia and Skripitsina, Zhilina also felt it relatively easy to shape agendas, adding that on the committee for the budget she had learnt a great deal and had to confront challenging questions 'that before I had never had to. For example, I wanted to change the tax situation quickly to make conditions better for investors.' But due to serious problems of collecting taxes and due to the pressing need to protect citizens and ensure defence and medical budgets, 'this was not possible'.[35]

Difficulties, however, had beset the committee for health protection. Its membership, according to Martynova, had fallen to a mere eight deputies. In fact, two male deputies from the Liberal Democratic Party of Russia had left in the first week. Martynova laughed, 'see who the weak sex is'. Lacking the prestige of some other committees and requiring hard work on often intractable domestic problems, this committee brought neither foreign trips, status or easy successes. Martynova lamented that despite the large number of doctors in the Duma, perhaps seventeen or twenty, there was reluctance to serve here. As a specialist in the field of drugs, she felt at least able to bring her knowledge to bear.[36]

In 1994 and 1995, then, deputies in Women of Russia participated in a wide range of committees, not restricted to stereotypically female areas. Although most women gravitated towards committees for which they enjoyed professional expertise, they none the less admitted to learning a great deal on them.

How did women deputies see their work in the Duma?

The information bureau of the Union of Women of Russia was keen from the start to emphasise the importance of a consensus-building approach. Natal'ia Sinitsina volunteered that 'The main question before us is how woman can live in this society, how to help her. Differences between us do not help.' In 1994, she was adamant that the Union of Women of Russia did not really wish to become involved in politics because it was a 'social' rather than a 'political' organisation. Necessity, however, spurred political action – 'We had to get involved in order to change the position of women.' The Union of Women of Russia saw its role as one of helping the faction in parliament. Sinitsina believed that the faction could affect women's lives for the better and act as a link between parliament and women in the public.[37]

When asked about relations with other parties, the Union of Women of Russia reacted with caution. 'We are not close to any party. We have no political orientation. Our aim is work, legislation, routine.' The main aim, Sinitsina insisted, was to fulfil election promises by getting the business done. For this, a 'balanced approach' was needed. She characterised arguments as counterproductive.[38]

Members of the feminist movement who are critics of Women of Russia have accused the parliamentary faction of voting closely with the Liberal Democrats and with the Communist Party. In response, Sinitsina argued, 'Why not support Zhirinovskii or the communists if their suggestions are good for society? It all depends on the idea under discussion. We must weigh up the options.'[39] Putting the same point differently, Natal'ia Malakhatkina said, 'We are centrist. We are ready to support left or right in order to reach agreement.'[40] Or, as Antonina Zhilina put it, 'People do not always understand us. Zhirinovskii oscillates. Who has not at some time voted with Zhirinovskii? Reformers have, communists have, we have.'[41] And, Marina Dobrovol'skaia noted, when Zhirinovskii created a scene in the Duma in September 1995 by pulling the hair of a female deputy from Iaroslavl' who was unattached to Women of Russia, the faction none the less wrote a press release condemning unseemly behaviour in parliament.[42] Interviewees insisted that members of Women of Russia were far from uncritical supporters of Zhirinovskii.

Perceptions of success

Deputies overwhelmingly agreed that among their greatest successes was painstaking work on laws, whether on the new family law now completed or on working towards legislation on vital topics such as alternative service to the draft.

Malakhatkina gave very high priority to Women of Russia's social policy. 'First of all, we defined social problems and developed a programme around them.'[43] She stressed the importance of pushing for finance for the programme 'Children of Russia'. By contrast, Parshentseva focused on her own speciality, that of security: 'We raise lots of questions about security, about the budget. We defend rights, including those of prisoners. We need parliamentary control of security. The Federal Service needs to be better defined. We put questions about this and defend our position.'[44] When I pressed Parshentseva on whether Women of Russia had the respect of other deputies and on whether the faction had influence over other factions, she insisted 'yes. Through our position. From our authority. Others support us because we work.'[45] Parshentseva, for example, had before May 1995 been twice to Chechnia, especially concerned about human rights.

The theme of growing respect for Women of Russia was repeatedly voiced. And although Zhilina drew attention to male derision of women in the parliament, she simultaneously saw an increasing awareness of women as a political force. Evidence for this was the already mentioned point that, before the 1995 elections, other parties had begun to include more female candidates on their party lists and also to put them higher up the list than before. This, Zhilina announced, was 'our little due to each of the parties'. Moreover, one clear success was that 'we set a precedent'.[46] Male deputies may not have liked it, but could not ignore it. Dobrovol'skaia agreed: 'Before it was fantastical to list women. Now Iavlinskii has put a woman third on his party list and Ziuganov has put one second. Zhirinovskii and Gaidar have included more women, even Rybkin has.'[47]

Women felt that respect for them was growing due to the visibility of their hard work. Zhilina's name, for example, had been put forward for the Council of the Central Bank which clearly should be regarded as an achievement. Women deputies, such as Parshentseva and Dobrovol'skaia, were visiting the troublespots of Chechnia, Bosnia and the Tadzhik/Afghan border. Women were not shying away from responsibility and danger, and, according to Dobrovol'skaia, sometimes other deputies and the press asked on any given question, 'And what about Women of Russia?' There was a belief that 'Women won't do bad things', and, moreover, 'Our voice is heard'.[48] Fedulova also believed that her important and visible role as deputy chair of the Duma 'certainly increased respect both for the faction and in general for the position of women in Russia'. She hastily added that it was not important who held this post. What mattered was that it was a woman.[49]

A more cautious response was given by Raisa Skripitsina who felt successes 'were few' and 'nothing to brag about'. But, like the others, she admitted, 'we can value our work on laws'. Moreover, the women did support each other. They celebrated birthdays and discussed their own family issues.[50] Vybornova also drew attention to 'a feeling of collectivism'.[51]

These, then, are the main reactions in interview with a Westerner to questions about achievements over a two-year period. Inevitably one has to consider the likelihood of self-congratulation and a striving to present as positive an image as possible. However, as their perceptions of shortcomings indicate, self-criticism was not absent.

Perceptions of shortcomings

Some deputies in Women of Russia readily acknowledged lack of parliamentary experience. For instance, Malakhatkina declared that 'We lacked "deputies' experience" [*deputatskii opyt*]. We are doctors, teachers, entrepreneurs, from industry.' Thus women had to grasp how to be deputies. She added that 'we had to study quickly, like children'.[52] Zhilina elaborated that 'we did not know the mechanisms of power. We lacked connections. Women came "from below"'.[53] Valentina Martynova similarly confessed that very quickly they had to learn how to put a question and what terminology to use. She believed it took half a year to learn how to be politicians.[54] Most deputies were very reluctant to talk about their internal divisions and disputes. Malakhatkina considered that 'there are no arguments or disagreements in the faction. Rather, we have working quarrels [*delovye spory*] which get results. We then reach agreement. We take a vote and the majority wins.'[55] Discussions took place at weekly meetings held on Tuesday mornings and Thursday afternoons.

Dobrovol'skaia laughed that many had expected Women of Russia to be the first to fracture. This had not been so, despite the need to 'paint over' certain differences.[56] Irina Vybornova and Valentina Martynova, however, readily volunteered that two women had left the faction. But this, Vybornova added, 'was highly insignificant in comparison with other factions'.[57] When I had earlier spoken on the telephone to the two women concerned, Larisa Babukh and Irina Novitskaia, they were reluctant to discuss why they had departed.[58] Babukh, in fact, had left to set up her own movement concerned with education and Novitskaia, in a second telephone interview, declared, 'I did not like the way in which the faction worked.'[59] It was clear, however, when subsequently talking to Fedulova that Novitskaia was not considered to be an energetic participant in the movement.[60]

More forthcoming than Vybornova, Martynova commented that there were ultra-radicals in the faction as well as very strict communists who would undo some of the reforms if they could. But when pressed to identify them, Martynova declined, admitting only that she herself had never been a communist.[61] Differences, therefore, on policy matters did exist. Martynova, however, stressed that 'one goal united us, effectively to bring some domestic comfort [*domashnyi uiut*] to Russia, to bring women's wisdom and reason to pacify fighting men'.[62] A strong feeling existed that male politicians were not helping women nor the country.

Another shortcoming readily identified was 'the need to work more with voters and with the media'. The former was especially difficult, suggested Skripitsina in October 1995, because 'Russia is so big. We cannot travel everywhere. There are now twenty-one in our faction, but Russia has eighty-nine regions.'[63] And greater participation in the media demanded time which was already too scarce. Vybornova reiterated the problem of inadequate time, but added 'we have many shortcomings, but not sharp ones. I do not see deep problems. They are temporary ones, not strategic ones.'[64]

Thus problems, difficulties and shortcomings were identified by deputies, but everyone interviewed could have been more forthcoming. A certain guardedness surrounded internal arguments, although this is typical of political parties worldwide.

The 'female' contribution to politics

When Women of Russia first formed their parliamentary faction inside the Duma, they were immediately criticised for being an all-female grouping. Yet, as Antonina Zhilina observed, 'parliament is constructed on sexual lines. We must get away from that and have women as well as men.'[65] Fedulova painted a broader picture. In a press interview, she reflected, 'Our society always looks on life with one eye – a male eye. But we want it to start looking with two; then the world will be better.' The problem was that 'there is no understanding of woman's contribution to our life. As a result, women's problems are underestimated.'[66] Moreover, in Zhilina's view, male deputies often looked upon women 'with great disdain'.[67]

Women deputies often felt that women and men approached problems in different ways. As Vybornova put it, 'Women's work methods differ from men's.' When probed further, she elaborated, 'woman is less aggressive, less envious, more progressive and more productive'.[68] Skripitsina felt that women were 'more painstaking' in their approach as well as 'scrupulous and conscientious, seeing problems through to the end'.[69] Zhilina talked about women's 'consistency, virtue and precision' whereas Svetlana Orlova insisted that 'women work harder than men and are more pragmatic'.[70] Lakhova boldly stated that 'men formulate problems differently';[71] Dobrovol'skaia believed that differences in nature were relevant. With regard to Chechnia, she commented, 'by nature women are against war. They want a peaceful path. Others do not always like our views. We wanted money for soldiers' wives. We visited all the hospitals where men with wounds lay. We gave presents and talked to them.'[72]

Dobrovol'skaia, however, stressed the complementarity of the sexes. Whenever she was told women were better than men, 'I say, "No dear. We must find a common language with men".' Against feminist separatism, she advocated 'harmony' by working together.[73] Martynova went so far as to say that only because male politicians had been incapable of 'caring for us and for the elderly' did women enter the political arena. Otherwise they would have preferred to stay at home. Instead, 'women came – not with indifference'. Martynova later laughed, 'Let men get used to the idea that a woman is also a person.'[74]

By 1995, however, Lakhova had begun to stress that women had to work separately because they had special problems, best worked on by themselves.[75]

From a movement not to a party?

The issue upon which deputies voiced the widest range of views concerned the future of their movement and whether or not it should become a party. In May 1995, Parshentseva said that she expected Women of Russia to become a party in four years' time, whereas one year later Orlova declared that it would happen, but laughed 'not until the twenty-first century', since Russia was not Sweden.[76] At the other extreme, Zhilina foresaw a time when Women of Russia would cease to exist. In October 1995 she said, 'If, in the next four years, women become active and join other different parties, then we shall calmly disband our faction.'[77] In response, I asked Zhilina if the question of disbanding the faction had been on the agenda from the start or whether it was a new consideration. She replied that it was indeed a 'new question' recently debated in the faction now that it had accumulated enough experience to look two or three steps ahead.[78] Fedulova in December 1995 echoed Zhilina:

> I do not think our movement will grow into a party. More likely, it will exhaust itself having fulfilled its tasks, and then women can, according to their desires, join the ranks of other parties. Today this is not the case. And the mood to become a party is not here.[79]

When pressed if some women did want a party, Fedulova admitted that this had been the case. She would not name the women concerned but noted that they were women from the regions who had enjoyed least contact with the movement before.[80]

Vybornova held an intermediate position: 'Become a party? Let's wait and see. It depends upon what legislation demands and upon what time requires. For a party to develop we need a particular political culture. We need to travel more, write, speak, participate in the media. We need to work on that.'[81] Skripitsina, likewise, advocated neither disbandment nor a party: 'To become a party soon is not so important. And is it worth it to build a women's party? Is it needed? We would have done it already had it been needed. At this stage it is not expedient.'[82] Looking back in 1996, Zhanna Lozinskaia confirmed that different positions had been taken on whether or not Women of Russia should become a party.[83]

It seems, then, that debates on the nature of Women of Russia and on its fate are dynamic and shift in emphasis. If at first Women of Russia was, for many of its members, 'social' rather than 'political', it soon became 'political' for the majority. And if at first the faction was deemed to have a long life, within the space of two years the idea developed that, once more women were present in parliament in all parties, then might be the time to disperse into other parties rather than persist as a grouping based upon the 'female' alone. This latter view had crystallised before the poor election result of 1995 and at a time when expectations of electoral success were high. Martynova, however, characterised the question as one of lively debate not rigid line.[84]

In sum, one tendency among members was to stress that women and men should work together, not separately. Another view held that a women's movement, not a women's party, was still needed.

The 1995 election campaign and results

Deputies in Women of Russia went into the 1995 campaign with some excitement. Although all ten women whom I interviewed at length in 1995 were reluctant to predict the percentage of the vote that they hoped to receive, most were confident that they would pass the 5 per cent barrier. In response to the question, 'What do you expect from the 1995 elections?', most were counting on being re-elected. Women campaigned hard and considered that their two years' experience in the Duma prepared them to work well in the next parliament. Most also felt that voters respected their record.

Limited funds, however, meant that Women of Russia purchased little television time for advertisements. In the week before the elections, Ziuganov's Communist Party of the Russian Federation, Zhirinovskii's Liberal Democratic Party, Chernomyrdin's Our Home is Russia and Iavlinskii's Iabloko enjoyed a greater visibility than Women of Russia. Fedulova admitted that more sponsors were needed and noted that they had enjoyed just one hour of free television advertisements.[85] Valentina Martynova revealed that she had been lucky enough to receive 65 million roubles of support for her campaign in Pushkin, just outside Moscow, but this was not even enough for posters and paperwork. She lamented that 'Five to ten million roubles is just half a minute of radio time.'[86]

The campaign was also fought amid the frequent hurling of patriarchal insults against women's participation in politics. Almost nightly, the arrogant misogynist Nikolai Lysenko, leader of the National Republican Party, told viewers how he had a good mother who 'knew her place' and a father who educated him in nationalist ideas. Some other parties, then, delivered strong anti-female messages, propagandising that women belonged at home. In a television interview upon the launch of her political autobiography, Lakhova adeptly rebutted such views, noting that it was quite usual for women over forty-five to have a place in politics, as in the West. In addition, men in politics, she observed, often behaved badly whereas Women of Russia intended to make politics 'softer and cleaner'.[87]

When the result of 4.61 per cent on the party list came in, it was clear that Women of Russia had failed to attract the male vote and had not expanded its base of female supporters. Although their humorous television advertisement with its catchy jingle was geared to men especially, it proved to be unsuccessful. It had shown a women in working clothes cleaning a window, thereby conveying the idea of toil and domestic order. The woman in overalls then became transformed into a well-dressed woman, who waved down at the men on the street below. She looked professional and caring. To the disappointment of its candidates, however, Women of Russia ranked fifth on the party list behind the Communist Party of the Russian Federation (22.3 per cent), the Liberal Democratic Party of Russia (11.18 per cent), Our Home is Russia (10.13 per cent) and Iabloko (6.89 per cent). Support, however, varied across the Federation. In many areas, Women of Russia was comfortably above the 5 per cent margin. The movement won a high 10.48 percent of votes in Evenkiiskii autonomous oblast, over 8 per cent in nine oblasts and okrugs, over 7 per cent in a further nine oblasts and okrugs, over 6 per cent in eleven oblasts and krais and over 5 per cent in fourteen regions. In forty-five 'subjects', however, support was under 5 per cent, falling to 2 per cent in Karachaevo-Cherkessaia republic and 2.17 in North Ossetia. Popularity was low in Moscow and St Petersburg where Women of Russia won just 2.45 and 2.75 per cent of the votes on the party list respectively. Uneven support across a huge land mass did not help the electoral chances of Women of Russia.[88]

When asked how the women candidates reacted to this result, Lozinskaia in 1996 said, 'Everyone is lamenting', and 'Lakhova suffers a lot'. Lozinskaia reflected that perhaps the leaders of Women of Russia had been too confident with the high expectations of 17 per cent in some regions. In her view, it had been a mistake to 'go it alone', refusing to make alliances with other groupings.[89] Orlova, however, disagreed, believing that 'we should have done nothing differently. They hurled dirt at us.'[90] In Orlova's view, blame was due to others' smear campaigns, not to Women of Russia's actions.

Right before the election, however, press articles drew attention to Women of Russia's contradictory voting behaviour in the Duma, which may have influenced some voters. *Izvestiia* noted that Women of Russia had voted in 1995 against an inflationary budget but, soon after, supported inflationary proposals. Moreover, the faction's position on privatisation seemed to vacillate. Likewise, some members of Women of Russia wanted war in Chechnia prohibited, but none the less the faction refused to support a bill stopping finances for military acts in Chechnia.[91] If there was logic in these apparently inconsistent voting patterns, Women of Russia seemed unable to convince sufficient voters. Statistics suggest that they failed to broaden their support base in an election which showed increased voter turnout and which was also complicated by forty-three parties and movements participating, compared with thirteen in 1993.

In 1996 just three candidates from Women of Russia took seats in the Duma: Ekaterina Lakhova, Svetlana Orlova and Zhanna Lozinskaia. They had all been deputies in the previous Duma. Thus, from their starting high of twenty-three deputies in 1994, representation from Women of Russia now plummeted to three. A fourth re-elected deputy, Anna Vlasova, had this time run as an independent, not having been included on Women of Russia's party list.

Political differences between these women were immediately apparent. Now that Women of Russia did not exist as a faction, Lakhova and Orlova joined the Deputies' Group of the Regions and both became active in Ivan Rybkin's Socialist Party, which enjoyed its own women's movement. Lozinskaia, by contrast, had become part of Nikolai Ryzhkov's *Vlast' Narodu* (Power to the People) and, according to Orlova and Lakhova, was closer to former communists.[92] Ryzhkov had been prime minister under Gorbachev. Anna Vlasova, now not officially of the movement Women of Russia, was closer to the Agrarian Party. Although Lakhova, Orlova and Lozinskaia sat next to each other in sessions of the Duma, according to Lozinskaia they did not engage in the lengthy discussions that they once had.[93] Although the idea of running again as a movement in the next elections to the Duma is still alive, the re-elected deputies are already pulled apart from each other due to their varied political leanings. In fact, in mid-1996, Lakhova and Orlova no longer viewed Lozinskaia as a member of the movement, although in interview Lozinskaia contradicted this claim.[94] Should they all, none the less, come together again to fight in the next elections to the Duma, their participation in committee work will contribute further solid parliamentary experience from which Women of Russia can benefit. Table 9.3 shows their current responsibilities.

Table 9.3 Positions of responsibility in the Duma in 1996 held by deputies in the movement Women of Russia

Member of the committee for regulations and organisational work of the Duma	Ekaterina Lakhova
Member of the committee for CIS states	Zhanna Lozinskaia
Member of the committee on the budget, taxes banks and finance	Svetlana Orlova

Sources: Interview with Zhanna Lozinskaia in the Duma (25 April 1996) and telephone interviews with Svetlana Orlova (29 May 1996) and with Ekaterina Lakhova (31 May 1996).

The campaign for presidency

Throughout 1995, some deputies in Women of Russia were extremely cagey about whether or not there would be a female candidate for the presidency in the 1996 race. By the autumn, statements were becoming bolder. Fedulova asserted that 'the time is not over the hills. Men have already exhausted their potential, and woman so far has remained in the shade.'[95] One ongoing difficulty, however, was mockery of women in politics. Fedulova refused to name possible candidates too soon to prevent attacks on them. In an interview in October, Zhilina reiterated this position. It was by then already clear that if Women of Russia received a respectable percentage of votes in the December elections to the Duma, then a female candidate for the presidency would follow. Zhilina admitted, 'We plan that. But under no condition will we name her now. We don't want people to throw stones on her candidacy in advance.'[96] Dobrovol'skaia gave similar indications.[97]

Raisa Skripitsina, however, was more sceptical. 'Society is not ready for that.' When I asked when it would be, she retorted, 'It is difficult to say. Women must work hard and develop into leaders. Lakhova, our leader, is well prepared, but not everyone knows her.'[98] Vybornova also made it clear that if anyone would be a candidate for the presidency, Lakhova possessed both the energy and the will.[99]

By December 1995, Fedulova was questioning the wisdom of putting forward a candidate from Women of Russia. In a press conference and in interview, she noted that Ella Pamfilova had emerged as a possible female candidate.[100] In 1996, however, Pamfilova did not apply for candidacy. Galina Starovoitova did, but her request to run for president was turned down on the grounds that some of the necessary supporting signatures gathered had been falsified.

Possible disagreements within Women of Russia about the appropriate candidate may have fuelled Fedulova's hesitancy. Certainly, by December, Lakhova was projecting a dynamic and modern image. She was wearing long dangly earrings, her hair was always well coiffured and she launched a book on her life in politics.[101] Rumours were circulating about tensions between Fedulova and Lakhova, but both insisted that they had good working relations, despite being women of different backgrounds, ages and specialisms.

After the elections of 1995, the office of the faction of Women of Russia would not be drawn on whether or not a female candidate would be put forward.[102] In February 1996, the information bureau of the Union of Women of Russia stressed that the movement would definitely support *a* candidate in the June elections, but whether or not it would be the movement's own candidate or a woman from another movement or party would have to wait for their official announcement on 26 April.[103] In the end, no one from Women of Russia attempted to run as a candidate in the presidential elections: the results of the 1995 elections had put an end to that idea. Only if Women of Russia had done well in 1995 would serious thought have been given to entering the presidential race. The unfortunate fate of Galina Starovoitova's attempt to run (not as a member of Women of Russia) is described by Olga Lipovskaya in the next chapter. As Orlova put it, just over two weeks before the presidential election, 'We support Yel'tsin.'[104] Lozinskaia, however, had already made clear that she was not a supporter of Yel'tsin's government and neither were some other members of Women of Russia.[105] Economic policy, then, and future political course, divided women in the movement more than they had been publicly willing to admit.

Conclusion

The years 1994 to 1995 saw the first all-female faction in the Russian parliament. Such a development would have been unthinkable in the USSR since factions within the CPSU were banned and divisions according to sex were considered divisive of working-class unity. Indeed, the very idea of all-female organisations smacked of 'bourgeois feminism'.[106] Moreover, women's factions in 1995 were still a rarity in most liberal democratic systems.

Coming very close to the 5 per cent hurdle in 1995, Women of

Russia almost entered the second Duma of the Russian Federation in respectable numbers. The first 1996 edition of the movement's newspaper engaged in soul-searching about the reasons behind the missing and crucial 0.4 per cent on the party list. Lakhova put it down to several factors: low media profile, failure of Women of Russia to make the movement's achievements well known, unpreparedness for the smears against Women of Russia which were hurled in the election campaign, incorrect views held about Women of Russia's position on the war in Chechnia and, above all, the difficulty of winning popularity for Women of Russia's indispensable 'centrist pragmatic course'.[107] Lakhova also posed the question whether the 1995 elections were 'temporary bad luck or defeat'. Certainly, just three deputies in parliament meant a loss of 'political weight', but on the other hand, Women of Russia had been more readily accepted by voters than had Russia's Choice and the Agrarian Party. She concluded that, as in medicine, the principle 'do not do harm' was relevant in politics. Women of Russia would 'go forward', widening the movement.[108]

While many political commentators may have written off Women of Russia as a credible political force in Russia, the movement still exists outside the Duma and its members intend to continue to play a political role. Although its resources are scarce compared to some other well-sponsored parties and movements, commitment to political action remains. According to Orlova, 'Many women will run for the Duma in four years' time', and the poor showing in 1995 does not stop Women of Russia as a movement from playing its 'normal role'.[109] Lakhova concurred, noting that the movement was broadening and that a new organisation, *Budushchee bez SPIDa* (A Future Without AIDS), had just subsumed itself under their umbrella, which could only strengthen Women of Russia further. Lakhova insisted that 'the movement will definitely fight in the elections'. If, however, the legal situation changed and only parties were permitted to run, it might conceivably form a bloc with a 'like-minded' political party.[110] This could well be Rybkin's Socialist Party. Women of Russia thus intend to return to the political arena with renewed vigour in the twenty-first century.

Among the prerequisites for success, however, are careful strategy, an injection of younger women into the movement, a more coherent economic policy, the construction of a dynamic media image and an ability to attract male voters who hitherto, overall, have given Women of Russia a cool reception. Yet were female supporters alone to increase in large numbers, that would be sufficient to surmount the 5 per cent hurdle. But the huge disadvantage for Women of Russia four years hence is the fact that their representation has dwindled in the Duma, thus their legislative record will be scant. This is at a time when other political parties are consolidating themselves, despite instabilities in the party system, and thus other political actors will have much greater experience to offer voters and perhaps be more appealing. A pragmatic alliance with another party, then, may be the most expedient path open to Women of Russia, and much, too, depends upon the pace at which resilient partiarchal attitudes in Russia which demean women's abilities in the public sphere can be eroded.

Notes

I am grateful to the Hayter Fund of Edinburgh University for a trip to Moscow in December 1995. Thanks are also due to the ESRC for a one-year research grant to work on rural stakhanovism. This enabled me to be in Moscow in October 1995 and in April–May 1996. Earlier versions and sections of this chapter were presented as papers at CREES, University of Birmingham, 28 February 1996 and at the Annual Conference of the Political Studies Association, 10–12 April 1996. Thanks are due to those present for comments. Special gratitude must be expressed, however, to Natal'ia Sinitsina for her solid help over recent years and to those deputies who found time in their very busy schedules to meet me. Particular debt is owed to Alevtina Fedulova for her readiness over the years to be interviewed and to the office of Ekaterina Lakhova.
 1 Svetlana Polenina, 'Zhenshchiny, vlast', demokratiia', *Rossiiskaia Federatsiia* 5, 1994, pp. 44–5.
 2 Soviet Women's Committee, *Soviet Women's Committee* (Moscow: Soviet Women's Committee, 1983), p. 2.
 3 Mary Buckley, *Soviet social scientists talking: an official debate about women* (London: Macmillan, 1986).
 4 *Izvestiia*, 2 July 1998, p. 10. For elaboration, see Mary Buckley, *Women and ideology in the Soviet Union* (Hemel Hempstead: Harvester/Wheatsheaf; Ann Arbor: University of Michigan Press, 1989), pp. 202–3.
 5 See Mary Buckley, 'Pukhova' in Archie Brown (ed.), *The Soviet Union: a biographical dictionary* (London: Weidenfeld and Nicolson, 1990), p. 304; and also Zhenshchiny Rossii, *Informatsionnyi biulleten'* 5, September 1995.
 6 Interviews in June 1990 and in May 1991 with Zoia Pukhova and Alevtina Fedulova at the headquarters of the Soviet Women's Committee, Moscow (subsequently the headquarters of the Union of Women of Russia). For further details, see Mary Buckley, 'Political reform', in Mary Buckley (ed.),

Perestroika and Soviet women (Cambridge: Cambridge University Press, 1992), pp. 67–8.
7 Interview with Pukhova, in the headquarters of the Soviet Women's Committee, June 1990.
8 Interview with Fedulova in the headquarters of the Soviet Women's Committee, May 1991.
9 *Ibid.*
10 Interview with Ekaterina Lakhova, Russian parliament, April 1991.
11 Interview with Ekaterina Lakhova in the Kremlin, March 1992.
12 Telephone interview with Ekaterina Lakhova, 16 May 1995.
13 Buckley, 'Political reform', pp. 55–8. See, too, Stephen White, *Gorbachev in power* (Cambridge: Cambridge University Press, 1990), p. 46.
14 I am grateful to Irina Kovrigina of the then Soviet Women's Committee for these statistics and others.
15 Polenina, 'Zhenshchiny, vlast', demokratiia', pp. 44–5.
16 *Ibid.*, p. 44.
17 By contrast, female success in the elections to the Federation Council was tepid. In all, 9 women were elected out of 178, amounting to 5.1 per cent.
18 *Vestnik Tsentral'noi Izbiratel'noi Komissii Rossiiskoi Federatsii* 1, 1995, pp. 3–56, 85–99, 113–32. In all, Iabloko was fielding twenty-six female candidates, The Democratic Choice of Russia 23, Our Home is Russia thirty-four, the bloc of Ivan Rybkin thirty-three and the Liberal Democratic party of Russia seventeen.
19 Interview with Alevtina Fedulova in the headquarters of Union of Women of Russia, 14 December 1995.
20 Interview with Valentina Martynova in the Duma, 12 December 1995.
21 Interview with Irina Vybornova in the Duma, 23 October 1995.
22 Telephone interview with the former office of the faction of Women of Russia, 15 January 1996; telephone interview with the information bureau of the Union of Women of Russia, 26 February 1996.
23 Interview with Natal'ia Sinitsina, information bureau of the Union of Women of Russia, Moscow, 26 September 1994.
24 Women of Russia's official television advertisement on 'Voters' Hour' in the run-up to the 1993 elections.
25 *Ibid.*
26 *Ibid.*
27 Svetlana Aivazova, ' "Zhenshchiny Rossii" – politicheskaia elita novogo vremeni', paper delivered at the Fifth Congress of ICEES, Warsaw, August 1995.
28 Zhenshchiny Rossii, *Informatsionnyi biulleten'* 1, 1994, p. 4.
29 *Ibid.*
30 Interview with Raisa Skripitsina in the Duma, 23 October 1995.
31 Interview with Marina Dobrovol'skaia in the Duma, 13 October 1995.
32 Interview with Skripitsina in the Duma, 23 October 1995.

33 Interview with Dobrovol'skaia in the Duma, 13 October 1995.
34 Interview with Skripitsina in the Duma, 23 October 1995.
35 Interview with Antonina Zhilina in the Duma, 25 October 1995.
36 Interview with Valentina Martynova in the Duma, 12 December 1995.
37 Interview with Sinitsina, information bureau of the Union of Women of Russia, 26 September 1994.
38 *Ibid.*
39 *Ibid.*
40 Telephone interview with Natal'ia Malakhatkina, 17 May 1995.
41 Interview with Zhilina in the Duma, 25 October 1995.
42 Interview with Dobrovol'skaia in the Duma, 13 October 1995.
43 Telephone interview with Malakhatkina, 17 May 1995.
44 Telephone interview with Galina Parshentseva, 18 May 1995.
45 *Ibid.*
46 Interview with Zhilina in the Duma, 25 October 1995.
47 Interview with Dobrovol'skaia in the Duma, 13 October 1995.
48 *Ibid.*
49 Interview with Fedulova in the headquarters of the Union of Women of Russia, 14 December 1995.
50 Interview with Skripitsina in the Duma, 23 October 1995.
51 Interview with Vybornova in the Duma, 23 October 1995.
52 Telephone interview with Malakhatkina, 17 May 1995.
53 Interview with Zhilina in the Duma, 25 October 1995.
54 Interview with Martynova in the Duma, 12 December 1995.
55 Telephone interview with Malakhatkina, 17 May 1995.
56 Interview with Dobrovol'skaia in the Duma, 13 October 1995.
57 Interview with Vybornova in the Duma, 23 October 1995.
58 Telephone conversations with Larisa Babukh and Irina Novitskaia on 20 and 19 October 1995 respectively.
59 Second telephone conversation with Irina Novitskaia, 8 December 1995.
60 Interview with Fedulova in the headquarters of the Union of Women of Russia, 14 December 1995.
61 Interview with Martynova in the Duma, 12 December 1995.
62 *Ibid.*
63 Interview with Skripitsina in the Duma, 23 October 1995.
64 Interview with Vybornova in the Duma, 23 October 1995.
65 Interview with Zhilina in the Duma, 25 October 1995.
66 *Moskovskie Novosti* 69, 8–15 October 1995, p. 6.
67 Interview with Zhilina in the Duma, 25 October 1995.
68 Interview with Vybornova in the Duma, 23 October 1995.
69 Interview with Skripitsina in the Duma, 23 October 1995.
70 Interview with Zhilina in the Duma, 25 October 1995; and telephone interview with Svetlana Orlova, 29 May 1996.
71 Telephone interview with Lakhova, 16 May 1995.

72 Telephone interview with Dobrovol'skaia, 16 May 1995.
73 Interview with Dobrovol'skaia in the Duma, 13 October 1995.
74 Interview with Martynova in the Duma, 12 December 1995.
75 Telephone interview with Lakhova, 16 May 1995.
76 Telephone interview with Parshentseva, 18 May, 1995; and telephone interview with Orlova, 29 May 1996.
77 Interview with Zhilina in the Duma, 25 October 1995.
78 *Ibid.*
79 Interview with Fedulova in the headquarters of the Union of Women of Russia, 14 December 1995.
80 *Ibid.*
81 Interview with Vybornova in the Duma, 23 October 1995.
82 Interview with Skripitsina in the Duma, 23 October 1995.
83 Interview with Zhanna Lozinskaia in the Duma, 25 April 1996.
84 Interview with Martynova in the Duma, 12 December 1995. For a fuller discussion of the question of movement versus party, see Mary Buckley 'From faction not to party: Women of Russia in the Duma' in Sue Bridger (ed.), *Women and political change: perspectives from East–Central Europe* (London, Macmillan, forthcoming).
85 Interview with Fedulova in the headquarters of the Union of Women of Russia, 14 December 1995.
86 Interview with Martynova in the Duma, 12 December 1995.
87 Russian television channel two, 7 December 1995, 8.30 pm.
88 For these statistics I am grateful to the office of Ekaterina Lakhova in the Duma.
89 Interview with Lozinskaia in the Duma, 25 April 1995.
90 Telephone interview with Orlova, 29 May 1996.
91 *Izvestiia*, 5 November 1995, p. 4. I am grateful to Mike Berry for drawing this article to my attention.
92 Interview with Lozinskaia in the Duma, 25 April 1996; and telephone interview with Orlova, 29 May 1996.
93 Interview with Lozinskaia in the Duma, 25 April 1996.
94 *Ibid.*
95 *Moskovskie Novosti* 69, 8–15 October 1995, p. 6.
96 Interview with Zhilina in the Duma, 25 October 1995.
97 Interview with Dobrovol'skaia in the Duma, 13 October 1995.
98 Interview with Skripitsina in the Duma, 23 October 1995.
99 Interview with Vybornova in the Duma, 23 October 1995.
100 Press conference filmed in the headquarters of the Union of Women of Russia, 14 December 1995; and interview with Fedulova there on the same day.
101 Ekaterina Lakhova, *Moi pyt' v politiku* (Moscow: Izdatel'stvo 'Aurika', 1995).

102 Telephone interview with the former office of the faction of Women of Russia, 15 January 1996.
103 Telephone interview with the information bureau of the Union of Women of Russia, 25 February 1996.
104 Telephone interview with Orlova, 29 May 1996.
105 Interview with Lozinskaia in the Duma, 26 April 1996.
106 For fuller discussion of this point, see Buckley, *Women and ideology in the Soviet Union*, pp. 44–57, 63–105.
107 Ekaterina Lakhova, 'Shag nazad? Dva shaga vpered!', *Zhenshchiny Rossii* 1(12), March 1996, p. 1.
108 *Ibid.*
109 Telephone interview with Orlova, 29 May 1996.
110 Telephone interview with Lakhova, 31 May 1996. In fact, this interview was conducted through Lakhova's aide due to the difficulty of making direct contact with Lakhova. Questions were left with Valeriia Borisovna two days earlier; she then put them to Lakhova who wrote down the answers which were relayed to me by her aide. This was a most expedient way of interviewing an elusive politician when answers to very specific questions were sought. It would not have been a useful technique for a long open-ended interview.

10 Women's groups in Russia

OLGA LIPOVSKAYA

After the collapse of the USSR

From 1992 to 1996 there were considerable changes in the development of public, non-governmental activity in Russia. Economic reform, changes in the Russian government's foreign policy and the opening up of borders together provided more favourable conditions which facilitated this.

More and more organisations began to appear, spanning a wide range of social and political issues. If, before 1991–2, there were mainly political movements which had a common name of 'informals' (*neformaly*) and who dealt with problems of human rights, politics and ecology, after 1992 different small organisations began to appear, based on particular social needs. These included economic survival, health, religious and spiritual fulfilment, family problems, the difficulties faced by the handicapped (children and adults) and homelessness.

After 1991, when the USSR ceased to exist, the structures which had previously prevented direct contacts between Russian public groups and activists with their Western counterparts were no longer there. An important role was played by Western journalists who worked very energetically in Russia, establishing contacts with political leaders and social movements. Journalists played the role of mediators, bringing together initiatives from both sides.

The 'third sector'

Thus, social and political activism began to change. The idealism and romanticism of the first years of perestroika were gradually transformed into a realisation of the need for an institutionalisation of non-governmental movements. Their stable and effective functioning depended upon economic survival, and the term 'third sector' appeared, becoming a part of the Russian vocabulary. 'First sector' refers to governmental structures and 'second sector' means the private sector. The coining of 'third sector', the non-governmental organisations (NGOs), confirmed its social reality. One consequence was that large Western foundations from the USA and Western Europe opened their offices in Russia. The Soros Foundation was the first, dealing mainly with scientific research and cultural matters; next came MacArthur, Eurasia, Ford and, in 1993, programmes of the European Council TACIS (Technical Aid to the CIS).

These developments caused changes in the context in which voluntary organisations formed and sustained themselves. Important prerequisites of survival and success for social groups and organisations became knowledge of foreign languages (especially English and German), practical experience with computers and awareness of cultural differences. Non-governmental activism became rationalised, and inexperienced or less-motivated groups and individuals disappeared from the front lines of the third sector. More pragmatic professionals, however, entered it.

Among the first projects which appeared were the Centre for Civil Initiatives (a Russian–American organisation in St Petersburg which provides training and seminars for local NGOs), a German–Russian exchange (a German project in St Petersburg with similar aims to those of the Centre for Civil Initiatives, which also publishes guides and directories for and about NGOs) and Interlegal (a US-sponsored organisation in Moscow which gives free legal consultations for NGOs). These organisations provide fundraising information and give practical training on organisational management to socially active groups. In this manner, they play a crucial role in the formation of civil society.

The women's movement

A similar dynamic is observable in the women's movement.[1] In 1991, the first contacts with Western colleagues were established by Moscow feminists in the Centre for Gender Studies, which resulted in the organisation of the First Independent Women's Forum in 1991 and of a Second Forum in 1992. These were held in Dubna, a small town near Moscow. The first Dubna conference brought together about one hundred women from different regions of the USSR and initiated an information network, ZHISET (Women's Information Network).

In November 1992, the Second Dubna Forum was a gathering of more than 500 women from the former Soviet Union and the West. The Forum declared the necessity of working out mutually beneficial strategies and joint action. This idea, however, has not yet been fully applied in practice, although a tendency towards its instigation does exist.

Since 1992, the number and diversity of women's organisations has increased considerably. Their classification varies, linked as it is to a variety of factors. The first and major classification divides the groups into 'introvert' and 'extrovert'. The former refers to groups and organisations that try to solve the socio-economic problems of their members. They are usually less developed in political and gender consciousness, small in number and focus on narrow problems. Some arose when the Western community started providing humanitarian aid to the CIS, dealing mainly with the distribution of food and goods to their members. The latter category of 'extrovert' groups embraces those which try to deal with a wider range of social and political issues and which have larger memberships. They possess a more developed political and social consciousness.

Introvert groups

Introvert groups include the Single Mothers' Association, local groups of mothers with big families, mothers with handicapped children and the Widows' Association.[2] Their structures are not usually very well defined and members tend to be passive consumers of what is offered by leaders and activists. After humanitarian aid had disappeared or was reduced, some of the groups managed to find their own way of surviving economically. They either provided members with small business opportunities or organised charity fairs, as did the Organization of Handicapped Women in the St Petersburg region, an example of a well-structured and highly motivated group. This group also organised cultural events for their members and persuaded local government to support them.

Some 'introvert' groups pursue charity and try to solve serious social problems that are overlooked by the government. A good example is the girls' shelter, 'Euphimia', in St Petersburg which provides a roof, food, and medical and psychological support for homeless adolescent girls, mothers and prostitutes. This is a unique organisation, the only one of its kind in Russia. Its work is indispensable, although the problem of girls' homelessness needs far more resources than the shelter can provide, offering as it does places for about one hundred.[3]

Another group which works effectively is 'Nadezhda' (Hope), also based in St Petersburg. It is an organisation for women with cancer, its efficiency and determination being attributed to the strong motivations of its two leaders, who are women who survived breast cancer operations. They transformed this traumatic personal experience into active support for women with similar diseases, giving both psychological and practical help. Although dealing with specifically individual problems related to cancer, they have managed to acquire resources and obtain information from different organisations, groups and individuals in Russia and abroad. Unfortunately their efforts to win access to state and local government structures have not been very successful.

Extrovert groups

Extrovert groups include various types of organisation. There are professional associations such as the Association of Women in the Media (with its headquarters in Moscow), the Association of Women and Business in Russia (based in St Petersburg but with similar groups in Moscow, Perm and in other regions), the Association of Policewomen (in St Petersburg) and the Russian Association of University Women. There are also educational and cultural organisations which provide lectures, seminars, psychological training and professional retraining for women. Good examples are the Petersburg Centre for Gender Issues, the International Institute of Women and Management in St Petersburg, the organisation 'Femina' in Naberezhnye Chelny and the Congress of Women of the Kola Peninsula.

New types of groups and organisations have also sprung up. The first independent lesbian group, MOLLI (an abbreviation for the Moscow Organisation of Lesbian Literature and Art) introduced itself at the Dubna meeting in 1992. Two additional groups in St Petersburg should also be mentioned here: Sappho-Petersburg (which split away from the mixed gay–lesbian Chaikovski Foundation), and a Club of Independent Women which provides a newsletter for contacts and personal advertisements for lesbian women (and gay men) around Russia. Sappho-Petersburg organises cultural events and has developed an educational programme. It aims to challenge homophobia and to alter social consciousness.

New developments can also be observed in the appearance of the first few crisis centres and hotlines for women (and men) who have experienced sexual or domestic violence. These organisations adopt a feminist ideology. The first centre, 'Syostry', resulted from the initiative of a US organisation, the Consortium of Women USA–CIS. This centre opened in Moscow in 1994 and a second one followed in St Petersburg in 1995. There are now about fifteen such centres all over Russia and they are all connected in information networks.

One example of how hotlines have been used is that of 22 May 1995, when the St Petersburg Crisis Centre, working with the Russian Association of Psychological Aid Hotlines, organised a special 'Day of Hotline Telephone Calls', supported by the Ford Foundation. Constituting the first event of its kind, it aimed to gain a fuller picture of the problem of violence against women. It endeavoured to educate women about human rights, to collect more accurate statistics and further to promote the psychological crisis services for women in Russia.[4] Altogether, twenty-four cities participated in this day and the results will be published along with the broader consequences for crisis services. This illustrates a successfully functioning network in the area of voluntary organisations.

The most inspiring and successful example of the social and political voluntary activity of women is provided by the Committee of Soldiers' Mothers of Russia (CSMR), also discussed by Kathryn Pinnick in chapter eight. It is inspiring partly because of the severity of the social problems with which they deal, concerning a large number of Russian women. The committee was founded in 1989 and worked with some positive results to improve conditions in the Russian military.[5] Its members have contacts or regional branches in fourteen of the former Soviet republics. The overall structure of the organisation is democratic with horizontal connections and a very effective network. One successful event was a Mothers' March for Life and Compassion to Chechnia in March 1995; hundreds of soldiers' mothers were given emotional welcomes in every town they visited. The CMSSR has managed to organise lobbying of military and governmental authorities and has persuaded them to negotiate. The International Peace Bureau nominated the CSMR for the 1996 Nobel Peace Prize.[6]

Feminist groups are a small but developing category among women's groups. In 1991, in Dubna there was only one registered organisation with an institutional base, namely the Moscow Centre for Gender Studies. Another group called SAFO (abbreviated from the Free Association of Feminist Organisations) was established just a year before, but did not develop. Members of this group formed their own organisations later, including the Petersburg Centre for Gender Issues, FALTA (Feminist Alternative) in Moscow and 'Syostry'. Today one can count more than ten organisations which openly apply the feminist label to themselves. Among them are the already mentioned 'Femina' in Naberezhnye Chelny, Women's Light in Tver, the Karelian Centre for Gender Studies and the Femin Club in Kemerovo.

Feminist organisations are more experienced than non-feminist groups in cross-cultural relations with Western counterparts, have a better knowledge of foreign languages and were the first to set up projects that cooperated with Western organisations and which benefited from funding. They play, or attempt to play, a role which coordinates women's activity in Russia today. Developing such coordination, however, is not simple and the dynamic is complicated.

Problems of feminism in Russia

The first problem facing feminism is that it is still not very popular in Russian society and many women activists try to disassociate themselves from feminist ideology. Second, the process of institutionalising non-governmental activity, particularly institutionalising specifically women's NGOs, inevitably causes opposition between pragmatists and idealists. This very common phenomenon is now experienced in Russia, too.

Pragmatism is a desirable quality in social and political activism, as are idealistic values. But a sustainable balance between them is necessary. In post-Soviet Russian reality, where a hierarchical and dependent mentality is still very strong, it seems that pragmatists have a greater chance of survival and greater ability to influence non-governmental movements. The dynamic is obvious: when access to funds was recognised, there were more and more newcomers to the women's movement who were seeking jobs and were not very concerned or informed about feminist and women's issues and ideals. They quickly grasped the value of information and resources and began to accumulate and control them.

Of course, there were enough human resources to put together projects, to define the ideas of different groups and individuals and to gather information. These pragmatic women were also successful in writing grant proposals, receiving the money and having full control over its distribution. They achieved considerable status and repeated this strategic cycle again and again.

There is, none the less, a positive outcome of such activity. Increasing numbers of women are coming together for seminars and activities organised by this '*nomenklatura*' and gradually more information is being disseminated. But on the negative side there is a devaluation of ideals and an establishment of hierarchies which have a serious impact on the broader movement.

A third problem is that feminist activity in Russia seems to be mainly in the area of theoretical research and study and less concerned with social and political activism. This is a pity because feminists as a group still have more experience and greater theoretical knowledge than non-feminists. This preoccupation can be explained by divisions and by a lack of trust between women activists and feminists and well as among feminists themselves.

The future of the women's movement, however, is positive. Educational programmes have appeared within the movement which provide for the spread of knowledge about organisational management. There are also legal consultations for women's groups and for individuals, consciousness-raising groups, psychological training in leadership skills and assertiveness, as well as information passed on about communications technology.

An important role was played here by international contacts through feminist groups. A very successful project has been the Network of East–West Women (NEWW), with its headquarters in Washington D.C., which unites more than fifty organisations in East-Central Europe, the CIS, USA and Western Europe by electronic mail. This large project is the most successful international cooperation between different feminist and women's groups in the East and West.

Another large and fruitful project which grew out of the NEWW was the formation in 1995 of a Russian Legal Committee and then of a Legal Committee of the CIS. This is a network of professional lawyers, feminists and political activists, working together in advocacy and in support of women's human rights. The work of the Legal Committee is a qualitative leap towards recognising the importance of political participation. Part of the project is establishing Committees on Gender Expertise of legislative bills, which amounts to a civilian supervision of the legislative process in terms of gender equality.

Recognition of the importance of joint action and of a unification of the women's movement is reflected in the appearance of an increasing number of regional associations. Examples include the Association of

Humanitarian Initiatives in Mirny, Sakha republic (formerly Yakutia), the Association of Women's Organisations of the Voronezh Region, "Ne ZhDI' (Don't Wait), the Council of Women of the Don region, the Women's Union of the Baikal region and many others.

The exchange of information is also growing and over the last three years a growing number of independent women's and feminist newsletters, bulletins and journals have been published. The bulletin *All Men are Sisters*, issued twice yearly since 1993 by the Petersburg Centre for Gender Issues, is 300 pages long and 1,000 copies have been distributed free in many regions of Russia. The literary feminist journal *Preobrazhenie* is published as an almanac by a group of the same name in Moscow. In Volgograd a feminist newspaper, *Women's Games*, has appeared. In Moscow, ZHIF, or Women's Innovation Fund, has put out a bi-monthly newsletter *Woman Plus/Zhenshchina Plius* (in English and in Russian). The periodical *Vy i My* (You and us) is published in Russian in the USA by a joint Russian–American editorial board. There are also on-line conferences, *Sisters* in Glasnet (in Russian) and *Network East–West Women* (in English). These all constitute important steps in the further integration of the women's movement in Russia.

Political consciousness and the Duma

The political consciousness of Russian women in general and of women activists in particular is yet to be developed. The results of the elections of 17 December 1995 to the State Duma (*Gosudarstvennaia Duma*) showed a decline in elected female members. Before the elections of December 1993, a new political movement, 'Women of Russia', was organised.[7] It was formed from an alliance of three organisations which provided them with federal status (that is, they had departments in more than twenty-two subjects of the Russian Federation), thus allowing their participation in the elections. The three organisations were the Union of Women of Russia (the former Soviet Women's Committee), the Association of Women Entrepreneurs of Russia and the Union of the Women of the Navy (which actually refers mainly to the wives of navy officers). Since all three organisations had a well-organised structure throughout Russia, official connections and access to finances, they were capable of finding enough supporters among voters.

So the proportion of women in parliament rose to 11.9 per cent, including independent candidates. But within the space of two years the alliance 'Women of Russia' did not manage to present a clear political platform, had not shown any positive results from their legislative work and, as a result, failed to win the necessary 5 per cent on the party list of the elections of 1995. This can partly be explained by their vote in the Duma in support of the war in Chechnia, which probably deterred many women from voting for them. They fell short, by 0.39 per cent, of the 5 per cent barrier on the party list for entering the Duma as a political faction.[8]

None the less, it should be noted that the number of women candidates in the previous elections of 1993 was twice as small – a mere 7 per cent of those standing, not including 'Women of Russia'. In 1995 the figure rose to 14 per cent. Similarly, the number of political parties and political movements putting forward candidates rose from thirteen to forty-three.[9] Many of these electoral blocs and political alliances included women candidates near the top of their party lists, which was not the case in 1993. These were Iabloko (Apple), Obshchee Delo (The Common Cause), Narodnyi Soiuz (the People's Union), the bloc Pamfilova-Furiev and others.[10]

The facts, however, do not illustrate a general acceptance of women's political participation by Russian society. Women of Russia's failure suggests that ordinary voters do not favour women deputies; indeed, the general trend in society is just the opposite. We are now witnessing the revival of patriarchal tendencies in Russian society and of the traditional image of motherhood.

So we are still waiting for a qualitative step towards the recognition of the basic and important right of women to be equally represented in politics. The first step towards this, however, has been taken, since there are growing numbers of women who understand this necessity. All in all, the poorer performance of Women of Russia on the one hand and the appearance of more politically active women from independent newly formed organisations and political unions seems to be positive, as they indicate changes in old political structures. The old guard is leaving and its space is gradually being occupied by a new generation.

Simultaneously, we must not overlook the fact that members of Women of Russia did not constitute a homogeneous group. Most members possessed a certain level of political experience which could have been used more effectively if they had had a clearer goal and sharper political platform, and had cooperated more with non-governmental organisations of women (although some of its members, such as Liudmila Zavadskaia, were very open to contacts with women activists and women's NGOs).

Moreover, a positive feature of Women of Russia's existence is that it is an example of a movement based on the gender principle, which seems to be a necessity in a society with such a strong patriarchal tradition. Most of the television programmes and articles in the media which covered the elections expressed, either directly or indirectly, a certain level of misogyny: political commentators, politicians (including Anatolii Sobchak, mayor of St Petersburg) and showmen referred to the physical or sexual appearance of women in Women of Russia and paid practically no attention to their political programme.

Successful candidates of a 'new' type

Characteristic of one type of election campaign run by a woman is that of Valentina Cherevatenko, a candidate of a 'new' type and co-founder of the women's association, Union of Women of the Don.[11] She stood as an independent candidate for the Duma, organising her campaign with very few financial resources and based mainly on the collective voluntary efforts of her supporters. Her opponents were very strong, representing the Communist Party of the Russian Federation and the political bloc of Prime Minister Viktor Chernomyrdin which enjoyed state financial support.

Her clear political position stressed the importance of women's participation in politics because 'the world in which we live consists of Men and Women'.[12] Cherevatenko argued that women's political participation was necessary for the peaceful solution of military conflicts and for social welfare provision for everyone. Her positive political record as a deputy in the city soviet of Novocherkassk, her committee experience concerned with women, motherhood and childhood and her formation of the Union of Women of the Don in 1993 were not sufficient to help her win a seat in the Duma. She came third. This lends credence to the finding of Elena Kochkina and her colleagues in their *Report on the legal status of women in Russia*. Kochkina convincingly shows that the probability of independent candidates (that is, those not belonging to any political or electoral blocs) winning is less favourable for women than for men due to a lack of access to financial resources from state funds.[13]

Galina Starovoitova is another interesting woman politician. In the 1995 elections she competed successfully against twenty-four male candidates in a local constituency of St Petersburg. Her track record in all elections since 1989 has been good: she became a deputy of the Supreme Soviet in 1989 and was the first in parliament to refuse the 'Socialist Way of Development'. She underwent fierce resistance from most politicians in the Supreme Soviet. Starovoitova's professional education made her an expert in ethnic/national relations and she was advisor to Yel'tsin on ethnic and nationality problems in 1990–2. Back in 1989, she was insisting on the elimination of the quota system for women in parliament. But after her bitter experience of sexism from Russian politicians, and after some time spent in the West (once she had been dismissed by Yel'tsin), through contacts with Western feminists she began to perceive the existence of discrimination against women in politics.

In the first half of 1996, the campaign for the presidential elections began. Debates among political scientists and journalists totally excluded the possibility of a female candidate since they focused on the hostilities between democrats and communists. Unexpectedly, however, the democratic alliance nominated Starovoitova as a candidate. The first stage of the campaign included the collection of signatures in support of all registered nominees: in order to be included on the voting list, nominees had to collect 1 million signatures in all, and no more than 70,000 from each region or subject of the Russian Federation. Thus signatures had to come from a spread of regions.

Starovoitova, however, was accused of having falsified signatures on her list, so on 26 April she was not accepted as a candidate by the Central Electoral Commission. She and her support group appealed against this decision, but the appeal was rejected in early May by the Supreme Court. Interestingly, some of the male candidates rejected on the same grounds, such as the millionaire Vladimir Bryntsalov, won their appeals and therefore became registered candidates for the presidential election. After the rejection of Starovoitova's candidacy, the initiative group which had supported her in the first place issued an appeal to women to express their dissatisfaction with the process of registration.

The women's movement, however, despite now being more developed and connected through information networks, was not prepared to start a campaign in support of Starovoitova. Even those who recognised the importance of this were not able to do it through lack of time and insufficient human resources; others did not accept the idea of a woman president at all. Most of the arguments voiced against her were based either on her gender or upon her appearance –

she was considered not attractive enough. Nobody referred to her political platform, to her career or to her professionalism.

Here may be the proof that Russia's women's and feminist movements are not yet prepared for real political action. The reasons include a lack of human resources, insufficient social consciousness about gender equality, an intensity of patriarchalism in Russian society, and poor access to economic resources for women in general and for women's groups in particular.

Conclusion

In sum, women's activism between 1992 and 1996 was growing. If at the beginning of 1993 there were about one hundred registered women's organisations all over Russia, by the end of 1995 there were already more than 400.[14] There are also even more grassroots organisations and groups working without official registration. In addition, due to the development of information technology and growing social consciousness, there is a greater convergence of groups. Many associations are being formed at local, regional and inter-regional levels. Increasing numbers of new independent women's and feminist publications, newsletters, bulletins and newspapers are being published and distributed, thereby exchanging information and sharing experiences.

None the less, the development of civil society in contemporary Russia is positive. Since 1992 the women's movement had grown significantly. Increasing numbers of women realise that current changes in social and political life affect them seriously, and the diversity of orientation and goals of these groups is also growing. Women's voices are increasingly expressed in the media, such as on television programmes, in women's pages of the democratic press and in independent women's publications.

Connections are also being established between women's organisations and feminist organisations. Practical work provided by the more advanced feminist projects on organisational skills, information technology, political lobbying, consciousness-raising and education contribute to developing the political consciousness of Russian women.

Discussions about civil society in the West may be different because the level of development there is not comparable with that of Russia and other states of the former Soviet bloc. Western feminists and political scientists can argue about definitions and merits of the idea, but it is obvious that, in our contemporary situation, civil society and its development are an ABC learning experience and a foundation for the social and political survival of society, the state and individuals. And the women's movement, the NGOs and the activists are all playing significant roles in this process, providing a basis for future generations, for democratic structures and for equality of the sexes.

Notes

1 For discussion of earlier developments under Gorbachev, see Olga Lipovskaia, 'New women's organisations' in Mary Buckley (ed.), *Perestroika and Soviet women* (Cambridge: Cambridge University Press, 1992), pp. 72–81.
2 The examples are taken from *The directory of women's organisations* (St Petersburg: Petersburg Centre for Gender Issues, January 1996).
3 The shelter 'Euphimia' was closed at the end of March 1996 by a decision of the city's mayor, Anatolii Sobchak, because of Euphimia's refusal to accept official surveillance from the mayor's office. This was announced by Sobchak on local television on 13 March 1996. Euphimia's refusal was motivated by the impossibility of getting funds from Western foundations and charity groups if they become a governmental structure. In fact, the case of Euphimia is characteristic of the relationship between governmental institutions and social groups. Bureaucratic structures try to impose control over non-governmental groups without providing the necessary support, in order to pretend that social issues are being dealt with.
4 Larissa Korneva, Alla Shaboltsa, Ol'ga Kochiarian, Natal'ia Khodyreva, 'Report on the work of the Petersburg Crisis Centre', delivered at a conference in Repino on 'Feminist theory and practice: east–west', organised by the Petersburg Centre for Gender Issues, 6–9 June, 1995.
5 For a description of the Organisation of Soldiers' Mothers in Ukraine, see Solomea Pavlychko, 'Between feminism and nationalism' in Buckley (ed.), *Perestroika and Soviet women*, pp. 94–5.
6 Information received from the on-line conference opened by the Network of East–West Women, 1 February 1996.
7 For a fuller discussion of this movement, see Mary Buckley's preceding chapter.
8 Elena Kochkina, Elena Ballaeva, Nadezhda Kuznetsova, Elena Tiuriukanova, *Report on the legal status of women in Russia: contemporary debates*. This is an independent report provided for a Project of the Legal Committee of the NEWW, April 1996. It has not yet been published.
9 Data from Svetlana Aivazova, presented at a seminar on 'From results to perspectives', December 1995, Moscow, organised by the Women's Information Project ADL and the Information Centre of the Independent Women's Forum.

10 Elena Kochkina, '0.39 per cent of power', *Nezavisimaia Gazeta*, 28 December 1995, p. 5.
11 Cherevatenko's career also includes setting up a private business in 1992 with her husband. This is significant since the careers of many women politicians in Russia today are combined with business. It can be assumed that women with certain economic and political status and experience easily recognise the necessity of political influence.
12 Brochure of Valentina Cherevatenko's 1995 election programme.
13 Kochkina, *et al.*, *Report on the legal status of women in Russia*.
14 *Ibid.*

PART 2

Women outside Russia in newly independent states

11 Women in changing societies: Latvia and Lithuania

NIJOLE WHITE

The process of national awakening which had begun in the Baltic republics of the Soviet Union in earnest in 1988 led to declarations of independence in 1990 in Lithuania and in 1991 in Latvia. Following these there began the so-called 'period of transition', a transition from Soviet political and economic structures and way of life to full democracy and market-based economic relations. General changes affecting the populations at that time also had a profound effect on women.

The situation of women in Latvia and Lithuania is well documented. There are many women academics who have been doing research in women's issues, and there is much activity in women's organisations which have been set up since independence. Large numbers of women journalists have been promoting awareness of the problems women face. In a relatively short time they have together amassed a considerable body of information on the situation of women in their respective countries. The present essay draws on some of this material.[1]

Before going on to examine various aspects of the situation of women since independence, it is useful to note that although Latvia and Lithuania are relatively more detached from the other former republics (they have not joined the CIS) and more Western-oriented (as they were while still part of the USSR), the commonality of their Soviet experience has ensured that changes which have been taking place there are, in the main, very similar to what is happening in Russia and some other parts of the former Soviet Union.

Between Latvia and Lithuania there are many similarities, but there are also some significant differences. The similarities stem from their common ethnic origins – both are descended from the Baltic tribes and speak languages which belong to the same linguistic group (though Lithuanians do not understand Latvian and vice versa). The differences have been determined by lengthy periods of existence under different foreign domination. The most noticeable of these differences is religion: Lithuanians are Roman Catholic, through association with Poland, whereas Latvians are Lutheran Protestant – Latvian culture developed under the influence of Germans and Swedes. Latvia also has more heavy industry than Lithuania and a much higher proportion of its population is comprised of 'foreigners'.[2] The proportion of males and females in their populations, however, is very similar. In January 1994, women made up 53.6 per cent of the population of Latvia which at that time numbered 2.5 million, and 52.7 per cent of the population of Lithuania which was 3.7 million.[3]

Women and work

Women's participation in the work force is a fluctuating figure with a tendency to decrease as economic reforms create rising levels of unemployment. In Lithuania, in January 1995 women made up 50.1 per cent of the work force; in 1993 this figure was 52.4 per cent. In 1985 it had been 52.2 per cent. In Latvia, in 1993 women made up 47.8 per cent of those in work, compared with 54.9 per cent in 1985.

Women worked in such traditionally feminised sectors as health (in Lithuania they made up 84 per cent of all health workers, and in Latvia 81.7 per cent), education (75 per cent in Lithuania, 77.7 per cent in Latvia), hotels and catering (87 per cent in Lithuania, 70.7 per cent in Latvia), trade (81 per cent in Lithuania, 65.2 per cent in Latvia), and also in manufacturing (53 per cent in Lithuania, 46.4 per cent in Latvia).[4] In many occupations, even in teaching, there existed an 'occupational pyramid', or vertical segregation: the number of women, which may have been large among non-promoted posts, decreased at the top. In Lithuania, for example, in 1991 women teachers made up 85 per cent of the total, but only 32 per cent of heads of secondary schools were women.[5]

In both Latvia and Lithuania, women were proportionately better educated than men. More girls stayed on in the senior classes of secondary schools, more entered higher education. In 1995 young women made up 56 per cent of students in higher education in Latvia and 55.2 per cent in Lithuania.[6] However, this did not bring them commensurate material rewards. The professions with high numbers of women – such as doctors, teachers and architects, which required the highest educational qualifications – were still poorly remunerated, just as they had been in Soviet times.

In the first quarter of 1994 in Latvia, women's and men's average earnings were 53.7 and 69.7 lats a month respectively. Men on average earned 1.3 times more than women. In every sector of activity, women's wages were lower than the average for that sector. For example, in education average pay was 51.3 lats, with women earning 48.8 lats a month and men, 58.8.[7] In Lithuania the average income for men was 1.4 times higher than it was for women.[8]

In Lithuanian urban areas in 1994, 3.5 per cent of men and 3.1 per cent of women were unemployed,[9] but according to the official data provided by the Lithuanian Labour Exchange, unemployed women comprised two-thirds of the total numbers of the unemployed.[10] In Latvia official unemployment was also low and approximately equal for males and females at 6 per cent. Women constituted 53 per cent of the unemployed.[11] Hidden unemployment in Latvia was estimated to be in the region of 12 per cent, and 'disproportionately female'.[12]

In the climate of economic reform when jobs are becoming increasingly scarce, there is a tendency to think that men have more right to a job than women. Lithuanian survey figures on this show that this view, predictably, is held by more men in the sample (72 per cent) than women (54 per cent).[13] There is evidence to suggest that women continue to place a high value on having a job and that losing their job is as traumatic for them as it is for men.[14]

Finding out how many people have started their own business or are working in the private sector as employees is problematic because private sector employers are apt to conceal the real numbers and the gender of their employees in order to avoid paying social insurance and other taxes. In Lithuania in 1993, women accounted for 47.7 per cent of all the private sector employees and employers.[15] Data from Latvia indicate that only very small numbers (under 10 per cent) have started their own business[16] and that men in this sector outnumber women by 2.5 or even 3:1.[17]

Discrimination against women in employment appears to exist but is difficult to document. Gender- and age-specific job advertisements are frequently published in the press both in Latvia and in Lithuania, although when questioned in a survey in early 1994, Latvian employers asserted that selection of staff was determined by applicants' professional qualifications and not by their gender.[18] A Lithuanian survey conducted at the same time found that only 12 per cent of women had experienced discrimination at work or at the time of being selected for a job.[19] The authors of the report explain this low number not by absence of discrimination but by low awareness: it tends to be expected and is therefore not noticed. There exists, however, a popular belief that employers, especially those in the private sector, prefer to appoint young, attractive and compliant women who would also be ready to provide sexual favours.[20]

In the new economic context the relative importance of work and family to women has undergone a slight change. While family and children are still placed at the top of the scale of values by a majority of women, work is catching up. Survey data from Lithuania show that, in 1990, 42 per cent of women rated work as 'very important', in 1992 the figure was 47 per cent, and in 1994 it went up to 63 per cent.[21] Earning an income remains an economic necessity for women, and for some it is also important as a way of realising their potential, of 'fulfilling themselves'. However, a considerable number of women – 56 per cent – still say that, 'circumstances permitting', they would 'prefer not to work, and to devote themselves to their families'.[22]

Within the family, the unequal distribution of household responsibilities between husband and wife remains, although the phrase 'double burden' is no longer used. In Lithuania Giedrė Purvaneckienė, a sociologist from Vilnius University, has established that in three-quarters of families, food preparation and laundry are done by women, and in two-thirds they do the cleaning. In only 20 per cent of families do husband and wife perform some the tasks together.[23] In Latvia popular opinion does not associate the unequal distribution of household tasks between husband and wife with women's rights or with their opportunities, and sees it as an acceptable traditional division of labour.[24]

Women's employment opportunities have been adversely affected by the curtailment of state child care provision, and also by fee increases to unaffordable levels for the remaining facilities. The Latvian report prepared for the Fourth United Nations World Conference on Women in Beijing recognises that 'maternal responsibilities' limit women's employment, noting at the same time a 'sharp reduction in the number of kindergartens'[25] and the fact that 'during the transition years pre-school enrolments have dropped by half'.[26] The Lithuanian report states that by 1990 'every child was assured day care services': the provision then was 1,681 day care centres (813 in urban areas and 868 in rural areas). In 1993 the overall figure had dropped to 928, with an especially sharp decrease in rural areas – down to 292, while in urban areas it was down to 626.[27] Both reports note that public opinion tends to frown on women who want to send their children to childcare establishments. In Lithuania, in the past 'using day care centres was considered unpatriotic, because it was part of Soviet reality'.[28] In Latvia, day care facilities had only been available to 61 per cent of children and were of poor quality. They were held to be a factor in creating 'fertile ground for the idealisation of the patriarchal family structure' and even for 'casting the usefulness of women's gainful employment into doubt'.[29]

Abortion

Given the fact that family, and children especially, are very important to women in both societies, it is paradoxical that abortion has been so widespread. In Soviet times it was viewed not as a right, a freedom for a woman to control her reproduction, but as a painful economic necessity, an injustice that the system had inflicted on women because it was unable to provide them with more humane methods of contraception. In post-independence years the level of the use of contraceptives has remained very low: a full range of these is now available, but they are either too expensive or unacceptable. Abortion – which a report on Lithuanian women prepared by Giedrė Purvaneckienė refers to as 'a woman's main problem'[30] – remains the chief method of regulating reproduction. In Latvia for every 100 births there are 120 to 130 abortions.[31] In Lithuania the figure is lower – 80 abortions per 100 births.[32]

Both countries have significant anti-abortion movements and support groups for women, especially single mothers, who decide not to terminate an unwanted pregnancy. For example, 'Action "Life"' is one of the directions of the Latvian charity Misija Pakāpieni, a Christian organisation, which offers advice to women who are experiencing an unwanted pregnancy. It also appeals to 'good people' to open the doors of their homes to those young mothers who have nowhere else to go immediately after they give birth.[33]

The attitude to abortion in Lithuania is partly dependent on individual disinclination to resort to it and is partly influenced by the Catholic Church, the Catholic press, Catholic women's organisations and the Lithuanian affiliate of the World Federation of Doctors 'Pro-Human Life'. A study of the population's attitudes to abortion conducted in 1994[34] has shown that in most cases both women and men disapprove of abortion. This is especially the case among older and less educated people. The index of approval/disapproval used in this survey was calculated on a scale of 1–10, where 1 equalled unconditional approval and 10 unconditional disapproval. The result was 3.5 for men and 3.4 for women. However, when the sample were asked if they would support complete prohibition or severe limitation of abortion, only 27 per cent of men and 25 per cent of women said they would. Among those who did not wish to ban abortion but who thought that the population should be informed about alternatives to it, were 36 per cent of men and 38 per cent of women in the sample. Women's right to choose was supported by 32 per cent of men and 34 per cent of women. Against the expectations of the Church, the overwhelming majority do not condemn abortion in cases where a mother's health is threatened (94 per cent), or where the baby is expected to be born with a physical or mental abnormality (88 per cent).

In the process of transition towards full democracy in their societies, the Baltic states wish to follow the West, and especially Scandinavian countries, in providing opportunities for family planning. In September 1994, Lithuania's Ministry of Health approved a programme of family planning. As part of this programme the Republic Family Planning Centre was established in Vilnius. The centre hopes to 'improve women's physical and emotional well-being and thus also their quality of life'.[35]

Women in politics

Women's participation in decision-making in the political structures of the states of Latvia and Lithuania is consistent with trends in all post-communist societies. In the post-independence or 'transition' period it has declined sharply compared with Soviet times. This is not viewed as a great loss for women, since in Soviet times numbers had been high only in those structures which had no real power – the Supreme Soviets and the local soviets. There had never been significant numbers of women either at the top level of the Communist Party or in the government, where real decision-making took place.

In Lithuania the number of women in parliament (Seimas) in 1990 was fourteen – they made up 10 per cent of the total membership of 141 (down from 35.7 per cent in 1985).[36] In 1993 there were ten women in the Seimas (7 per cent of its membership).[37] In Latvia in 1993, women members in their parliament (Saeima) comprised 15 per cent compared to one-third in 1980. In local government after the municipal elections of May 1994, women's representation was higher

– 39.1 per cent, compared to 49.2 per cent in 1980.[38] In Lithuania the figures for local government are shown only for mayors – all fifty-five of them are men – and for heads of municipal councils – one woman and fifty-four men.[39]

The numbers of women in top government positions (with the exception of Lithuania's Prime Minister Kazimiera Prunskienė, who held her office from March 1990 to January 1991) remain insignificant. In 1994, in Lithuania there was only one woman deputy minister and one ambassador.[40] In Latvia there were no women in the first two post-independence governments, but since 1994 the situation has improved: there is one minister – Vita Tērauda, minister for state reform; one state minister and four state secretaries are women; and there are five women diplomats. Women occupy such positions as director of the First Political Department in the Ministry of Foreign Affairs (Argita Daudze), director of the Saeima Information Department (Anita Dūdiņa) and state secretary at the Ministry of Welfare (Maija Poršņova). Women members of the Saeima are respectively chair and vice-chair of parliamentary committees on human rights (Ieva Arbidāne) and budget and finance (Aija Poča).[41]

In analysing the reasons why women's representation is so low, researchers cite factors such as the election system where voting is for party lists on which women's names are usually far down the list, and also lack of respect in society for women politicians which means that voters are reluctant to give their support to women candidates. A study conducted in Lithuania in 1994 to ascertain the population's attitude to women in politics established that their absence from the corridors of power was neither noticed nor deplored.[42] Forty-two per cent of those questioned thought that women's participation should remain at current (low) levels, 27 per cent did not want them to participate at all, while those who wanted women's participation to increase made up 23 per cent.[43] In considering measures which could help to increase women's participation, 42 per cent of the sample thought that women should strive to get their names entered nearer to the top of political parties' lists. The same percentage were of the opinion that women should be educated to want political participation. Devising a quota system for women was supported by 35 per cent. A more radical measure of women-only electoral lists attracted the least support – 25 per cent. Even those people who favoured increased participation by women did not advocate radical change: rather they were for a slow, 'natural' increase.[44]

Increasing the numbers of women in politics is viewed as imperative by many Lithuanian and Latvian women who are prominent in the field of women's studies. For example, Giedrė Purvaneckienė emphasises that women's participation is a 'must': without a proportionate participation their young democracy will not be a true democracy, nor will it be possible to achieve a society more favourable to women than the existing one. Society based on men's experience alone, which is very different from women's experience, cannot be favourable to women.[45]

Women's organisations

While women appear only infrequently in the structures of political power, public life in Latvia and Lithuania is by no means devoid of their representation. Women who had been active in laying the foundations of their respective independent states in 1917–18 and who subsequently founded numerous organisations to promote women's interests and women's rights, served as an inspiration for the generation who took an active part in the 'singing revolution' of 1988–90. In 1995 there were some thirty women's organisations in Lithuania and fifteen in Latvia. Some of these grew out of the broad independence movements – the Latvian Popular Front and the Lithuanian Sąjūdis – when these began to split into more clearly defined political groups, political parties and other organisations. Others were revived or re-created pre-war organisations, such as the Lithuanian University Women's Association (LUMA) and the Latvian Association of Academically Educated Women (LAISA), and organisations of religious or patriotic orientation. The desire for unity gave way to a diversity of views: there appeared party-affiliated women's organisations, and also ethnically based groups of Polish and of Jewish women. Latvian and Lithuanian businesswomen have established their own organisations: the Businesswomen's Association of Lithuania and, in Latvia, the Women's Business Club.

Many of these organisations share a common aim – promoting women's rights and the advancement of women.[46] They are also aware that unity would make them more effective, and therefore they have sought to coordinate their activities. The Latvian Women's Organisations' Cooperative Council was created in the autumn of 1992, following the example of such cooperation in the inter-war years; each organisation was to send two authorised members to the council which would endeavour to work on the principle of consensus, leaving any matters not acceptable to the individual organisations for them to resolve by themselves.[47] A similar coordinating role in Lithuania is played by the Lithuanian Women's Association, created in 1992.[48]

A conference of the Lithuanian Women's Association held in January 1995 was devoted to examining the work of women's organisations and their perspectives. Some 200 participants of the conference heard a proposal voiced by a businesswoman and media personality from Kaunas, Dalia Teišerskytė, that a women's political party be set up in Lithuania. She reported that preparatory work had brought in some 700 letters of intent to join such a party. The aims of this emergent party are to foster women's ability to express themselves, to develop their sense of citizenship and to attract as many women into politics as possible. It hopes to influence public opinion so that more people are in favour of a real chance for women to take part in the running of the state. The new party will stand for creating equal opportunities for women and men.[49]

A coordinating body – the *ad hoc* coordination committee of Lithuanian Women's Organisations, set up in autumn of 1993 – later took on the responsibility for preparatory activities for the Fourth United Nations World Conference on Women. As the conference remit required preparation at two levels – governmental and non-governmental – an artificial division was created and some duplication of effort occurred. In Lithuania the *ad hoc* 'non-governmental' committee asked the government to establish a 'governmental' National Preparatory Committee. At about the same time, the position of state counsellor on women's issues was created at the Office of the Prime Minister of Lithuania. Giedrė Purvaneckienė, a prominent academic, became the occupant of this position. A governmental National Preparatory Committee for the Fourth UN World Conference on Women was also set up in Latvia in 1994. It included a number of women in the government of Latvia (it was chaired by the minister for state reform), several women academics and two women MPs as well as leading members of some women's organisations. The report they produced was an example of close cooperation between governmental and non-governmental levels of women's activity.[50]

Preparations for the conference were accompanied by an increase in awareness of women's issues in Latvia, and especially in Lithuania, where they also stimulated new research. Special projects aimed at collecting the latest data for presentation in the national report on women were initiated, financed by the UN Development Fund and by the Lithuanian government. A newsletter of activities was published in

Lithuanian (*Moters Pasaulis*) and in English (*Woman's World*). In the run-up to the event in Beijing there was an upsurge in conferences, summer camps and workshops, held by many women's organisations in Lithuania and in Latvia. The enthusiasm surrounding this stemmed from the fact that, for women from the Baltic states, this was the first time they were to appear as independents in the international arena: as part of the Soviet Union, global strategies for dealing with women's problems and for advancement of women elaborated at the three preceding UN conferences had bypassed them.[51]

Women's studies

Research activity associated with preparations for Beijing built upon a rich tradition that goes back some twenty-five to thirty years. When study of society was resurrected in the Soviet Union in the 1960s, the Baltic republics were at the forefront. Among the key themes were the problems of the family and marriage, this interest being encouraged by the government which was concerned over the declining birth rate, especially in the European part of the USSR. Under the general umbrella of 'family', women's issues also began to be studied.[52]

A gender-specific approach remained strong in the tradition of the study of society that developed in the 1970s and into the 1980s. As their states gained independence, the orientation of scholars in Latvia and Lithuania began to change to involve comparisons with Central and West European and especially with Scandinavian countries. This was due to their desire to re-join Western culture, and also because of contacts with women of Latvian and Lithuanian origin who had worked in the USA, Canada, Germany, the UK and Sweden, as well as contacts with Western feminists. These were developed at international conferences and symposia.

The first academic conference at which work on women's issues was publicised took place in September 1991 in Riga. The conference had a general theme, 'Woman in space and time', and was organised by the Department of Sociology of the Latvian Academy. Its proceedings were published in a substantial volume entitled *Fragments of reality: insights on women in a changing society*.[53] The conference attracted many participants from Latvia – the Academy Institutes of Philosophy and Sociology and of Economics, the Latvian University, Riga Technical University, the University of Agriculture and other institutions – and also guest speakers from the USA, the UK, Sweden and Finland. The stated aim of the organisers was to 'bring together empirical and theoretical research on women's changing activities, behaviors, values and ideals' and to provide 'psychological, sociological and statistical portraits of women'.[54] The conference marked the beginning of women's studies in Latvia.

The beginning of women's studies in Lithuania was marked by two events: the international congress 'Woman in the changing world' which was held in May 1992, and the conference 'The paths of women: East and West', organised in August 1993. The latter event was the first academic conference on gender issues in Lithuania. Abstracts of papers presented at it were published in Lithuanian, English and German.[55] Conference participants included established women scholars from Lithuania, the USA, Canada, Mexico and Norway, as well as several students. The themes covered ranged from issues of women's health, education, women in philosophy and literature, women in the labour market and in politics, culture and science. There were also papers on value orientations of women and other aspects of identity.

Contact with Western feminists and increasing familiarity with gender discourse in the West introduced a new dimension to the study of women's issues. Experience of international women's studies was available in Lithuania in the person of Karla Gruodis: educated in the West, she taught various aspects of feminist theory at Vilnius University and was also researching ways to create an interface between the needs of Lithuanian women and 'foreign' feminism and women's studies.[56] To facilitate this work she prepared an anthology of feminist texts translated into Lithuanian from English and French.[57]

An important landmark in the development of research on women was the setting up of dedicated interdisciplinary Women's Studies Centres. In Lithuania the first such centre was initiated in 1992 by the Lithuanian Association of University Women at Vilnius University, followed by one at Kaunas Technological University. In 1992–3 the Vilnius centre was running a number of courses and seminars for students: feminist theory, women and culture, women and society and women in Lithuanian and world literature. In 1993 the main research themes of members of the centre were the sociology of women and the family (Giedrė Purvaneckienė); women and work (Vida Kanopienė); gender and Lithuanian national identity (Karla Gruodis); and various aspects of gender in literature (Marija Aušrinė Pavilionienė, Viktorija Daujotytė).[58]

The Latvian Women's Studies and Information Centre takes its inspiration from the tradition of women's studies in the Nordic countries. The centre states that it has 'all the preconditions' for such work; in particular, a tradition of research into 'socio-demographic' topics – research done in Latvia between 1966 and 1992. The list includes ten polls focused on such subjects as childbirth, marriage motivation, women with 'fatherless' children, time budgets, health, family and work. Latvian researchers recognise the continuity of their research tradition, but its drawbacks are also noted: this research was not focused specifically on women, it tended merely to list men's and women's views on a subject without generalisation or conclusions.[59] The Latvian centre was created in 1993 on the initiative of researchers working at the Institute of Economics and the Institute of Philosophy and Sociology of the Latvian Academy of Sciences. The centre is not involved in teaching; the main thrust of its activities is research ('to gather and disseminate sociological research results about the women of Latvia and women's organizations'), but it also organises seminars and discussions, collects publications, memoirs and photographs of women in Latvia and makes these materials available for consultation at the centre. Undertaking research projects and collecting statistics are part of its interests, too. Advice is available to those who wish to embark on research into women's issues and women's movements in other countries and the centre also advises on women's rights. Related to these activities are the centre's contacts with research establishments in Latvia and abroad as well as with Latvian women's organisations through their Cooperative Council.

A collection of articles and memoirs produced by members of the Latvian centre, *Women of Latvia – 75*, was published in Riga in 1994. As the title suggests, it is intended to cover women's situation over seventy-five years from the time a Latvian state was first created, but the bulk of the collection concentrates on women and the effects of economic and political change in the present. The work published in this collection provided much of the material used in the compilation of the Latvian National Report to the Fourth UN World Conference on Women.

Conclusion

Preparations for the Beijing conference were instrumental in mobilising for action the existing strengths of women researchers, women's organisations, women in parliament and in government. Two main strategic goals have been identified: work to put in place equal opportunities legislation and to create a framework for monitoring and enforcing such legislation, and a broad programme to educate women and society in general to view equal opportunities as the norm, to make society more aware of and more responsive to women's needs. The preparatory committees have stated the intention to continue to play their coordinating role since, as Giedrė Purvaneckienė put it, 'Most important is that after the conference the work should not stop there ... After the conference comes the most difficult stage; that is, putting into effect the tasks that were identified.'[60]

In the future, cooperation with women's movements outside the Baltic states is likely to continue to play a major part in shaping the strategy of the movements in Latvia and Lithuania and also in lending them support, both moral and material. The movements in the Baltic states are not inclined to follow the example of the women's movement in Russia because of their recent experience of Russian domination, preferring their inspiration to come from the Scandinavian countries or from North America. However, the women in the Baltic and the women in Russia have two major things in common: the Soviet experience which they are trying to leave behind, and the Western models of feminism which they strive to emulate to a greater or lesser extent. Therefore their goals and the forms of their activities are rather similar.

Indications are that the women's movements in Latvia and Lithuania are already sufficiently strong to be able to influence the process of policy making in their respective countries so that the policies that emerge are more favourable to women and help them to satisfy both their desire to have children and/or their wish to have a job and to play a part in public life.

Notes

1 The author wishes to acknowledge her gratitude to Argita Daudze and Terēze Svilane of the Latvian Ministry of Foreign Affairs, researchers at the Women's Studies Centres in Riga and in Vilnius, and especially to Dr Inna Zariņa and Dr Marija Aušrinė Pavilionienė. Special thanks go to Aija Tūna and Irena Litvinaitė of the Latvian and Lithuanian National Preparatory Committees for the Fourth UN World Conference on Women, Beijing 1995.

2 At the time of the 1989 Soviet population census, Latvians made up only 52 per cent of the population, compared with 80 per cent of Lithuanians in Lithuania. Karen Dawisha and Bruce Parrott, *Russia and the new states of Eurasia: the politics of upheaval* (Cambridge: Cambridge University Press, 1994), p. 338.

3 Sources of most of the statistical information presented here are: *Latvia: national report on the situation of women*. Latvian National Preparatory Committee for the Fourth UN World Conference on Women (Riga: 1995), hereafter referred to as *Lat. NR*; *Women in Lithuania: The national report to the Fourth UN World Conference of Women* (Vilnius, 1995), hereafter referred to as *Lith. NR*; *Lithuania: Women in a changing society. Report compiled by Lithuanian non-governmental women's organizations to be presented at the Fourth United Nations World Conference on Women in Beijing, 1995* (Vilnius: 1995), hereafter referred to as *Lithuania: Women*.
4 *Lat. NR*, p. 28; *Lith. NR*, p. 26; Marija Karalienė, 'Women in Lithuania (a statistical survey)', *Woman's World* 1, July 1994.
5 *Lith. NR*, p. 20.
6 Andris Bērziņš, 'Statement of the delegation of the Republic of Latvia to the Fourth World Conference on Women', p. 3 of typescript; *Lith. NR*, p. 21.
7 *Lat. NR*, p. 28. 1 lat is equal to 1.7 $US.
8 *Lith. NR*, p. 16.
9 *Lith. NR*, p. 26.
10 *Ibid.*
11 *Lat. NR*, p. 16.
12 Bērziņš, 'Statement', p. 2.
13 Giedrė Purvaneckienė, 'Women in the Republic of Lithuania', *Woman's World* 2, October 1994, p. 5.
14 Ilze Koroleva, 'Young women's attitude towards work: options, opportunities and reality' in *Women of Latvia – 75* (Riga: Zvaigzne, 1994), p. 35.
15 Karalienė, 'Women in Lithuania'.
16 Brigita Zepa, 'Women in times of economic change' in *Women of Latvia – 75* (Riga: Zvaigzne, 1994), p. 17.
17 *Lat. NR*, p. 14.
18 *Lat. NR*, p. 16.
19 *Lith. NR*, p. 14.
20 *Lat. NR*, p. 16.
21 Giedrė Purvaneckienė, 'Lithuanian women and the family' in *Lithuania: Women*, p. 41. The sum of all the percentages quoted here makes a variable figure well in excess of 100, indicating that more than one sphere of activity out of six – family, work, religion, friends, leisure and politics – could be cited as 'very important'.
22 *Ibid.*
23 *Ibid.*
24 *Lat. NR*, p. 14.
25 *Ibid.*, p. 16.
26 *Ibid.*, p. 10.
27 *Lith. NR*, p. 18.
28 *Ibid.*

29 *Lat. NR*, p. 10.
30 Purvaneckienė, 'Women in the Republic of Lithuania', p. 6.
31 Bērziņš, 'Statement', p. 3.
32 *Lith. NR*, p. 31.
33 'Misija Pakāpieni' leaflet.
34 Giedrė Purvaneckienė, 'Lithuanian population's view on abortion' in *Lithuania: Women*, pp. 44–5.
35 Dr Vytautas Klimas, 'Family planning: problems, goals and ways' in *Lithuania: Women*, p. 40.
36 Ona Voverienė, 'Women Parliamentarians' in *Lithuania: Women*, p. 18.
37 *Lith. NR*, p. 10.
38 *Lat. NR*, p. 24.
39 *Lith. NR*, p. 10.
40 *Ibid.*
41 *Lat. NR*, p. 39, list of members of the Latvian National Preparatory Committee for the Fourth UN World Conference on Women.
42 *Lith. NR*, p. 11.
43 Purvaneckienė, 'Women in the Republic of Lithuania', p. 2.
44 *Ibid.*, p. 3. The study also breaks down each response by gender; for example, opposition to women's participation in politics is higher among men (31 per cent) than among women (23 per cent); support for women-only lists is lower among men (21 per cent) than among women (28 per cent).
45 Giedrė Purvaneckienė, 'Nepamirškime – mūsų dauguma' (Let us not forget – we comprise the majority), *Moters Pasaulis (Woman's World)* 1(5), January–February 1995.
46 Giedrė Purvaneckienė, 'The Lithuanian women's organisations', *Woman's World* 1, July 1994.
47 Appendix ('Essential information') in *Women of Latvia – 75* (Riga: Zvaigzne, 1994), pp. 227–30.
48 Irena Litvinaitė, 'Demokratija negali galioti tik vyrams' (Democracy cannot be valid just for men), *Moters Pasaulis* 1(5), January–February, 1995. The Association is described in greater detail in 'Women's organisations' in *Lithuania: Women*, p. 60.
49 Irena Litvinaitė, 'Moterys išeina į didelį kelią' (Women join the mainstream), *Moters Pasaulis* 1(5), January–February, 1995.
50 Bērziņš, 'Statement', pp. 2–3.
51 *Lith. NR*, p. 7.
52 The first symposium on the family and related issues was held in Vilnius in 1967. The published materials of the symposium included such papers as 'The role of working woman in everyday life' and 'Woman's work and problems of leisure' in *Problemy byta, braka i sem'i* (Vilnius: Mintis, 1970).
53 *Fragments of reality: insights on women in a changing society* (Riga: Vaga, 1992).

54 Ilze Trapenciere, 'Preface', *Fragments of reality*, p. 3.
55 *Moters kelias: Rytai ir Vakarai*, referred to as *The paths of women: East and West* (Vilnius: 1993).
56 Karla Gruodis, 'Studying Lithuanian women', *The paths of women*, p. 8.
57 *Feminizmo ekskursai* (Excursions into feminism) (Vilnius: Pradai, 1995), compiled by Karla Gruodis.
58 Vilnius University Women's Studies Centre leaflet.
59 Inna Zariņa, 'The formation of the Latvian Women's Studies and Information Centre' in *Women of Latvia – 75* (Riga: Zvaigzne, 1994), pp. 199–200.
60 Giedrė Purvaneckienė, 'Why is the Beijing Conference important to us?', *Woman's World 5*, August 1995.

12 Progress on hold: the conservative faces of women in Ukraine

SOLOMEA PAVLYCHKO

The collapse of the Soviet Union and the declaration of independence were a fundamental turning point in the history of Ukraine. 1990 and 1991 were years of enormous political and social optimism, and at this time there was mass participation in the euphoric demolition of the totalitarian, imperialist, politically closed and economically bankrupt state. Over 90 per cent of Ukraine's population voted in favour of independence in the referendum on 1 December 1991 in the belief that they would be better off in a new country called Ukraine rather than in the USSR. The first parliamentary election of March 1990 and the presidential election of December 1991 showed high levels of electoral turn-out. Civic life was vibrant, new political parties emerged one after another, hundreds of NGOs were formed, laying the foundation of democracy and civil society. In this stormy process, new leaders emerged and, for the first time, alongside men's voices, women's voices were heard.

Crisis in Ukraine

The enormous crisis – sharp decline in production, inflation, widespread corruption and government prevarication when it came to reform – radically altered the situation in Ukraine in 1992–4. Words such as 'market', 'democracy', 'independence' and 'the West' began to lose their currency. It turned out that the market economy in its Ukrainian variant resembled a bazaar, and democratically elected parliaments were the main obstacle to reform. The West fixed its attention on Russia and took scant notice of the newly independent states. Old Soviet institutions and bureaucratic practices were preserved in the new Ukraine. The transition period became so stretched out that it seemed it was becoming permanent. The enthusiasm associated with the destruction of the old was replaced by uncertainty and a sense of the pointlessness of individual and social efforts.

Political parties and organisations, including women's organisations, continued to spring up as before. However, their role and popularity in society diminished. The democratic movement, which in 1990 counted millions of active sympathisers, fragmented into scores of small associations and organisations. Gradually the society was eaten away by apathy. Symptomatic of this was the March 1994 elections: parliament has 450 seats of which only 394 have been filled; the rest remain vacant because of low level of electoral interest and Ukraine's bizarre electoral law. (To be elected, a member of parliament has to win more than 50 per cent of the votes with more than 50 per cent of eligible voters participating in elections.) Out of twenty ridings in Kiev, seventeen seats remain vacant because of voters' apathy. This in a city which four years earlier witnessed mass demonstrations involving hundreds of thousands of people.

Women's voices

The role, status and the general life and problems of Ukrainian women in the last few years must be understood within the overall societal context. Between 1989 and 1991, women first appeared on the political scene of Ukraine not as a statistical mass but as an independent force with an independent voice. It was as if the eternally quiet, second-class majority all spoke at once. These were women political prisoners and dissidents who demanded freedoms, anti-militarist activists, ecological activists who demanded the shut-down of Chernobyl and the distribution of honest information about the consequences of the 1986 nuclear disaster. Women's voices were very audible in religious and cultural movements. They demanded the legalisation of the Ukrainian Catholic Church and the restoration of rights of the Ukrainian language. Amongst cultural organisations, especially in the Taras Shevchenko Ukrainian language society (which today is called the 'Prosvita' society), women did not, as a general rule, advance their claim to leadership positions but they were, and remain, the basic moving force of local organization, especially in eastern Ukraine where they face the most formidable challenges. Within the academic community, women raised awareness of the feminist tradition in literature, rediscovered the indigenous Ukrainian feminist tradition hitherto suppressed by the Soviet regime, and argued for the need to introduce women's studies in universities. The first centres for gender studies were founded and the first gender research in sociology undertaken. On television and radio the first programmes about Western feminism were aired, and family violence, rape and even the existence of the lesbian and gay movement were discussed. There were few women on the national political scene but a number did achieve national reputations as members of parliament.

Women's organisations became those grassroot formations where, for the first time, it was possible to speak about political opposition to the communist regime, the threatening environmental situation, the appalling conditions of life for tens of thousands of Ukraine's orphans and about one of the world's highest abortion rates. The main perspective was that of the protection of children. In this, woman as mother was the dominant concept of the role of a woman. Women set up the country's first charitable organisations. The second perspective – the political aspect of the vast majority of the women's organisations – was opposition to communism and totalitarianism. Women's organisations as a political force and individual women personalities contributed significantly to the collapse of the USSR.

Although the ideologists of women's organisations accepted the role of women as mother, thus repeating the totalitarian stereotype, it appeared, none the less, that women began seriously to fight for a new social status and planned to exert genuine influence on the political and social life of their country. Moreover, there was no doubt that women were a new, bold and dynamic social force and that, ultimately, their values would be humanistic values as the feminist theoretical tradition states. Thus, in 1992 there was much ground for an optimistic prognosis. One cannot say that all expectations have been shattered, since in all respects the distance between post-perestroika 1990 and 1996 is immense. Society continues to change even though the tempo has subsided.

Women's organisations and women activists were the tip of the female iceberg. As we see today, however, the phenomenon known as 'Ukrainian women' is contradictory. It has become clear that one cannot speak about women in Ukraine as a homogeneous group. Neither can we speculate about a single women's identity or the overall political priorities of women, let alone about typical electoral behaviour. It has become apparent that differences among women are no less sharp that those between women and men. For example, it has transpired that women members of parliament in reality do not represent women, have little interest in women's issues apart from the traditional concepts of motherhood and are even somewhat ashamed of their sex. It is obvious that the development of the women's movement will not follow Western patterns: the approaches of Western feminism cannot be copied blindly when analysing the condition of post-Soviet women.

Women in politics

At the beginning of the 1990s it appeared that women would become a significant political force and, moreover, one which would be unequivocally democratic and progressive. The début of women on the political scene provided grounds for this view, but today if one asks whether there is a serious women's voice in Ukrainian political discourse, the answer is an unequivocal 'no'. And this is in spite of the fact that there are over seventy women's organisations in Ukraine today whose representatives attended the Fourth United Nations World Conference on Women in Beijing in September 1995; in spite of the fact that in parliament there are seventeen women deputies, whereas in the previous parliament there were thirteen; in spite of the fact that the educational level of women is higher than that of men; in spite of the fact that women form 54 per cent of Ukraine's population and 52 per cent of the work-force.[1]

As a general rule, all discussion about the political status of women begins with analyses of their representation in the organs of power. Let us examine the Supreme Rada – Ukraine's parliament. The seventeen women members of parliament represent 4 per cent of deputies. Of them, three belong to the Communist Party, two are socialists, two are members of the agrarian faction – in other words, seven are members of the left-wing bloc. Only one woman belongs to Rukh (People's Movement for the Revival of Ukraine), and the rest belong to faceless centrist factions. In Ukraine's first democratically elected parliament, a number of women belonged not only to the democratic bloc, Narodna Rada, but they were also among the most active and eloquent advocates of independence and economic and political reform. In the first parliament, five women were members of Rukh. Brilliant personalities such as Larysa Skoryk and Iryna Kalynets are no longer to be found in the Supreme Rada. In the second parliament the fact that so many women belong to the communist and socialist bloc has meant that the women's political voice no longer advocates democracy and the development of civil society.

There are no strong women personalities in political parties, in government organs or in parliament today. No women have national reputations. Ukrainian political parties, be they left- or right-wing, are exclusively male clubs. Most democratic political parties endorse the general rhetoric of the state about 'the return of women to the family' or, as it is sometimes called, 'the renaissance of the patriarchy'. It does not seem to bother democrats that this position is at odds with their other democratic ideas. Among left-wing parties there is an inconsequential proportion of women and no women at all in the leadership. Perhaps the only exception is Natalia Vitrenko of the Socialist Party, who is a member of parliament and adviser to the head of parliament on economic affairs. She is the most vocal amongst the most conservative, anti-democratic, anti-market reform and anti-Ukrainian wing of the political spectrum. In October 1995, she elaborated an alternative to the government economic programme which was characterised by its hostility to privatisation and the market, and by its nostalgia for Soviet-style state control. However, in January 1996 she was expelled from the Politburo of the Socialist Party, and later from the party itself, for her criticism that the socialists were too timid in their opposition to the president's and the government's course of reform. In May 1996 she founded the progressive Socialist Party which upholds 'genuine Leninist principles'. The fact that Vitrenko is the most vocal political woman has served to discredit women's voices in politics.

That there are no women political leaders is not surprising in view of the fact that 97 per cent of women do not belong to any political organisation.[2] (There are no data on men's participation in the research cited, but it is not very substantial either.) At the same time, sociologists note that the consciousness of women is quite politicised. This politicisation lies in the fact that they actively follow political events; however, they rarely show partisan political sympathies. Interestingly, the political orientation of women is virtually the same as that of men.[3]

The Supreme Rada is the only higher organ of power where women are represented at all. There are about sixty-five ministers and heads of state committees in Ukraine's government: not one is a woman. There are some 270 deputy ministers and only six are women. In Ukraine's constitutional order, ministers are appointed and, as a rule, are not members of parliament. The majority of the public service consists of women, yet only 3 or 4 per cent are to be found in the upper echelons. Sociological surveys show that 'serious representation at the level of decision-making is to be found only in medicine (39 per cent) and science (29 per cent)'.[4]

At the same time, women as civil servants are often the symbol of the ineffective, conservative, prevaricating Ukrainian state. Thus, as previously mentioned, women not only form the majority of state functionaries, but in a number of spheres and a number of ministries they are a dominant majority. Their numerical preponderance in some ministries (headed, of course, by males) has few parallels in Western countries. In Table 12.1 we give data for a number of ministries. It should be noted that support staff (secretaries and the like) are excluded from the quoted figures.

Table 12.1: Percentages of female employees in Ukrainian ministries

Ministry of the Economy	67.2
Ministry of Finance	80.1
Ministry of Justice	87.3
Supreme Court	76.2
Higher Arbitration Court	83.9
Ministry of Statistics	93.9
Ministry of Social Welfare	95

Source: Statistics from Public Service Commission. Cabinet of Ministers Report (unpublished mimeo), 1 June 1995.

Professions which in the West are traditionally masculine – courts, the justice system, banks, economic ministries – in Ukraine are feminised. These women, under certain conditions, could become a substantial force of the feminist message, could change the stereotype about the status of women. They are well educated and professionally qualified but in the political sense they are the most inert and silent, and are the furthest removed from the women's movement of whatever orientation. Beneath the surface they really believe that motherhood and marriage is the height of a woman's career, that women must be charming and take good care of men, that 'nature' made it thus. In other words, there is a deep assimilation of traditional male rhetoric by these women. The problem lies in the fact that thousands of women – civil servants, women in parliament and professional women in general – belong to that type which could be called 'a woman-man', who achieve high positions but do not change the nature of authority and its ideology in the interest of women. The thousands of women found in this category are lost in the mass of over 25 million Ukrainian women who belong to totally different social layers, groups which, irrespective of education or work, exist beyond the decision-making sphere, beyond prestigious employment, status and high incomes.

Women, work and discrimination

Women are traditionally concentrated in spheres outside serious decision-making – in agricultural labour, construction, industry and education. Moreover, the lower and the less well paid the positions, the greater the chance of finding women in them. A high level of unemployment among women is characteristic of the situation in post-Soviet countries. In Ukraine 70 per cent (some data suggest 80 per cent) of the unemployed are women, two-thirds of whom have higher education. Women were the first to lose jobs in the stress of the period of the transition from a planned to a market economy. Moreover, many women are stuck in physical labour, which itself is a form of hidden discrimination. The average income of women is substantially lower than the average income of men. According to the Human Development Report sponsored by the United Nations, the average income of women in industry as compared to that of men in 1993 ranged from 45 per cent in the energy sector to 90 per cent in light industry.[5]

The state does everything it can to avoid shedding light on facts which point to discrimination. The data cited earlier exist only in materials prepared under pressure from international organisations and circulated in research and policy papers. For internal purposes the state, through its senior members of parliament or ministers, constantly repeats the patriarchal rhetoric of 'return women to the family'. In fact, this rhetoric is a badly masked attempt to hide and justify high levels of unemployment and discrimination against women, which has become much worse in the last three years.

The few women politicians who exist stubbornly refuse to acknowledge social and economic discrimination against women and refuse to include the women question in their programmes. The official women's discourse in Ukrainian society is generally restricted to topics concerning motherhood, children and family matters – the last parliament, for instance, had a Commission on the Family, Motherhood and Children. The new parliament abolished this commission but, under pressure from women's organisations, a Committee on

Women's Affairs, Motherhood and Children was established by the president's administration. In daily life women's discourse consists of the kitchen, fashion, make-up, health and sex. Not surprisingly, a 'serious' woman politician will try to demonstrate before society that she is not interested in this kind of question and, in fact, is no different from her male colleagues. The message of the woman leader or of a successful woman in a men's world is construed thus: first, by upbringing, education, behaviour and views ('women's things are trivial'), I am the same as you – that is, I am man, only of a different sex: second, however, I can, when necessary, use my feminine charm.

Alexandra Kuzhel', a member of parliament from Zaporizhzhia, 'a capitalist' and head of an accounting firm who does not hide her ambition to become the next president of Ukraine, recently said the following:

Whenever some woman member of parliament goes abroad we get together and discuss what to wear, how to be attractive. This is very important. When I travelled to England I bought myself a very expensive suit because I knew that otherwise I would not be accepted in their parliament. I don't like to be together with too many women. I feel much more comfortable in the company of men.[6]

When asked if it is difficult to compete with men and whether men take her less seriously because she is a woman, she answered, 'No. I cannot complain about serious negative attitudes towards me. Of course, sometimes I confront haughtiness but this is an exception, not the rule.'[7]

It is not only women politicians but the entire society that stubbornly refuses to recognise discrimination against women. Recent public opinion polls showed the information given in Table 12.2, which demonstrates that the majority of respondents do not know about the discrimination against women and almost half consider men and women to have equal rights and equal chances.

Analogous results could be drawn from twenty-five interviews from women of the eastern Ukrainian industrial city of Luhansk. Only two of them 'explicitly acknowledged having been subject to discrimination as a woman'.[8] Interestingly, most of the interviewed women lacked any Ukrainian (linguistic, cultural, political or regional) identity and all felt that the Russian language had to be accepted as a state language along with Ukrainian. Those with business orientations were advocates of economic union with Russia and Belorus. Most of them felt that their life was materially better in former times (presumably in the times of the USSR); however, most of them were 'unwilling to try the private marketing operations which offered scope for much higher earnings'.[9] Although only twenty-five women were interviewed, their answers show a typical complex of feelings and ideas of Ukrainian women in this region – the justifiable despair, lack of political and national identity, and some latent political conservatism. The most active opponents of the granting of the collective farm lands to individual farms in 1993 (when this farming movement emerged) were women from collective farms – the most oppressed, uneducated and underpaid strata of women in Ukrainian society.

Table 12.2: Social attitudes on gender roles in 1995 (replies given in percentages)

(1) Is there any change in the level of involvement of women in Ukrainian society?	
Increasing	27.8
Remains the same	39.1
Diminishing	13.6
Difficult to say	19.5
(2) Do men and women have equal opportunities for job promotion?	
Women have better opportunities	3.8
Men have better opportunities	44
Opportunities are equal	43.8
Difficult to say	8.5
(3) Have you noticed in recent years instances of discrimination against women?	
Yes	17.8
Can't recall	19.5
No	53.5
Difficult to say	9.3

Source: Socis-Gallup, Ukrainian Political and Economic Index. Report no. 14, May 1995, pp. 24–5.

In general, recent surveys of opinion point to a marked decrease in women's political activity. In the 1980s and the early 1990s, women's political activism was on the upswing. Three leading Ukrainian sociologists conclude:

On the whole, most important today for the majority of women is how to survive the sharp price increases (67 per cent of women and 55 per cent of men consider this a primary concern). For men, much more important than for women is concern to influence decision-making (men – 27 per cent; women – 19 per cent) ... One can conclude on the basis of the latest data that men are much more politically literate than women. Women in Ukraine provide simplistic solutions (all their interests are focused on the survival of their families) and their only expectations of assistance is that which the relatives can provide.[10]

However, there is another side of these sociological data, not noticed by its authors. Taking on themselves the whole burden of economic survival, women give men a chance to be parasites on women and to be free to dedicate their effort to ideas and ideals.

Table 12.3: Responses on jobs for which men and women are most suited

	Most suitable for women (%)	Most suitable for men (%)
Pre-school education	67	33
Household chores	65	35
Service sector	58	42
Medicine	57	43
Schools	53	47
University	48	52
Scientific research	44	56
Agriculture	42	58
Industry	38	62
Civil service	32	68
Politics	30	70

Source: Iu. Saienko, E. Plisovs'ka, M. Linovytska, 'The status of women in the political, social and economic life of Ukraine', *Politychnyi portret Ukrainy* 13, p. 18.[11]

The public opinion survey which is cited in this chapter provides interesting data on perceptions of what is considered suitable employment for men and women, shown in Table 12.3. The data speak for themselves. What is important to add, however, is that women considered all jobs as suitable for both sexes equally. It was men who focused on household work, the service sector, pre-school education, schools and medicine as the most suitable for women, and regarded scientific research, public administration and politics as male spheres.[12]

Two of the three authors of the sociological survey cited are women; despite this, that study contains not a few sexist remarks in the analyses of the survey results. Thus, when the survey shows that women, more than men, preferred to work under the leadership of an experienced boss, the authors remark, 'this of course corresponds to a woman's nature'.[13]

Women's organisations

The women's movement could be playing a role in the mobilisation of women and in raising public consciousness as to the status of women. The unofficial women's movement in Ukraine has a six-year history. It started in 1990 with the Women's Community of Rukh (which later split from Rukh), the Union of Ukrainian Women and others. They emerged at the end of perestroika and were part of the social awakening and birth of new political ideals, one of the most exciting moments of this century. It was only later that it became clear that the patriotically inclined women's organisations lost their sense of mission with the collapse of the USSR and with the emergence of an independent Ukraine. Their political programme had won. When a new programme had to be advanced, problems started. Instead of focusing their energies on the struggle for equal rights, the organisations, by and large, swallowed the rhetoric of national revival and were lost among the scores of political and community organisations advancing similar goals.

During the last five years the number of women's organisations has increased to seventy; Kiev itself has some twenty organisations. However, their influence on society remains modest and the women's movement in Ukraine has little political influence. Most women's organisations have small memberships and are regionally based. As a rule, the women's movement does not involve young women or women from the agricultural and industrial milieux – almost without exception, members of these organisations are women with higher education, middle-aged if not elderly, often housewives. The leaders of the two most influential groups (Women's Community and the Union of Women of Ukraine) are wives of Ivan Drach (former head of Rukh and a member of parliament) and Viacheslav Chornovil (acting head of Rukh). Feminism occupies virtually no place in their discourse and if they mention feminism, they will quickly add a footnote distancing themselves from it.

Women's organisations can be divided into two categories: first, political and, second, service/community groups. The political women's organisations are Women's Community (Zhinocha Hromada), the Union of Women of Ukraine, Ukrainian Christian Women's Party and others. These represent the democratic spectrum. The communist spectrum includes the Union of Women of Ukraine, which was formally the Committee of Soviet Women, and the newly created Women of Crimea group. The former support Rukh or are aligned to the republican, democratic, Christian-democratic, liberal or other centrist parties; the latter support the unreconstructed communists. Common political action of women's organisations in Ukraine is thus impossible to achieve.

In the spring of 1994, during the elections to parliament, Zhinocha Hromada made an attempt to unite women's organisations into a common electoral bloc. Among the priorities of the bloc were: 'strengthening Ukraine's independence, freedom, democracy and rule of law, rapid economic reform, social protection of the population, defence of the political, economic and social rights of women, guaranteed rights for families ... the propagation of humanistic values in education and in the mass media'.[14] The programme of the women's bloc was vague, to put it mildly, and could hardly compete with men's parties and blocs.

There is a wide panorama of service/community women's organisations. It includes groups such as the All-Ukrainian Federation of Mothers With Many Children (those with more than three); the organisation of Jewish women, Rachamim, which helps elderly Jews; 'Mama–86', an organisation which helps the child victims of Chernobyl; or professional groups such as the Association of Women Film-makers. Recently, women involved in business and in the mass media, or the wives of the *nouveaux riches*, have organised themselves into groups such as the Odessa Ladies Club. Also, recently the institution of girls' schools has revived, whose purpose is to educate a spectrum of ladies, from governesses to the wives of rich men – a mission fundamentally different from that of girls' schools at the turn of the century, whose goal was to provide women with an excellent education.

Traditionally, the women's discourse of motherhood has a chance to become sharply politicised if a woman has a son serving in the army, as Kathryn Pinnick has shown in chapter eight. The Soldiers' Mothers for the New Army is a group dedicated to ensuring that human rights are respected in the army and to highlighting cases of brutality in the armed forces. 'Mama–86', a curious name, given its activism, is, in fact, an organisation campaigning on issues of environmental protection and on the shut-down of Chernobyl.

The independent state

In independent Ukraine, the state has simply neglected women's issues and made little effort to win women's support. In the presidential campaign of June 1994, Leonid Kravchuk, who was seeking re-election, met with women only on the night before voting took place. With the approaching UN conference in Beijing, the Ukrainian state decided that it could not be bypassed in this important event. In the spring of 1995, a National Conference of Women's Organisations was hastily convoked to prepare for Beijing, and a National Committee organised. The National Committee was headed by deputy prime minister for social policy, Ivan Kuras, who also headed the Ukrainian delegation to the women's conference in Beijing. On the eve of his departure to Beijing he gave an interview to the magazine *Women* (*Zhinka*), where he indicated that, under the leadership of the National Committee, two programmes were being developed: 'Family planning' and 'Children of Ukraine'. Questions of women's rights or discrimination against women were not mentioned in the interview. In the deputy prime minister's mind, the status of women is inextricably bound up with the defence of the rights of the family, motherhood and childhood.[15]

In short, government policy remains the same, as does its rhetoric. The more they speak of defence of women in the role of the mother and wife, the deeper is the open and covert discrimination against women.

In the meantime, millions of Ukrainian women distance themselves from problems of discrimination and ignore the political rhetoric surrounding women's issues by avidly watching Mexican, Brazilian or Portuguese soap operas which flood Ukrainian television, while remaining the objects of sexual abuse in the family, sexual harassment at work and victims of an antediluvian health system. Most do not see themselves as objects of discrimination, most do not have independent ideas or voices and accept the stereotypes peddled by the mass media.

The media have generated two main stereotypes which have remained the same since the beginning of glasnost (the end of the 1980s). The first is woman as icon (wife, mother, the backbone of the family and of the country, a national shrine and the Hearth Mother). The second stereotype is that of the glamorous woman – beautiful, well-dressed, chic, – whose life-style is advertised in countless women's magazines from the Russian edition of *Cosmopolitan* to the Ukrainian language *Women's Secrets*, published in Lvov. Whereas the first stereotype is rooted in local, national values, the second is identified with the West. The national icon and glamorous woman are the beloved clichés of television and the tabloid press (a press which outnumbers all other types of newspapers). Every media consumer has an opportunity to select the myth of his or her choice.

There is not much that one can say about men in this connection. The arguments and rhetoric of Ukrainian males have remained the same in recent years, even though the individual words may have changed. Communist and former political prisoners, writers of the older generation and young assistants to the president – all speak in the same voice: women are a delightful, venerated, respected sex in general, and in Ukraine in particular, and the only problem is that they are forced to work. Accepting the blame for this condition, men hope for a better future where women will be freed from labour. In the recent past I have not heard a single public interview with a man who would acknowledge discrimination against women. But you have to give Ukrainian male politicians their due. Unlike in Russia, they have not raised the question of the introduction of polygamy: Christian traditions in Ukraine are too strong for that.

Conclusion

To summarise, contemporary Ukraine shows two tendencies: first, the strengthening of discrimination against women in all spheres of social life and the workplace; and, second, the unwillingness or inability of society in general, and women's organisations in particular, to understand this phenomenon and to challenge it.

It is characteristic of the situation in Ukraine that a man led the Ukrainian delegation to the Fourth UN World Conference on Women in Beijing, a delegation hand-picked by the state apparatus. It is typical of the situation in Ukraine that the quite substantial number of Ukrainian delegates (which also included activists who attended the NGO events) remained silent throughout. This silence is characteristic of the political discourse of Ukrainian women. Of course, there are individual voices – generally academics and artists – which sound dissonant chords. There are a number of feminists, and Simone de Beauvoir's *The second sex* recently appeared in Ukrainian translation. One hopes that these voices will strengthen and become more authoritative – 54 per cent of the country's population cannot remain mute forever.

A couple of years ago one could have ended on this optimistic tone. But today the main question remains – what will the women's voices be like? Whom will women support? Will they become a base of support for communists, since they have been most affected by the transition to the market and long for the past as it appears to some that they lived better under the old regime? Or will they support democratic reforms notwithstanding unheated flats, unemployment, the growth of crime and insane price rises? Today one can speak of certain tendencies to support the former (although since there is no single women's identity, equally there is no single political choice). Exhausted women, manipulated by male demagogues, blinded by stereotypes and locked in unprestigious employment, especially on collective farms, have the potential for serious political conservatism. Nationally conscious and democratically oriented women, who, by and large, live in cities and have higher education, as a rule profess the patriarchal ideas of woman as Hearth Mother which in itself is also a manifestation of deep cultural conservatism. The only effective antidote to these tendencies will be quick transition to democracy and market economies, a transition which today has stalled and which has given rise to archaic discourses, one of which is women's conservatism.

Notes

1 *Ukraine. Human development report 1995* (Kiev: PROON, 1995), pp. 35–6.
2 N. Lavrinenko, 'The women's movement in post-communist Ukraine: achievements and slips' in *Politchnyi portret Ukrainy* 13 (Bulletin of the Research Centre, 'Democratic Initiatives') (Kiev: 1995), p. 11.
3 E. Plisovs'ka, 'The women's movement in the world and in Ukraine' in *Politychnyi portret Ukrainy* 13, p. 6.
4 *Ibid.*, p. 6.
5 *Ukraine. Human development report 1995*, p. 36.
6 Alexandra Kuzhel', 'Husbands who put up with such women as I am are kamikaze', *Vseukrainskiie Vedomosti*, 28 October 1995, p. 3.
7 *Ibid.*, p. 3.
8 W. Michael Walker, 'Changing lives: social change and women's lives in east Ukraine' in Sue Bridger (ed.), 'Women in post-communist Russia' in *Interface* no. 1 (Bradford, Summer, 1995), p. 102.
9 *Ibid.*, p. 109.

10 Iu. Saienko, E. Plisovs'ka, M. Linovytska, 'The status of women in the political, social and economic life of Ukraine' in *Politychnyi portret Ukrainy* 13, p. 16.
11 The results of this study are based on a survey of 1,197 respondents in ten oblasts (596 men and 601 women).
12 Saienko *et al.*, 'The status of women', p. 18.
13 *Ibid.*, p. 17.
14 Lavrinenko, 'The women's movement in post-communist Ukraine', pp. 10–11.
15 'Unity of efforts in everything', *Zhinka* 8, 1995, pp. 4–5.

13 Out of the kitchen into the crossfire: women in independent Armenia

NORA DUDWICK

Gender as ideology and its practice in Armenia

Gender, as a socially defined category which links biological sex to a particular set of social obligations and cultural expectations, has important ideological and practical consequences for families and societies. This chapter will examine how the abrupt political and economic changes of the last few years have intersected with Armenian and Soviet constructions of gender to shape the lives of Armenian women.

For Armenians, the family represents the centre of affective life and, no less importantly, the means by which they resisted cultural assimilation and physical destruction as a people through centuries of onslaught by Arabs, Mongols, Turks and other ethnically or religiously alien peoples. Countless proverbs express the centrality of the family to ethnic 'survival', and the complementarity of men's and women's roles in this joint endeavour. Armenians often describe the family as a 'fortress' – man, the 'outer wall', wards off external danger, while woman, the 'inner wall', preserves domestic order and harmony. The organic relation of each part to the whole is also expressed in the analogy of a married couple to a body, in which man is the head, and woman is the neck. When invoking this comparison, people frequently point out that although the head supposedly makes the decisions and controls the body, in fact, women subtly control the head, for 'as the neck turns, so turns the head'. Both proverbs stress the supportive and subordinate nature of women's relationship to men. Armenian women do not necessarily accept or conform to these stereotypes, but they must still contend with them, whether to defy, subvert or adapt them.

Enormous economic hardships and disorienting social changes have accompanied the disintegration of the Soviet state, with its centralised, planned economy, into separate republics. In this context, women in Armenia are feeling the increased pressures of such stereotypes, which are now invoked to exclude women from public and economic life. A 1995 survey of 800 women in three cities, undertaken by the Women's Council of Armenia, found that an overwhelming majority of respondents felt their position in economic and public life had worsened during the transition.[1] This deterioration results from a cluster of factors, including large-scale unemployment and underemployment, the reduction of subsidies and benefits, the collapse of infrastructure, agricultural privatisation, male labour migration, ongoing war with Azerbaidzhan and, finally, rising nationalism which seeks to rediscover 'national' identity in the reaffirmation of traditional gender relations.

Sovietisation and gender relations

If industrialisation and the spread of capitalism reduced the power of the patriarch in extended Armenian families, Sovietisation reduced the significance of the family itself as a productive unit as individual farms and businesses were nationalised or destroyed, and individuals entered the industrial labour force and collective farm brigades. The state also tried to reorganise gender roles in the family, thereby further eroding the patriarch's authority and replacing it by a 'quasi-familial dependency' on an increasingly patriarchal socialist state.[2] For example, state-run nurseries and municipal services took over some household chores so that women could enter the labour market. Ultimately, the state's inability effectively to distribute goods and services gave the large, closely knit extended Armenian family a new importance as a functional alternative to official distribution networks.

Nevertheless, during the Soviet period, women's role in the family gradually changed. By the late 1980s, Armenian women were completing higher education in equal numbers to men and working in every profession, although they rarely occupied management positions. Prevailing Soviet paternalism, which distinguished between professions best suited to men and women, became combined with the Armenian patriarchal ethos – largely accepted by Armenian women –

which sees women as the pre-eminent guardians of the 'ojakh' or hearth, with all that this role entails in terms of reproduction, child care, cooking and housework.

The trauma of transition: economic collapse and war

Every post-Soviet republic has its claim to unique hardships. For Armenia, these consisted of the devastating 1988 earthquake and the war with Azerbaidzhan. The impact of these events, along with consequences of the Soviet state's collapse, reverberated through society, plunging a large proportion of the Armenian population into poverty, and disrupting gender relations in the family, economy and polity. Armenia experienced a particularly severe economic decline as a consequence of its dispute with Azerbaidzhan over control of the Nagorno-Karabakh autonomous oblast, a conflict which catalysed inter-ethnic violence, a two-way flood of refugees between the two republics and a blockade of Armenia by Azerbaidzhan.

The 7 December 1988 earthquake in north-west Armenia (which destroyed one-third of the republic's industrial capacity), the closure of the Metsamor nuclear power plant and disruptions in the once tightly integrated Soviet economy halted production and caused widespread unemployment. When government fuel supplies ran out in 1991, the population, including refugees and earthquake victims living in schools, hotels, metal containers and other buildings never intended for habitation, shivered through harsh winters without heat, cooking gas, or more than a few hours of electricity – if that – a day. As the Karabakh conflict escalated into war and the blockade continued, many people resorted to the traditional Armenian pattern of labour migration.

By July 1993, according to UNICEF estimates, approximately 1 million (from a 1.7 million-strong labour force) were either formally unemployed or on involuntary forced leave.[3] People received their diminished salaries late; industrial workers sometimes received wages in the form of the goods their factory produced rather than as cash. Many people continued to work to preserve routine, from a sense of duty, to socialise with colleagues, or to retain access to public resources, information, humanitarian aid, professional contacts, potential contracts, even bribes.

In 1991, the overwhelming majority of Armenians voted for and greeted independence enthusiastically, and expressed verbal enthusiasm about 'democracy' and the 'free market'. Yet, like most former

Soviet citizens, Armenians retain basic assumptions and expectations about 'social justice', which includes a sense of entitlement to jobs, education, subsidies and benefits. The employment crisis, sharply increasing economic differentiation, reduction of social entitlements, hyperinflation, loss of savings, unemployment and non-payment of salaries, and, not least, shame at their visible poverty, have left all but the new elite bewildered and nostalgic for the idealised predictable and secure life they used to live.

In the absence of a civic tradition of cooperative public endeavour in the pursuit of shared interests, the extended family remains the primary indigenous social unit capable of effective cooperation. Armenians' response to the current economic crisis has consisted largely of individual and family coping strategies and a reliance on local and transnational kinship networks, partially supplemented by international humanitarian aid programmes. The painful restructuring of the economy and the day-to-day hardships have therefore increased the importance of the family to social survival, while simultaneously destabilising family relations and sharpening gender differences.

Redefining gender responsibilities

The family carries great importance in Armenian society. Without a respected, well-connected family, people feel socially and economically vulnerable. For most Armenians, the family rather than the state was, and still is, the most reliable form of social insurance. A family's ability to protect its members, however, depends in part on the respect in which it is held in the community. This respect is tied up with local notions of family honour, which requires a man to earn enough to support his wife and children and to maintain the family's position in the community by public demonstrations of prosperity. Likewise, family honour requires that women behave modestly and play a subordinate role in the family economy.

Before 1988, Armenia as a whole enjoyed a relatively high standard of living, aided by its flourishing second economy. Armenian female-headed households were rare; marriage rates were high, divorce rates the lowest in the Soviet Union. Unmarried women – a marginal category with low social status – almost always remained with parents or married siblings. Men composed the base and women the superstructure in the Armenian economy, in that men dominated positions in heavy industry, metallurgy, mining, the upper echelons of party and government, and the army and police, while the textile, electronics and food-processing industries, service sector, and health, education and culture — except for top administrative posts — were 'women's work'.[4] This gendered division of labour corresponded to pay differentials averaging 500–700 roubles a month for male occupations, and 120–130 roubles a month for 'women's work'.

Despite women's level of educational attainment — 51 per cent received high education, 28 per cent were awarded the 'candidate degree' (roughly comparable to a Western Ph.D or slightly below), and 35 per cent of those working at the Academy of Sciences were women — few of them challenged the assumptions underlying the gendered division of labour. Most gave precedence to their family responsibilities, even if it meant leaving the labour market for years to raise young children. Others combined home responsibilities with work by seeking less demanding jobs with fewer hours and accepting lower pay, a process which further contributed to the feminisation of professions such as teaching and office work.[5]

Men's reduced ability to support their families and either women's inability to make a cash contribution to the household, or, alternatively, her economic activism, have in some cases reversed the traditional sexual division of labour, destabilised relations of authority and responsibility between men and women, and transformed the extended family into a broken family, a single-parent family, a transnational family, even a polygamous family.

Shifting labour patterns

Between 1991 and 1994, production fell by 60 per cent. The massive restructuring of the economy affected people according to their social group, place in the social hierarchy, and gender-determined relation to reproduction and production. As in other post-socialist countries, unemployment hit women, whether urban or rural, more seriously than men, and women have found it harder to enter the new private sector, except at the lowest level. Moreover, the closure of child care facilities, steep increases in the price of transportation and difficulties in daily life enormously complicated the task of combining work and family.[6]

No matter what a woman's status as a worker, she continues to bear the brunt of responsibility for child care, cooking and cleaning. Especially in urban settings, lack of cooking gas and the irregular electricity supply have forced women to cook over kerosene or wood-burning stoves (a slow, dirty and often headache-producing procedure). Women more than men have changed their daily routines, often rising in the middle of the night when electricity goes on to prepare meals, heat water for washing clothes, and bathe. Women, aided by their children, also bear the brunt of carrying water – traditionally a woman's task – up to high-rise apartments when lack of electricity shuts down water pumps.

For the rural population, subsistence agriculture has become an important survival strategy. Armenia's radical 1991 land privatisation programme broke up the republic's state and collective farms. By the end of 1992, Armenia had 280,000 independent farmers. Many new farmers had never worked in agriculture before, while experienced farmers were often unable to raise cash crops, given the high price of seed, fertiliser, pesticide, fuel and rental of heavy machinery.[7] As a result, many families now subsist on their garden plots.

Privatisation made the position of rural women both difficult and insecure. Land was awarded to families, and preliminary research suggests that customary law may still dominate, awarding the land to the husband in cases of divorce.[8] As in town, few industries in the countryside still function, which means that most families with land now survive from subsistence farming and barter rather than wage labour. Since operating heavy equipment is considered a male domain, women lack the opportunity of those equipment operators who managed to acquire privatised equipment and can now rent their services out for cash.

As subsistence farmers, women have added the additional burden of physical labour in the fields and care of livestock to housework, which is already made difficult by the irregular energy supply. Generally, the poorer the family and the fewer labour hands, the more women add to their own tasks (such as preserving fruits and vegetables, milking and fetching water), physically demanding tasks generally considered men's work (such as working with draught animals, ploughing, harrowing the soil, sowing, harvesting grain, even operating big machinery).[9] In the words of a local ethnographer, despite the current importance of their unpaid labour on the family plot, women without outside employment have become like 'household slaves' – their housework has increased enormously, while their inability to contribute cash to the family economy has reduced their authority and independence in the family. Reduction of social services previously provided by the state, such as kindergarten, has added to their burdens, for many men are unwilling to pay for new private kindergartens when their wives do not have formal paid employment.[10]

Large numbers of men have now resorted to a traditional Armenian coping strategy – labour emigration, especially from rural regions. Up to a million people are thought to have left the republic since 1991. Approximately 10 per cent have left as families, but the overwhelming majority of migrants are able-bodied men between the ages of eighteen and sixty. Working as contract labourers in Russia and other Slavic republics, most men bring their earnings home at the end of a season, or try the riskier proposition of sending it home with acquaintances.

Their absence has created numerous problems for wives and children left behind, who often subsist without news or remittances for months on end. In some cases, young wives who have just moved into their husbands' homes have been forced into sexual relations with their fathers-in-law or brothers-in-law. The rate of abandonment has risen, along with anecdotal reports of suicide among abandoned wives. The peculiar phenomenon of the 'second family' has emerged, as men who have been working for several seasons outside Armenia move in with local women and start new families. In some cases, they continue these families on their return, or even bring them to Armenia. Their Armenian wives are forced to swallow the pain and humiliation this entails, since they and their children depend on their husbands' income. They are also prevented from seeking male companionship in their husbands' absence by the conservative rural morality which quickly brands such women as 'prostitutes'.

Male labour emigration, as well as the emigration of young men seeking to avoid the new army draft, have created a radical disproportion of men to women, reducing marriage prospects for women. Early marriage – before twenty-five – has long been an Armenian preference; today, the number of teenage marriages is increasing, as well as the age gap between husband and wife. Privatisation of higher education and lack of employment prospects have encouraged some parents to conclude that there is little point in daughters postponing marriage for higher education. There is no evidence of forced marriages, but girls experience greater pressure than ever from parents to choose their husband according to his family's prosperity.

Widespread unemployment and male migration has forced women to search for new and alternative sources of income, since it is no longer possible to support themselves and their children on a single salary and government benefits, as they did during the Soviet era. In towns and cities, women of every educational level and profession have become visible in the one economic enterprise which has flourished since 1991, that of petty trade and commerce. Travelling with friends, kin or organised groups, women have borrowed money from acquaintances or professional money-lenders, and travelled to Iran, Turkey, Syria, the Gulf states, Greece, Eastern Europe, even Vietnam and China, to purchase consumer items to sell at open-air markets in the city or through acquaintances in villages. Some women have managed to earn enough to support their families. Others combine trading trips with short periods of work abroad, even as prostitutes (an activity to which very needy families may turn a blind eye). Women have also made use of knitting, sewing, embroidery, potting and baking skills, operating small, unregistered businesses which they publicise by word of mouth.

Few women have achieved 'elite' status in the business world. For the most part, this position is occupied by a male trading elite who import expensive equipment and appliances on order from the Gulf states. While women most frequently operate modest businesses in their homes, larger-scale free enterprise has taken on the character of a ' "macho capitalism" dominated by young male entrepreneurs ... ex-members of the old Soviet *nomenklatura*, and mafia-like networks of extortion and enforcement'.[11] As elsewhere in the former Soviet Union and Eastern Europe, female entrepreneurs tend to be less successful; they have less access to these old and new networks, and tend to be more law-abiding.[12] In chapter four, Marta Bruno has also highlighted differences between male and female entrepreneurial cultures in Russia. In Armenia, women who do aim high are often criticised for violating gender norms. Thus, while Armenians may attribute male entrepreneurial success to 'connections', when women use the same means, they are labelled 'prostitutes' for their alleged use of marriage or informal alliances to powerful men to further their business careers.

This reasoning, combined with the sharpened economic competition for jobs, has given rise to the frequently heard slogan now addressed to women, to 'leave work and return to your families and children'. According to the poll cited earlier, 49 per cent of the respondents supported this demand, although many added they were not able to leave their jobs at present. Others sharply disagreed with the sentiment, but as answers to other questions suggest, even those who actively seek careers outside the home feel stymied by 'patriarchal attitudes', assumptions that businesswomen achieve success through 'immoral' means, or by their own lack of confidence.[13]

In addition to the development of commerce, the expanding foreign diplomatic and international aid community also created a window of opportunity for women. Once over-represented in the liberal arts such as philology and foreign languages, women who previously earned modest salaries as foreign-language teachers now find themselves in demand for comparatively highly paid jobs as translators, interpreters, guides and office managers. Many of these women have become the economic mainstay of their families, although they may find themselves squeezed out by the young men now graduating from language courses who offer the advantage of their greater comfort in the public sphere, not to mention their practical skills, such as driving. In the context of growing economic differentiation, women appear at a disadvantage. To the extent that women participate in the economy, they form 'quasi-class fractions' forming a 'buffer zone' between men of their own class and men of the class below them in the hierarchy.[14]

Women and public life

Not only have women become economically marginalised, they find it increasingly difficult to participate in political life. The nationalist movement of 1988 began as a 'genderless festival'[15] of goodwill and optimism which brought men and women onto the streets to demonstrate, march and chant in support of political change. As in Eastern and Central Europe, although women were absent from the core leadership, they took part in public discussions, worked as campaigners in the first democratically run electoral races, and wrote, reproduced and distributed illegal literature.[16] When the Karabakh Committee – including Levon Ter-Petrossian (president since 1991) and other prominent members of government and opposition – were imprisoned, their wives and sisters actively and publicly campaigned for their release.

But when the nationalist movement effectively transformed into the first post-communist government, women found themselves virtually excluded. Despite the government's European orientation and adoption of radical economic reform, they have done little to encourage women's participation in political or public life. In comparison to their largely pro forma (but 30 per cent) representation in local and central government and the Communist Party during the Soviet period, today they comprise only 8 per cent of parliament, and one of the twenty four ministerial posts. As the leader of a women's organisation explained, the Soviet quota system harmed the women's movement by appointing compliant rather than capable women, thereby delegitimising their participation in government.

While several small 'women's parties' have formed, women figure in very insignificant numbers in the larger political parties, none of which have shown interest in 'women's issues' or women's rights. The reduction of women serving in politics has occurred in most post-socialist regimes, to a greater or lesser degree, in part as a reaction against Soviet-era quotas. Perhaps, as Chatterjee suggested was the case in Bengal,[17] the rejection of gender equality in political life represents an attempt by Armenian nationalists to defend what Chatterjee termed an 'inner domain of sovereignty' against a perceived onslaught of alien Western values, using idealised 'traditional' gender relationships to represent the essence of Armenian uniqueness. Armenian nationalists realise that to compete effectively in the world market-place as a Western nation (such as they believe Armenia to be), they must accommodate to Western ways of doing business. As a result, defending an idealised 'national' culture allows them to feel they retain control over some aspect of life.

Some women have reacted to this socialist-era political and economic manipulation by suggesting that women are better suited by their nature to play a backstage supportive role in politics. Those women who try to participate in political life face many obstacles. Several small women's parties, including one headed by an initiator of the 1993 teachers' strike and by a former representative to the All-Union Congress of People's Deputies, were prevented from registering for the 1995 Armenian National Assembly elections due to various 'technicalities'. Given the extremely managed nature of elections, few members of the public accept this explanation, but ascribe the rejection of at least one of the parties to its slightly oppositional platform.

The only women's party which did participate, and which, to everyone's astonishment, won eight out of the forty seats allocated to candidates elected from party lists, was the mysterious Shamiram (named for the Assyrian Queen Semiramis who unrequitedly loved and ultimately murdered the Armenian King Ara the Beautiful), which came into existence only months before the election. Many people argued that Shamiram had won due to an anomaly of the very confusing election ballot and the Armenian public largely discounted the party as a serious political endeavour. Composed as it was of the wives, daughters, friends and alleged lovers of the intellectual and political elite, Shamiram is widely viewed by a large part of the public as the means by which the ambitious minister of the interior hoped to place 'his' people in the National Assembly. The public (of both sexes) has reacted to Shamiram in the same terms as they assess the unexpected success of female business entrepreneurs: by dismissing them as 'prostitutes'. The origin and progress of Shamiram reveal the difficulties which face women in politics. For women to enter political life without male approval and support – overt or covert – is hardly feasible, while women who make use of such support reaffirm popular prejudice that women in politics are simply the tools of men. The actual extent to which the members of Shamiram were made use of by the powerful men to whom they are related, or the extent to which they exploited these men to obtain an entry to political life, remains to be seen.

Blocked by the practical as well as moral difficulties of participating in politics, many active women have moved into the new and still only vaguely defined realm of non-governmental organisations. Yet despite the existence of over thirty women's organisations, none have what Westerners would consider a feminist agenda, and only a few take up the issue of women's rights at all. Like Shamiram, the majority are run by the wives, sisters and daughters of the elite – the only ones with sufficient power, resources or time. Some organisations appear intent on competing for Western resources such as expensive equipment and trips abroad; others have responded to nationalist appeals directed to them as mothers and defenders of the weak.

A few women's organisations have a slightly more political agenda. The Women's Council, the continuation of its Soviet predecessor which Gorbachev revived in 1987 and which has branches throughout the republic, defines its aims as researching and proposing legislation aimed at protecting women and children. Self-consciously espousing a 'centrist' and 'constructive' policy, the organisation ratifies an essentialist view of women as equipped by nature to mediate between extreme political positions. The newly formed Democracy Union has taken up the traditional women's issue of children to turn attention to the new category of homeless urban children, as well as to the problem of female prisoners' rights. Its leadership has also proposed construction of an information centre concerned with women's legal rights. Perhaps the majority of 'women's organisations', however, have devoted themselves to channelling assistance to families of men killed or injured in Nagorno-Karabakh, helping needy families and encouraging large (patriotic) families. As such, they have subordinated the problems of women to that of the nation, in a gesture of sacrifice that may never be rewarded.

Women and war

The war in Nagorno-Karabakh and on the Armenian–Azerbaidzhani border has affected the position of Armenian women in obvious and less obvious ways; for although war appears to be a largely male activity, it makes very specific demands on women. As Iveković points out, although women are complicit in war as part of the system and symbolic order which supports it, men define the 'interests' of war and organise the fighting.[18] A small number of women accompanied the men to front-line areas as cooks or nurses, on rare occasions as fighters or as prostitutes. For the most part, however, a revived discourse of genocide (harking back to the large-scale 1915 slaughter of Armenians in the Ottoman Empire) and ongoing threats to Armenian survival appealed to women to remain home, maintain the family economically and morally, inspire their men with patriotism and give birth to future soldiers.

The division of labour in war has resulted in a division of labour in suffering as well. Men have been killed or handicapped, and many of the latter are now unemployed. Their deaths and injuries are, in the first instance, an emotional tragedy for their families. Secondly, given distinct gender roles which make it harder for women to enter the public sphere, the absence of an able-bodied man in the family, or the presence of an invalid, leaves wives, mothers and children economically and morally vulnerable.

To the extent that war benefits individuals, however, these individuals are largely men. One case in point concerns both the widespread looting that occurs in emptied villages, towns and enterprises; a second case concerns war-profiteering, by which Armenian dealers in petrol have taken advantage of the Azerbaidzhani blockade to sell, at a large profit, fuel purchased in Azerbaidzhan and elsewhere. A third case concerns Armenia's construction of an army. While this state-building undertaking has been triggered by the national sense of vulnerability shared by men and women, it has created an expensive new bureaucracy which offers careers and well-paid jobs mainly to men, as officers, and provides lucrative opportunities, either connected with supplying the army, or from bribes paid by prospective conscripts trying to evade the draft.

The government also uses the construction of the army and defence of Armenian borders to justify the underfunding of traditionally feminine areas of the economy such as education. In 1993 and 1994, when the largely female teaching force appealed to parliament for funds to improve abysmal teaching conditions – unheated, unrepaired schools, lack of textbooks and teaching materials, and low salaries – they were told, in the words of one teacher, that 'we sympathise, but first Armenia must develop its military capacity'.[19] Teachers argued in vain that without the moral and patriotic instruction they provided students, Armenian boys would not have volunteered to defend Karabakh in the period preceding the construction of the army. The teachers ultimately gave way to the government's arguments, however. As the head of the Women's Council explained, 'in our blood there is a memory of genocide ... [and] the feeling of danger. The theme of war and women should start with the fact that we have a national complex of vulnerability.'[20] These words echo a sentiment expressed by many women, that although they deplored the impact of the war on the lives of their families, they viewed Armenians as victims simply defending their right to a national existence.

Many widows have bitterly questioned the purpose of their sacrifice, following the government's and army's failure to provide them pensions or child support. But in contrast to the former Yugoslavia, where feminist organisations actively participated in peace movements, Armenian women – with a few well-known and well-travelled exceptions – have not openly questioned or protested the conduct of the war. Nor do women feel they have much say over their husbands' involvement; their resistance, if any, has largely taken the form of hiding sons from the army or sending them abroad. Even the virtual press-ganging of Armenian youth in which the Armenian army has indulged has failed to catalyse any organised resistance to the war.

Conclusions

Describing women's situation in Armenia, the head of the Women's Council deplored the impact of the economic crisis on women, but felt women should act as a buffer between political opponents rather than aligning themselves with either the government or the opposition. In the current situation, she explained, 'when war has been forced upon us in Karabakh ... we can't open up an internal front; we put up with things that for the women of Armenia are practically impossible to put up with, but we don't wish to be guilty of creating an unpredictable situation in Armenia.'

With some exceptions due to specificities of history, culture and region, political and economic change has had a similar impact on Armenian women as it has had on women throughout the post-socialist world. Rising nationalism, fuelled by war, reinforces psychological obstacles impeding development of an independent women's movement. Despite the ceasefire of 1994 and popular exhaustion with the war, an historic memory of genocide constantly appealed to and refined by nationalist leaders makes it particularly difficult for women to assert their own interests, and to see how and in what context goals quite antithetic to these interests are pursued in the name of defending wives and children. In addition to its drain on the economy, the war also has the impact of reinforcing a conservative siege mentality and a retreat to 'national' values. Many Armenian men and women feel overwhelmed by economic catastrophe and political instability in their society, which they tend to associate with 'capitalism', 'free markets', and 'democracy'. In the present chaotic conditions, women's retreat to the comforting traditional picture of the Armenian woman as nurturer is a retreat from bad working conditions, corrupt politics and overwork, rather than a rejection of change.

Notes

Research for this chapter was completed as part of a project funded by the Harry Frank Guggenheim Foundation, and written while I was a research associate at the Institute for European, Russian, and Eurasian Studies at George Washington University. I would like to thank both institutions for their support.

1 I would like to thank Nora Hakopian, president of the Women's Council of Armenia, for very generously making available to me a copy of this unpublished poll, which was carried out by the organisation's members.
2 Katherine Verdery, 'From parent-state to family patriarchs: gender and nation in contemporary Eastern Europe', *East European Politics and Societies* 8(2), 1994, pp. 227–30.
3 Wolf Scott, 'Emergency and beyond: a situation analysis of children and women in Armenia', Geneva: UNICEF (January 1994), no pagination, section 22.
4 Igor Barsegian, 'Woman as superstructure: Armenian women after communism' (paper delivered at the American Anthropological Association annual meetings, Washington D.C., 1995).
5 Hana Havelková, ' "Patriarchy" in Czech society', *Hypatia* 8(4), 1993, p. 93.
6 The following discussion draws on Nora Dudwick, 'A qualitative assessment of the living standards of the Armenian population', Armenian Poverty Assessment Working Paper No. 1, The World Bank, 1995.

7 Sharon Holt, 'Using land as a system of social protection: an analysis of rural poverty in Armenia in the aftermath of land privatization', The World Bank, 1995.
8 *Ibid.*
9 *Ibid.*
10 Save the Children – US, 'Participatory assessment of Martuni region' (unpublished report, 1995), p. 27.
11 Beth Holmgren, 'Bug inspectors and beauty queens: the problems of translating feminism into Russian' in Ellen E. Berry (ed.), *Postcommunism and the body politic* (New York: New York University Press, 1995), p. 25.
12 *Ibid.*, p. 25.
13 From the unpublished poll carried out and provided to me by the Women's Council of Armenia.
14 Michael Mann, 'A crisis in stratification theory?' in Rosemary Crompton and Michael Mann (eds.), *Gender and stratification* (Cambridge: Polity Press, 1986), p. 47.
15 Barsegian, 'Women as superstructure'.
16 Valentine M. Moghadam, 'Introduction. Gender dynamics of economic and political change: efficiency, equality, and women' in Valentine M. Moghadam (ed.), *Democratic reform and the position of women in transitional economies* (Oxford: Clarendon Press, 1993), p. 3.
17 Partha Chatterjee, *The nation and its fragments: colonial and postcolonial histories* (Princeton: Princeton University Press, 1993), p. 119.
18 Rada Iveković, 'Women, nationalism and war: "Make love not war"', *Hypatia* 8(4), 1993, pp. 114–15.
19 From an interview conducted at a teachers' strike meeting in the town of Vaik, 1994.
20 From an interview conducted in September 1995.

14 The women's peace train in Georgia

TAMARA DRAGADZE

The role of women, as both perpetrators and victims in the tragedies of so-called 'ethnic cleansing', is so complex that it will take many inter-disciplinary, cross-cultural studies in order to establish any general patterns and correlations. We have become increasingly aware of this form of warfare through global media and some progress has been made in fields such as clinical work with the female victims of rape and violence. However, the interplay has yet to be identified and systematised between women's given roles in the societies to which they belong and the roles they take on in situations of 'ethnic conflict'.[1]

The turmoil that has swept through conflict-torn, post-communist Europe is exceptionally perplexing in so far as in Western Europe the media had, to a certain extent, identified with fellow-Europeans, even Eastern ones, in a way that was not characteristic of coverage of the Rwandan conflict, for example. Recent suggestions of the violent participation of female church members, let alone secular women, in the Rwanda massacres will undoubtedly yield insights into the nature of this interplay of gender-related social roles and their breakdown or, perhaps, re-interpretation in certain conditions.

The role of women in violent events in Eastern Europe can be examined in at least three ways: as perpetrators of violence, as victims and as 'peacemakers'. It is their role as peacemakers which will be briefly examined here.

As a general point, it appears that only rarely are women able to step outside their defined roles and challenge the male-dominated political arena. In those East European countries where education was advanced and where women had played an important role in civilian and economic life, there was a challenge for women to confront those within their own society who were involved in the conflicts. There were many grounds for them to argue with political leaders that there were more important issues at stake than personal profit and power on the one hand and the expression of ethnic pride on the other. In most cases, however, it appears that not only were the women unable to identify those responsible for the conduct of the armed conflicts but also that they were unable to avoid being manipulated in the larger arena.

Peace movements led by women were an appropriate ideological expression of their role in society, as nurturers, protectors, the givers of life. However, despite the sincerity of their feelings they did not have the sufficient distance from their own society to plan strategy carefully and to target the unusual. In other words, atrocities were being committed against the most vulnerable, those in the domain to which women have often been assigned as custodians and carers, and yet women were unable to use their role to confront and dispose of such practices of cruelty and terror, either by persuading women in the 'enemy camp' to join forces with them to stop the fighting or by challenging their own politicians to find a political, instead of a military, solution to the disputes.

There are a few rare exceptions in Eastern Europe. Some of the women's movements against the war in Chechnia have learned to challenge some of their societies' accepted values, both Russian and Chechen. Indeed, since the Chechen war began in December 1994, it is the women's peace movements – or at least some of them – which alone have been visible.[2] Either it is more acceptable in Russia and Chechnia at large that women join across the ethnic divide to stop the war or else (and this is much more likely) the war in Chechnia is not an 'ethnic' war at all, so that the women's joint protests have a completely different character.[3]

There have been other examples, however, where women are so closely enmeshed in a patriarchally dominated political situation and conform so readily to the expectations that society holds of them, that women's peace movements which would have challenged the *status quo* would have been impossible to develop. The case I will use to illustrate this point is that of the Women's Peace Train which was organised in the republic of Georgia and which started on 20 September 1993. My sources are based on personal interviews with eye-witnesses and a filmed sequence of events shown on Georgian television.

The Women's Peace Train event is not an illustration, in my judgement, of anything uniquely Georgian or even post-Soviet, but rather the event demonstrates a much more general position where women can usually transcend neither the idioms of expression nor the political strategies of patriarchal societies when these are engaged in armed conflict.

Background

Since 1921, Georgia had lost its independence to Soviet domination and a powerful movement to restore independence developed as soon as Gorbachev's reforms permitted it. As a result, some of the problems which Soviet nationalities policy had created and kept alive with one hand while suppressing protest with the other began to surface. These included the relationships between the Georgian and Abkhazian peoples and relations between the Union Republic of Georgia government and the Abkhaz Autonomous Republic within Georgia and, with it, a whole panoply of opportunities for the Moscow government to manipulate and intervene in. This included delivering weapons, directly or indirectly and very selectively, to various groups to serve their purpose. At the same time, the use of force was resorted to by the Soviet central government itself with impunity. In Georgia the role of women in the independence movement was noted when Soviet troops hacked to death women demonstrators with sharpened spades in April 1989. The ages of the women had ranged from sixteen to seventy-two and their portraits and coffins were carried through the streets. It created anger that the Soviet government had chosen the 'weakest' sex to massacre, and the women were praised for their bravery in having taken part in a peaceful protest knowing, as all Soviet citizens did, that their government could take ruthless measures whenever they wanted to. Highly misplaced, however, was the Georgians' expectation that Western governments would be so outraged that women had been specifically targeted for violence that they would sever diplomatic relations with Gorbachev's government.

At the end of 1991, the Soviet Union was dissolved and Georgia regained its independence with a nationalist president at the helm, Zviad Gamsakhurdia, who seemingly did not want to cooperate with the former colonial masters in Moscow. He was ousted through internal political conflict at the beginning of 1992 and in March the former Soviet foreign minister, Eduard Shevardnadze, returned from Moscow to his native Georgia and took power. He was mindful of being seen as a Moscow lackey and intended Georgia to pursue a policy of 'active neutrality' by not joining the Moscow-led Commonwealth of Independent States. The Russian Federation was displeased and was able to exert its privilege as custodian of the Soviet heritage by fulfilling or disregarding its obligations as it pleased, under the Tashkent Agreement it had signed, to share out the Soviet military hardware among the successor states. The Georgian government was permeated with uncontrollable rogue figures who presented themselves in the role of what should have been a national army on the one hand and, on the other hand, there was a Russian government eager, as its defence minister, Pavel Grachev, said, to extend its Black Sea coast. The dispute between the Abkhaz local government and that of Tbilisi was therefore bound to escalate out of all proportion. There had been decades of Abkhaz resistance to Georgian domination. Various minorities accounted for half of the province's inhabitants; by the time of the conflict, barely 17 per cent of the province's population were Abkhaz. The Abkhaz leadership had for a long time seen rapprochement with Russia as the only viable alternative for them, which the Georgians, being half of the total population of the province, were likely to refuse. Romantic young Georgians from the main cities, many from the intelligentsia, went to fight for Georgian sovereignty without any training; the Abkhaz volunteers armed themselves as best they could and obtained what support they could muster from non-Georgian minorities as well as the Russian military base conveniently located there. What started as the Abkhaz population's response to the indiscriminate raids by intrepid and indisciplined Georgian armed bands escalated into a full-scale conflict in the summer of 1992. The Georgian ill-equipped government tried to hold the capital of the Abkhaz Autonomous Republic, Sukhumi, while the Abkhaz volunteers fought back with determination and superior organisation, and with more advanced weaponry supplied by various Russian sources whose interests they served. To compound the dangers of violence, the ousted Georgian president had returned to Mingrelia, the Georgian province neighbouring Abkhazia, hoping to seize back power as soon as the incumbent government was sufficiently weakened. This is the background against which the Georgian women's peace train was organised.

The peace train departs

In Tbilisi, Georgian families with young sons were desperate, often because they could not stop them from rushing to Abkhazia as a patriotic gesture. By and large, however, this was not judged to be an empty gesture because preserving the territorial integrity of Georgia was seen by them as a matter of survival. It was felt very strongly that the ethnic assertiveness of the non-Georgians and their territorial claims for separation were manipulated by Russian imperialist forces who wished to weaken, and then end, Georgia's sovereign independence. Among the Georgian opinion-formers, little imagination was employed to attempt to understand and respond positively to the Abkhaz fears and demands, manipulated or not.

By tradition, in most of the Caucasus, honour should force men in combat to put down their weapons if women got between them, especially if they removed their white headscarves and threw them between the men. Women wanted to stop this war and this tradition of the past was resurrected for the occasion.

Soviet tradition was different. Women had been asked to fight at the Front during the Second World War; the Soviet image of Soviet Woman was universal: a muscular proletarian who created a new socialist paradise and defended her homeland. On this occasion, however, there was an ancient tradition ready for use in a way that would serve politicians well in Georgia. The idea was to get the women to shame the Abkhaz men and their mercenaries and backers to lay down their arms, or some such gesture; the anxiety was not to be addressed to the Georgian fighters at all, except to obtain permission to let them in to make their protest near the war zone.

Keti Dolidze, of the Georgian Film Actors' Theatre, called on all sincere and peace-loving women to come on a train, specially hired for the occasion, to travel to Abkhazia and demand peace. The hope was that up to 60,000 women would gather; although figures are so inexact that I will not make a guess. Probably, only several thousand mounted the train and arrived in Abkhazia.

Not to seem nationalistic, the women organisers were happy when a few representatives of other nationalities joined them; for example, a Russian woman (who accused Russia of being behind the war) and a Latvian woman (who said the whole world would have to wake up to what was going on) came on board.

The whole event was filmed for television and shown on the official channel. In the film a man's voice solemnly intoned Shevardnadze's message written to the participants in the women's peace train, whom he admired: 'Mothers, sisters, children, grandchildren, you want to stand between the fighters in Abkhazia.' He added a warning that reactionary forces in Russia were causing the war and it would eventually bring chaos to the rest of the world. One Lithuanian woman said that what was happening in Abkhazia was a struggle between Georgia and fascism and 'separatism' which must be stopped. The women felt their mission was far-reaching and noble, but they undertook it alone as an unilateral action.

It is important to note that there are Abkhaz women's peace rallies which had taken place in the region's capital, Sukhumi, where they demanded that the Georgians stop attacking them. The possibility of forming an alliance with Georgian women across the ethnic boundaries simply to stop the violence, whatever the causes, was not part of the agenda. Likewise, on the occasion of the Georgian women's peace train meetings, according to the statements of the women which have been recorded and are accessible, no attempt was made to separate out the Abkhaz 'people' from the fascists and imperialists to whom they were apparently allied. They too did not call the 'enemy' by any other names than those in their national press. What will never be known, however, is whether this was because the endeavour to create peace when the war was already at its peak was started too late by the Georgian women, or whether it was simply not part of the universe of discourse at that time.

The train's journey

The train, full of women who were mostly middle-aged, many of whom were going out to look for their sons at the same time, started off from Tbilisi with much fanfare and tears. Some of them had white gauze scarves round their shoulders (it being too hot in September for headscarves). There was trepidation, too, because the growing lawlessness in the country made any journey unpredictable.

The train stopped in Khashuri. Keti Dolidze, the organiser, who had already anticipated difficulties when they reached that province, said 'We will go through Mingrelia with love, only with love.' Another woman, a well-known actress, forcefully told people that they should not worry or fear. All along the route, the train was met with women who either mounted the train or brought food for them.

By the time the train reached Kutaisi, the second-largest city in Georgia, Keti Dolidze talked about Georgian unity, and not about peace between the Georgians and the Abkhaz. She did mention unity among all the nationalities in Georgia but, although she probably targeted her attention to them, she did not mention the Abkhazians by name. It is interesting to note, however, that when it was her turn to address the public at Kutaisi railway station, the woman world chess champion, Nana Alexandria, said their pain was mostly connected with war in Abkhazia but also said that Georgians must stop fighting each other, undoubtedly referring to the deposed president and his men who hoped to take back power by force, having lost it by force previously.

At this point, a woman poet read out some lines she had just written; 'The women are coming. Stop! The women are coming. Stop! Drop your weapons. The women are coming!' But here, almost, uniquely, it seems, she evoked the commonality of mothers both Abkhaz and Georgian, because she also recalled an old Georgian poem about the mothers of a slain tiger and a slain hunter who joined together to mourn the loss of both their sons who had killed each other. She also noted that she wished she herself were a mother so she could be like the hunter's mother who sought out his slain enemy's mother to weep with her. She stirred sympathy from the gathered crowds, it being considered a great tragedy among Georgians for a woman to be childless.

In Samtredia, another town in western Georgia, a woman said through the loudspeaker, 'We will go as far as we can and will stop where the men tell us to.' The organisers also asked for more women to join, whatever the cost, because it was necessary for everyone to see how many women stood for peace and unity. Another woman was more radical in her words: she said she was joining the train because she wanted to be with the children fighting, with the young men, instead of those older men who sent them there but themselves sat at home in Tbilisi and elsewhere. Another mother said that they were taking the fruit they had been given generously in Samtredia to Abkhazia.

It was at this point that General Tenguiz Kitovani, one of the Georgian commanders (at the time of writing, May 1996, under arrest for treason relating to the Abkhaz war) arrived at the station with a band of men ostentatiously brandishing their kalashnikovs. He told the women to turn back the peace train because Kobalia, the deposed president's military commander, and other henchmen would not let the train through the next province, Mingrelia, which separated them from Abkhazia. When the film came to be shown on television, the apparently recorded voice of the deposed president, Gamsakhurdia, was heard saying, 'Prostitutes are coming from Tbilisi, as if to stop the war in Abkhazia but they really want to make trouble in Mingrelia. Let our women stand on the rail tracks by [the town of] Tskheniskali and show pictures of their children who have been killed. Let them throw the pictures at the women.' He referred presumably to people who had been killed in the civil war rather than in Abkhazia. At the time, the women did not know that Gamshakhurdia had apparently spoken in this way.

To the peace train women, however, General Kitovani said, 'The Mingrelian women will fight you because their children have been killed.' This statement may be used in evidence against him in his forthcoming trial to prove that at the time he was really in alliance with Gamsakhurdia rather than with Shevardnadze. The television programme showed him nonchalantly lighting a cigarette and saying that he had come specially to meet the women on the peace train to ask them to turn back because he knew that the Mingrelian women would stand on the rail tracks and that chaos would ensue.

Interestingly, however, most of the women did not believe him: this was one moment of defiance. There were several Mingrelian women in the peace train who did not accept that there was any division between the people in the province of Mingrelia and the rest, as they asserted that all were Georgian. One woman shouted 'We must stand by our children everywhere.' They then distributed white headscarves, the symbol of women's peacemaking, and the train moved on, with some of the women actually shouting to Kitovani that he and his armed men were 'provocateurs'.

The television programme showed nothing of the peace train as it went through Mingrelia. Eyewitnesses, however, have told me that it sped rapidly and without difficulties, and when it occasionally stopped they took on more women, some of whom, admittedly, simply wanted to join their families in Abkhazia.

The train arrived in the Gali region of Abkhazia which had a majority Georgian population. There was a large meeting at which women chanted 'Georgia, Georgia' and there was a further rally where the cry was 'Georgians, Georgians!' Some women asked where their sons were, with whom they had lost contact. One woman said that the body of her slain son had been found with his eyes gouged out and nails torn out and she wanted to go where he was. Another woman asked for all the regions to be united, adding 'May there be peace, unity; I believe that Georgia will survive.'

At the rally in Gali, undoubtedly reminding people of the need to change direction, the chess champion Nana Alexandria said that 'We have so many sins on our hands that we are afraid of each other.' This point was not discussed further; instead, a poem in praise of Georgia was read out, written by Ana Kalandadze, one of the most famous

Georgian woman poets. The overwhelming feeling at the rally was that Georgia itself was threatened and that the peace had to be brought about to save it.

Even at this peace rally, a man rushed up with the news, which later proved false, that the deposed Gamsakhurdia's military leader, Kobalia, had set aside his differences with the present Georgian government and was going to fight side by side with them to preserve Georgian territorial sovereignty against the Abkhaz separatists and their allies. Hopes were raised in vain. The rhetoric, it should be noted, was about somehow winning the war rather than stopping it in its tracks.

Representatives of the women's peace train visited a house where a young boy's body was laid out, ready for burial; inevitably, there was a sense of helplessness and impending doom. One woman said her children were fighting – God help Georgia. All the women shared their grief but were unable to channel it against the violence of war in general.

They stood by a train full of men going off to fight and they dutifully clapped their hands as it pulled away, following the Georgian tradition that you do not cry when men leave to fight, so they would not take tears with them. Ominously, some Georgian women refugees driven out of other parts of Abkhazia were already arriving in Gali when the peace train left for Ochamchire which also had a sizeable Georgian population. There the effects of 'ethnic cleansing' were already being felt when one refugee said, 'The Abkhaz are no longer our brothers, because they have killed our children, even one nine-year-old.' One angry woman said, 'The army is standing outside Sukhumi and not fighting, so let us go and force them to go in. We've lost our friendship with the Abkhazians.'

Obviously, at this point, the Georgian Peace Train women would not feel this was the moment for seeking peace and contrition, for Georgian women to find Abkhaz women to swap horror stories about how each side had damaged the other. The mood was one of deep despair. One of the women from the peace train shouted out, 'Forgive us that we cannot help', particularly because they were surrounded by women asking for news of their sons.

By 24 September, when the fighting was reaching its final stage, outnumbered and with markedly inferior weaponry and organisation, the Georgian government was about to lose the battle and withdraw completely from Abkhazia. The women were told they should leave the area as soon as possible but, through a combination of difficulties caused by the war itself and the threatening presence of the deposed president in the neighbouring province, the train was only able to leave at 4 a.m.. It returned rapidly to Tbilisi, with a passenger list of defeated and desperate women who then glued themselves to their televisions to learn the outcome of the last battle.

Aftermath

Around a quarter of a million ethnic Georgians were driven out of their homes in Abkhazia. Many of them were forced to walk through a high mountain pass over 4,000 metres in altitude in the cold October weather, and several died on the way. The international community turned a conspicuously blind eye on the whole affair, as Russian interests were felt to be too important to confront. Peace initiatives themselves were considered too challenging at the time.[4]

At the present time, nearly four years later, the re-population of Abkhazia with non-Georgians has not taken place as their leaders might have hoped. The political fate of Abkhazia is dependent on Russian decision making and continues to be uncertain. Most of the local population now live in extreme hardship, although it may be some consolation to them that they are able to run their own affairs without recourse to the Georgian capital, Tbilisi. There is still no joint Abkhaz and Georgian women's movement to reach across the ethnic and political divide to create peace and reconciliation.

Conclusion

After the end of Soviet rule, women were able to have recourse to their traditional roles to express their emotions and to attempt to play some part in the fateful events which had overtaken their country. In the Caucasus, women, particularly mothers, were recognised as having the right to intervene to stop men fighting. In the case of the women's peace train which hoped to stop the war in Abkhazia, the fighting there was no longer of a traditional kind. It was, instead, a war linked to issues of modern geopolitics with powerful elements in Russia supporting one side, admittedly well motivated and organised, with modern weapons, satellite photography and other means for a small population to engage in a battle well beyond its original capacity. The Georgians were in disarray and weakened by civil war and military incompetence and insubordination, but their country's independence and Shevardnadze's courting of his Western acquaintances had appeared to be a threat to Russia. Superpower mentality was at work and the means at its disposal for action were not at a level easy to target by a civilian peace campaign. This was not an arena where women's peace trains could play much of a role without a carefully thought out strategy. This would have involved building bridges with dissident Abkhaz women who would have had to be against the principle of using violence of any sort. Even then, as elsewhere, such challenging demonstrations of unity among women representing both sides would have had to be unusually large-scale in order to halt the use of violence. This has yet to happen anywhere, let alone in Georgia. Until now, group solidarity among fellow ethnics and the desire to defend them against any perceived threats seem to outweigh the wish to create long-term strategies for peaceful living.

Notes

1 See Sharon Macdonald, Pat Holden and Shirley Ardener, *Images of women in peace and war* (London: Macmillan, 1987); and Rosemary Ridd and Helen Callaway, *Women and political conflict: portraits of struggle in times of crisis* (New York: New York University Press, 1987).
2 A European tour, for example, is being undertaken by two pairs of women, one Chechen and one Russian, campaigning for support for peace.
3 Protest against the war in Chechnia can thus be compared to the anti-Vietnam war movement or to the anti-colonial wars that won sympathy in some sections of the British population.
4 Even the UN office in Sukhumi, according to *The Times* correspondent, made no attempts at intervention or to give humanitarian aid even when people took refuge in the building in which they had premises.

15 Between tradition and modernity: the dilemma facing contemporary Central Asian women

SHIRIN AKINER

Introduction

By the end of the nineteenth century a huge part of Asia had been brought under Russian rule – in terms of surface area, a territory far larger than that encompassed by modern India. The indigenous population was almost entirely Muslim, of the Sunni sect. In the north (approximately equivalent to the territory of present-day Kazakhstan and Kyrgyzstan) and the south-west (present-day Turkmenistan), the local peoples followed a nomadic or semi-nomadic way of life. Religion here tended to be syncretic, only superficially Islamicised. In the oasis-river belt of Transoxiana (present-day Uzbekistan and western Tadzhikistan), there was an ancient urban culture. The cities in this region had long been famous as centres of Muslim scholarship. There were hundreds of *madrassah* (religious colleges) and thousands of (male) students of Islamic law. The focal point of the social as well as the religious life of the community was the mosque, at least one of which was to be found in every hamlet or town ward. Folk traditions and customs were inextricably intermingled with Islamic practices. At the popular level these were reinforced by the authority and prestige of representatives of the mystic orders – Sufi adepts, wandering dervishes (*kalendar*) and local holy men (*ishan*) – who were frequently credited with possessing supernatural powers of healing and soothsaying.

Under Soviet rule, Central Asia underwent an intensive process of modernisation. In effect, the region was wrenched out of Asia and thrust into Europe. Traditional culture was either destroyed or rendered invisible, confined to the most intimate and private spheres. In the public arena, new national identities were created, underpinned by newly fashioned languages and Western-style literatures and histories. Universal compulsory education was introduced, at first at primary level, later extended to secondary level; medical and social welfare networks were established, as a result of which health standards were greatly improved and average life expectancy raised by several years. Society was secularised: Islamic legal and educational institutions were abolished and Islamic beliefs and practices almost obliterated. Western-style cultural amenities such as museums, art galleries, opera and ballet companies and theatres took the place of traditional forms of artistic expression, thereby altering the social, cultural and intellectual environment. These and the many other changes that were set in motion at this time were ideologically driven and underwritten by major allocations of human and financial resources from the central government. This degree of official support (accompanied, from time to time, by ruthless coercion) enabled substantial progress to be achieved within a remarkably short period.

It was against this background of dynamic transformation that the campaign for female emancipation – or more precisely, for gender equality before the law, in the home, in education and at work – was launched. Thus, the struggle to redefine women's rights did not take place in a vacuum, but as part of a larger process, and was strengthened and amplified by other reforms that were implemented concurrently. The basic aims were underpinned by a variety of practical measures that gave substance to these new rights and opportunities for women. These might appear to have been optimum conditions in which to bring about a radical change in the position of Central Asian women. Yet this was only partially achieved: despite the very real improvement in facilities and range of choices, and the greater visibility of Central Asian women in public life, in the private sphere older patterns of behaviour continued to dominate gender relations. Soviet-style modernity was accepted by the indigenous population, but subtly transformed (or subverted) so as to accommodate traditional concepts of social order and propriety.

Today, since the collapse of the Soviet Union and consequent disintegration of the political and economic framework within which the modernisation of Central Asia was accomplished, many aspects of the Soviet legacy are being re-examined. In each of the newly independent states a new phase of nation building has been initiated and a redefinition of the national identity is under way. Traditional cultural and social values are now being emphasised and Islam is again beginning to play a prominent role in public life. At the same time, this region, which until very recently had almost no direct access to non-Soviet sources of information, is suddenly experiencing a flood of exogenous influences: foreign films and publications, businessmen from all parts of the world, tourists, international civil servants, aid workers and missionaries (representing every shade of Islam and Christianity, as well as other faiths or sects such as the Baha'i and Hare Krishna) are introducing new ideas and helping to shape new aspirations. Attempts at economic and political reform are also creating an impetus for change.

The emancipation movement was one of the defining elements of the ideological construction of Soviet Central Asian identities. It is not surprising, therefore, that as part of the current, post-independence process of refashioning national identities, the validity of the Soviet view of gender relations is being called into question. However, the situation is in flux. It is by no means clear whether the newly independent Central Asian states, individually or as an integrated group, will choose to remain within the European socio-cultural orbit that they have inhabited for the past half century, or whether they will seek to associate themselves more closely with their earlier, Islamic/Asian heritage. Central Asian women themselves are caught between conflicting impulses: some feel the need to return to their 'authentic' roots, with a renewed emphasis on traditional domestic obligations; others, to continue along the road to greater personal independence and freedom of choice. The great majority, however, would like to retain the balance between tradition and modernity that was reached, slowly and sometimes painfully, during the Soviet period. The dilemma that now confronts Central Asian women, poised between two value systems, subscribing in part to both, but not wholly to either, can only be understood in the context of the rapid, enforced, and not fully internalised, transition from a pre-modern to a modern society. It is therefore necessary to take a broader chronological perspective when dealing with this region than with other parts of the former Soviet Union, where the discontinuities have not been so profound. Hence, this paper begins by briefly reviewing the position of Central Asian women in the pre-Soviet period; it then looks at the relevant aspects of the Soviet emancipation movement; and, finally, at the challenges that are confronting Central Asian women in the post-Soviet states.

The term 'Central Asian women' is here used to refer collectively to the women of the titular peoples of these states, namely, the Kazakhs, Kyrgyz, Tadzhiks, Turkmen and Uzbeks. Ideally, were space to permit, each of these national groups should form the subject of a separate study. However, they do still share a sufficient number of common features – in large part the legacy of a shared Soviet experience – for it to be possible to make some valid generalisations about their present situation. This may not continue to be the case in the future, but as yet the divergences are quite slight. The issues that affect the position of women in the settler communities are rather different and it is beyond the scope of this paper to consider these groups. Likewise, indigenous peoples such as the Bukharan Jews, who have a different cultural background from the majority of the population, are not covered here.

Central Asian women in pre-Soviet society

Central Asia was incorporated into the tsarist empire over a period of some 150 years, beginning with the creeping annexation of the Kazakh steppes in the early eighteenth century and ending with the subjugation of the Turkmen tribes in the deserts of the south in the late nineteenth century. Russian policies towards their new subjects varied over time and from one area to another, but, in general, they were less interventionist than those of other European colonial powers. The tsarist government was mainly concerned with the creation of an effective administrative apparatus and the development and exploitation of the economic potential of the region. The local rulers were generally deposed (in most cases to be coopted into the service of the new regime), but the emir of Bukhara and the khan of Khiva were allowed to retain semi-independent status. Even in the areas that came under direct Russian rule, there was very little interference with traditional institutions. In the legal sphere, the most serious crimes were transferred to the jurisdiction of the Russian courts, but in all other cases *sharia* (Islamic canon law) and *adat* (customary law) continued to regulate the lives of the indigenous population. Although some Russian and Russo-native schools were opened, education, too, remained predominantly Islamic.

Information on pre-Soviet Central Asian society (or more accurately, *societies*, since there were many different groupings, all of which had their own traditions and customs) is very sparse. Moreover, it is almost entirely confined to the 'outsider's' view, as recorded in the accounts of tsarist officials and ethnographers, West European and American travellers, and Soviet field researchers of the 1920s.[1] The evidence they present is valuable, but it is incomplete, and informed by very particular cultural biases. Inevitably, this has given rise to misunderstandings and distortions. Indeed, such material generally reveals more about the prejudices and ideals of the writers than about Central Asian perceptions of their own society. However, despite the inadequacies of these sources, it is nevertheless important to review the picture they provide of Central Asian life at this period, since this construct has formed the basis for two, mutually contradictory, mythologising projects: that of the Soviet activists, who used it to promote a negative image of traditional society; and that of anti- and post-Soviet nationalists, who created from it an idealised image of a 'golden age', uncorrupted by Europeanising/Russifying influences, and hence an inspiration, if not a model, for the future development of the region.

In this period (that is, the nineteenth century), large extended families were the norm amongst nomads as well as sedentary peoples.[2] Several married groups, spanning at least two generations, would form a single entity, living, working and, in the case of the nomads, migrating, together. Marriages were arranged by close relatives in accordance with the rules of Islamic and customary law; neither the bride nor, generally, the bridegroom had any say in the choice of their future partner. There was frequently a considerable difference in age between husband and wife, since the financial obligations incurred by the male were very heavy, especially the payment of the 'bride price' (*kalym*); only young men from the wealthiest families could afford this. The minimum age set by Islamic law at which a girl could be given in marriage was nine years. Islamic law permitted a man to be wedded to up to four wives at any one time (on condition that all were treated equally), but local practice in some places allowed many more.[3] Concubinage was also not uncommon. In theory, both husband and wife had the right to initiate a divorce, but in practice it was invariably the husband who took such action.

Female members of the family made an important contribution to the family economy, producing foodstuffs, clothing and furnishings. However, child-bearing was probably their most important function. Large numbers of sons were considered to be vital for the security and prosperity of the household, but proverbs suggest that daughters were regarded as a burden.[4] Female mortality was very high;[5] this was probably owing to frequent pregnancies starting from a very young age, but it is possible that girls were given less care and nourishment than boys. Medical help was minimal, for the most part restricted to the services of local holy men who were credited with supernatural healing powers, occasionally enhanced by some knowledge of traditional remedies.

In urban communities, girls and women led a segregated existence, contact with males being restricted to close relatives. Within the family home they had their own quarters; when they went out, they wore a cloak-like over-garment (*parandzha*) and a waist-length horse-hair veil (*chachvan*) which concealed their faces. In nomad and semi-nomad communities, and possibly in remoter settled areas, women were not veiled, although they did wear some form of headgear which also covered part of their upper body. They did not have segregated dwellings, but there was a strict division of labour which served to mark out the boundaries of male and female space. Given the paucity of source material, it is impossible to gain a coherent picture of regional, social and economic variations. It is generally supposed that women in nomad communities enjoyed a greater degree of freedom. This may not have been the case at the lower end of the social scale, but amongst the ruling elites, women appear to have been able to act with a substantial degree of autonomy.[6] In settled communities, women were probably subjected to greater formal controls, although those who were skilled artisans could possibly acquire some independence through membership of craft guilds.[7] By the early twentieth century, there were some facilities for the education of girls. For the most part, these took the form of elementary religious schools run by the wives of the local *mullah* (religious functionary). In middling and upper-class circles women received a fuller education; a few became accomplished literary figures in their own right.[8]

Almost nothing is known about intra-family relationships and the way in which they affected the position of women. By analogy with societies that have similar traditions (for example, in Afghanistan and Pakistan) and also with modern, post-Soviet family structures, it seems reasonable to assume that although there was strong patriarchal control, and overall gender asymmetry in terms of authority and prestige, within their own domain women had parallel hierarchies that were as rigidly ranked and almost as powerful as those of the male world. Moreover, as wives, and the mothers of sons, women would have been able to exert very considerable influence not only within the family unit, but also in external affairs.

Soviet gender politics

In the aftermath of the Russian revolution, Central Asia, as other parts of the tsarist empire, was swept by civil war. The main contenders were various Slav military and political factions, but in some areas contingents of foreign (mainly British) interventionists played an active role; there were also nationalist movements that sought to establish autonomous states in Kazakhstan and Kokand, and amorphous bands of rebels, known as *basmachi*, under the leadership of local warlords. By 1920, Soviet power had been firmly established in most areas, though the *basmachi* continued to offer a guerrilla-type resistance for almost a decade longer. They claimed to be fighting a 'holy war' in defence of Islam and traditional values. Although they rarely represented a serious military threat, their influence amongst the indigenous population was so strong, especially in the 1920s, that the Soviet authorities were forced to temper their reformist zeal with a degree of caution, and to delay for some years the full implementation of programmes such as the emancipation of women and the campaign against religion.

Nevertheless, a number of measures were introduced at this time which laid the foundations for later developments. The most important of these was the National Delimitation of 1924–5, whereby administrative-territorial units were created on the basis of the ethnolinguistic affiliations of the main indigenous peoples. Two of these units, Uzbekistan and Turkmenistan, immediately acquired the status of full Union republics, while Tadzhikistan, Kazakhstan and Kyrgyzstan were elevated to this status some years later. These formations were entirely new, with no basis either in the tsarist provincial divisions or in the pre-colonial khanates. The reasons for this exercise in territorial division are debatable, but certainly it was more successful in consolidating the main ethnic groups within a single unit than were similar boundary-drawing projects enacted by other colonial powers in Asia and Africa. Without any movement of peoples, an average of some 90 per cent of the Uzbeks, Turkmen, Kazakhs and Kyrgyz were included within the borders of their respective titular units.[9] The Tadzhiks fared less well: they were so closely intermingled with the Uzbeks that it was impossible to make an equitable territorial division of the land they both occupied; the new borders deprived them of the historic centres of Bukhara and Samarkand, and, as a result, over a third of the ethnic Tadzhiks were brought under Uzbek jurisdiction.[10] In addition to the indigenous Central Asian peoples, there was already a sizeable Slav (mainly Russian) presence in the region;[11] the percentage share of the titular people in the total population of each of these republics decreased during the first decades of the Soviet period owing to the constant influx of migrants from other parts of the Soviet Union, especially from the European republics.[12] This helped to dilute further the traditional culture and to accelerate the process of social and economic change.

Creating the legal and operational infrastructure

Ideologically, the campaign for the emancipation of Central Asian women grew out of Russian Marxist feminism, drawing inspiration and moral support from leading activists such as Nadezhda Krupskaia, Klara Zetkin, Inessa Armand and Aleksandra Kollontai (who is sometimes credited with being the instigator of the movement in Central Asia).[13] The project was organised and monitored by the central organs of the Communist Party in Moscow. From the earliest days of Soviet rule it was regarded as a strategic priority. There were three main reasons for this. Firstly, there was genuine horror and disgust at the social injustice: to Russian eyes, the treatment of Central Asian women in traditional society seemed tantamount to slavery. Secondly, there was a political imperative to create a 'surrogate proletariat' to engage in the class war and also the related war against religion.[14] Thirdly, there was an economic necessity to draw women into socialised production.

During the first years of the emancipation campaign (c. 1918–26), the main emphasis was on the creation of an organisational infrastructure. One aspect of this was to establish a legal framework that codified women's rights, as well as the measures that could be used to enforce them. Islamic courts, using the *sharia* and *adat* legal systems, functioned alongside Soviet courts until 1928, but their powers were circumscribed and in some areas of family law they ceased to have any jurisdiction in the early 1920s. Laws and decrees passed by the state took precedence over the provisions of all other codes. In 1918, the official registration of marriages, births and deaths was made compulsory. Also, the option of having recourse to Soviet divorce law instead of the *sharia* code was introduced, in an effort to give women greater protection. Between 1921 and 1923, laws were passed banning such practices as polygamy, the payment of *kalym* and marriage without the consent of the bride; the minimum age for marriage for girls was set at sixteen years, for boys at eighteen years. Any violation of these laws was treated as a criminal act and subject to severe penalties. The land and water reforms of 1925–9 gave women an independent entitlement to a share of these resources, thereby emphasising their autonomous status in law and in society. Great efforts were made to publicise these new legal provisions: the laws were translated into the local languages and the texts disseminated widely. Public meetings and rallies were held to explain women's civil and constitutional rights. Moreover, Central Asian women were urged to take an active part in the legal process. Several were given basic training in Soviet law and attached to the courts as People's Assessors. Later, longer courses were provided and towards the end of the 1930s they began to enter the judiciary.[15]

Another aspect of the work of these years was the training of local cadres. The first activists were almost all young Russian communists;[16] few of them had any knowledge of the local languages or customs. Gradually, however, from about 1925 onwards, they were joined by Central Asian supporters. These were mostly young girls from poor backgrounds who, for one reason or another, had become isolated from their families; they joined the Communist Party and became actively involved in the emancipation movement.[17] By 1920, a number of women's sections (*zhenotdely*) of the Communist Party had been organised in Central Asia. At first they made little impact on the lives of the indigenous population, but they were later to play an important role in strengthening and consolidating the emancipation movement. Much of the practical support and training for Central Asian women in this period of transition was channelled through these bodies; they also acted as watchdog committees, monitoring working conditions and ensuring that local officials and employees fulfilled their statutory obligations towards women. They were likewise responsible for ideological education and were much involved in consciousness-raising activities among the local women.

One of the most important areas of the work of the women's sections was the organisation of social clubs exclusively for women. Here they were able to provide a secluded, protected environment in which Central Asian women could feel at ease outside their own homes. The first such club was established in the old quarter of Tashkent in 1924; others soon appeared throughout the region, even in remote, rural areas.[18] The clubs offered a range of medical, legal and educational services; other activities included sewing and reading circles; amateur dramatics, devoted mainly to the performance of playlets on contemporary themes; consultations on nutrition, hygiene and child care; and also lectures, film shows and concerts.[19] Given the very controlled and segregated conditions of female existence in Central Asia at the time, the clubs were a remarkable innovation. They represented the first tentative step towards women's full participation in public life.

Casting off the veil

The decision to intensify the emancipation campaign by initiating the mass unveiling of Central Asian women was taken in Moscow in the autumn of 1926.[20] The organisation and preparatory propaganda work was delegated to specially constituted regional party committees, but the overall strategy continued to be formulated and directed by the central authorities. By this time some 25,000 Central Asians had joined the party and almost 55,000 were members of the Young Communist League; thus there was a body of 'shock troops' in place to carry out the operation.[21] In Uzbek it was known as the *khudzhum* (the attack), and indeed it was conceived in terms of a military exercise. The key target areas were the densely populated cities of Uzbekistan, where the practice of wearing the veil was most deeply entrenched.

The first large-scale public displays of unveiling took place in 1927, on International Women's Day (8 March). Preliminary estimates claimed that on that one day 8,500 had cast off their *parandzha* and *chachvan* and ceremonially incinerated them on giant bonfires.[22] In reality, the figure of those who unveiled was far lower; moreover, of those who did make this gesture, many, including several Young Communist League members, redonned the veil the following day. However, this did not deter the party-state authorities. The wearing of the veil was not banned by law (although some activists were in favour of this), but a variety of so-called 'administrative' measures were used to further the campaign. Special privileges were given to women who discarded the veil; the husbands of those who did not were liable to be penalised.[23] In some enterprises it was a condition of employment that women should be unveiled. On occasion, more ruthless methods were used; women were intimidated into unveiling, or unveiled by force.[24] Meanwhile, there was ceaseless ideological indoctrination through newspaper articles, films, posters, lectures and even house-to-house visits.[25] The results of these efforts was that by the mid-1930s it was increasingly rare to see a fully veiled woman. However, in country areas or in the old quarters of the cities, women continued to cover their heads and shoulders with large headscarves.

The *khudzhum* was a definitive episode in the social transformation of the region. To the Russians, the *parandzha* symbolised everything that they were fighting to eradicate: oppression, ignorance, injustice and human degradation.[26] However, from the little contemporary and circumstantial evidence that is available, it would seem that, for

Central Asians, the veil had a very different range of associations. It was a protection against unwanted contact with strangers and also against the physical grime of the environment. It could be, too, a status symbol, indicating social standing.[27] Most importantly of all, it was a statement about the fundamental ordering of society: the nature of gender relations, the division between public and private space, the conventions of civility. For the Russians, the success of the *khudzhum* was an ideological victory. For the Central Asians, it was a defeat and a brutal rape: the honour and dignity of the community was suddenly and monstrously violated. No other measure of Soviet policy – not the closure of the mosques, the sedentarisation of the nomads, collectivisation or the purges – provoked such violent and outspoken resistance. Even senior party officials at first refused to allow their wives to unveil.[28] Women who did throw off the *parandzha* were often rejected by their families. More than a thousand unveiled women were murdered, either by their relatives or by the *basmachi*, in these years.[29] It was not, however, only men who were opposed to the *khudzhum*. Published Soviet sources generally present the reaction of Central Asian women to the campaign to cast off the veil in very enthusiastic terms. Occasionally, though, there are hints that there were some who were prepared to speak out openly against it.[30] However, the terror that was unleashed in the 1930s effectively put an end to any further opposition. The trauma of the *khudzhum* was suppressed, buried in the sub-conscious, as were so many of the other tragedies of this period. A new generation of women grew up in a world in which Soviet values had already become the accepted norm: for them, the discarding of the veil took on the significance of a rite of passage that marked the entry into a new era of progress and enlightenment. Concomitantly, the former way of life was made to seem very remote, alien and primitive, an attitude which facilitated the inculcation of a negative evaluation of traditional society as a whole.

Political and economic mobilisation

The Soviet authorities regarded education as an essential component of political and economic mobilisation. In Central Asia, in the early 1920s, the level of literacy amongst the indigenous peoples (as estimated in Soviet sources) ranged from an average 7 per cent amongst the Kazakhs, to just over 2 per cent amongst the Turkmen and Tadzhiks; in rural areas it was lower, and amongst women, scarcely above 1 per cent. One of the first priorities of the new state was to remedy this situation. Special ABC (*likbez*) courses were set up in railway coaches, tents, factories and every other conceivable venue. Great efforts were made to reach the female population. The women's sections were especially active in this field, but the trade unions (*profsoiuzy*), Young Communist League and other socio-political organisations also contributed to the campaign. At the same time, the network of schools and teacher-training colleges was expanded, while the Islamic educational institutions were gradually phased out; by 1927, the entire educational system had been Sovietised.[31] In the larger towns and cities most of the schools were co-educational, but in rural areas many families refused to allow their daughters to attend mixed establishments. Fully integrated education was not achieved until the 1930s.

Primary schooling was made compulsory for boys and girls alike by about 1930. This was later expanded to an eight-year (incomplete secondary) course;[32] eventually an optional two to three years (higher secondary) were added. Central Asian girls began to embark upon tertiary education in significant numbers in the late 1930s and thereafter to enter the professions, particularly law, medicine, teaching and scientific research. Nevertheless, in the 1970s the proportion of Central Asian women with higher education was still considerably lower than the average for the Soviet Union as a whole.[33] The chief obstacle to raising the level of attainment was the tendency of Central Asian girls to leave school early in order to marry. Some later returned to full- or part-time education, but the majority did not progress beyond the minimum school-leaving qualifications.

School was not only the place where a general educational programme was provided; it was also the channel through which the values and goals of communism could be inculcated in the younger generation. The educational process was also used to challenge inherited conventions regarding the role of women in society. As one former Soviet citizen put it, 'they constantly told us that women must be fully equal with men, that women can be flyers and naval engineers and anything that men can be'.[34] Central Asian girls were encouraged not only to study, but also to take part in physical training and team sports; in performing arts such as ballet, acting (on stage and in films) and singing; and in occupations requiring technical skills such as tractor driving. Perhaps nothing so vividly illustrates the changes that were taking place at this time as the appearance, in the 1930s, of the first female parachutists in a society in which only ten years previously women had been heavily veiled.[35]

During the same period, energetic efforts were made to involve Central Asian women in the political-administrative process. Female delegates were elected to represent their communities in public meetings at local and republican level. Activists were sent for training to the Communist University, the Turkic School of Soviet and Party Work and other such institutions.[36] In the early 1920s, Central Asian women began to join the party, some no doubt impelled by idealism and belief in the reform programme, but others by a realisation of the practical benefits that would accrue from such a move. In percentage terms their participation remained low, but actual numbers were quite high, given their lack of previous political experience; in Uzbekistan, for example, by the beginning of 1929 there were over 1,000 Uzbek women party members.

In response to Lenin's injunction that more women should be elected to the soviets, Central Asian women gradually came forward to stand as candidates. However, progress was slow; not only were the women reluctant to take part in elections, but there was much covert opposition from the male members of the community. Nevertheless, the authorities continued to press for an improvement in the situation. There was a constant monitoring of the proportion of women in senior managerial posts, and shortcomings as well as successes in this field were widely publicised.[37] Positive discrimination was used to accelerate promotion and a quota system was introduced whereby women were allocated approximately a third of the posts in government and in party-administrative organs. This, along with the effusive public acclaim that was accorded to women's achievements in other fields such as the arts, sports and science, provided a high degree of female visibility in society. It created a range of positive, 'progressive' role models with whom Central Asian girls could identify.

Another important aspect of the political mobilisation of Central Asian women in these years was their role in the anti-Islamic campaign. Since women were regarded as the chief victims of religious oppression, it was they who were selected to take a leading part in the campaign to eradicate Islam. The *mullahs* were equated with the wealthy peasants and represented as both class enemies and the enemies of progress. Branches of the Godless League (later renamed the 'Militant Godless League') were set up in all the Central Asian republics. They grew rapidly in the frenzied, fear-dominated atmosphere of the day. In Uzbekistan, for example, in 1928, 3,500 Uzbek women were members of the League; by 1931, the number had reached 27,000. Anti-religious circles were set up in most enterprises and about 80 per cent of the members were local women.[38]

The result of this onslaught was that knowledge of the religion was reduced to a minimum. Almost all that survived were some of the rituals connected with the major life-cycle ceremonies (male circumcision and burial rites, for example), and some semi-folk, semi-Islamic practices such as visits to the graves of revered individuals, where prayers and sacrifices were offered up in the hope of securing benediction. Women remained active in keeping such informal aspects of Islam alive. So far as more orthodox beliefs and practices were concerned, some of the older generation of women continued to perform as best they could some of the prescribed ritual prayers and to observe at least a part of the fast of Ramadan. However, few of the generation that grew up after the Second World War maintained this tradition. Islamic prohibitions on the consumption of pork products and alcohol were increasingly disregarded by Central Asian men, many of whom spent most of their working lives in multi-ethnic environments, where they were under constant pressure to conform to the norms of Soviet society; women, however, protected by the privacy of their homes, were able to observe these dietary laws more strictly.[39]

The first steps to draw women into socialised labour were made through women's cooperatives. These were organised in the early 1920s, and represented a half-way stage, enabling women to continue practising their traditional tasks, such as weaving, sewing and dairying, but outside the family home, in a group environment and for financial reward. Special shops and consumer cooperatives were set up through which women could sell their products directly, without the intervention of middlemen.[40] Towards the end of the decade there was a proliferation of light industrial enterprises, and increasing numbers of local women found work in factories concerned with food-processing, silk-spinning and the production of garments and hosiery. Heavy industry was developed somewhat later, but relatively few female workers were employed in this sector since conditions were considered to be unsuitable for women for physical as well as psychological reasons.

By contrast, the agricultural sector was regarded as eminently suitable for female labour and a concerted effort was made to draw Central Asian women into the work-force. In the north, this was mainly devoted to various forms of animal husbandry, while in the south, the chief areas were cotton cultivation and silk-worm breeding.

Women's involvement in the development of the cotton-growing industry was the most problematic area, and subsequently attracted much adverse criticism. By 1934, women were involved in almost all aspects of the production of the cotton crop; however, the majority were employed on a seasonal basis for the back-breaking job of harvesting the cotton by hand.[41] Their achievements in helping to secure 'cotton independence' for the Soviet Union were praised in the mass media and those who exceeded their set norms were rewarded with medals and special privileges. The other side of the coin was that work conditions in the plantations were very arduous and that the women were, in effect, used as human tools.

Central Asian girls were taught that it was their right, and also their duty, to seek useful and gainful employment in the public sector. As adults, most of them were to have some experience of work outside the home, but the period of employment was often quite limited, owing to the almost continuous cycle of child-bearing and child-rearing. Moreover, the goal of gender equality at work was never fully attained. Here, as in other parts of the Soviet Union (and in many other countries, too), employers were reluctant to take on female workers on the grounds that they were less productive than their male counterparts; there were also complaints about the length of the statutory maternity leave. Women were frequently (and illegally) paid less for the same work as men; they were also not given as many opportunities for in-service training to raise their qualifications.[42] As a result, many remained trapped in low-paid, unskilled or semi-skilled jobs. This made them vulnerable to redundancy when more efficient technology was introduced.[43]

The main motivation for the economic mobilisation of Central Asian women was undoubtedly the need to boost the labour force at a time of major industrial and agricultural expansion. However, it was seen, too, as a means of reinforcing the emancipation movement, since it gave women the possibility of achieving financial independence through waged work. It also provided them with an opportunity to experience new conditions, and to come into direct contact with people from different social and ethnic backgrounds. In most parts of the world, the move to paid employment outside the home has had an important impact on the way women regard themselves, as well as on their position in the family and in the broader community. In Central Asia, however, this did not happen to any significant degree. There was scarcely any redefinition of gender roles, scarcely any extension of the traditional kin-based networks of friendship, solidarity and support.

This is less surprising than it might at first appear: Central Asian women (and men), confronted with the headlong pace of change in the public sphere, reacted by holding on yet more firmly to the order they knew in the domestic sphere, where they had a greater degree of control. Thus, Central Asian women did not in fact assume the role of a revolutionary force to destroy traditional society. Rather, they colluded in its preservation: by accommodating external pressures through the adoption of additional identities, appropriate to the public sphere, they deflected intrusions into the private domain, thereby protecting the integrity of the older disposition of family roles. This is not to imply that the public identities were a sham; on the contrary, all the indications are that they were the product of genuinely held perceptions and aspirations. However, they were confined to one area and were not permitted to penetrate beyond that space, and thus could not bring about the radical change of society that had been anticipated.

Family and community

Family and community relations were (and remain) the most conservative areas of Central Asian society. Even in cities, amongst the most educated and travelled groups, there was relatively little structural change during the Soviet period; in rural areas, social conventions were even more strongly preserved. Hence, there were perceptible continuities with the pre-Soviet period. The extended family networks remained powerful. The actual size of cohabiting units fell sharply, owing to such pressures as the nature and availability of accommodation, changes in employment patterns (including, of course, collectivisation) and the general regimentation and homogenisation of life under Soviet rule. Nevertheless, close contact was retained amongst the members of the larger family even when they were physically dispersed through frequent (wherever possible, daily) visits and telephone calls.[44] Adult sons would often continue to live at home even after they had married. In such cases, it remained customary for them to hand over their wages, as well as any earnings of their wives, to the head of the family to use as he pleased. The absolute authority of the father was mirrored by the less formal, though perhaps psychologically yet more compelling, authority of the mother. In accordance with the Islamic precept, 'Happiness lies at the feet of the mother', sons treated their mothers with huge respect, regarding her every word as a sacrosanct command. This honoured status gave her as great a degree of control over their lives, and over the lives of their dependents, as she herself wished to exercise.

Within the family unit there was a high degree of order. This expressed itself through a strong, almost ritualised, code of civility which regulated every aspect of behaviour. Children were socialised in this environment to accept their place in the hierarchical structure, with the attendant obligations, responsibilities and privileges. Constructions of masculinity and femininity were internalised at this stage and gender roles assigned. A strong sense of sibling solidarity was fostered, as well as respect and affection for the older members of the family. Habits of obedience, conformity and submission were fostered in girls and boys alike; the latter may have had greater freedom of action outside the home, but within the family both genders were equally bound by strict conventions. Discipline was maintained through positive encouragement in the form of praise and little gifts. Corporal punishment was very rare: patriarchal authority was clearly enough understood, even by very young children, for a warning tone of voice and a stern demeanour to serve as a sufficient reprimand. There was still a residual preference for sons, though in terms of care, affection and opportunities, daughters no longer appeared to be less privileged than sons.

On marriage, brides moved to the patrilocal residence. From the outset, they were expected to conform to the conventions of their husband's home. Attitudes towards the newcomer were often harsher and more demanding than towards the children of the family. For the young bride, the mother-in-law's word was final. If there was a dispute, the husband would almost always side with his mother, even if he sympathised with his wife's position, and this could cause the young bride to feel very isolated. Her defencelessness was underlined by the fact that her husband would normally take control of any money she might earn, giving back to her only what he considered to be an adequate allowance (thereby defeating the Soviet aim to give women economic independence through waged work). A girl would often not be able to visit her family without her husband's permission. In case of a complete marital breakdown, however, she would normally return to her parental home. There was no social stigma attached to divorce or to remarriage. A wife's status in the family improved with time, with the birth of children, also with the arrival of other daughters-in-law, the wives of younger sons. Initially, the experience of learning to live in the new household could be difficult. However, there was usually a great deal of encouragement and support from other female members (including, sometimes, the mother-in-law herself) and normally the bride was assimilated into the new environment quite quickly.

Community relations usually involved extended kin-networks as well as neighbours. There was a high level of group solidarity, reinforced through numerous joint activities. The practical preparations for such events as a wedding or a wake were undertaken by the community as a whole, thus relieving the strain on the individual family. These were often huge affairs, requiring vast quantities of food (80 kg each of meat and rice were not uncommon provisions), chairs, tables, crockery, and pots and pans. The utensils and furniture were all provided from the communal stock. Women, whatever their status and professional qualifications, would take their place at the stove and the chopping board. These occasions provided an important opportunity for gossip to be exchanged, a family's reputation and standing in the community to be monitored, problems to be aired, and advice to be given and received. Thus, the community helped to offset the possible isolation of family life. In cases of major family disputes, the senior female of the community would act as counsellor and arbitrator, guiding the different sides towards a compromise. The community also provided additional opportunities for socialising children in traditional values, supervising them when they were out of the home and reinforcing habits of civility, consideration and courtesy. The positive aspect of community life was that it provided a highly effective, informal and very sensitive social security network. The negative aspect was that it was very difficult to escape from its all-embracing control.

Marriage and fertility

It has become an accepted axiom, confirmed by evidence from all over the world, that rises in female literacy rates are accompanied by a decrease in birth rates. Central Asian women, however, have to date proved to be an exception to this rule. Under Soviet rule the crude birth rate remained very high. Consequently, the age structure of the titular peoples of the Central Asian republics continued to conform to the model of the broad-based demographic pyramids of countries such as India, Kenya and Nigeria, with well over half the population under twenty years of age. There are a number of reasons why this pattern was maintained, but principally it was the result of a convergence between pro-natalist attitudes in traditional and Soviet society.

Custom, mediated through family and peer pressure, ensured that marriage, preferably at an early age, remained the natural goal for Central Asian girls.[45] As in the past, children were regarded as a blessing, the foundation of the family's happiness and prosperity. Moreover, within the family unit, the young wife's status was to a large extent still determined by the number of children, especially boys, that she produced. At the same time, with improved medical care, female life expectancy rose and hence the period of fertility was extended. Since infant mortality was likewise reduced, the result was a high level of natural increase. The financial strain of a large family was relieved by the state provision of child and maternity allowances. The lump sum allocation at birth, as well as the monthly welfare benefit, increased in accordance with the number of children. Thus, a mother who had only one child received a considerably smaller sum for that one child than she did for her fourth or fifth child; for the eleventh child and above, the benefits were quite large.[46] In the European republics, where wages were generally higher and families smaller, these allowances were not of great importance. In Central Asia, however, they could constitute a substantial contribution to the family budget.

There were also other forms of state support for motherhood. There was a statutory obligation for employers to provide sixteen weeks' paid maternity leave, as well as entitlements to further unpaid maternity leave without loss of job or seniority. The status of motherhood was reified by the ceremonial award of honours, medals and privileges. The highest rank, that of 'Heroine Mother', was bestowed on those who had borne and reared ten or more children. In Uzbekistan alone, by 1987 over 100,000 women had been given this title; over a million had been awarded the order 'Mother's Glory' (seven to nine children) and over 2 million that of 'Medal of Maternity' (five or six children).[47] The holders of these honours were treated with great respect, their maternal achievements noted in the press and praised in party reports, alongside accounts of industrial and agricultural successes. Thus, motherhood, or rather, the child-bearing aspect of motherhood, was set on a par with other important contributions to society. By contrast, the domestic routine of child-rearing was regarded as an obstacle to full emancipation, hence to be eradicated as soon as possible through the provision of a full range of socialised welfare services. In fact, this goal was not realised and Central Asian women continued to be childrearers as well as child-bearers for a large portion of their lives.

In addition to these pro-natalist measures, there were other factors which also helped to perpetuate the tradition of large families. Close-knit kinship networks ensured that there were generally other females available to help with child care and other domestic chores.[48] Women who wished to pursue professional careers, therefore, did not have to make a choice between having a family or continuing to work. At the same time, the close proximity of senior relatives meant that they were able to exert continued psychological pressure on the younger wives to produce children.[49] This, coupled with a high level of ignorance about sexual matters, very little medical counselling on family planning and a very inadequate supply of contraceptives, meant that even those who wished to limit their pregnancies were unable to do so.

Ill-health, domestic violence and self-immolation

For most of the Soviet period the campaign for the emancipation of Central Asian women was described in very positive terms, with great emphasis on the achievements, and a glossing-over of mistakes and unfulfilled goals. In the mid-1980s, however, during the period of perestroika and glasnost, a more critical attitude began to emerge.[50] One of the issues that attracted wide coverage, both in Moscow and in the Central Asian republics, was the use of harmful substances to sustain the cotton monoculture, and the effect that this was having on the health of the workforce, the great majority of whom were women and schoolchildren (who every autumn spent several weeks assisting with the cotton harvest). It was revealed that a highly toxic chemical, similar to Agent Orange, was being used to defoliate the cotton. Immediately after the spraying had been completed, women and children were sent into the fields to pick the cotton with their bare hands, without any protective clothing. Another malpractice was the use of huge quantities of chemical fertilisers, pesticides and herbicides to boost the yield; these then leached into the soil and water and in turn contaminated the food chain.[51] Concerns were voiced at this time as to the possible long-term effects of measures such as these on the health of the population. Some feared that irreparable damage had already been inflicted on their immune systems; the term 'ecological AIDS' was coined to describe this condition.

Some of these reports undoubtedly owed more than a little to journalistic licence. There was also an element of political manipulation, with this and other examples of environmental mismanagement being used by the liberal-reformist lobby as a stick with which to beat the Soviet system as a whole. Until further, unbiased, medical research has been carried out it will be impossible to assess the full gravity of the situation. It is, nevertheless, beyond dispute that there was gross exploitation of women and children and that this was causing major health problems.

More attention also began to be paid to shortcomings in the domestic sphere. As elsewhere in the Soviet Union, there was criticism of the heavy 'double shift' of work that women had to endure. In Central Asia, the burden was the more onerous owing to the prevalence of large families, relatively low provision of communal amenities such as crèches, canteens and laundries, and, outside the main cities, the chronic scarcity of labour-saving devices such as washing machines and electric vacuum cleaners.[52] Concerns were voiced, too, about the dangers of frequent, closely spaced pregnancies and the debilitating effect this was having on the physical and mental well-being of Central Asian women, as well as on the health of the nation as a whole. The question of family planning began to be raised in public in the second half of the 1980s, though was soon dropped on account of strong local opposition.[53]

At this time, there was also some discussion of the psychological pressures that were inflicted on women within the confines of the family. There was little specific mention of physical violence, but anecdotal evidence suggested that it was quite widespread, indicating that it was an accepted, or at least acknowledged, feature of marital behaviour. The one aspect of domestic violence that did come to light was the horrifying and baffling incidence of suicide by self-immolation. According to official sources, in Uzbekistan, in one year alone (1986–7), 270 girls and young women killed themselves in this way.[54] It was generally agreed that the actual figure was probably far higher and that many such deaths were being passed off as accidents. The phenomenon appeared to be limited to Uzbekistan and Tadzhikistan.

Some commentators believed that it was the relentless drudgery of women's lives, compounded by oppressive patriarchal attitudes in the family, that were to blame; others sought an explanation in a possible nutritional deficiency (a lack of protein, for example), which might cause depression and disorientation. It was also suggested that the practice might have its origins in some form of religious belief. However, Islam is categorically opposed to suicide. The more ancient faith of Zoroastrianism, which in pre-Islamic times had many adherents in Central Asia, did involve the practice of fire-worship, but the flame was regarded as holy and pure, not to be defiled by any form of live sacrifice. Animistic cults regarded fire as a cleansing force, but there is no evidence that they sanctioned human immolation. Interviews with the local population revealed a wide variety of reasons, or at least triggers, ranging from persistent bed-wetting among young teenagers to quarrels with best friends; from aspersions cast on the virginity of a young bride to arguments over the payment of the bride price. The method of death, by the girl dousing herself with oil, then setting it alight, was excruciatingly painful; the very few who survived were dreadfully disfigured. Yet this did not seem to act as a deterrent, but rather as a goad to others to take more care with the preparations. Visitors to areas where there had been recent instances of self-immolation described an atmosphere of contagious, almost physically palpable hysteria.[55] Whether this phenomenon was in any way provoked or stimulated by conditions that were specific to the Soviet regime must be a matter of speculation. What it does indicate, however, is that even after more than sixty years of Soviet rule, there were areas of Central Asian life that were still unknown and unfathomable to outsiders.

Post-Soviet readjustments

The Central Asians acquired political independence not as a result of a struggle for national independence, but as a consequence of the disintegration of the imperial power. In January 1992, the governments of the new states inherited, almost literally overnight, direct responsibility for a formidable array of problems. Other former Soviet republics encountered similar difficulties, but in Central Asia the situation was rendered more acute by a number of factors that were specific to the region. One of these was the high level of specialisation in the production of primary commodities and the relatively low level of industrialisation; these republics were thus more dependent on inter-republican exchanges than were other regions. They were also poorer and therefore more reliant on budgetary transfers from the central government to help support their welfare services. The geographic location of these states, surrounded by steppes, deserts and mountains, and over a thousand kilometres in any direction from an open sea, was an added disadvantage. Moreover, the transport and communication links that had been developed during the Soviet period tied the region to Russia; there were virtually no direct connections of any sort with the world beyond the borders of the Union.

The difficulties of transition from Soviet republics to independent states are today being compounded by social problems. The rapid rate of demographic increase is placing ever greater pressure on the resources of the new states. There is a high ratio of dependents to wage-earners, thus the rise in unemployment has affected the living standards of a wider section of the population than in the European regions of the CIS, where families are far smaller. The economic deterioration has likewise contributed to a heightening of inter-ethnic tensions. The settler communities feel threatened and many thousands have chosen to emigrate. In some ways this has helped to defuse the situation, but the sudden loss of large numbers of senior managers and technical personnel has inflicted substantial damage on the nascent post-Soviet national economies of the region.

The most potentially dangerous effect of the collapse of the Soviet Union was that it created an ideological vacuum. It was not only that the economic and administrative framework within which the modern Central Asian states had been developed abruptly ceased to exist, but that the theoretical justification for their formation was discredited. Consequently, the physical boundaries of the new states, and even the validity of the national identities that had been crafted during the Soviet period, were suddenly open to question. The result could have been the instant Balkanisation of the region. However, with the exception of Tadzhikistan (arguably the most flawed of the Soviet nation-building projects), this has not happened. The instinctive response to the threat of chaos has been a reassertion of the most conservative features of society. There has been no transfer of power to new leaders: on the contrary, it is because of their links with the previous regime that incumbent ruling elites are regarded as guarantors of stability. Equally, the majority of the population are prepared to accept a high degree of authoritarian control in order to guard against the perceived danger of social and regional fragmentation.

In all the Central Asian states, some appearance of political pluralism is currently permitted, but in reality, only those parties that support government policies are granted official registration. Genuine opposition movements have been suppressed, either, as in Uzbekistan, Tadzhikistan and Turkmenistan, by formal bans, or, as in Kazakhstan and Kyrgyzstan, by indirect, but scarcely less effective, controls (for instance, by restricting access to the media or creating obstacles to registration). Yet even without these curbs, it is unlikely that dissident groups would attract much support. In the late 1980s, their efforts to draw attention to political and social abuses were welcomed, but today they are regarded as perilously divisive. The emphasis now is on conformity and solidarity. A form of self-censorship has re-emerged, stifling the discussion of potentially controversial questions. Thus, for example, it is acceptable to discuss mother and child welfare, since these are matters that relate to the health of the nation as a whole; moreover, problems in these areas can be blamed (with some justification) on the shortcomings of the Soviet system. Domestic violence or the phenomenon of female self-immolation, however, are issues which do not fit easily into the idealised image of traditional family life; also, they cannot easily be resolved without the public examination of questions that are still regarded as essentially private, falling within the domain of the patriarchal family. They are therefore treated, as in the pre-perestroika period, as taboo subjects.

New parameters for gender relations

Nation-building projects in the newly independent Central Asian states are drawing on three main elements: the reinstatement of Islamic values as the guiding ethic for society; the rearticulation of the national culture by such means as the rewriting of the historical narrative to establish linkages between the pre-colonial past and the post-Soviet present, and the reviving of 'authentic' traditional institutions, symbols and concepts of propriety; and the reassertion of patriarchal authority through the symbolic identification of the head of state as the 'Father of the Nation'. All three elements are contributing to a redefinition of the parameters of gender relations.

The Islamic resurgence in Central Asia began in the 1970s with the emergence of a small-scale revivalist movement in the Ferghana Valley (eastern Uzbekistan, southern Kyrgyzstan, northern Tadzhikistan). A second and stronger impetus was provided by a sudden shift in government policy towards Islam. Previously, Islam had been condemned as a pernicious force, inimical to progress. At the end of the 1980s, however, there was evidence of a more conciliatory attitude. This was partly the result of a greater tolerance to religion throughout the Soviet Union, but was also an attempt to combat the perceived threat of Iranian influence by fostering a sense of pride in an indigenous Islamic tradition. More mosques were opened in 1989 than in the whole of the previous decade, the public celebration of Islamic feast days was given official support, and copies of the Qur'an and records and cassettes of Qur'anic recitations suddenly began to appear in state-run kiosks. The number of Soviet Muslims allowed to perform the *hajj* (prescribed annual pilgrimage to Mecca) rose from thirty in 1989 to 1,500 in 1990, and, in general, links with Muslims in other countries increased. These measures did not result in a mass return to religion, but they did reintroduce Islam into the public arena. Islamic symbols and references became an accepted part of life: Muslim clerics were accorded a new respect and invited to contribute to the process of perestroika.[56]

After independence, the re-Islamicisation of the social environment was used as a substitute for the liberation struggle that had not taken place. There was a triumphalist fervour in the rash of mosque building that took place in the immediate aftermath of the collapse of the Soviet Union. In Turkmenistan, for example, there were only four mosques open for worship in the 1980s; by 1994, there were 181, with 100 or more at the planning stage; in Uzbekistan there were 300 in 1989, but over 5,000 by 1993.[57] There was a similar proliferation of mosques in the other republics. Schools and voluntary bodies began to teach the Arabic script (abolished in Central Asia in 1930) and to give instruction in reading the Qur'an. *Madrassah* and Islamic cultural centres were opened throughout the region. The finance for these undertakings was provided jointly by local Muslim communities, district authorities and charitable donations from Muslims abroad.

Today, although most Central Asians welcome the reintroduction of Islam into the public space, the majority do not want it to assume a regulative function: they still feel strongly that religion and the state should be separate. Nevertheless, a core of active and committed believers has begun to emerge. Quite a large proportion are from villages and provincial towns, or the poorer quarters of the capital cities, but there is also a substantial number of university students and young professionals. The proportion of women who actively espouse an Islamic way of life is as yet very small in relation to the total population of each of the five states. However, the fact that they have so categorically rejected the Soviet model of female emancipation (and likewise the more recently proffered Western versions) has a significance that goes far beyond mere numbers. Some interpret it as a portent of an imminent mass return to Islam. It is too early to predict whether or not this will happen, but certainly there has been an upsurge in the demand for a Muslim education for girls. In response to this, several women's *madrassah* have been opened and courses at some of the men's *madrassah* now accept women.[58] Women are also beginning to go abroad for further training to Islamic universities in Turkey, Egypt and other Middle Eastern countries.

Muslim women's organisations in Central Asia have not so far been very successful. Fledgling 'Leagues of Muslim Women' were founded in Uzbekistan, Kyrgyzstan and Kazakhstan soon after independence. However, the Kazakh organisation collapsed within months, owing to financial improprieties in the handling of its accounts; the other two groups are now also moribund. Schoolgirls and young university students have begun to wear the *hejab* (Muslim headscarf) and ankle- and wrist-length clothes, but this practice is still rare, especially in the cities; in the Ferghana Valley, a few of the older women have resumed the full *parandzha*.[59] As yet, however, the veil is still regarded as a symbol of a personal commitment to Islam. It has not become politicised as has been the case elsewhere.

While some women are certainly adopting an Islamic way of life of their own volition, in some areas there is a growing tendency for men to impose Islamic norms on women. This is most noticeable in the Ferghana Valley and in Tadzhikistan. Here it is men who set the standards for female modesty in behaviour and dress. It is also the men who decide whether or not women should be allowed to attend the mosque or to play an active role in religious undertakings outside the home.[60] The women here are more vulnerable because not only is the protection offered by the state now much weaker, but usually these women do not know their rights in Islamic law and are therefore unable to argue their case on those grounds.

The second element in the post-Soviet nation-building process – that of a rearticulation of the national culture – has not brought about a qualitative change in gender relations, but it has given renewed respectability to attitudes and practices that, during the Soviet period, were regarded as socially and politically unacceptable. This is most marked in matters concerning the family. The traditional power balance – patriarchal control allied to maternal authority – is now acknowledged with a sense of pride rather than decried as a vestige of primitive practices of the past. This new mood was vividly illustrated by the comment of a young Uzbek, who, when asked recently what were the qualities that had most attracted him to his bride-to-be, answered without hesitation, 'That she should be as a floor-cloth to my mother, then to my elder brothers' wives, then to me.'[61] The phrasing is, of course, crude, and more urbane Central Asian males would certainly not formulate their view of their relationship with their wife in such terms. However, the very fact that anyone should voice such sentiments in public is in itself a sign of the changing times: a decade ago, this would have been inconceivable.

Other indications of the shift in attitude include a greater readiness to admit to the continued existence of a practice such as polygamy: this is still illegal, but the fragmentary evidence that is now emerging suggests that it is quite widespread and, moreover, not regarded with the disapproval that characterised Soviet writings on the subject.[62] The positive aspects of traditions such as the payment of the bride price – now usually presented in the form of gifts of clothes, jewellery and household items – are also stressed. Likewise, participation in large-scale family and community functions, formerly frowned upon by the authorities, is now regarded as a positive feature of social life. In Uzbekistan, the role of the local neighbourhood (*mahalle*) in poverty alleviation and other social welfare projects has been institutionalised through the allocation of government funds and the formal recognition of the authority of community elders. Finally, the centrality of motherhood is being reaffirmed, but with a telling shift of emphasis: during the Soviet period, the maternal role was divorced from domesticity. Now, the domestic context has been reinstated and child-rearing is being accorded the same importance as child-bearing. Concomitantly, the role of women as the moral educators of the new generation is being highlighted.

The third element, that of the cult of the father-leader, is yet another reversal of a fundamental tenet of Soviet ideology. The image of the head of state as the loving but stern, wise but generous, head of the family-nation firmly reinstates the patriarchal discourse. This was implied in the personality cults that evolved around Soviet leaders, but in Central Asia today, especially in Uzbekistan and Turkmenistan, the notion has been elaborated far more comprehensively. The concept of male guardianship has now been re-established as a parameter of private as well as of public life. Society has finally freed itself from the emasculation imposed by the *khudzhum*. From a traditionalist perspective, it might be said that order and propriety are being restored. The result has been that gender asymmetry in power and status has re-emerged in unashamedly vigorous form, giving rise to a rapid masculinisation of the positions of authority. Today, women in Central Asia are not excluded from public affairs, but their participation is dependent on male sufferance.[63] Nevertheless, as in other male-dominated societies, individual women, especially those who are closely related to the ruling elites, may be accepted as honorary males in the highest echelons of the power structures with relatively little difficulty. It is those lower down the social scale who are beginning to experience the brunt of gender discrimination.

Economic pressures

The dislocation of supplies, services and trade which followed the collapse of the Soviet Union has had a devastating effect on the newly emergent national economies of the Central Asian states. Prices for industrial and domestic commodities continue to soar; transport networks have been decimated owing to fuel shortages. Many industrial plants have been forced to close down, or to introduce sweeping redundancies, because of lack of supplies, loss of markets and huge debts. Unemployment has spiralled. Welfare benefits, including child and maternity allowances, have been increased at regular intervals, but have been unable to stave off severe material hardship for large sectors of the population. Education and medical care have also been severely affected; standards have fallen dramatically, while the introduction of 'hidden charges' to services that were formerly free has further reduced the scope of welfare provision. Poverty and malnutrition are now becoming serious problems.

Women have been the chief victims of the shrinking labour market. It is not only the unskilled or semi-skilled workers who have been savagely hit by redundancies, but also the trained professionals. The quota system and positive discrimination that operated in support of female employment during the Soviet period have been abandoned. Now, whenever there is a choice between employing a male or a female, the former is automatically given precedence, on the grounds that he is the main breadwinner in the family. At the same time, features in the mass media and the pronouncements of public figures are helping to alter social opinion, creating a climate in which the home, rather than the shop floor or the office, is regarded as the 'right place' for a woman. Even in Kyrgyzstan, where official attitudes towards working women are still generally favourable, it was estimated that by mid-1993 almost 70 per cent of the unemployed were women; the economic crisis has deepened considerably since then and it is very likely that the present position is a great deal worse. However, it is difficult to gain an accurate picture of the situation in any of these states since, firstly, definitions of joblessness are abstruse, designed to conceal rather than reveal the true state of affairs (a phenomenon that is by no means unique to Central Asia); secondly, women are often retained on the staff of an enterprise or institution, but rarely given any work and paid, if at all, a nugatory salary.

Economic pressures are also beginning to have an adverse effect on female education. Schooling used to be free, compulsory and of a reasonably high standard. Today, the quality of tuition in the state schools is so poor that those who can afford it send their children to private schools. These are very expensive. The state schools, too, though still nominally free, require so many extra contributions from parents that even this form of education is becoming a financial burden for poor families with large numbers of children. In these cases, it is the daughters' education that is sacrificed. The girls become semi-permanent truants, and are often set to work selling assorted oddments on street pavements in order to supplement the family income.

There are rumours that in return for a substantial down payment to the parents, some young girls are being sent to the Gulf states to work as household servants;[64] this may be utterly untrue, but the level of material deprivation is reaching such a point that even if this is not so, it is already taking shape as a fantasy solution. Female (and, to a lesser extent, male) prostitution is on the rise in Kazakhstan and Kyrgyzstan; for students, it is sometimes the only way of financing their studies.[65] In Kyrgyzstan, questions have been raised in parliament as to the desirability of licensing brothels, in order to limit the risk of spreading sexually transmitted diseases. The majority of those who are involved in prostitution are Slavs and members of other immigrant groups, but there are also quite a few Kazakhs and Kyrgyz. In the other Central Asian states it is uncommon for women of the titular groups to work as prostitutes. However, in the capital cities of the region (and perhaps in other large urban settlements), sexual conventions are no longer as strict as they once were and it is not unknown for local girls to enter into extra-marital relationships in return for financial benefit.[66]

Another consequence of the economic crisis has been to bring about changes in attitudes to family planning. In urban areas, at least among the professional classes, young couples are beginning to worry about the cost of rearing a large family. Before, this was not a consideration, since all the major expenses were covered by the state. Now, it is not only that the price of essentials such as health care and education are rising, but that many more choices are available in terms of optional extra-curricular activities, fashionable clothes, toys and electronic gadgetry. Parents in these circles are coming to feel that they will only be able to provide the type of upbringing that they would wish for their offspring if they limit the size of their families to two or, at the most, three children.

In rural areas, especially in Uzbekistan and Tadzhikistan, birth rates are still amongst the highest in the world (over forty per thousand per year). Since in all five countries the great majority of the titular peoples live in the countryside, it is not surprising that in most areas there has been a relatively small fall in the average rate of natural increase over the last three decades.[67] The governments in the newly independent Central Asian states are beginning to realise the economic implications of this high level of expansion. To date, however, it is only in Uzbekistan that an official family planning policy has been launched. This has involved intensive preliminary research into social attitudes, followed by education and information campaigns. The scheme is still too new for it to be possible to evaluate the likely impact. It is also difficult to know how the related scheme of (semi-) compulsory pre-marital medical counselling for young couples will develop. It is intended to raise awareness of health, sex and family welfare issues, but as it is formulated at present, with the emphasis on producing a population that is sound in mind and body, there is a hint of an underlying eugenic agenda.

External influences

In the immediate aftermath of independence, there was an influx of missionaries and various cultural delegations from Islamic countries. Such events were a novelty and aroused great interest. Now, however, the visits of delegations have become more of a routine activity and are greeted with less pomp, while the missionaries are, in most areas, subject to close state supervision. In all, the impact of Islamic countries on the Central Asian states has been considerably weaker than had originally been anticipated. The chief sources of external influence, particularly so far as women are concerned, are Western. There are two very different areas in which the effects of this pressure are felt: concepts of glamour and concepts of human development.

Little is known of traditional Central Asian concepts of female beauty other than the stereotyped descriptions of classical literature and the elegant, stylised figures in miniature paintings. These, however, are almost entirely images conceived by men; female perceptions of style and fashion, and attitudes to luxury, beauty care and physical perfection, are largely uncharted territory.[68] During the Soviet period, new stereotypes were introduced, projecting robust workers and indefatigable mothers as the ideal models, but how, why and for whom these women beautified themselves – or even if they did – was regarded as a matter too inconsequential to merit attention. Over the past two to three years, this has changed: the region has been inundated with Western soap operas, video cassettes of the latest feature films, fashion magazines, advertisements for hair and skin treatments (sometimes even the actual products), and, most recently, beauty parlours and aerobics classes. Initially, Central Asian women were very cautious in their response to these blandishments, but, as with the women's clubs of the early Soviet era, they are gradually being overcome by curiosity and in the larger cities are starting to try these new recipes for health, beauty and a shining future. If the appearance of female parachutists and tractor drivers symbolised one turning-point in the modern history of Central Asia, then perhaps the appearance of the first be-swimsuited beauty contests may be said to have marked another.[69]

A very different form of potential Western influence is diffused through aid and technical assistance programmes. These are administered through international organisations, the agencies of national governments, and also through non-governmental organisations (NGOs). Most have a brief to integrate women into development programmes. In principle, this may be a helpful approach; in practice, however, it often misfires. Central Asians, both men and women, deeply resent what they regard as the patronising attitude of some of the administrators of these programmes. The schemes the latter propose often have little relevance to local conditions; in particular, they frequently fail to take account of the existing high levels of literacy, indigenous professional experience and relatively wide range of modern amenities (albeit that these are now under threat owing to the economic crisis).

Another cause of irritation is the implicit, or even explicit, bias that some Western (or Western-trained) staff display against Islam and traditional society.[70] The message, in effect, is that the Central Asians must adopt Western institutions and norms since their own culture is characterised as 'underdeveloped'. However, many Central Asians now travel abroad and have access to the Western media, and thus are able to form their own opinion of Western societies. They find much to admire but, equally, are appalled by the social problems, especially those caused by the breakdown of the family. Thus, it is galling for them to have to endure the disparagement of their own values by those who, in their opinion, have been even less successful in creating an acceptable social environment. By contrast, respect for the achievements of the Soviet period are growing. As one Uzbek writer, formerly known for his outspoken criticism of the Soviet regime, commented recently, 'These Western activists are just like the Soviets, but at least the Soviets gave us schools and hospitals along with their ideology, these give us only the ideology.'[71] Similar sentiments are to be heard with increasing frequency throughout the region.

A third cause of complaint is the 'packaging' of Central Asian issues for the international community. Inevitably (and again as with Soviet activists in the 1920s), foreign aid and development programmes try to enlist the support of local women. However, since project organisers are often more interested in pursuing their own agendas than in gaining an understanding of local conditions, still less of local culture, what they seek is confirmation of their views. Those who would work with them, sometimes out of conviction but sometimes, inevitably, as a means of securing the per diem allowances and other fringe benefits, reflect back what their sponsors want to hear. These are the women who then become the 'independent representatives' of the community and are invited to international conferences and seminars in order to articulate the required position.[72] Translators and interpreters compound the problem, encasing their words in a straitjacket of jargon that effectively extinguishes any spontaneity or genuine insight into the situation. It is little wonder that such women tend to be regarded as opportunists by their compatriots. The fact that they receive such attention is viewed as additional proof of the insincerity (or at the very least, naïvety) of Western agencies. This severely undermines the credibility, and hence the efficacy, of programmes that might otherwise have much to offer.

Passivity: a coping strategy?

There has been strikingly little attempt on the part of Central Asian women to articulate their views on what their rights should be. In the Soviet period, this passivity could be explained by the fact that they had no option but to support official policies. Now, however, they have a greater awareness of possible choices, and it might have been expected that they would take the initiative in gaining more control over their lives and in extending their political, economic and social demands. Yet to date there has been little sign of this. In 1991–2, a few women's movements made a fleeting appearance, most notably, the Uzbek-based Tumaris (the female wing of the opposition party Birlik). The Muslim Women's Leagues referred to above fared little better, also proving to be unsustainable.

Since independence, throughout the region semi-official Women's Committees have been formed, closely modelled on the women's councils (*zhensovety*) of the Soviet period. These are chiefly concerned with the dissemination and implementation of official social welfare policies relating to women. There are also bodies that are specifically devoted to mother and child health care. These organisations are mostly staffed by women and, indeed, provide one of the main outlets for female participation in public affairs. However, although they may have some input into policy formulation, their sphere of action is circumscribed by the fact that, as members of these committees, they have an official function. Consequently, they do not have the same degree of independence as representatives of NGOs in Western countries.

On an individual level, some women are exercising choice in the lifestyles or careers that they follow. Some have entered the private sector and are becoming successful entrepreneurs. Regional Businesswomen's Associations are beginning to appear; these, however, are professional bodies that, for the most part, focus on issues relating to the general business environment and not specifically to conditions for women. A number of women are engaged in careers that take them to foreign countries for study or training; a few have taken the opportunity to remain abroad for relatively long periods. In the larger cities, more typically in Kazakhstan and Kyrgyzstan, some younger women (generally those who have spent a considerable time in study or work away from home) have distanced themselves somewhat from their families and kin-group networks in order to lead a more independent existence; such a choice often entails the corollary of rejecting, or postponing, marriage. In a very different way, those who have opted to follow an orthodox Islamic way of life have also taken control of their lives.

The above examples of Central Asian women's attempts to establish their own space may seem insignificant when compared with developments elsewhere in the former Soviet Union, but even these are exceptional in the context of the region. The great majority of women have not shown any inclination to exceed the limits sanctioned by society. This apparent apathy is often regarded by outsiders as a sign of 'backwardness', from which Central Asian women need to be liberated. Yet they themselves view their situation in a very different way. They are conscious of being part of an organic whole, no one particle of which can be altered without the whole being affected. It is not that Central Asian women see their situation as perfect – indeed, they have as many complaints as women elsewhere – but that they perceive that it has compensations as well as shortcomings, that it offers good-neighbourly support as well as social constraints.

Central Asians are today under greater strain than at almost any other period in recent history. Under Soviet rule, despite all the external changes, these societies remained, in Durkheimian terms, largely 'mechanical', with a high degree of homogeneity, conformity and group solidarity. Now, faced with massive economic, social and environmental pressures, they are in danger of sliding towards anomie – the loss of shared values and the consequent breakdown of social controls. The civil war in Tadzhikistan has provided a dramatic example of how easily and quickly this could happen. There is an acute awareness that the same process could be repeated elsewhere. This has provoked an almost maniacal insistence on the need to preserve stability; all other freedoms are seen as of secondary importance. This is not mere political rhetoric: it is a constantly recurring theme in private as well as public discussion.

Against this background, the 'passivity' of Central Asian women may be seen as a positive rather than a negative stance, a choice rather than a failure to choose. Today, as during the Soviet period, women are instrumental in moderating the pace of change, helping to mediate the effect of external influences. The perceived passivity could be interpreted as a sophisticated coping strategy for protecting the central values of society in a time of flux and stress, thus a crucial contribution to community life, and of fundamental importance in maintaining continuity and identity. It may of course be argued that even if this is so, the women are nevertheless involuntary victims of the system, trapped in a vicious circle of dependency and self-sacrifice. This does not seem to be borne out in practice. There are undoubtedly cases of abuse and oppression here, as in any other part of the world but, in general, Central Asian women, whether in urban or in rural areas, appear to be able to negotiate a position that is, to them, acceptable. If they do not take a public stand to articulate their demands this does not necessarily mean that they are too weak or too ignorant to do this: it could equally well indicate that they believe they are able to operate more effectively by working in an indirect way, using the social levers that are available to them within their families and their communities. This could change in the future: if there were to be a breakdown of society, then they might be forced to take a more independent position, to fight for their rights. Under such conditions, politicised feminist movements, either of a Western or an Islamic orientation, might emerge. It is, however, noteworthy that this does not, as yet, appear to have happened to any significant degree even in Tadzhikistan. The upheavals of the war and the experience of the refugee settlements have not acted as a mobilising impetus. Rather, there has been a consolidation of existing networks and of established patterns of behaviour.

Conclusions: Eurasia revisited

Central Asia lies at the heart of the Eurasian landmass. Once, it was the nodal point on the 'Silk Roads' of antiquity, the global trade network of the day. Today, after years of partial isolation on the periphery of Europe, the region is regaining its centrality: the old, long-suspended ties with neighbours to the east and to the south are being restored through modern transport and communications links. This does not mean that the Central Asian states will sever relations with Russia or reject the Soviet heritage. The complex network of personal and professional, political, economic, cultural and educational linkages that has been established over the past seventy years will certainly not be erased in the near future, though in time it may become a less dominant feature of contemporary Central Asian life. Similarly, many of the aspirations that were nurtured during the Soviet period, such as, for example, that of gender equality, will continue to shape people's hopes and expectations, even if they are not actively promoted. It is also very unlikely that contacts with the West will diminish. On the contrary, the Central Asian states have signalled their desire to remain a part of this world through numerous trade and diplomatic missions, as well as through membership of organisations such as the Organization for Security and Co-operation in Europe (OSCE) and NATO's Partnership for Peace programme. Western-sponsored aid and development projects, whatever their shortcomings, will no doubt continue to be implemented. Informal channels of Western influence, such as the media, will likewise continue to be a major source of influence.

However, these new states are also looking in other directions and finding points of reference and mutual understanding in, for example, China, Korea, Japan, Indonesia, Malaysia, India and Pakistan. These countries present models that differ very greatly one from the other, as well as from those of Western countries. Yet they also have some common characteristics, loosely described as 'Asian values', which include an emphasis on the importance of the family, on the interests of the community rather than those of the individual, and on consensus rather than confrontation. Central Asians recognise here a sense of social priorities similar to their own. Over the past few years it is this discovery of sympathetic cultural echoes in the east and south which has perhaps had the greatest effect on the morale of the Central Asian states, giving them new confidence in the validity of their traditional values. This might well foster the emergence of more conservative trends in the future.

There are still too many uncertainties for it to be possible at this stage, scarcely five years after the traumatic transition to independence, to predict how these new states will develop. However, in view of their past history, it seems likely that there will be a very cautious and gradual recalibrating of the balance between public and private spheres, leading to a greater emphasis on traditional structures, eventually, possibly, of a revivalist hue. It is unlikely that there will be a qualitative change in the position of women in the near future. Further ahead, however, it is possible that in some of the states there may be a move towards a more Islamic way of life, with a reintroduction of the constraints, but also of the freedoms and rights, that Islam gives women. In the north-eastern parts of Kazakhstan and northern Kyrgyzstan, where there has long been influence from the settler communities, it is possible that there will be a more pronounced Westernisation of society, at least in the public sphere. However, much will depend on the resolution of present economic problems. If the recession continues to deepen, there could be a very rapid unravelling of society, with consequences that are impossible to predict, except for the very obvious point that in such conditions it is invariably the women and children who are the most vulnerable and are therefore likely to suffer a major deterioration in their situation. In these circumstances, perhaps the present preoccupation with stability is no bad thing.

Notes

Conventional systems of transliteration have been used for foreign words. It should be noted, however, that in a term such as *khudzhum*, which is here transcribed from the Cyrillic script (as used, for example, for Uzbek), since it refers to a specifically Central Asian phenomenon, the sound *j* (as in 'John') is rendered by *dzh*; however, in Arabic words which refer to general Islamic practices and are already, therefore, in use in English (e.g. *hajj*), the same sound is rendered by *j*, since this is a more familiar spelling.

1 Good surveys of tsarist/Soviet source material relating to this period are given by Ol'ga A. Sukhareva, *Bukhara: XIX – nachalo XX v* (Moscow: Nauka, 1966), pp. 3–22; Tahira Kh. Tashbaeva and Mane D. Savurov, *Novoe i traditsionnoe v bytu sel'skoi sem'i uzbekov* (Tashkent: Fan, 1989),

pp. 3–10. The most informative Western source for this period is probably Annette Meakin, *In Russian Turkestan: a garden of Asia and its people* (London: George Allen, 1903).

2 Bukhara appears to have been an exception in this regard in that the available evidence suggests that average family sizes were small, consisting of 4–6 individuals (Sukhareva, *Bukhara*, pp. 106–11). However, the definition of terms is not always clear, hence it is difficult to draw firm conclusions.

3 Bibi Pal'vanova, *Emansipatsiia musul'manki* (Moscow: Nauka, 1982), pp. 7–8.

4 E.g. 'Qiz bola tuqqandan kora tosh tuqqan iakhshiroq, negaki, tosh hech bolmasa devor qurishga iaraidi-ku' ('It is better to give birth to a stone than a girl-child, because at least you can build a wall with a stone'). Quoted by Z. R. Rahimboboieva, in her speech to the 'First Uzbekistan Women's Conference', March 1958, published in *Ozbekiston khotin-qizlarining birinchi s'iezdi: stenografik hisobot* (Tashkent: Uzbek SSR Davlat Nashriioti, 1960), p. 16. Meakin (*Russian Turkestan*, p. 97) confirms that disappointment was the usual reaction to the birth of a daughter.

5 Sukhareva (*Bukhara*, p. 105) gives some statistical information on female life expectancy in Bukhara. In 1920, the percentage ratio of females to males in the Turkestan region was 47.7 to 52.3 (Pal'vanova, *Emansipatsiia*, p. 49). Cf. Russia in 1926, where the percentage ratio was 52.8 to 47.2, thus with a preponderance of females, unlike the situation in Central Asia, where there was a preponderance of males. (Source: Soviet Census of 1926, cited in Shirin Akiner, *Islamic peoples of the Soviet Union* (2nd edn, London: Kegan Paul International, 1987), under the relevant ethnic entries. Note: the information in this book is drawn from Soviet statistical material; for ease of reference, the ultimate sources of data are not cited in this article unless they are of particular interest.)

6 For example, Khansha Pupai, the wife of Abulkhair, mid-eighteenth century khan of the Kazakh Little Horde, seems to have played an active role in steppe politics; see Begezhan Suleimenov (ed.), *Kazakhstan v XV–XVIII vekakh* (Alma-Ata: Nauka, 1969), p. 141.

7 Very little information is available on this subject. Meakin (*Russian Turkestan*, pp. 100–2) indicates that several of the educated women in urban areas were engaged in trade, generally of objects that they had produced themselves. Zbigniew Jasiewicz, 'Professional beliefs and rituals among craftsmen in Central Asia: genetic and functional interpretation' in Shirin Akiner (ed.), *Cultural change and continuity in Central Asia* (London: Kegan Paul International, 1991), p. 173, speaking of a somewhat later period, mentions the existence of 'a certain form of organisation' amongst craftswomen of the region, notably women potters in the mountains of Tadzhikistan.

8 In the early nineteenth century, there were a number of talented female poets at the court of the khan of Kokand, including Nadira (b. 1790), the wife of the ruler, Umar Khan; they were presumably not merely literate, but highly educated. On girls' schools in the early twentieth century see, for example, Meakin, *Russian Turkestan*, p. 87. However, literacy rates varied greatly from one place to another. According to Sukhareva (*Bukhara*, p. 104), in 1926, 13.4 per cent of the female population of Bukhara were literate, compared with 46 per cent of the male population. The overall average literacy rate for the Uzbek SSR as a whole, though, was only 3.8 per cent (Akiner, *Islamic peoples*, p. 280).

9 According to the 1926 Soviet census, 84.5 per cent of Uzbeks were included within the territory of the Uzbek SSR, 94.2 per cent of Turkmen in the Turkmen SSR, 93.6 per cent of Kazakhs in the Kazakh ASSR, and 86.7 per cent of the Kyrgyz in the Kyrgyz ASSR. For a summary of the regional distribution of these peoples, see Akiner, *Islamic peoples*, under the relevant ethnic entries. (Reference is made here to Kazakh ASSR and Kyrgyz ASSR because at the time of the census they were Autonomous Soviet Socialist Republics, not yet full Soviet Socialist Republics.)

10 In 1926, 63.1 per cent of the Tadzhiks were included within the territory of the Tadzhik ASSR, which at that time formed a subordinate administrative unit within the Uzbek SSR; there were a further 35.8 per cent located elsewhere in the Uzbek SSR (see further Akiner, *Islamic peoples*, p. 306). These figures are based on the official ethnic designations as recorded in the 1926 census; some would claim that they do not accurately reflect the population's self-perception of their historical ethnic origins. The negotiation of territorial rights was by no means a smooth and amicable affair: there were many bitter arguments over border regions, especially those with mixed populations. A detailed account of this process is given by Rakhim Masov, *Istoriia topornogo razdeleniia* (Dushanbe: Irfon, 1991).

11 In 1926, Russians numbered 1,279,979 (19.7 per cent of the total population) in the Kazakh ASSR; 116,436 (11.8 per cent) in the Kyrgyz ASSR; 5,638 (0.7 per cent) in the Tadzhik ASSR; 75,357 (7.7 per cent) in the Turkmen SSR; 246,521 (4.7 per cent) in the Uzbek SSR. By 1959, these figures had increased to 3,972,042 (42.7 per cent of the total population) in the Kazakh SSR; 623,562 (30.2 per cent) in the Kyrgyz SSR; 262,611 (13.3 per cent) in the Tadzhik SSR; 262,702 (17.3 per cent) in the Turkmen SSR; 1,092,468 (13.5 per cent) in the Uzbek SSR. (See further Akiner, *Islamic peoples*, under the relevant ethnic entries.)

12 By 1959, the percentage share of the titular group in the total population of their eponymous republic was as follows: Uzbeks 62.1; Turkmen 60.9; Tadzhiks 53.1; Kyrgyz 40.5; Kazakhs 30.0 (Akiner, *Islamic peoples*, under the relevant ethnic entries).

13 Richard Stites, *The women's liberation movement in Russia: feminism,*

nihilism, and Bolshevism 1860–1930 (Princeton: Princeton University Press, 1978), p. 332. For an account of the broader Soviet context of female emancipation see Mary Buckley, 'Soviet interpretations of the women question' in Barbara Holland (ed.), *Soviet sisterhood* (London: Fourth Estate, 1985), pp. 24–53.

14 The term was coined by Gregory Massell, *The surrogate proletariat* (Princeton: Princeton University Press, 1975); this is the first, and to date only major study by a Western scholar on the politics of female emancipation in Central Asia.

15 For accounts of the creation of the legal infrastructure, see Dilorom A. Alimova, *Reshenie zhenskogo voprosa v Uzbekistane 1917–41 gg.* (Tashkent: Fan, 1987), pp. 11–12; Shodmon M. Masharipova, *Raskreposhchenie zhenshchin Khorezma i vovlechenie ikh v sotsialsisticheskoe stroitel'stvo* (Tashkent: Fan, 1990), pp. 12–13; Aleksandr M. Lobachev, *Protiv t'my* (Tashkent: Uzbekistan, 1990), pp. 32–6; Pal'vanova, *Emansipatsiia*, pp. 26–36; Rakhima Aminova, *The October Revolution and women's liberation in Uzbekistan* (Moscow: Nauka, 1977), pp. 37–8, 59–60.

16 Leading Russian activists included: Ida Finkel'shtein, widow of the Tashkent commissar; Lidia Dvorkina; Berta Bendetskaia (b. 1898); Lukiia Shumilova (1873–1939); Lidiia Otmar-Shtein (b. 1899); Eustaliia Ross (b. 1896). Serafima Liubimova (b. 1898), who was sent from Moscow to Tashkent in June 1923 to head the women's section of the Central Committee of the Turkestan Communist Party, was responsible for creating an infrastructure of social organisations to support the emancipation movement. See further Pal'vanova, *Emansipatsiia*, pp. 49–57; Alimova, *Reshenie*, pp. 14–15; Aminova, *October Revolution*, pp. 12–15; R. Ia. Radzhapova, *et al. Khhdzhum – znachit nastuplenie* (Tashkent: Uzbekistan, 1987), pp. 117–87.

17 These included Risoliat-khon Alieva (b. 1898); Shamsikamar Gaibdzhanova (b. 1897); Tadzhikhon Shadieva (b. 1905). See further Pal'vanova, *Emansipatsiia*, pp. 62–7; Lobachev, *Protiv t'my*, p. 136; Masharipova, *Raskreposhchenie*, pp. 14–17.

18 Pal'vanova, *Emansipatsiia*, p. 106.

19 Masharipova, *Raskreposhchenie*, p. 37; Pal'vanova, *Emansipatsiia*, pp. 108–10.

20 Pal'vanova, *Emansipatsiia*, p. 165.

21 *Ibid.*, pp. 97, 147–8; Masharipova, *Raskreposhchenie*, pp. 61–2; Aminova, *October Revolution*, pp. 63–4; Alimova, *Reshenie*, p. 61. Dilorom A. Alimova, *Zhenskii vopros v Srednei Azii* (Tashkent: Fan, 1991), p. 25.

22 Aminova, *October Revolution*, p. 95.

23 Alimova, *Zhenskii vopros*, p. 23; Alimova, Reshenie, pp. 30–2; Aminova, *October Revolution*, p. 121.

24 Pal'vanova, *Emansipatsiia*, p. 168, also personal communications made to the present author by Professor Pal'vanova in London, in 1992.
25 Lobachev, *Protiv t'my*, p. 40.
26 This was not only a Russian view; see, for example, the comments by Joshua Kunitz, *Dawn over Samarkand* (London and New York: Lawrence and Wishart, 1936), p. 274, where he describes the garment as 'monstrous and degrading', resembling 'a gray or dark-blue coffin standing stiffly on end, covered with a black, bulging, heavy lid'.
27 Meakin (*Russian Turkestan*, pp. 128–9) noted that '"the man in the street" can generally tell at a glance the social standing of a woman by the quality and condition of her *parandzha*; those worn by the rich were often made of silk, but the majority were of cotton. The usual colour was a dull grey, but Tatar women would sometimes wear bright colours, such as canary yellow or bright red. Only women from the lowest strata of society (e.g. beggars) would venture out of the house without a veil.'
28 Alimova, *Zhenskii vopros*, pp. 25–8; Aminova, *October Revolution*, pp. 92–103.
29 Alimova, *Zhenskii vopros*, p. 76; Masharipova, *Raskreposhchenie*, pp. 23, 32, 51–6; Aminova, *October Revolution*, pp. 49–57.
30 Aminova, *October Revolution*, p. 92.
31 Alimova, *Reshenie*, p. 55; Aminova, *October Revolution*, pp. 179–92.
32 The move to an eight-year course was completed by 1962/63; see K. F. Fazylkhodzhaev (ed.), *Deiatel'nost' kompartii Uzbekistana i usileniiu sotsial'noi aktivnosti zhenshchin: Sbornik dokumentov i materialov (1959–1975 gg.)* (Tashkent: Uzbekistan, 1986), p. 26.
33 The numbers of women of the titular groups of the Central Asian republics who possessed higher (tertiary) educational qualifications in 1970 were as follows (per 1,000): Uzbeks 13; Kazakhs 20; Tadzhiks 7; Turkmen 10; Kyrgyz 15; cf. Soviet average of 37 (Akiner, *Islamic peoples*, under the relevant ethnic headings).
34 H. Kent Geiger, *The family in Soviet Russia* (Cambridge, Mass.: Harvard University Press, 1970), p. 130.
35 Aminova, *October Revolution*, pp. 211–12.
36 *Ibid.*, pp. 17–18.
37 Pal'vanova, *Emansipatsiia*, p. 270.
38 Alimova, *Reshenie*, p. 55.
39 Probably the best study to date on Soviet Islam is Tolib Saidbaev, *Islam i obshchestvo* (Moscow: Nauka, 1984); see also A. Ahadov, *Islom zamonga moslashganda* (Tashkent: Uzbekistan, 1989). For more recent developments, see Shirin Akiner, 'Islam, the state and ethnicity in Central Asia in historical perspective' in *Religion, state and society: the Keston Journal* 24 (2–3), December 1996 (forthcoming).
40 Alimova, *Zhenskii vopros*, pp. 35–8.

41 Alimova, *Zhenskii vopros*, pp. 47–9; Lobachev, *Protiv t'my*, p. 55; Pal'vanova, *Emansipatsiia*, p. 244.
42 Pal'vanova, *Emansipatsiia*, p. 205; Darikha Saburova, *Zhenshchiny Karakalpakstana* (Nukus: Karakalpakstan, 1989), pp. 37–46; Alimova, *Zhenskii vopros*, p. 46. The problems over equal pay, conditions and opportunities for women were not of course restricted to Central Asia; for the broader Soviet context see Alastair McAuley, *Women's work and wages in the Soviet Union* (London: George Allen and Unwin, 1981), especially pp. 11–31.
43 Alimova, *Zhenskii vopros*, p. 112.
44 This section is based mainly on material contained in Tashbaeva and Savurov, *Novoe i traditsionnoe*; also on personal interviews conducted by the present author 1985–95. Although the section is written in the past tense, since in the context of this article it refers to the Soviet period, the conditions described here are very much the same today, in post-Soviet Central Asia.
45 This is also part of the Islamic heritage; see, for example, Lois Beck *et al.* (eds.), *Women in the Muslim world* (Cambridge, Mass.: Harvard University Press, 1978), pp. 87–8; Parveen Shaukat Ali, *Status of women in the Muslim world* (Lahore: Aziz, 1975), p. 21. In 1959, the percentage of married girls of the titular group in the age group 16–19 years was as follows: Uzbeks 31.8; Kazakhs 28.7; Tadzhiks 36.6; Turkmen 32.0; Kyrgyz 44.2; cf. Russians 9.3. By 1970, the percentage of married girls in this age group had fallen to the following levels: Uzbeks 21.7; Kazakhs 12.3; Tadzhiks 24.9; Turkmen 19.1; Kyrgyz 20.1; cf. Russians 9.1 (Akiner, *Islamic peoples*, under relevant ethnic groups).
46 For the pre-1981 provisions see Bernice Madison, *Social welfare in the Soviet Union* (Stanford, Ca.: Stanford University Press, 1968), pp. 61–70; for post-1981, see Jo Peers, 'Workers by hand and womb: Soviet women and the demographic crisis' in Holland (ed.), *Soviet sisterhood*, pp. 116–44, especially p. 136. In 1981 the lump sum payment for the first child was set at 50 roubles, for the eleventh and subsequent children at 250 roubles each.
47 Tashbaeva and Savurov, *Novoe i traditsionnoe*, p. 38.
48 Geographic mobility was low, hence kin-groups generally continued to live within the same village, neighbourhood or collective farm. The level of urbanisation among the titular groups within their eponymous republics also remained low; in 1970, it was less than 30 per cent for four of the groups (only 14.5 per cent for the Kyrgyz), and only just over 30 per cent for the Turkmen (Akiner, *Islamic peoples*, under relevant ethnic groups). Mixed marriages between different ethnic groups were also comparatively uncommon, especially in rural areas.
49 Such is the preoccupation with fertility that even visiting strangers will be interrogated in great detail about the number of children they have, or

intend to have. According to an Uzbek informant, mothers-in-law in rural areas would often accompany their sons' wives on visits to the doctor to ensure that they did not seek contraceptive advice (communication to the author, Tashkent, 1996). For a comparative international perspective, see Helen Ware, 'The effects of fertility, family organization, sex structure of the labour market, and technology on the position of women' in Nora Federici *et al.* (eds.), *Women's position and demographic change* (Oxford: Clarendon, 1993), pp. 257–84.
50 See, for example, Saburova, *Zhenshchiny Karakalpakstana*, p. 49.
51 A great deal has been written on this subject in recent years. A fairly comprehensive account is given by Boris Rumer, *Soviet Central Asia: 'A tragic experiment'* (Boston: Unwin Hyman, 1989), pp. 62–75. See also Aleksandr Minkin, 'Zaraza ubiistvennaia', *Ogonek* 13, 1988, pp. 26–7; Aleksandr Minkin, 'Posledstviia zarazy', *Ogonek* 33, 1988, p. 25; Shirin Akiner, 'Environmental degradation in Central Asia' in Reiner Weichhardt (ed.), *Economic developments in cooperation partner countries from a sectoral perspective* (Brussels: NATO, 1994), pp. 255–63.
52 See, for example, Saburova, *Zhenshchiny Karakalpakstana*, pp. 71–80; Tashbaeva and Savurov, *Novoe i traditsionnoe*, p. 67.
53 Alimova, *Zhenskii vopros*, p. 118.
54 *Ibid.*, pp. 118–19; E. Gafurov, 'The flames of feudalism', *International Pravda* 2(7), 1986, p. 24; Pal'vanova (*Emansipatsiia*, p. 8) indicates that the practice was not unknown in pre-Soviet times.
55 Personal communications to the author in Tashkent in 1990 by an Uzbek film-maker, Shukhrat Makhmudov, and his Kazakh wife.
56 Shirin Akiner, 'Islam in post-Soviet Central Asia', *Harvard International Review* 15(3), 1993, pp. 18–21. The article was written on the basis of information gathered by the author from informants in the Central Asian republics 1989–92.
57 *Aziia*, 11 June 1994, p. 24; *Nezavisimaia gazeta*, 6 January 1994, p. 3.
58 Anara Tabyshalieva, *Vera v Turkestane* (Bishkek: AZ-MAK, 1993), p. 123; *Slovo Kyrgyzstana*, 30 November 1993, p. 3.
59 These are subjective assessments, based on the author's personal observation made in the course of several visits in 1994–6 to Tashkent, the Ferghana Valley, Bishkek and Almaty. Some other observers feel that this is an underestimation and that both the *hejab* and the *parandzha* are becoming far more common. This perception may be influenced by the fact that such observers (local and foreign) regard the resurgence of Islam as a threat. It should be noted that the wearing of the *hejab* is a new phenomenon, imported from other Muslim countries; the traditional Central Asian covering is the *parandzha*. To some extent, these different interpretations of the Muslim dress code reflect divergent trends in Islam in Central Asia today. Wearers of the *hejab* tend to favour a more reformist, modernist approach to the religion, while wearers of the *parandzha* are

generally more conservative. However, regional and social factors also play a role here, hence no firm conclusions can be drawn about a woman's religious orientation solely on the basis of her outer garments.

60 Gillian Tett, in an unpublished paper on 'Women and Islam in Tadzhikistan', presented at the conference on 'Social change, demographic trends, family structure and gender relations in Muslim societies – with special reference to Central Asia', held at the School of Oriental and African Studies (SOAS), University of London, July 1992, made the point that while it was women who 'de facto carried the greatest religious burden during the Soviet years, it is now men who dominate Islam in the public sphere' and that it is men who are setting the agenda for what Islam should 'mean' for women.

61 Comment made to the author by a young Uzbek of about twenty-four years of age, with secondary schooling and further educational training, in the Ferghana Valley in 1994.

62 Tatiana Savelieva, in an unpublished paper presented at the conference on 'Social change, demographic trends, family structure and gender relations in Muslim societies – with special reference to Central Asia', at SOAS, July 1992, gave an account of recent fieldwork carried out in Uzbekistan; in one village, she reported, almost 20 per cent of the unmarried women were integrated into polygamous families.

63 In June 1995, the senior government posts held by women included the following: in Uzbekistan, deputy prime minister, chairman of parliament (*Olii Madzhlis*), deputy chairman of parliamentary committee on labour and social security, deputy minister of labour, first deputy minister of social welfare; in Kazakhstan, deputy minister of trade and industry; in Tadzhikistan, deputy prime minister, deputy minister of health; in Kyrgyzstan, minister of foreign affairs. No information was available on the situation in Turkmenistan.

64 Personal communications to the author in Bishkek, 1996.

65 In one evening, a student can earn at least 30 US dollars, the equivalent of some six times the value of a monthly stipend. (Personal communications to the author in Bishkek, 1996.) In Kazakh and Kyrgyz newspapers of 1994–6 there have been several reports on rising levels of prostitution and other criminal activities carried out by women. See, for example, Gul'mira Arbabaeva, 'Na kollegii MVD otmechen rost zhenskoi prestupnosti', *Panorama* 29, 23 July 1994, p. 9; Kanapiia Gabdullina, 'Bezrabotitsa s zhenskim litsom', *Dzhuma: Piatnitsa* 17, 20 October 1995, p. 2.

66 Personal communications to the author in Bishkek, Almaty and Tashkent, 1996.

67 Levels of natural increase (per 1,000 of the population) in the five republics in 1960/1987 respectively were as follows: Uzbekistan 33.8/30.1; Kazakhstan 30.6/18.0; Kyrgyzstan 30.8/25.3; Tadzhikistan 28.4/34.9; Turkmenistan 35.9/29.3. (Source: *Naselenie SSSR 1987*, Moscow: Finansy i

statistika, 1988, pp. 132–42.) The largest change was in Kazakhstan, where the birthrate fell quite steadily in rural and in urban areas until 1980; thereafter it began to rise again. A similar pattern was to be observed in Kyrgyzstan. These two republics have long had large settler populations; the birthrate in these non-indigenous communities was significantly lower than amongst the titular peoples, hence the overall slower rate of increase. In Uzbekistan and Tadzhikistan the rate of increase is such that, according to some estimates, in the near future for every ten people who leave the ranks of the working age group, some thirty-five will enter it (Viktor Perevedentsev, *Moskovskie novosti* 41, 11 October 1992, p. 9).
68 Meakin, *Russian Turkestan*, pp. 120–8, is one of the few writers to comment on this aspect of the lives of Central Asian women.
69 See, for example, the report on the 'Kazakhstan Queen of Clubs – 95' beauty contest, *Delovaia nedelia*, 11 August 1995. *Dzhuma: Piatnitsa*, published in Kazakhstan, is a typical new-style women's paper, full of advertisements for stylish lingerie, cosmetics and beauty treatments.
70 This phenomenon has been noted elsewhere. See, for example, Angela Gilliam, 'Women's equality and national liberation' in Chandra Mohanty *et al.* (eds.), *Third World women and the politics of feminism* (Bloomington, Ind.: Indiana University Press, 1991), pp. 215–50, especially p. 218; also Chandra Mohanty, *ibid.*, pp. 51–80, 'Under Western eyes: feminist scholarship and colonial discourses'.
71 Personal communication to the author by a member of the banned opposition party *Erk*, in Germany, 1995.
72 Cf. Gilliam, 'Women's equality', p. 227, where the question is posed: 'Which Third World Women speak for which Third World women?'

Index

Abkhazia, war in, and the Georgian peace train 253–60
abortion
   in Latvia and Lithuania 207–8
   in Ukraine 221
   women's right to 88
Afghanistan war 143–4
   afganki 11, 13, 144, 150–3
   coming to terms with 154–5
   widows and mothers of soldiers killed 147–50
age
   of economically inactive men and women 26
   structure in Central Asia 278
   of women voting for Women of Russia 164
Agrarian Party 162, 177, 180
agricultural production
   and private allotments 49, 52
   and private farms 38
   see also rural areas
aid programmes, in Central Asia 291, 292
Aivasova, Svetlana 164
Akiner, Shirin 12, 14
Alasheev, Sergei 23, 33
alcohol, anti-alcohol campaign 47
alcohol abuse
   and rape 106
   in rural areas 51, 53
      and forced migrants 133, 134
   and violence against women 101
Alexandria, Nana 256, 257
allotments
   and migrant workers 129–30
   private 49–53
Anika 11, 150–3, 154
Antonian, Iu. M. 103–6
Arbidāne, Ieva 209
Armand, Inessa 268
Armenia 9, 10, 13, 235–48
   earthquake (1988) 237
   economic collapse 237–8
   families in 235–7, 238–9, 241
   gender roles 235–7, 246
   Nagorno-Karabakh conflict 13, 237, 245, 246
   nationalist movement 243
   Sovietisation and gender relations 236–7
   women
      and public life 243–5
      and war 246–7, 248
      and work 239–43
Arslanova, Fanuza 165, 166, 168
Ashwin, Sarah 9
Association of Women Entrepreneurs of Russia 64, 65–6, 70, 71, 158
Association of Women Writers 64
Attwood, Lynne 10–11
Azerbaidzhan 13, 237, 246

Babukh, Larisa 172
backlash, feminist 7
Baltic states 12
   links with outside world 4
   see also Estonia; Latvia; Lithuania
basmachi rebels in Central Asia 267, 271
battered wives *see* domestic violence
beauty
   and images of the ideal woman 81–2, 94

305

beauty (*cont.*)
  and Western influence in Central Asia 290–2
Beauvoir, Simone de, *The second sex* 232
Benjamin, Walter 56
bereaved mothers, of soldiers killed in Afghanistan 147–50, 154
birth rates
  and attitudes to motherhood 88–9
  in Central Asia 278–80, 289–90
Bowers, Elain 9
Brezhnev, Leonid 77
Bridger, Sue 9–10, 59
Brownmiller, Susan 109
Bruno, Marta 10, 242
Bryantsalov, Vladimir 196
Buber, Martin 56
Buckley, Mary 11–12
Budushchee bez SPIDa (A Future Without Aids) 180
bulletins, feminist 193
businesswomen *see* entrepreneurs

cancer, 'Nadezhda' (Hope) organisation for women with 189
capital punishment, and rape 111
capitalism
  and the culture of consumption 62–3
  de-contamination of 63–7
  Russian transition process 58–61
Catholic Church
  and abortion in Lithuania 207–8
  Ukrainian 220
Central Asia 261–96
  community relations 278
  emancipation campaign (1918–26) 268–71
  families in 265–6, 276–82, 286–7
  forced migrants returning to Russia from 120
  and Islam 14, 261, 262, 263, 264
    anti-Islamic campaign 273–4
    law 265
    resurgence of 284–6, 296
  legal framework 268–9
  links with outside world 4, 295–6
  National Delimitation (1924–5) 267
  nomad communities 265, 266
  post-Soviet readjustments 282–95
    and 'Asian' values 295–6
    demographic problems 283
    economic pressures 288–90
    external influences 290–2
    and gender relations 284–7
  relations with Russia 295
  Soviet gender politics 266–82
  Soviet rule in 261–2
  Tadzhikistan 13, 14, 267, 281
  women
    casting off the veil 270–1
    education 262, 266, 271–2, 285, 288–9
    entrepreneurs 293
    and ill-health 280–1
    and Islam 285–6
    marriage 265, 268, 277–80, 287
    motherhood 276–7, 279–80, 287
    passivity as coping strategy 292–5
    political and economic mobilisation 271–6
    in pre-Soviet society 264–6
    self-immolation 281–2, 284
    and work 274–5, 279, 280, 288–9
  women's organisations 12, 269, 292–3
  see also individual countries, e.g. Uzbekistan
Centre for Civil Initiatives (St Petersburg) 187
Chatterjee, Partha 244
Chechnia, war in 143, 155
  soldiers' mothers 11, 144–7, 190
  and Women of Russia 170, 171, 173, 177, 180
  and women's peace movements 251
Chepurnykh, Elena 165, 167
Cherevatenko, Valentina 195
Cherniakhovskaia, Anna 111
Chernomyrdin, Viktor 163, 175, 195
Chikova, Galina 64, 65, 71
child care
  in Armenia 239
  in Latvia and Lithuania 206–7
  and women in work 21
childbirth, in Central Asia 265, 279–80, 281, 287
children
  in Central Asia 277
  and the Democracy Union in Armenia 245
  as migratory push factor 122–5, 136
  protection of, in Ukraine 221
Children of Russia programme 170
Chornovil, Viacheslav 229
Chubkova, Galina 167
Church, the *see* religion
CIS (Commonwealth of Independent States) 3, 12
civil servants, Ukrainian women 224

Index

civil society, development in Russia 197–8
collective farms *see* rural areas
collectives *see* labour collectives
commerce, Russian attitudes to 65
Committee of Soldiers' Mothers of Russia (CSMR) 145–6, 190
Communist Party
  of the Russian Federation 163, 169, 175, 176
  of the Soviet Union (CPSU)
    and Central Asia 268, 269
    and domestic violence 102
    and labour collectives 29–30
    and the Soviet Women's Committee 159, 160
  Ukraine 222
community relations, in Central Asia 278
Congress of People's Deputies 161
conscription, and the war in Chechnia 146
consumption, culture of, and women entrepreneurs 62–3
contraception *see* family planning
coping strategies 14, 15
  in Armenia 13, 238, 240–3
  in Central Asia 292–5
corruption, and women entrepreneurs 71–2
Cosmopolitan, Russian edition of 232
cotton-growing industry, in Central Asia 274–5, 280–1
CPSU *see* Communist Party, of the Soviet Union
crime *see* organised crime
CSMR (Committee of Soldiers' Mothers of Russia) 145–6, 190
cultural adaptation, and forced migrants 132–5, 136–7

Daudze, Argita 209
Daujotytė, Viktorija 213
day care facilities, in Latvia and Lithuania 206–7
Democracy Union (Armenia) 245
Democratic Choice of Russia 163
diplomatic community, and employment for Armenian women 242–3
disabled women, in rural areas 46–7
discrimination against women
  in Central Asia 288
  in Latvia and Lithuania 205–6
  migration workers 128
  in politics 196–7
  in Ukraine 12, 225–9, 231

divorce
  in Armenia 238
  in Central Asia 265, 268, 277
  and working women 92
Dobrovol'skaia, Marina 165, 166–8, 169–70, 171, 172, 173
  and the presidential campaign (1996) 178
Dolidze, Keti 254, 255
domestic violence 99–100
  in Central Asia 281–2, 284
  and gender roles 99, 100–3, 107–8, 111–12, 113
  and housing 102–3
  spousal murder 10–11, 99, 107–8
  women's crisis centres 111–12, 190
  writings on 107–8, 112–13
Dostoevskii, Fiodor 64
double burden 77, 85, 206
  of women in Central Asia 281
  and women in rural areas 131
double standards of morality 10
Drach, Ivan 229
Dragadze, Tamara 13–14
Dubna Forums 187–8
Dūdiņa, Anita 209
Dudwick, Nora 9–10, 13
Duma *see* parliaments, Russian

earnings *see* wages
economic mobilization, women in Central Asia 274–5
economic reforms
  capitalism and market relations 58–61
  effects on women 4–5, 59
  and rural areas 38–40, 42–5, 50–1
  and unemployment among women 4–5, 21–2, 59
  and Women of Russia 164
education
  in Central Asia 262, 266, 271–2, 285, 288–9
  girls' schools in Ukraine 230
  in Latvia and Lithuania 204–5
  'The ethics and psychology of family life' course 79–80, 83–4, 85
  women in Armenia 236, 239, 246–7
  of women voting for Women in Russia 166
elections
  1993
    women candidates 194
    and Women of Russia 11, 157–8, 162–3

elections (*cont.*)
    and Yel'tsin 6
    1995, and Women of Russia 12, 158, 163, 175–8, 179–80
    1996, and Yel'tsin 6–7
    Armenia (1995) 244
    Ukraine 219
    women candidates 195–7
electoral reform (Russian Federation) 161–3
employment *see* unemployment; work
entrepreneurs
    differences between male and female 64
    images of women 94–5
    in Latvia and Lithuania 205, 210
    men
        Afghan veterans 150
        Armenia 242
        Russia 57, 64, 67, 71, 129, 130
    and migrant workers 129–31
    and monetary relations 68–9
    New Russians 63, 67
    and the transition to capitalism 58–61
    women in Armenia 241–2
    women in Central Asia 293
    women in Moscow 10, 56–73
        and the fashion industry 63, 65–6
        and networks 62, 70–2
        and organised crime and corruption 71–2
        street-traders 58, 67, 68, 69, 70, 72
        and *za dushoi* (for the soul) 63–7
Estonia 4, 12
    anti-conscription movement 146
ethnic cleansing 250
    Abkhazia 258, 259
ethnic conflict, fear of, as migratory push factor 121, 122, 123, 124, 125, 136
'Euphimia' girls' shelter, St Petersburg 188–9
European Council, TACIS (Technical Aid to the CIS) 187

Faludi, Susan, *Backlash: the undeclared war against feminism* 7
families
    in Armenia 235–7, 238–9
        and 'second families' 241
    in Central Asia 265–6, 276–82, 286–7
family planning
    in Central Asia 280, 281, 289–90
    in Latvia and Lithuania 207, 207–8, 208

farming *see* rural areas
fashion industry, women entrepreneurs 63, 65–6
father-leader, cult of in Central Asia 287
Federal Migration Service of Russia *see* FMS
Federation Council 162
Fedulova, Alevtina 160–1, 163, 164, 165, 166, 167, 172, 173, 175
    on the future of Women in Russia 174
    and the presidential campaign (1996) 178, 179
feminism
    hostility of Russian women to 61, 191
    in Latvia and Lithuania 215
        and women's studies 212–14
    problems of in Russia 191–3
    in Ukraine 220–2, 232
feminist groups 12, 190–1, 197
fertility *see* birth rates
FES (Federal Employment Service) 24, 25
FMS (Federal Migration Service of Russia) 119, 120, 121, 126, 131
food production, and private allotments 49, 52
forced migrants (Russian speaking) 11, 119–37
    and cultural adaptation 132–5, 136–7
    gender and employment 127–32, 135–6
    push factors in 121–5
    resettlement of 125–6
fuel supplies, Armenia 13
Funk, Nanette 22
Future of Russia 162

Gaidarenko, Nataliia 108, 110
Gamsakhurdia, Zviad 252, 256–7
gender roles
    in Armenia 235–7, 246
    in Central Asia 265–6, 275, 277–8, 286–7
    and images of the ideal woman 80–1
    in Ukraine 227
    and violence against women 99, 100–3, 107–8, 111–12, 112–13
'genderquake', 7
Georgia 4, 9, 13
    anti-conscription movement 146
    independence movement 252
    women's peace train 13–14, 250–60
German-Russian exchange 187
glasnost 77
    and soldiers' mothers 145
    and the Soviet Women's Committee 159

Index

Gorbachev, Mikhail 3, 159, 245
  anti-alcohol campaign 47
  and electoral reform 161
  and farm leasing 40
  and Georgia 252
  on women and work 22
Goskomstat, unemployment statistics 23, 24, 25
Grachev, Pavel 253
groups *see* women's groups/organisations
Gruodis, Karla 213

health workers, in Latvia and Lithuania 204
homeless women, 'Euphimia' shelter in St Petersburg 188–9
homemakers, images of women as 84–6
hotlines 190
household responsibilities, unequal distribution of 77, 85, 131, 206
housewives, and domestic violence 101–2, 111
housework
  in Armenia 239–40
  attitudes to 27–8
  and gender roles 85
housing
  and domestic violence 102–3
  and forced migrants 128–9, 132, 136
  in rural areas 44, 47, 48
Humphrey, Caroline 62, 67

Iabloko 175, 176, 194
Iakovleva, Liubov′ 150, 151, 152, 153
ideal man, women's perceptions of the 10, 85
'Ideal Russian Woman' stereotype 78, 80–1
ideal woman, images of the 10, 77–96
  and beauty 81–2, 94
  as caretakers and givers 83–4
  and gender roles 80–1
  as homemakers 84–6
  and marriage 86–7
  and men 82–4
  and motherhood 87, 88–90, 95
  and the 'Perfect You' competition 10, 78–9, 85–7
  women politicians 95
  and work 90–3, 95
  young women's perceptions 83, 84
IMF (International Monetary Fund) 5
incomes
  of Ukrainian women 225
  see also wages

individuality, and the 'Ideal Woman' 96
industrial capacity, Armenia 13
Interlegal 187
international aid community, and employment for Armenian women 242–3
Islam in Central Asia 14, 261, 262, 263, 264
  anti-Islamic campaign 273–4
  and marriage 265
  as migratory push factor 124, 125
  resurgence of 284–6, 296
Ivanova, Alexandra 147
Iveković, Rada 246

job advertisements, and women's physical appearance 82, 103
journals, feminist 193

Kalandadze, Ana 257–8
Kalynets, Iryna 222
Kanopienė, Vida 213
Kay, Rebecca 10
Kazakhstan 9, 261, 267, 283, 289, 296
  forced migrants returning to Russia from 122
  Islam in 286
Kemerovo oblast, unemployment in 24
Khodyreva, Nataliia 110, 112
Kirgizia *see* Kyrgystan
kitchens, nostalgia associated with Russian 22–3
Kitovani, General Tenguiz 256, 257
Klimantova, Galina 165, 166, 167
Kobalia (military commander) 256, 258
Kochkina, Elena 195
Kokand 267
Kollantai, Aleksandra 268
Korosteleva, Marina Vladimirovna 91
Kosmarskaia 128
Kotenov, Alexander 153
Kozhukhova, Valentina 167
Kravchuk, Leonid 231
Krest'ianka magazine 152–3
Krupskaia, Nadezhda 80, 268
Khrushchev, N. 88
Kuras, Ivan 231
Kuzhel', Alexandra 226
Kyrgystan (formerly Kirgizia) 9, 261, 267, 283, 286, 288, 289, 296
  forced migrants returning to Russia from 120

labour collectives 23, 24, 27, 28–30

labour force *see* work
Lakhova, Ekaterina 95, 161, 164, 165, 166, 167, 173, 176, 178, 180
  and the 1995 election 176, 177, 180
  and the presidential campaign (1996) 178, 179
Latvia 4, 12, 103, 203–15
  abortion 207–8
  anti-conscription movement 146
  compared with Lithuania 203–4
  declaration of independence 203
  period of transition 203
  women in politics 208–10
  women and work 204–7
  women's organisations 210–12
  women's studies 212–14
Lebed', Aleksandr 6, 7
Legal Committees (Russia and the CIS) 192
Lenin, V.I. 273
lesbian women's groups 189–90
Liberal Democratic Party of Russia 162–3, 168, 169, 175, 176
life expectancy, and gender 26
Lipovskaya, Olga 12, 179
Lissyutkina, Larissa 21, 22–3, 27, 30
Lithuania 4, 12, 103, 203–15
  abortion 207–8
  anti-conscription movement 146
  compared with Latvia 203–4
  declaration of independence 203
  period of transition 203
  women in politics 208–10
  women and work 204–7
  women's organisations 210–12
  women's studies 212–14
living conditions
  on former state and collective farms 42
  in rural areas 46–9, 51
  in Ukraine 233
  and women in the home 23, 27–8
living standards
  Armenia 238
  and economic reforms 59, 60
  and private allotments 50
Lozinskaia, Zhanna 167, 174, 176, 177, 178, 179
Luiblinsk Internationalist-Servicemen Museum 148
Lysenko, Nikolai 175

Malakhatkina, Natal'ia 165, 166, 167, 170, 171–2
Maliutina, Tatiana 64, 66

Mama–86 230–1
managers
  farm managers 39, 43–4
  female, redundancies 22
  male, and women's work 30, 31–2
'Maria' (women's group) 144
market reforms *see* economic reforms
marriage
  in Armenia 238, 241
  in Central Asia 265, 268, 277–80, 287
  and forced migrants 131
  and 'The ethics and psychology of family life' (secondary school course) 79
  women's attitudes to 10, 86–7
Martynova, Valentina 167, 168, 171, 172, 173, 175
Marx, Karl 101
Marxist-Leninist ideology, and women in the labour force 77
'masculinisation' of Russian women 80
maternity leave 21
  in Central Asia 279
  and migrant workers 129–30
media
  and the *afganki* 152–3
  and farm leasing 40
  images of women 10, 78–9, 81–3
  and work 90–1, 95
  treatment of violence 11
  in Ukraine, stereotypes of women 231–2
  on women's work 21
  see also press, the; rural press
men
  age of economically inactive 26
  in Armenia
    and gender ideology 235–6
    and war 246
  attitudes to women's work 30–3
  attitudes to work 25–6
  effects of economic change on 4, 5
  entrepreneurs
    Armenia 242
    Russia 57, 64, 67, 71, 129, 130, 150
  forced migrants
    and cultural adaptation 133–4, 136
    and push factors in migration 121–3
    and work 120, 127–8, 129, 130, 131
  ideal man, women's perceptions of the 10, 85
  and images of women 82–4
  and migration 241
    from rural Armenia 10, 11

Index

profiting from war 13
in rural areas
  and alcohol abuse 51, 53
  and 'commerce' 50–1
  and private farms 40–1
in Ukraine 232
and unemployment 23–4, 25, 26, 30
and violence against women 10–11, 99–113
wages 23
and working women 92
metallurgy, percentage of female employees 25
Mezentseva, Yelena 22, 25
migration
  gendered aspects of 11
  labour emigration in Armenia 241
  to Central Asian republics 267–8
  of young people into towns 47
  see also forced migrants
mines, lamp room workers 28, 29, 31, 33
ministries, women employed in Ukrainian 234
Monousova, Galina 33
moral superiority, attributed to women 84
morality, double standards of 10
Moscow
  Centre for Gender Studies 187, 190–1
  museum on the Afghanistan war 154–5
  women entrepreneurs in 10, 56–73
  and Women of Russia 176
  women's crisis centre ('Sisters') 108, 109, 110, 113
Moscow Council of Mothers and Widows 147–8, 149–50
Moscow Image Centre 78–9
Moshak, G.G. 107
motherhood
  in Central Asia 276–7, 279–80, 287
  and 'The ethics and psychology of family life' (secondary school course) 79
  women's attitudes to 10, 87, 88–90, 95
  in Ukraine 221, 222, 225
  see also soldiers' mothers
murders
  of women by husbands/lovers 10–11, 99, 107–8
  of women in Central Asia 271
  of women demonstrators in Georgia 252

'Nadezhda' (Hope) 189

Nagorno-Karabakh conflict 13, 237, 245, 246
National Republican Party (Russia) 175
Nedelia newspaper, and domestic violence 102–3
networks, and women entrepreneurs 62, 70–2
New Russians 63, 67
  and domestic violence 101–2, 111
new technology, and print workers 33–4
newly independent states 9, 12–14
  leaders of 4
  see also Central Asia; individual states
newspapers *see* press, the; rural press
NEWW (Network of East-West Women) 192
NGOs (non-governmental organisations) 186–7, 198
  in Central Asia 291
nomad communities, in Central Asia 265, 266
Novitskaia, Irina 172

occupational sectors
  and gender differences, in Ukraine 228
  in Latvia and Lithuania 204
Orel region (Central Russia)
  forced migrants 120, 124
  and work 127, 130–1
organisations *see* women's groups/organisations
organised crime, and women entrepreneurs 71–2
Orlova, Svetlana 165, 168, 173, 174, 176, 177, 178, 179, 180
Our Home is Russia 163, 175, 176

paid work *see* work
Pamfilova, Ella 178
Parekh, B. 125
parenthood *see* motherhood
parliamentarianism versus presidentialism debate 3–4
parliaments
  Latvian 208–9
  Lithuanian 208
  Russian 161–3
  and political consciousness 193–5
  Ukraine (Supreme Rada), women members 221–3
Parshentseva, Galina 165, 167, 170, 171, 174
part-time work 90
Party of Russian Unity and Concord 162

passivity of women
  as a coping strategy 14, 15
  in Central Asia 292–5
Pavilionienė, Marja Aušrinė 213
Pavlychko, Solomea 12
peacemakers
  women as 14
    peace train in Georgia 13–14, 250–60
peasant (private) farms 9, 38–9, 40–2, 49, 52, 53
pensioners
  forced migrants 126
  in rural areas 46, 47–9
perestroika 3, 59
'Perfect You' competition 10, 78–9, 85–7
Pilkington, Hilary 11, 22
Pinnick, Kathryn 11, 13, 190
Pisklakova, Marina 111
Plazk, Miroslav 85
Poča, Aija 209
police, and domestic violence 111
political activism 12
  in Latvia and Lithuania 208–10
  in Ukraine 222–5, 227–8
  women politicians 95
political consciousness, and the Duma 193–5
political mobilisation, of women in Central Asia 273–4
political parties
  and parliamentary factions 159
  representation of women in 162–3
  Ukraine 12
  Armenia 13, 244–5
  see also Women of Russia
polygamy 232, 287
Poršņova, Maija 209
post-modernism 8
poverty
  and economic reform 60
  media articles on 91
  in rural areas 45–9
power feminism 7
pragmatism, and feminist groups 191–2
Praust, Rudolf 53
presidential campaigns
  (1996), and Women of Russia 178–9
  Ukraine (1994) 231
presidential power in Russia 3–6
press, the
  feminist 193
  and stereotypes of women 232
  and violence against women 102–3
  and women's crisis centres 112
  see also rural press
print workers
  attitudes to women's work 28, 29, 30, 31, 33
  and new technology 33–4
private (peasant) farms 9, 38–9, 40–2, 49, 52, 53
private sector workers, in Latvia and Lithuania 205
professional women
  in Armenia 236
  in Latvia and Lithuania 204–5
  in Ukraine 234–5
'prostitutes', women labelled as 13
prostitution
  and the Afghanistan war 151
  in Central Asia 289
Prunskienė, Kazimiera 209
Pukhova, Zoia 159, 160
Purvaneckienė, Giedrė 206, 207, 210, 211, 213, 215

radical feminism 96
rape 11
  and capital punishment 111
  and the law 101
  Russian literature on 103–6, 112–13
  statistics 99
  and women's crisis centres 109–11
REAP (Research, Education and Advocacy Project) 109–10, 111, 112
redundancies 21–2, 25, 78
  in Central Asia 275
refugees 119, 120, 121, 126
  see also forced migrants
Regent, Tat'iana 126
religion
  in Latvia and Lithuania 204
    and abortion 204
  in Russia, and bereaved mothers of soldiers 148
  and suicide by self-immolation 281–2
  see also Islam
'revolutions' in 1989 3
Rimashevskaia, Natal'ia 21, 25
roles see gender roles
Rukh, Women's Community of 229, 230
rural areas 9–10, 38–55
  alcohol abuse 51, 53
  in Central Asia
    and agriculture 274–5
    birth rates 289–90

Index

forced migrants resettling in
  and cultural adaptation 132–5, 136
  and work 127–8, 129–32
former state and collective farms 38, 39, 42–5, 130
  Ukraine 227
  in Latvia and Lithuania 206
  and market reforms 38–40, 42–5
  private allotments 49–53
  private (peasant) farms 9, 38–9, 40–2, 49, 52, 53
  subsistence farming 9, 10, 46, 47, 50,
  in Armenia 240
  unemployment and poverty in 9, 45–9, 127, 128
rural press
  advertisements for women 41–2
  on alcohol abuse 51
  on farm managers 43–4
  on poverty and living conditions 46–7, 48
Russian Association of Crisis Centres for Women, REAP Project 109–10, 111, 112
Russian Centre for Public Opinion Research (VTsIOM) 26
Russian Federation 9–12
  failed coup of August 1991 5, 157
  forced migrants returning to 119–37
  and Georgia 252–3
  images of the ideal woman 10, 77–96
  parliaments 161–3
  rural areas 9–10, 38–55
  violence against women 10–11, 99–118
  women entrepreneurs in Moscow 10, 56–74
  Women of Russia 11–12, 13, 95, 157–81, 193–5
  women's groups 12, 186–98
  and women's work, attitudes to 21–37
Russian Movement for Democratic Reforms 162
Russia's Choice 163, 164, 168, 180
russkii absurd (Russian absurd) 60
Rwandan conflict 250
Rybkin, Ivan 163, 177, 180
Ryzhkov, Nikolai 177

St Petersburg
  Psychological Crisis Centre for Women 110, 190
  'third sector' projects 187
  and Women of Russia 176
  women's groups 188–9, 189–90

Sakharov, Andrei 144
Scientific Research Institute on the Family 92
self-employment *see* entrepreneurs
sexual abuse/harassment, of women at work 103
Shakhrai, Sergei 162
Shamiram (Armenian women's political party) 13, 244–5
Shapiro, Judith 25
Shestakov, D.A. 107–8, 112
Shevardnadze, Eduard 252–3, 254, 257
Sinel'nikov, Aleksandr 92
Single Mothers' Association 188
Sinitsina, Natal'ia 163–4, 169
'Sisters' (Moscow women's crisis centre) 108, 109, 110, 113
Skoryk, Larysa 222
Skripitsina, Raisa 166, 167, 168, 171, 172, 173
  on the future of Women in Russia 174
  and the presidential campaign (1996) 178
social contract, breakdown of 60
social justice, in Armenia 238
social protection, and Women of Russia 164
Socialist Party
  Russia 177, 180
  Ukraine 223
soldiers' mothers
  Committee of Soldiers' Mothers of Russia (CSMR) 145–6, 190
  and the Georgian peace train 14, 256, 258, 259
  soldiers killed in Afghanistan 147–50, 154
  and the war in Chechnia 11, 144–7
Soldiers' Mothers for the New Army 230
Soros Foundation 187
Soviet Women's Anti-Fascist Committee 159
Soviet Women's Committee (SWC, later Union of Women of Russia) 11, 157, 159–61
Stalin, Joseph 100
Starovoitova, Galina 178–9, 195–7
state benefits, to forced migrants 126
street-traders 58, 67, 68, 69, 70, 72
subsidiary economic activities
  and men 24
  migrant workers 129–30
subsistence farming 9, 10, 46, 47, 50
  in Armenia 240

suicide by self-immolation, in Central Asia 281–2, 284

TACIS (Technical Aid to the CIS) 187
Tadzhikistan 13, 261, 267
  civil war in 14, 294–5
  forced migrants returning to Russia from 120, 133–4
  Islam in 286
  post-Soviet 283
  suicide by self-immolation 281
Tashkent Agreement 253
teachers, in Latvia and Lithuania 204
technical assistance programmes, in Central Asia 291
Teišerskytė, Dalia 211
television
  Georgian peace train on 251, 254–5, 259
  Ukraine 221
  and Women of Russia 164, 175, 176, 195
Ter-Petrossian, Levon 243
Tērauda, Vita 209
Tereshkova, Valentina 159
'third sector' (non-governmental organisations) 186–7, 198
Tkachenko, A. 103–4
Tolstoi, L.N. 80
towns
  forced migrants resettling in 128–9
  women in 10
trade, Russian attitudes to 65
Turkmenistan 4, 261, 267, 283
  mosque building 285

UAV (Union of Afghan Veterans) 150, 153
Ukraine 4, 9, 12, 219–33
  Commission on the Family, Motherhood and Children 225
  crisis in 219–20
  declaration of independence 219
  elections 219
  parliament (Supreme Rada) 221–3
  presidential campaign (1994) 231
  women in politics 162, 222–5
  women and work 225–9
  women's organisations 220–2
Ul'ianovsk (Middle Volga)
  forced migrants 120
  and work 127, 129
unemployment
  Armenia 13, 237, 239
  Central Asia 283, 288
  and gender 9
  Latvia and Lithuania 205
  media articles on 91
  men 23–4, 25, 26, 30
  redundancies 21–2, 25, 78
  registrations 23, 24
  Russian Federation 21, 23–7
  and subsidiary economic activity 24, 26–7
  and violence against women 103
  women 4–5
    debates on female 14
    and economic reform 21–2, 59, 60
    forced migrants 127–8
    and pressure to return to the home 78
    proportion of 23
    and representation in parliament 162
    in rural areas 9, 45–9, 127
    in Ukraine 225
  and women entrepreneurs 57
  and Women of Russia 164
Union of Women of the Don 195
Union of Women of Russia (formerly Soviet Women's Committee) 11, 157–8, 163
  see also Women of Russia
United Nations
  Fourth World Conference on Women (Beijing) 206, 211–12, 214–15
  and Ukraine 222, 231, 232
urban areas
  in Armenia 239–40
  and forced migrants 128–9, 132–3
  in Latvia and Lithuania 206
Uzbekistan 261, 267, 273, 279
  community relations 287
  forced migrants returning to Russia from 120, 125
  Islam in 285, 286
  post-Soviet 283
  suicide by self-immolation 281–2
  Tumaris 292
  women's presence in politics 162

Verdery, Katherine 62
victim feminism 7
victims, women as, and economic reforms 4–5
violence, women as victims and perpetrators of 14
violence against women 10–11, 99–113
  women's crisis centres 102, 108–12, 113
  see also domestic violence; rape

Index

Vitkovskaia, Galina 121–2, 123–4, 125, 126, 127, 128, 129
Vitrenko, Natalia 223
Vlasova, Anna 167, 177
Vodzakovskaia, Iuliia 110
voluntary organisations *see* women's groups
Vybornova, Irina 163, 165, 168, 171, 172, 173
   on the future of Women in Russia 174
   and the presidential campaign (1996) 178

wages
   in Armenia, differentials 239
   and economic reforms 59
   late payment of 25, 237
   in Latvia and Lithuania 204–5
   men 23, 24
   in rural areas 42–3, 51
   women 30–1, 32–3, 34
war
   Abkhazia 13–14, 253–60
   Afghanistan 11, 13, 143–4, 147–55
   Chechnia 11, 143, 144, 144–7
   civil war in Tadzhikistan 14
   men profiting from 13
   Nagorno-Karabakh conflict 13, 237, 245, 246
   see also soldiers' mothers
Western influences, in Central Asia 290–2
Western values 15
White, Nijole 12
widows
   in Armenia 247
   of soldiers killed in Afghanistan 147–50
Widows' Association 188
wife battery *see* domestic violence
Wolf, Naomi 96
'Woman in the changing world' (international congress) 213
'woman-man', in Ukraine 224–5
Women of the Fleet 158
Women of Latvia – 75 214
Women of Russia 11–12, 13, 95, 157–81
   on not becoming a political party 174–5
   in the Duma 166–9
      voting behaviour 176–7
   elections
      (1993) 11, 157–8, 162–3
      (1995) 12, 158, 163, 175–8, 179–80
   and the 'female' contribution to politics 173
   perceptions of shortcomings 171–2
   perceptions of success 170–1
   and political consciousness 193–5
   and the presidential campaign (1996) 178–9
women's cooperatives, in Central Asia 274
Women's Council (Armenia) 245, 247
women's councils (*zhensovety*) 158, 293
women's crisis centres 102, 108–12, 113
women's groups/organisations 12, 186–98
   Central Asia 12, 269, 292–3
   Islamic 286
   extrovert groups 188, 189–91
   introvert groups 188–9
   Latvia and Lithuania 210–12
   Ukraine 12, 220–2, 229–31
   see also Women of Russia
women's magazines
   and domestic violence 102
   Ukraine 232
women's movement 187–91
women's studies
   Latvia and Lithuania 212–14
   Ukraine 221
wood processing, percentage of female employees 25
work
   attitudes to 9, 10, 21–37, 90–3
   in Latvia and Lithuania 205–6
   'downgrading' of female labour 9
   gendering of jobs 32, 204, 228
   and men
      attitudes to women's work 30–3
      forced migrants 120, 127–8, 129, 130, 131
   strategies to reduce labour costs 24–5
   subsidiary economic activity 24, 26–7
   and women
      in Armenia 239–43
      attitudes to women's work 9, 21–37, 90–3
      in Central Asia 274–5, 279, 280, 288–9
      and costs of employing women 21, 32
      de-skilling 127–9
      forced migrants 127–32, 135–6
      government ideology and policy 59–60
      images of the ideal woman 90–3, 95
      job advertisements 82, 103
      in Latvia and Lithuania 204–7

work (*cont.*)
  media articles on 90–1
  pressure to give up paid work 77, 78, 84–5, 92–3
  right of women not to work 21
  in rural areas 10, 41–53
  and sexual abuse 103
  suitable employment 93
  in Ukraine 225–9
  see also entrepreneurs; unemployment
workers' collectives *see* labour collectives
working conditions
  in Armenia 237
  and private allotments 50
  rural women 42
  women industrial workers 30–1, 32, 33–4

Yel'tsin, Boris 38, 196
  and the 1996 election 6–7
  conflict with parliament 5–6
  government policy on women and work 59–60
  and the Union of Afghan Veterans (UAV) 150
  and the war in Chechnia 145
  on women 84
  and Women of Russia 179
young people, attitudes to parenthood 89–90
Yugoslavia, war in former 14

Zavadskaia, Liudmila 165, 167, 194
Zetkin, Klara 268
zhensovety (women's councils) 158, 293
Zhilina, Antonina 165, 166, 167, 168, 169, 170–1, 173, 174
  and the presidential campaign (1996) 178
Zhinocha Hromada 230
Zhirinovskii, Vladimir 4, 63
ZHISET (Women's Information Network) 188
Ziuganov, Genadii 6, 7, 63, 170, 175
Zoroastrianism 281